H.M.S Terrible and Her Naval Brigades

H.M.S. "Terrible." Spithead, 1898.

H.M.S Terrible and Her Naval Brigades
A Cruiser & Her Campaigns During the Boer War and Boxer Rebellion

The Commission of H.M.S. "Terrible"
1898-1902
George Crowe

The White Era
Fred T. Jane

H.M.S Terrible and Her Naval Brigades
A Cruiser & Her Campaigns During the Boer War and Boxer Rebellion
The Commission of H.M.S. "Terrible" 1898-1902
by George Crowe
The White Era
by Fred T. Jane

FIRST EDITION

First published under the titles
The Commission of H.M.S. "Terrible" 1898-1902
and
The White Era

Leonaur is an imprint of Oakpast Ltd

Copyright in this form © 2013 Oakpast Ltd

ISBN: 978-1-78282-197-7 (hardcover)
ISBN: 978-1-78282-198-4 (softcover)

http://www.leonaur.com

Publisher's Notes

The views expressed in this book are not necessarily those of the publisher.

H.M.S Terrible and Her Naval Brigades
A Cruiser & Her Campaigns During the Boer War and Boxer Rebellion

The Commission of H.M.S. "Terrible"
1898-1902
George Crowe

The White Era
Fred T. Jane

H.M.S Terrible and Her Naval Brigades
A Cruiser & Her Campaigns During the Boer War and Boxer Rebellion
The Commission of H.M.S. "Terrible" 1898-1902
by George Crowe
The White Era
by Fred T. Jane

FIRST EDITION

First published under the titles
The Commission of H.M.S. "Terrible" 1898-1902
and
The White Era

Leonaur is an imprint of Oakpast Ltd
Copyright in this form © 2013 Oakpast Ltd

ISBN: 978-1-78282-197-7 (hardcover)
ISBN: 978-1-78282-198-4 (softcover)

http://www.leonaur.com

Publisher's Notes

The views expressed in this book are not necessarily those of the publisher.

Contents

Introductory Remarks	9
Commissioning: Experimental Cruises	13
Voyage to the Cape: Crossing the "Line"	33
Résumé of South African History	46
Naval Brigade in South Africa: Anglo-Boer War 1899-1900	60
Arrival of Sir Redver's Buller in Natal	77
Relief of Ladysmith Operations	102
Battle of Colenso	118
Desperate Assault on Ladysmith	135
Arrival of Buller's Army at Spearmans	151
Spion Kop Operations	159
Retirement of Buller's Army to Chieveley	175
Ladysmith Relieved!	185
Return of the "Terribles" To Durban	206
Colonial Appreciation of the Navy	226
North China War	239
Story of the Six Days' Siege	257
Fall of the Native City	269
Chefoo and Wei-Hai-Wei	300

Return of the Naval Brigades	306
Reminiscences of China and Japan in H.M.S. "Terrible"	326
Homeward Bound	359
Life and Routine in a Modern Man-of-War	374
Appendices	398
The White Era	411

Respectfully dedicated
to
Commodore C. G. Robinson, A.D.C.
Captain Percy Scott, C.V.O., C.B.
And to
The officers and my comrades
of
His Majesty's Ship "Terrible"

Introductory Remarks

Nearly two years ago, (as at 1902), a book was published at Hong Kong entitled *From Portsmouth to Peking, via Ladysmith, with a Naval Brigade,* in which publication the operations for the reliefs of the besieged garrisons of Ladysmith, and the Foreign Legations in Peking were briefly narrated. In an explanatory note the reasons for its appearance were stated, also an assertion made that it was my intention, upon the expiration of the commission, to produce a more comprehensive work, which would be a commentary of the principal events in connection with H.M.S. *Terrible.* This book is therefore the outcome of that tentative promise, and also of the fact that my first literary attempt met with favour and unexpected success.

To avoid creating undesirable misconception of purpose, it is specially pointed out to the reader that the book throughout deals principally with the *Terrible's* particular history. An effort, however, has been made to logically and impartially narrate those events relating to the great Anglo-Boer and the North China wars, insomuch as concerns the naval participation in those two campaigns.

Certain subjects and matter, which may appear extraneous to the title selected for the work, have been briefly introduced, as being of possible interest to those with a limited acquaintance of actual naval life, and to those debarred from the opportunities of foreign travel. Where special experience or technical knowledge was essential to delineate the story, extracts from authorities have been quoted; but otherwise the writer is solely responsible for what has been adduced.

Obviously, much of the work is the result of intermittent labour, mostly penned during the silent hours of the night—after "pipe down." Concerning its literary merit, or demerit, the writer has a very tranquil mind, for instead of aspiring to perform the impossible with the pen, every effort has been put forth to render the diverse narratives of events, etc, of interesting perusal to service and civilian readers alike, devoid of literary garnish or vague technicalities. If this much has been accomplished, an object will have been fully achieved.

I am under great obligation to Messrs. Newnes, the (original) publishers, certain photographers, and others who have considerately allowed certain subjects to be reproduced in the book, which are specified; also to Chief-Armourer Burke, R.N., who has supplied most of the illustrations. Lieut. Hutchinson, R.N.R., produced the Tientsin map. Midshipman Wood that of the Ladysmith operations, and Midshipman Down the scientific sketches of the dredger-raising process.

It might be opportunely stated here that the naval service, with its anomalies, is often much at variance with the imaginative views and ideas regarding it which generally prevails outside the great naval ports. Almost every conceived notion or impression is widely astray from the real facts—especially those regarding the personnel As science has enforced a transitory system of improvements in shipbuilding and manufacture of armaments, it consistently follows that an analogous effect is produced among the personnel. Nelson's ships and mode of warfare, and his warrior-seamen, have been relegated to a glorious past, though the ardent spirit he created has remained.

The British naval men of the present period, (as at 1902), are totally dissimilar to the Nelsonian type of seamen, professionally and otherwise. *Then* they were generally recognised as volatile and illiterate seamen, whose only ambition was to excel in daring exploits at sea and in adventurous carousals on shore. *Now* they are mostly men with certain social refinement, with developed faculties and scientific attainments, as the result of the national compulsory education system, the comprehensive service training imparted, and of foreign travel; and, as has been recently attested, are as capable as ever of performing their duty to king and country. As of old the British seaman still glories in being led and commanded by capable officers, but, as ever, resents being driven or domineered. Admonitory or inspiring sentiments, judiciously expressed by a respected superior, will invariably produce any desired effect

It is most difficult to impress the perhaps well-intentioned—but too often much-meddlesome—philanthropist, that the British man-of-warsmen of this age are not the socially-forlorn type of humanity so vividly depicted in nautical novels, and that they view with deserved contempt and derision the "naval slumming" and the contents of the many tons of childish literature with which ships are futilely flooded. Any form of charitable intent is wholly repugnant to his real or acquired nature. Certainly in the navy, as also exists among each and every class of the community, there are a small minority of social pests and "ne'er-do-weels," but on the principle that "*a few swallows do not make a summer,*" neither do a few "King's hard bargains" debase the whole navy. Indeed it is very questionable, since the abolition of the short service or single commission engagements and the substitution of the continuous-service system, if the naval men do not develop into a superior type of manhood than their compeers on shore, after a few years of disciplinary service, otherwise the training to which he is subjected, and which is the nation's boast, counts for little or naught.

It is true that certain laudable naval institutions exist in each of our naval ports, which tend to promote and sustain the social and moral status of those who are styled foreigners, that is, men who do not reside locally, but there is a much vaster field for philanthropic work and mission labour among the degraded humanity of our large towns and cities than in His Majesty's Navy. Bluejackets do not profess to be saints, neither can they be classed as special sinners. On board they are disciplined machines of war; on shore they are law-abiding citizens in the fullest sense of the term.

No British youth, desirous of a sea-life, need have any qualms or compunction against entering His Majesty's Navy, for nowhere can a roving and adventurous life be more fully enjoyed than on a model British man-of-war, as is exemplified in these pages while relating the eventful commission of H.M.S. *Terrible*.

George Crowe.

December, 1902,

PART 1

CHAPTER 1

Commissioning: Experimental Cruises

From March, 1898, to September, 1899

Her Majesty's ship *Terrible* was commissioned at Portsmouth Dockyard, March 24th, 1898, by Captain Charles Grey Robinson, R.N., for particular service, and to undergo a series of experimental trials.

More than the ordinary amount of interest was taken in naval circles in this commissioning, owing to the fact that the ship was one of two sister-ships that were at this period the largest and most powerfully armed cruisers afloat; the other being H.M.S. *Powerful*, then in commission on the China Station.

It is worthy of note that these two ships should both, in their first commissions, have achieved reputations that have not—it is safe to assert—been surpassed during the iron age of the British Navy. Both were the cause of many animated discussions in the House of Commons respecting their general efficiency and sphere of usefulness. Both their names are inseparable from the early history of the great Anglo-Boer War, 1899-1902, mainly in respect of the operations for the defence and relief of Ladysmith. The names of both their captains[1] became familiar to the English-speaking peoples owing to the part played by each during the war; and both captains received the Order of the "Companion of the Bath" for distinguished services, while several officers and others in both ships received either war decorations, or special promotions, or were mentioned in despatches for gallant or meritorious service in the field.

---

1. Captain Hon. Hedworth Lambton (*Powerful*) and Captain Percy Scott, who had then succeeded to the command of the *Terrible*.

But the *Terrible's* war history did not cease in South Africa, for her crew afterwards took a prominent part with their guns in the stirring episodes of the China War of 1900, when the Great Powers conjointly suppressed the Boxer Rebellion.

Commissioning day is always an event of supreme importance in the Royal Navy, and was not less so on board the *Terrible* on this occasion. It is a date that is stamped on the memory of every member of the crews of H.M. ships. A birthday may be forgotten or ignored, but not this day, which is the time-pivot upon which all calculations, self-imposed abnegations, or future hopes of individuals turn; and is annually kept green by the anniversary dinner given in the officers' messes, and by a special performance of the ship's inevitable minstrel *troupe*.

Snow, several inches deep, covered the ground on the eventful March morning when the *Terrible's* crew left the Naval Depôt and marched to where their future ocean residence was then lying—a stately four-funnelled cruiser, the very antithesis of the old wooden hulks which constitute the *depôt*.

Few persons outside the navy, or, indeed, inside, know much of the apparently mysterious machinery, or method, employed to bring a ship from the Fleet Reserve and place it as a fighting unit fully equipped among the commissioned ships of our vast fleet, for much of the system lies deep below the surface open to ocular observation. The procedure adopted is practically the same for every ship, large or small, and a brief *résumé* of what actually occurs at commissioning will serve two purposes—to simplify a naval subject little understood, and also to start the ship's history.

The initial stage begins with the sending of an official communication from the Admiralty to the port admiral (otherwise termed the commander-in-chief) stating on what date a certain ship will commission, upon what service it will be employed, and to which squadron it will be attached. The ship will have been previously got ready for service by the dockyard authorities and by them reported to the Admiralty as in all respects ready for the "pennant." The captain and all other officers are appointed to the ship by the Admiralty, each receiving his official appointment by post—a document that must be acknowledged without delay as directed therein. Their names also appear in the leading London papers, which is often the first intimation an officer gets whether of an appointment or a promotion.

The coal and most of the stores, but not the ammunition, are invariably placed on board as soon as the ship is placed in the "Reserve" ready for active service, and an engineer officer, a gunner, boatswain, and carpenter are attached to the ship for the purpose of becoming acquainted with their respective departments prior to commissioning. The Port Admiral issues instructions to the captain of the *depôt* to prepare a crew, and also notifies the other officials interested. Now the task begins in real earnest. The drafting departments select the petty officers and men from the roster books, which contain a record of each man's qualifications, date of last foreign service, etc.

This duty demands great experience owing to the multifarious gunnery, torpedo, artisan, mechanical, and miscellaneous ratings now required for the complement of a modern man-of-war. The men selected are then detailed, and have to pass a medical examination, the severity of which is governed by the nature of the service the ship is ordered on. Then follows a kit inspection, after which, if the ship is to join a squadron on a foreign station, the "draft" (as they are now termed) are permitted to proceed on several days' leave to visit their friends.

On returning from "draft leave," the captain of the *depôt* will hold a "draft inspection," at which every man must parade dressed in his best uniform. This officer, with a wide experience in all things naval, accompanied by the staff of officials directly responsible for the drafting arrangements, carefully scrutinizes each individual with such keenness that nothing irregular, either in appearance or dress, can escape his notice. Inspection over, the great event of the morrow is awaited, which is to sever the draft from the methodical *depôt* life, and connect them with the rigorous *régime* peculiar to a British man-of-war.

Early next morning the "draft" will be busy packing their ponderous kits into waggons for conveyance to the ship, and, breakfast over, they are finally paraded and marched on board. On arrival they are officially handed over, together with all documents concerning them, to their future commanding officer—a commander or senior lieutenant, otherwise styled the executive officer.

It is upon this officer that falls the greatest amount of individual responsibility respecting the organisation of the personnel and economic regulating of a newly commissioned ship. For several days previously he has had to work hard, with brain and pen, preparing each officer's and man's numerous duties, besides devising general stations for important evolutions. These must fit like the movements of a clock for exactness, unless a state of chaos is to be brought about—undignified if only on drill, unjustifiable if on service. The senior engineer is similarly responsible for all duties strictly connected with his own department.

In the event of the ship being rammed or springing a leak, every watertight door must have responsible men stationed to close it, while the collision mat would have to be promptly got over the ship's side to check the inrush of water. To repel a midnight torpedo boat attack; comply with a sudden signal to "man and arm boats;" put out a fire, either on board or on shore; arrange stations for numerous other movements, etc., under various conditions—require a wide experience and a fertile brain. Not only have these stations to be carefully thought out (the heterogeneous types of ships prohibiting the adoption of a universal system), but the scheme has also to be imparted to the new crew by incessant drilling, to ensure promptitude and precision when reality supersedes drill. Often has a smart evolution been the sole factor whereby a grave danger has been averted, or perhaps a ship saved from a critical position—and even the tide of a battle turned.[2]

Proceeding with the subject proper, we shall find that the Royal Marines have also arrived from their barracks; "station cards," which concisely enumerate each man's special duties, have been served out, and the whole crew have been given a reasonable time to stow their kits, familiarize themselves with their duties, and otherwise prepare in good time for a busy day. In the meantime all officers will have reported their arrival on board, and have had their respective duties likewise assigned to them by the departmental "chiefs."

Shortly before 9 a. m., Captain Robinson arrived on board in his official capacity, being received on the gangway by the principal officers, who were severally introduced to him by Commander Limpus (the executive officer).

Punctually at nine, the ensign was hoisted on the flagstaff, the pennant let fly at the masthead, a general salute from the bugles was sounded, while officers and men faced aft and saluted; this impressive ceremony officially announcing that the ship was duly in commission.

The formal reading of the captain's commission of authority has long since been dispensed with, and relegated to past history, its importance ceasing with the introduction of the continuous service system which replaced the antiquated method of single commission engagements. This document was then read to impress the raw material

---

2. Appropriately applies to the naval gun episode at Ladysmith.

Captain Charles Grey Robinson, A.D.C.
Commissioned H.M.S. *Terrible,* March 24, 1898

and undisciplined with a sense of the dignity and power vested in the captain—perhaps a necessary reminder at the time, especially during the press-gang period, when many turbulent characters formed a portion of every crew.

Sufficient time having elapsed for compliance with the preliminary order, the whole crew assembled on deck, when "fire," "collision," and "general quarters" stations were read out and explained; the crew being afterwards exercised at them to make sure that they fully understood their individual and collective duties in each evolution. These are the principal stations invariably performed in every ship as early as possible, since the first two concern the ship's safety, and the last is the general fighting station for the entire crew when in action; but they form only a small fraction of the evolutions carried out in a man-of-war.

Filling up with stores, ammunition, and coal was finished as early as possible, and the ship prepared for the service for which she was commissioned. The foregoing is an account of the necessary preliminaries before the *Terrible* could start upon her eventful commission.

Eight hundred and sixty-one officers and men formed the complement of the ship, but before leaving harbour 120 boys and young stokers were embarked for training, giving a grand total that would compare favourably with the huge complements of a Nelsonian line-of-battle ship of three-decker size.

The customary commissioning inspection was made by Admiral Sir Michael Culme-Seymour, after which the ship proceeded to Spithead. While there the Duke and Duchess of York visited the ship, the captain conducting the royal visitors round the decks. The duke, himself a naval officer, proceeded below to inspect the powerful engines, and displayed keen interest in this leviathan among cruisers.

The programme to be carried out was extensive for such a large ship to undertake, but the experiments were essential in order to test fully the water-tube boilers with which she is exclusively fitted. These were now being largely introduced into the Royal Navy, and much controversial opinion respecting their efficiency then prevailed among engineering scientists.

Owing to dense fogs in the Channel two attempts to proceed with the trials were abandoned, but on May 4th the first 60-hours' trial was made and satisfactorily concluded; 5000 horse-power being the test limit for this run—the "first heat" of the "full-power race" which was to conclude the experiments.

Queen's birthday was celebrated in Portsmouth harbour on May 24th in the usual naval fashion. Each ship present dressed with flags and fired a royal salute at noon, Nelson's old flagship, the *Victory*, performing her annual function of directing the ceremonies on this propitious occasion. In the evening the Right Hon. George J. Goschen, M.P. (First Lord of the Admiralty), and Mr. Austin Chamberlain, M.P. (the Civil Lord), accompanied by Captain Fawkes, R.N., joined the ship for an official visit to Gibraltar. Leaving early next day, another trial, this time of 10,000 horse-power, was successfully carried out, the ship arriving at the famous British fortress on the 28th inst.[3]

Gibraltar is a high rocky promontory, connected with Spain by a low isthmus, styled the "neutral ground." It rises to a height of just over 1400 feet at its greatest elevation, is three miles in length, and about three-quarters of a mile in breadth. On the opposite African coast, about 15 miles distant, is Tangier, an important coast town of Morocco, where diplomatic representatives to that country reside. Gibraltar is a Crown Colony, the Governor being also the General Officer commanding the garrison. It was captured during the war of the Spanish Succession in 1704 by a combined British and Dutch force, commanded by Sir George Rooke, and in 1713 was formally ceded to Great Britain by the Treaty of Utrecht, since which date the "Rock" has remained continuously in British possession.

Several attempts, however, were subsequently made for its recapture, the most important being the historical siege in 1779-83, when the British garrison under General Elliott, successfully held out for three years and seven months against a combined French and Spanish force, enduring severe privations towards the finish. Its value as a strategical position is incalculable, for though the introduction of steam propulsion for fighting ships has somewhat lessened its power of control over the Straits, yet its own invulnerability remains as certain as it was in the glorious days of yore. It is the first link in the imperial chain of British possessions that encircles the globe, and is also the strongest, so that, should it snap, the remaining links might be seriously imperilled.

The docks in course of construction must infinitely enhance its value as a naval base, while the steady additions of long-range guns of great destructive power, together with the numerous torpedo craft

---

3. It being the writer's object to describe the commission of the *Terrible* in its entirety, a brief description of each foreign port or country visited will be inserted as occasion arises.

that would form the threshold over which a hostile fleet must pass in or out of the Mediterranean door, assure its title of being the strongest offensive and defensive fortress in the world. A magnificent breakwater affords substantial protection to a large fleet, and must prove invaluable in war time, providing as it does absolute immunity from torpedo attack and also from that latest ocean terror—the submarine boat. The population (mixed European and African) numbers about 20,000, who are mostly occupied with commerce and shipping. A strong garrison is always maintained here, and should history repeat itself, Gibraltar will not fail to uphold its traditional reputation for impregnability.

The Admiralty Lords having concluded their official inspection of the naval establishments and works in progress, the ship left for England on the 30th inst., arriving at Spithead without incident on June 3rd.

The next two months were spent in dockyard hands preparing the ship for severer experiments than it was originally intended should be carried out. The ship was having a midsummer vacation, an unexpected arrangement few found fault with, for Portsmouth in the summer, with all its attractions, is an agreeable place enough whereat to earn a pension. Whilst in dock, a distinguished party of members of the House of Commons, who were being conducted round the dockyard by Lord Charles Beresford, M.P., visited the ship. They were evidently much interested, several honourable members being visibly impressed, though, unfortunately for them, it was with navy wet paint on the tails of their frock-coats, the ship having been freshly painted throughout. It is proverbial that wet paint attracts the smartest clothing with the power of a magnet, but will repel old or dirty garments—at least, this is a theory which can easily be tested on Sunday mornings, as the result of that time-honoured touch-up for the "rounds" the previous night

Early in August the ship was again ready to proceed on her trials, and during the month two 60-hours' runs at 15,000 and 20,000 horse-power were made, success having again to be recorded. Previous to these two trials important alterations had taken place with the engines to try and solve an engineering problem concerning the excessive vibration, especially aft, from which the ship suffered when steaming at certain high speeds. The trials evidenced that a highly satisfactory solution had rewarded the engineers' skill, and likewise cured a defect that would have seriously interfered with accurate shooting

Commander Arthur Henry Limpus.

from the stern guns, when fired under those conditions. The next trial was made at 22,000 horse-power, which enabled a speed of 21 knots to be recorded.

The preliminary trials were all over, for—to use sporting terms—the ship was now to compete for the blue ribbon of her designed speed, the stokers having dubbed the final run as the steaming Derby. In some ways her trials for this big event resembled the preparation of a favourite horse for the classic race at Epsom.

On September 15th the ship was ready to proceed, and officials representing the departments interested assembled on board to note the result of this final full-power race against speed and time; 25,000 horse-power having to be maintained for four hours, and the ship also having to travel 100 miles in that limited time to satisfy her judges.

To propel a constructed mass of over 14,000 tons weight through the water at 25 miles per hour requires both physical and mechanical endurance of no mean order. The powerful engines derive their enormous horse-power from forty-eight boilers of the Belleville water-tube type, which were then receiving a rabid condemnation from the "anti-water-tubists." The coal expenditure for this special run averaged 25 tons per hour, which may appear a great quantity to consume, but it must be remembered that the coal-carrying capacity of the ship is over 3000 tons, and sufficiently large in proportion even to this consumption. It would require a personal visit into the stokeholds and engine-rooms fully to realise what a full-speed trial means in a large modern man-of-war.

Owing to the necessity of having an armoured protective deck over the engines and boilers, it follows that, for want of space, the piston stroke must be considerably reduced, so that these huge engines were compelled to revolve at the rate of 110 revolutions per minute to obtain the required speed. In the stokeholds it might be truly said there was as hazardous a risk to be faced as on a battlefield for those men who fed the furnaces. A mishap, fortunately rare, occurring below when steaming at full speed, would probably produce disastrous results. As steam was the greatest factor upon which success depended, the day was a real stokers' day, and three hundred of these men had practically the result of the race in their hands. Fleet-Engineer Rees was in the position of trainer, as he knew what the ship could, and should, do, providing everything below went well; but no one envied the position of this officer on trial days—this day in particular.

Owing to the Channel being enveloped in a dense fog, it was late in the afternoon before favourable weather allowed the run to take place. On the approach of dusk huge tongues of flame shot high out of the lofty funnels, becoming more vivid as the light waned, until they seemed actually to be licking the blackness of the sky overhead. Imagine the feelings of those on board an alien Atlantic liner, being chased up Channel by a *Terrible* in wartime, projectiles and flames drawing nearer with every mile, and the friendly port too far away to afford asylum. Yet this imaginative scene is what the ship may be destined some day to enact in reality.

Three hours of the trial had successfully passed, a uniform speed of 22½ knots having been logged, when the ship sprang into a fog-bank, so dense that the range of vision did not exceed the ship's length. To go tearing along the busiest waterway in the world at such a speed under such risky conditions spelt disaster to someone should a collision occur. The captain therefore decided not to accept the risk, and as the race thus far, and the pace maintained, had been so highly satisfactory, the engineering judges pronounced a verdict in favour of the ship. The *Terrible* had won the "blue ribbon" in easy fashion, and experimental trials and engineering troubles were at last over—so it was then fondly hoped, though unkind Fate decided otherwise, as will be seen later on.

A short cruise to Berehaven followed, the crew undergoing a fortnight's instruction in torpedo warfare and submarine mining operations. When returning to Portsmouth the first heavy gun practice took place, and although the firing was carried out on a rough sea, some excellent results were obtained; seemingly a precursor of the phenomenal prize-firing records subsequently established by the ship on the China Station.

From October 1st until towards the end of November the ship remained at Portsmouth making good defects developed at the last trial. The political barometer just at this period stood rather low. In the Soudan the *khalifa's* power had been smashed by Kitchener at Omdurman; but the fruits of his success had been somewhat spoiled by the surreptitious occupation of Fashoda, a town further up the Nile, by a French military mission. This was the incident that was attracting the serious attention of the nation—in fact, of Europe; the presence of French troops in that town being distinctly affirmed by the British Government to be an unfriendly act that could not be tolerated. However, diplomacy eventually closed an "*affaire*" that had touched national sentiment on both sides of the Channel, and Lord

Salisbury announced on November 4th that the French Government had decided to withdraw their clandestine mission from the Nile. The Fashoda incident was thus officially closed just as the *Terrible* had been put in working order!

On November 25th, a surprise order was received from the Admiralty for the ship to proceed to Malta, and take out a relief crew for the *Camperdown*. Several officers and men who were on weekend leave were recalled, and the Naval Depôt hurriedly prepared a draft to go out.

The ship left England two days later, encountering a fresh nor'-westerly gale while crossing the Bay, which caused exceptionally heavy rolling, while a continuous succession of green seas frisked about the upper deck until the waters immortalised by Dibden had been left well astern. Malta was reached at noon, December 2nd, the passage having been performed in 121 hours, which was then the record trip for a combined speed and distance trial of a man-of-war; the actual distance run being 2206 miles: an average speed maintained of 18 knots.

Malta probably occupies the most unique position of any of our Imperial possessions. In splendid isolation it stands across the course that leads to the Suez Canal and the East; its geographical and strategical position making the island the paramount naval base in the Mediterranean. It is the headquarters of our powerful squadron maintained on that station, and has also, except India, the largest military force under one command outside the British Isles. The island is strongly fortified, and Valetta provides an ideal harbour, whether as a safe refuge for shipping or protection for a fleet, its entrance being easily closed to hostile vessels of any sort, while the proposed breakwater will, when constructed, considerably enhance its value both in peace and war time. Extensive naval dock accommodation and important works and arsenals are situated in natural positions with absolute immunity from any sea attack, which enables the island to sustain its protective fighting strength, with its own resources, in the absence of the squadron.

Its history is of the most romantic description, the island having been occupied in turn by the ancient Phoenicians, Greeks, and Romans; in the Middle Ages by the Saracens and Moors; and at later periods by the Sicilians and Knights of St. John. In nearly all ages Malta was recognised as being of such immense value to its possessor that its occupation virtually meant supremacy of sea power in the Mediterranean Sea, though in the earlier days that power was used purely for

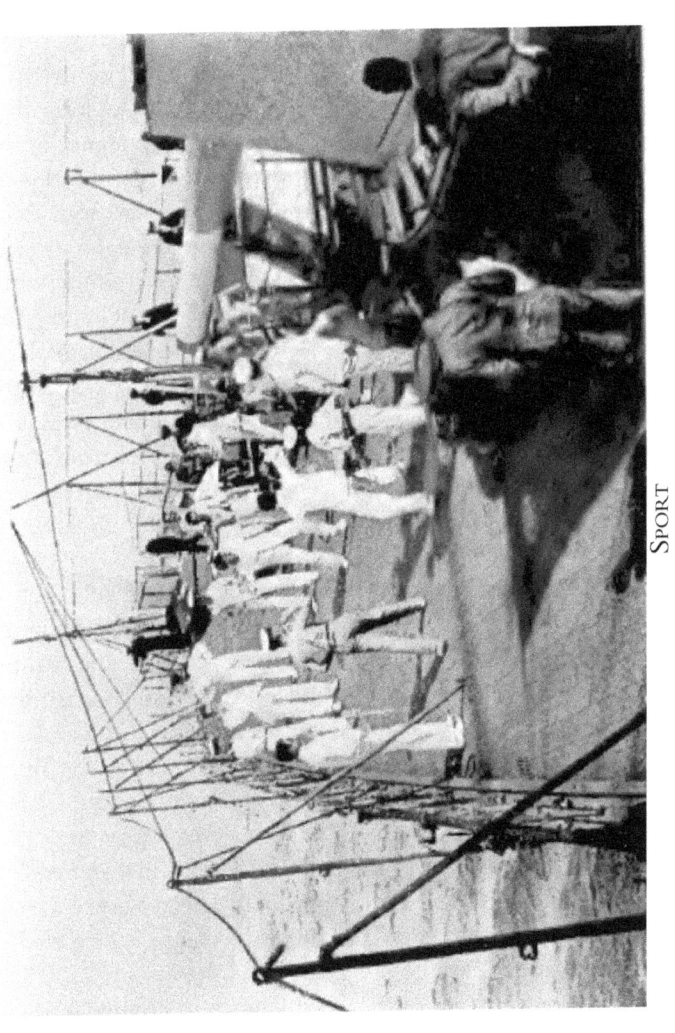

Sport

Junior officers of the "Terrible" engaged at the pastime of "swinging the monkey" at sea.

aggressive purposes. There is a spot on its coast marked by a statue of St Paul, where legend states the Apostle was shipwrecked in 58 *A.D.*, and catacombs may be visited inland, where the Christian inhabitants hid themselves from the persecution of successive *infidel* conquerors.

After passing through many centuries of turbulent history, occasioned by constant struggles for its possession, the island secured a new era of comparative peace when it was conquered by Sicily in 1090, and thereby brought under Christian rule. Until 1530 it belonged to that kingdom, after which it was transferred to the sovereignty of the Knights of St John of Jerusalem, who made the island their headquarters. Many attempts were subsequently made to wrest it from these stalwart supporters of Christianity; it was rigorously besieged in 1565 by the Turks, but all their efforts to capture it were successfully withstood. Its gallant defence was conducted by the famous Grand Master, La Valette, after whom the city of Valetta—the present capital—is named; the old capital of Citta Vecchia being abandoned as such the following year. The Knights now firmly established themselves, and expended their vast wealth in carrying out magnificent fortifications and other works, which are still in splendid condition, and erecting beautiful cathedrals, churches, and palaces, which are among the show places of Europe for old-world grandeur.

Until 1798 the Knights continued their beneficent rule, but in that year Napoleon brought his great power to bear upon Malta by expelling the Order. In 1800 the native Maltese revolted, and, assisted by British and Neapolitan troops, compelled the French garrison to capitulate, when Malta was occupied by the British; the island and its dependencies being formally ceded to Great Britain by the Treaty of Paris in 1814. Besides being a stronghold of supreme importance, Malta has also an enormous trade, its harbour being a port of call for the numerous vessels passing to and from the Suez Canal and eastern ports. The island is highly cultivated, producing nearly every variety of semi-tropical fruits and vegetables, much of which is exported to the London markets.

The principal occupation of the inhabitants is in connection with the shipping, government establishments, agriculture, and working of gold and silver, while the female element is largely employed in manufacturing the famous Maltese lace and embroidery. The island is about seventeen miles long, and nine in breadth, the colony including, the adjoining island of Gozo, and other islets. The population of the whole group is about 180,000, who, since they have enjoyed British rule, have become a prosperous and loyal community within the Empire.

The crews of the *Camperdown* having been exchanged, the ship left for England on December 8th, calling at Gibraltar *en route*; Portsmouth being reached on the 15th of the month.

Christmas, 1898, was spent in England; as many as could be spared going on ten days' leave, and the unlucky remainder spending the Yuletide season on board in the usual time-honoured naval fashion. Keen rivalry in mess decorations and culinary productions betwixt individual messes seldom fails to take place in men-of-war on this occasion. By Christmas Eve the spacious decks had been deftly transformed into a veritable fairyland by means of abundant supplies of evergreens, coloured lamps, and flags, with which the long gangways had been decorated in lavish style, while each mess had been converted into a fairy-like alcove. Arboreal arches, *naïvely* adorned with amusing or significant mottoes, were erected at the entrance of each mess deck, besides several mechanically worked representations of things nautical, some of which were specially designed to ambuscade the unwary inquisitor. The interior of the ship, when electrically lit up, presented a transformation scene of sumptuous splendour. On Christmas morning the tables were fairly bending with the weight of edible luxuries; the quantity provided not depending so much on the number of persons berthed in each mess, as on the length of the mess table!

It is an unwritten law that every inch of space must be covered with something; the viands and fruit being neatly interspersed with photographs representing various types of feminine beauty, from the gay *geisha*-girl of Japan to the modest maid of Devonshire. Punctually at noon, Captain Robinson, accompanied by all officers on board and several guests, and preceded by the ship's band, playing the "Roast Beef of Old England," made the customary tour round the mess decks. Stopping briefly at each mess, he exchanged the "Compliments of the Season" with the mess representative, and partook of certain delicacies from the proffered plates, which it were sacrilege to pass without due recognition of their contents. But a captain would require the digestion of an ostrich and the capacity of an elephant if he even sampled all that he feels it incumbent upon him to accept.

Yet it all disappears to some mysterious place, known only to a captain—and perhaps his vivacious coxswain. The day itself stands unique from all other days of the year, for from noon routine is suspended, and a sort of topsy-turveydom exists on the lower deck. The petty and non-commissioned officers will suavely perform the necessary routine work; the marine drummer-boy and a bluejacket boy for the nonce will supersede the sergeant-major and master-at-arms; the orders of these two embryo officials being humorously obeyed. These customs, however, and also that of carrying the principal officers round the decks after dinner, though still in vogue, are but a lingering survival of old naval lore, which before long will collapse into obscurity. Naval Christmas Days were formerly of a bacchanalian character, a form of celebration which finds but little favour with the present generation of "handy-men." Up till evening rounds at 9 p.m., the festivities continue, when at that hour routine and discipline displace revelry and decorations.

Weeks of doubt and speculation concerning our future movements were set at rest by the receipt of instructions for another voyage to Malta, to take out a relief crew for the *Royal Oak*. Leaving Portsmouth, February 22nd (now 1899), the ship arrived at Malta, without incident, on March 2nd. Exchange of crews having been effected, the ship left for England on the 8th, calling at Gibraltar as before.

It was on this homeward passage that Fate was to tarnish the ship's reputation, for an untoward mishap occurred that brought her unenviable notoriety. The passage both ways was being conducted at economical speed—twelve knots per hour—under very favourable conditions, when, without the slightest warning to indicate weakness, a water-tube in one of the boilers suddenly split, the full 180-lb. pressure of escaping steam violently blowing the fires from the furnace into the stokehold, the door of which had been inadvertently opened. Several men were badly scalded and burnt, one stoker (Edward Sullivan) so severely that he died a few hours afterwards. It is worthy of record that Stoker Parham, at considerable personal risk and entirely acting on his own initiative, shut off the main stop-valve of the damaged boiler, thereby minimizing the danger in that stokehold. For this service he was afterwards highly commended by the "Court of Inquiry," and promoted.

On arriving at Plymouth on the 15th, two days after the mishap, some of the details became public, and when Portsmouth was reached next day, it was found that the press had so magnified and twisted the real facts, that the ship was besieged with anxious friends of the crew, and scores of telegrams were awaiting delivery. "Sensational headlines" of present-day journalism have much to answer for. As was anticipated, both an inquest and an official investigation were held; an exhaustive inquiry into all the circumstances connected with the fatality resulting in the finding of both courts "that no blame was attributable to anyone." Full naval funeral honours closed the brief service career of another of the many victims claimed by science on its passage to a state of perfection. The accident, however, supplied fresh material for another hostile attack on the water-tube boiler, especially the now stigmatised Belleville type. Fierce opposition has invariably been the reception extended to scientific inventions in all ages. Few innovations receive an early welcome, but, as in the present instance of these particular boilers, the law which governs the survival of the fittest must prevail.

Great engineering authorities have stated that from a military standpoint the water-tube boiler is best suited for the Royal Navy, and therefore, if for no other reason than this, their adoption would appear to have been fully justified.

An opportune chance here presents itself of explaining in a few words the essential differences between the ancient and the modern boilers. The main point is that the one system is the exact converse of the other. Both are tubular boilers; the water in the cylindrical type is in the boiler space, the flames passing *through* the tubes, while in the water-tube boiler, the water—as the name implies—is inside the tubes, the flame playing *around* them. It is obvious that a greater heating area is obtained in the water-tube pattern, and consequently steam can be raised more quickly. But this boiler also satisfies many of those requirements which scientists are striving to provide for boilers of fighting ships. An important factor strongly in its favour is that it occupies less space, and is of far less weight than the cylindrical boiler, a matter of great moment in a man-of-war, as it enables a heavier armament or additional armour to be borne.

Moreover, the ability to raise steam quickly; the minimised loss of available power and risk of danger if penetrated by a shell or otherwise disabled; the ease with which it can be repaired or renewed; and its special adaptability for complying with the conditions that sudden changes of speed entail on boilers, render it too valuable for military purposes to be discarded. Yet the acme of perfection is apparently not attained at present, and the water-tube boiler remains among the list of modern inventions which are still in a state of evolution. Certain recommendations were advanced by experts at the public inquiry. These the Admiralty decided should be carried out forthwith, and as the improvements would occupy a considerable time to complete, the ship was placed alongside the dockyard to expedite the work. Harbour routine became the order of the day, the work being carried out not in the least interfering with the drills, instructions, and duties that are usually performed at other times. Southsea Common became as familiar with our field guns during this lay-up as the *kopjes* surrounding Ladysmith became a few months later.

During this long summer vacation (from sea life) the *Terrible* was the centre of attraction to the excursionists who invade the town during the season, several thousand visitors being shown over the ship. Among the many distinguished personages who crossed the gangway were the late Admiral H.R.H. the Duke of Edinburgh (Saxe-Coburg-Gotha), H.S.H. Captain Prince Louis of Battenberg, R.N., and the Duke and Duchess of Portland.

The marriage, on April 20th, of our highly esteemed captain was the one notable and interesting event to chronicle during the ship's temporary *hors-de-combat* existence. The nuptial ceremony was performed in London, Commander Limpus and several other officers from the ship accepting invitations, while the rites prescribed by ancient naval usage for such auspicious occasions were duly observed on board. Useful presentations from both officers and ship's company were made to the graceful bride, a lady who afterwards became deservedly popular with the whole crew for her genial personality.

The attendance of the Captain and Mrs. Robinson, Commander and Mrs. Limpus, Fleet-Engineer and Mrs. Chase, several officers, and a few invited guests, at a private commemorative dance given by representative lower-deck ranks, was a proof of the friendly relations existing throughout the ship, and these were maintained throughout a long commission. To the strains of the ship's string band, which discoursed enchanting music, dancing was briskly indulged in from early evening until midnight, at which hour a pleasant gathering dispersed.

As September approached, the refitting programme was nearing completion, and rumour became busy regarding the ship's future service—one week China, another week the Channel, then the "Straits" indeed, each station in turn was suggested as the place where the commission was to be taken up—or recommenced. However, the gift of prescience was a negative quantity with all the prophets, for the final sailing orders were totally at variance with every ventured prognostication.

Time—and the summer months of 1899—flew by all too quickly. The "all work and no play" policy found no favour with the *Terrible's régimé*. Leave unlimited, consistent with service requirements, was the rule instead of the exception, the most being made of an indulgence which was highly appreciated by the "Sailors of the Queen."

H.M.S. "Terrible," 1848.

Length, over all, 246 feet.   Beam. 42½ feet.
Displacement, 1,848 tons.   Indicated Horse Power, 2.400.
Guns:—Upper Deck—Four 56-pounders; Two 68-pounders.
Main Deck-Four 56-pounders: Four 68-pounders.

H.M.S. "Terrible," 1898.

Length, over all, 538 feet.   Beam, 71 feet.
Displacement. 14,200 tons.   Indicated Horse Power, 25,000
Guns—Two 9½-inch, Twelve 6-inch. Eighteen 12-pounders.
Twelve 3-pounders, Eight Maxims.

CHAPTER 2

Voyage to the Cape: Crossing the "Line"

September and October, 1899

Admiralty Orders were received early in September that the ship would probably leave England about the middle of the month for the China Station, to proceed there by the Suez Canal route. The distribution of the British Fleet is, of course, mainly governed by considerations of foreign policy, therefore the Admiralty, in disposing of ships, act mainly on this principle. It was just at this period that the political situation in South Africa was becoming acute in consequence of the apparently hostile attitude of the Transvaal and Orange Free State Republics towards Great Britain. To mention briefly here that the tone of the recently published despatches from both republics was producing an uneasy feeling in the country, and that war, even now at this juncture, appeared almost inevitable as the solution of the questions at issue, will suffice to explain the chain of events.

Definite instructions were received on the 10th to complete with coal and stores, and embark relief crews for the destroyers *Handy* and *Hart*, besides disposable supernumeraries for the China Station.

On September 14th the ship proceeded to Spithead to prepare for the voyage and undergo a short official trial to test the work just completed; and this proving satisfactory, the captain was able to report the *Terrible* "as ready in all respects for sea." On the 18th telegraphic instructions were received that the ship was to proceed to China via the Cape, to augment the squadron in South African waters, should circumstances render this course necessary on our arrival there. The *Powerful*, whose commission was expiring, was also ordered to return home from China by the same route for a similar purpose. Political considerations had altered the compass course of both ships. Precautionary military measures had also been taken by the despatch of strong reinforcements from England and India, the defensive strength of the British forces then in South Africa being wholly inadequate to cope with any aggressive action the republics might contemplate against the Colonies.

Numerous changes had taken place in the ship's complement during our inactive condition in dockyard hands among both officers and men. Lieutenant Hughes Onslow had relieved Commander Gillett as Navigating Officer; Lieutenant Drummond was now the Gunnery Officer, *vice* Lieutenant Molteno; Fleet-Engineer Chase had already relieved Fleet-Engineer Rees prior to the last voyage to Malta, and several officers of junior rank and a large number of men had also been exchanged for various service reasons. The selection of Captain Robinson for the important command of the Torpedo School (H.M.S. *Vernon*) was the change, however, that mostly concerned the entire crew. His departure was the occasion of much genuine regret, as is always the case when a popular captain vacates his command before the ship's term of service has expired.

During his eighteen months' reign in the *Terrible* the crew had enjoyed exceptional privileges and pleasurable service. In Captain Percy Scott, his successor, who had recently paid off the *Scylla*, we had an officer with a wide service reputation as an expert in gunnery and signalling, and a vigorous gunnery policy was the expected result of his appointment. Nor was the forecast a wrong one, as subsequent events will tend to prove. It is now matter of history how his name became associated with the 4.7 gun in the Anglo-Boer War, and again with heavy gun prize-firing records in China; but of these subjects more *anon*.

The signal, "Permission to proceed in execution of previous orders," being affirmed by the admiral, the ship left for Plymouth the afternoon of September 19th, arriving there early next morning. The embarkation of more supers brought the total number on board to 1133 officers and men; the sailing arrangements thus completed, the ship left at sunset for her destination. "Off at last!" was the ejaculation that escaped from many lips as the land was cleared, in token of relief apparently from some momentous suspense. It was in truth a happy relief to find that at last there was a definite objective to carry out instead of a monotonous return to spasmodic and inglorious trooping voyages. Besides, the nature of the mission now before us, and the possibilities in view, came as

Captain Percy Moreton Scott, C.V.O., C.B.

an agreeable sequel to the first act in the drama of our commission.

Our authorised speed of thirteen knots brought the ship to Las Palmas on the 25th, where the ship was coaled, the crew working continuously at this operation until 2000 tons had been shipped. Coaling a man-of-war is always performed as an evolution by the crew, rapidity in filling the bunkers being obviously only second in importance to fighting efficiency. Routine is of course suspended, which fact probably accounted for two youthful midshipmen, who will be termed Mr. S—— and Mr. B——, finding time to fight a mock duel with the historic dirk; the blade of Mr. B——'s dirk being neatly passed through his opponent's arm, inflicting a nasty flesh wound, as the result of this sham *affaire d'honneur*, "Honour" was satisfied, but not the captain, who issued a prohibitory edict against the sport of mock duels.

By noon, the 26th, the Grand Canaries, one of the few remaining links with the past colonial greatness of Spain, had been left well astern, and so had apparently the temperate climate; for real tropical weather had penetrated to a latitude far beyond the usual tropical limits, causing a general desire to camp out on deck both night and day. The heat below was so intense that the full benefit of a Turkish bath might be obtained in the auxiliary engine-room where the temperature then registered over 130 degrees, the stoker on watch finding even his bathing drawers a superfluous garment. One stoker humorously described the stokehold as being a training home, for a certain position, at a certain place, in another world. That may be.

Various ranks and ratings are often described as the backbone of the Royal Navy—a much abused and undesirable phrase. Yet few who are cognizant of the conditions under which the engineering staff perform their duty would deny that title (if it must be used) to them—engineers, artificers, and stokers alike, who, whether at sea or in harbour, in torrid or temperate climes, in peace time or war, have always risky and arduous duties to perform.

A diversion from routine and an occasional day devoted to sport tends to create good fellowship, and promote the popularity of a life on the ocean wave—a life vividly and romantically described by Marryat, whose famous stories have drawn many a British youth to a sea career.

"Crossing the Line" is an ancient nautical ceremony that always produces the maximum of fun if properly performed. The captain's permission having been obtained, preparations for carrying out this tropical carnival were immediately put in hand.

By the time the ship arrived near the equatorial line everything was ready for our nautical spectacular entertainment—the convivial spirits who were taking the characters displaying an almost fiendish delight in their endeavours to make the performance a success. The royal regalia of Neptune and Amphitrite were genuine works of art, resplendent with jewels obtained from the theatrical costume box, the robe worn by the latter being made from real Japanese silk. In fact, the costumes for each character, both in style and effect, were quite "Alhambrian." Every additional touch that was made served further to deepen the mystery which surrounded these mystic rites, and sharpened the curiosity of those who had never been in Father Neptune's mythological dominions before. Improbable yarns were spun, and strange rumours set afloat concerning the ceremony, which in the old sailing days was invariably accompanied by plenty of horse-play, and was also an occasion for slyly paying off old scores against disliked individuals—though nothing of this nature was expected, or did occur, in this instance. During the evening of the 2nd October, the prelude to the "official ceremony" that was to take place next day was performed, the ship actually crossing the Line about 7 p.m., according to reckoning.

The proceedings commenced by Chief Boatswain's-mate Bate hailing the bridge, and reporting to the officer of the watch, "Line right ahead," followed by the order for "Hands to clear away Line"; which was, by arrangement, piped in loud tones round the decks, and signalised the commencement of the fun, bringing every one below on deck with a rush. Father Neptune—represented by the biggest man on board—(Ship's Corporal Churchman), dressed in full regalia and using a megaphone, now hailed the bridge, asking the usual questions as follows:—"What ship is that?" "Where from?" "Where bound?" and "What is your captain's name?" each question is turn being correctly replied to by the officer of the watch. Neptune being apparently satisfied hailed the ship to stop, which demand was formally complied with, and a few minutes afterwards "His Majesty," accompanied by an impish-looking attendant, appeared on the starboard gangway— hitherto dark—and was introduced by a flood of electric light that made his appearance and regalia look very impressive.

He was received by the guard and band, the former using broomhandles for arms, the latter playing a few bars of a comic air as a salute when the guard came to the "present." Neptune gravely returned the salute, and then greeted the captain, who was present to receive him. After the usual courteous questions had been put and answered, "His Majesty" requested permission to visit the ship again next day, accom-

CROSSING THE LINE

The secretary reading a petition to Neptune from the novices desirous of becoming subjects of His Majesty

panied by his court in accordance with ancient custom. A favourable answer having been given, Neptune retired over the gangway, and was accorded the same honours as on entering, the sudden extinguishing of the electric light and burning of phosphorous fire, signalling his departure to his submarine kingdom.

The scene, which was highly appreciated by the nautical audience, might be termed both pretty and picturesque, yet the next day's ceremony was still enveloped with secrecy and mystery, which made it the more keenly looked forward to. Punctually at 10 a.m. next day, the grand procession moved off, the band playing a slow march during the parade, which started from forward, the space on the clear upper deck allowing the pageant to be seen to advantage. Father Neptune with the Amphitrite (Lieutenant Bogle, R.N.) in full royal robes and other regal insignia, attended by a page of honour and nymphs, were seated on a state car, drawn by the Bears, preceded by the Master of Ceremonies, and escorted by a body-guard of boys dressed in quaint costumes, and carrying tomahawks. They were followed by the Court in their order of precedence, each wearing a costume denoting the official position he held. On arriving on the quarterdeck, their "Majesties" were received by the captain and officers with mock official dignity; the M.C. introducing them as follows:—

> Your Excellency—
> His Majesty, 'Father Neptune,' who came on board last night, is now accompanied by his consort, the Lady Amphitrite; And they now wish in chosen words their pleasure to express, and by royal command the secretary will now read their address.

The secretary then came forward and read an amusing address, specially written in verse for the occasion by Neptune's "Poet"[1] Laureate," touching events which concerned the ship's history and other incidents, as follows:—

> *Your Excellency—*
> 1. *Right glad are we to visit your quadruple-funnelled ship,*
> *And enable our amphibious court to greet you on your trip. It is not often nowadays that we come up from below; But we are pleased to visit you with pomp and regal show,*
> 2. *Your noble ship we hear has been a source of great comment,*
> *And given cause for lots of talk in your House of Parliament; But now*

---
1. Composed by the author.

it is quite safe to say this soon will be forgot when her reputation is
retrieved—under Captain Scott.

3. Who has not heard of the Scylla's[2] fame—a feat that's worth repeating—
Bat what should now prevent your ship that brilliant record beating?
For even now we hear that you are endeavouring to impart
Scientific handling of her guns—a most important start,

4. For it is the 'man behind the gun,' and the accuracy of his fire,
That will vanquish England's enemies, when they threaten her Empire.
For that 'real thing' of which Kipling wrote—an oft-repeated phrase—
Britannia's sons will fight her guns, as they did in Nelson's days.

5. But history repeats itself, and great deeds soon decay.
Though down below our 'Court' oft speaks of those in Bantry Bay.
Dossiers and Bordereaus will fade, and Kruger's power must go;
But what will outlive every deed is the donkey named 'What Ho!'[3]

6. And now, Commander Limpus, we've something for your ear,
For it does not seem—at least to us—that your Notice [4] was quite clear.
Did you not state in '98—I think you will remember—
To the China Seas the ship would go, in the middle of September?

7. Now, when that Notice was put up, you couldn't have been sincere,
Or else had not consulted first, the ship's Fleet-Engineer;
But never mind, you are forgiven, and meant not to deceive,
For you spent the summer of '99, in the dockyard—giving leave!

8. But now we hope your ship's quite trim, and fit to take her place
Among the squadrons of the Fleet, ready for battle or the 'Chase.'[5]
For 'England's'[6] power is always felt upon the ocean 'Wilde,' [7]

---

2. Made 80 *per cent*, of hits with 4.7 guns at prize firing—a phenomenal record, which was closely emulated by the Terrible's 6-inch guns two successive years on the China Station.
3. An absentee in plain clothes disclosed his identity to a naval picquet, when passing them mounted on a donkey, by hailing, "What Ho!" whereupon he was chased and captured.
4. A notice was posted up in July, 1898, stating that the *Terrible* would probably leave for China in September, on conclusion of the experiments; but this proved a wrong forecast of events.
5/6/7 Fleet-Engineer Chase; Lieutenant England, R.N.; Lieutenant Wilde, R.N.; officers of the ship.

On land or sea, protection's free, to each imperial child.

9. Although our time is limited, and our greetings nearly done,
We cannot to our dominions go, and forget your 'Number One.'[8]
On New Year's Day, we're bound to say, that we have got a notion
'Their Lordships'—as a season's gift—will send him his promotion.

10. "We have often noticed sailors, when down below they come,
Belong not to I.O.G.T.,[9] and leave behind their rum,
Though we must confess it's tasty, when in battle or in breeze,
And makes one feel more frisky, than does vaccinated cheese.

11. Now, don't think that we're frivolous, or given to consoling,
But hope you'll have some stirring times—we don't mean always coaling—
For this is work that must be done, which hides the sailors' blushes
When they see the Jonty[10] prowling round (doing nothing) with the Crushers.[11]

12. 'Britannia rules the waves,' it's said, but her ruling seems so funny,
For mal-de-mer is well served out, so different from prize-money;[12]
But our advice to all on board, who suffer from such ills.
Is to listen to your 'squee-gee[13] band,' or take some Beecham's Pills.

13. "Now let all your gallant officers, and men of each degree.
Remember that 'Father Neptune' is the guardian of the sea;
And 'tis well known from experience, that many unpleasant things
Must be done—if promotion's won—when you've dropped the apron strings.

14. "If your men should land to fight, for England, home, and beauty.
Their Captain, I am sure, expects, that they will do their duty.
And emulate past naval deeds, and not return until—
Like Briton's sons, they've fought their guns, and avenged Majuba Hill.[14]

---

8. "Number One" is the naval expression which designates the first-lieutenant of a man-of-war.
9. The "Independent Order of Good Templars."
10/11. Lower-deck terms for the master-at-arms and naval police respectively.
12. Prize-money is paid by shares according to service rank—sea-sickness is no respecter of persons.
13. Term applied to a ship's drum-and-fife band; generally an unmelodious orchestra.
14. The *Terrible's* guns were especially mentioned in despatches by General Buller for the part they took at Pieter's Hill on Majuba day.

15. *Now, your Excellency, we have finished*
With our diatribe,
And with your kind permission
We'll your decks now circumscribe;
That we may view our subjects.
Before we open Court,
To receive that homage which is due:
May we hope for your support?
Our royal visit to a ship
Is not a new invention
But an ancient custom oft retailed
By old sea-dogs when on pension."

Note.—The whole of these verses were recited on the "Crossing the line" occasion, some, particularly 3, 4, 14, being true forecasts.

Presents of a smokable description were now handed to the members of the Court, after which the procession again formed up and completed the tour round the decks, finishing forward on the forecastle at the font—a huge canvas tank four feet deep filled with sea water into which a hose was kept running.

The secretary now called out the names of novices, who were brought forward by Neptune's own police, and introduced to their "Majesties" and Court, who occupied a raised platform overlooking the font. Each in turn was examined by the Court Physician, who thoughtfully pronounced them all fit to be made subjects, passing them on to the barber's assistant, who lathered each with his mystic mixture of soft soap and oatmeal. The barber completed the toilet, the shaving instrument used being fashioned from a piece of hoop-iron shaped as a razor. Thus prepared, they were plunged into the font, where the Bears finished off the ceremony of initiation, much to the relief of the candidate, who now became one of Neptune's subjects.

The fun was continued till noon, causing endless amusement, with an entire absence of ill-humour throughout, although each degree was made very impressive—especially to the candidate seeking (?) admission. Every officer, according to his seniority, who had not previously been south of the equator was made a victim; a selected number from each rating being taken from the rest of the crew owing to the large number borne. Several surprise initiations were made on unsuspecting onlookers by recently made subjects, which increased the fun.

One of these was the sudden pounce made by the midshipmen on the First-lieutenant, who had been directing operations from the fore bridge. He gracefully surrendered to his captors, and was gently (?) passed through each stage—the middies afterwards going in search of further prey. Another occasion was the sweeping of the whole Court, including Neptune himself, into the font towards the finish, which carefully planned scheme practically concluded the programme, the success of which fully justified the somewhat tentative permission given for its performance. The characters were taken by both officers and men, representing "Neptune," "Amphitrite," "Nymphs," "Doctor," "Barber" and "Assistant," "Policemen," "Bears," "Court Jesters," "Secretary," and "M.C.," a total of nearly fifty taking part. In the evening a smoking concert was held on the poop, which thus terminated a day entirely devoted to frivolity—a day out at sea.

Next day the ship encountered strong S.E. trade winds, which were in striking contrast to the glorious equatorial calm of yesterday, "*'Tis an ill wind that blows nobody good.*" In this instance the refreshing breeze cooled the ship and made life comfortable 'tween decks, but it also compelled the captain to alter course and head for St Helena to replenish with coal, in case of meeting with worse weather. Arriving there on October 7th, coaling ship immediately began, the evolution early indicating that a record for slowness was to be established, owing to the primitive method in vogue at this port.

St Helena is both picturesque and historic, its claim to the latter title being permanently established in the view of the whole world by its connection with the great Napoleon's last days. The emperor's tomb is situated in a beautiful spot a few miles inland at Longwood, and as it is the showplace of the island, many officers and others made a pilgrimage to the shrine, and also to the residence in which he spent his exile. By permission of the British Government, his remains were exhumed in 1840, taken to France, and amidst much pomp and ceremony due to his former imperial rank and greatness, placed in the "Invalides" at Paris, the national burying-place for distinguished Frenchmen. The island was discovered by Juan de Nova Castella, a Portuguese navigator, in 1501. It was colonised by the Dutch about 1645, who held it till 1651, when it was seized by the British East India Company, but was retaken by the Dutch in 1672.

The following year saw the island again in possession of the British, who have retained it ever since, it being governed by the aforesaid company until 1834, when it became a Crown Colony. Though only some 1000 miles from the Equator, the island, owing to its mountainous formation, possesses a most salubrious climate, and is the health resort of the West Coast Squadron. It was formerly an important place of call for shipping going to India and the Far East, but its prosperity was seriously diminished by the opening of the Suez Canal, which diverted the eastern trade route. Jamestown, the capital, is a prettily situated seaport, having a good anchorage, where vessels are able to lie close in shore. The island is about ten miles long, by six miles broad, with a mixed coloured population of about 4000. Agriculture and fishing form the principal occupation of the somewhat unprogressive inhabitants, apart from what the shipping provides. Its unique position in the Atlantic makes the island of strategical value to the Fleet Considerable numbers of Boer prisoners, including General Cronje, were exiled there during the continuance of the war.

The few hundred tons of coal required having been bunkered, the ship sailed for the Cape next day. Anticipation had at last reached the stage of realisation. Super-eminent skill in gunnery was the order. To obtain this result scientific lessons in aiming and firing at cunningly devised targets placed outside the ship had become the diurnal routine six days out of the seven. To attain proficiency with the rifle and pistol, one side of our lengthy upper deck was transformed into a miniature Bisley range, having variety butts complete, whereat instruction in shooting was imparted in "service hours," while keen private competitions were taking place every evening—a useful form of amusement The officers were also frequently exercising the hand and eye at revolver practice, some good shooting being made, as was evidenced one evening by a small hole being drilled through Lieutenant Lawrie's leg, which by some mischance had got in the line of fire, but the wound being only a flesh one, quickly healed.

On October 13th, the track chart showed that only 215 miles separated the ship from her destination, and speculation became rife as to what news the morrow would bring forth. Not since leaving England had any South African news been obtained to alter the situation as it then appeared; the news gleaned at St. Helena being of a very meagre description. Nevertheless, campaigning gear field accoutrements had been put in order, the latter having been served out to each individual, so that any apparent defect might be timely remedied.

Next day, October 14th, the *Terrible* steamed into Simon's Bay. The *Powerful*, having arrived the previous day from China, was now at Cape Town, discharging an infantry battalion, which had been brought from Mauritius with great promptitude.

The precipitate invasion of British territory and committal of hostile acts by the armed forces of the two republics had occurred on the 12th inst. The astounding manner in which war had displaced diplomacy had occasioned considerable surprise; not because such a result was wholly unexpected, but as having upset every preconceived idea formed on the situation. The Boers themselves had forced the crisis by offering a definite ultimatum of an uncompromising character, seemingly determined to end negotiations with war. This result one may safely opine was the inevitable and contemplated climax intended by them to secure the fruits of years of political aspirations—or conspiracies.

The ship's commission being largely associated with the Cape, the next chapter is assigned to a short account of South Africa, which may be found interesting perusal to those readers who are unfamiliar with the subjects dealt with therein. Considering the fact that the "Great Anglo-Boer War" ranks among the most important events in the history of the British Empire, this brief diversion from the story proper can scarcely be termed superfluous or out of place.

Chapter 3
Résumé of South African History

From 1486 to 1899

The Cape of Good Hope was discovered in 1486 by Bartholomew Diaz, a Portuguese navigator, when searching along the West African coast for a sea route to the East Indies. Eleven years later, Vasco da Gama, a compatriot of Diaz, sailed from Portugal and successfully completed a voyage to the East Indies by this route. In rounding the Cape, he touched at the place where Durban now stands, and as it was Christmas Day when he dropped anchor there, named the country Natal. The Portuguese, however, did not settle at the Cape, but subsequently established themselves on the island of Mozambique on the eastern coast They gradually extended their sovereignty to the mainland opposite, taking possession of the coast territory from Delagoa Bay northwards to Cape Delgado, about 900 miles in length—the whole possessions now designated as Portuguese East Africa, Lorenzo Marques, the mainland capital, is situated on the shores of Delagoa Bay, and is a port of considerable political and commercial value.

A railway running from here connects its system with the Transvaal lines at Koomatipoort, 60 miles distant on the frontier, thus giving the insulated Transvaal Republic a strategic opening to the sea other than by British routes. The importance of Delagoa Bay and its railway became more manifest during the war, as supplies were easily despatched from thence to the enemy, and moreover the line afforded safe conduct for them when closely pressed It was by this route that President Kruger escaped to the coast when his capture was becoming imminent, afterwards proceeding to Europe in a Dutch war-vessel. Situated 500 miles north of Delagoa Bay is the port of Beira, which place is also connected by rail with the British province of Rhodesia, about 180 miles distant As we possess ancient treaty rights of passage through this portion of Portuguese territory, a British force was despatched from here to help in the relief of Mafeking from the north—an equivalent to some extent for the use the Delagoa route was put to by the Boers.

Following the Portuguese in South Africa came the Dutch, in 1652, who then took possession of Table Bay, and established a fortified base for their shipping. The Cape from this time became an important place of call for vessels trading to the East Indies, until the Suez Canal changed the eastern route. The salubrious climate of the Cape is admirably adapted to Europeans, so that the colonizing Dutch quickly attached themselves to the country. Townlets and hamlets were gradually formed, and prosperity rewarded their agricultural and pastoral pursuits, their produce finding ready market with the passing shipping. Such was the beginning of Cape Colony.

Towards the end of the century a blend of population took place by the introduction of several hundred French religious refugees (Huguenots) into their midst, who had been compelled to leave France upon the revocation of the Edict of Nantes. This combination of European pioneers—with a sprinkling of Anglo-Saxon blood—was the source from which the present Boer race have sprung; probably the hardiest people among civilised nations. The government of the colony was vested in the Dutch East India Company, who retained their power until 1796, when, Holland becoming allied with France in war against England, the Cape was seized by a British force. By the terms of the Peace of Amiens, in 1802, it was restored to its former possessors, but was captured a second time by the British during the next war, in 1806, being formally ceded to the British Crown by the Netherlands Government in 1814. British history in South Africa practically dates from this period.

Cape Colony was now brought under British laws, after having been subject, with little interruption, to Dutch rule for over 150 years. The Dutch colonists soon showed discontent against British rule and customs, and, in 1816, the most rebellious spirits among them attempted resistance to certain laws, but the rising was quickly suppressed. Not so, however, its evil effects, for the Boer seed of racial hatred towards everything British had apparently germinated by this episode; the infliction of capital punishment on some half-dozen ringleaders of the revolt nurturing a bitter reminiscence, the sequel of which is to be found in the Slaagters Nek anniversary, and, perhaps, the present struggle. These sturdy Afrikanders had descended from a stock, who for generations had enjoyed certain forms of home-made laws, tolerated by the old governing authorities owing to the scattered condition of the communities, which prevented due enforcement of authority.

Rebellion had attempted to fight the law, the law had subdued the rebels, but an impressive penalty produced other results besides submission. A series of trekkings into the interior were the means whereby many disaffected sought to obtain their freedom from a progressive flag, and a place in which to indulge their mediaeval inclinations with impunity. But these dispersions were met by the British Government proclaiming their sovereignty over the whole of South Africa south of latitude 20° (the Zambesi), so that, unless the Boer trekkers crossed into Portuguese territory, they still remained British subjects

The landing of some 5000 British immigrants in 1820, and the steady flow that followed this influx, somewhat equalised the balance of numbers between the two races in the Colony. Four years later, a British settlement was established in Natal, hitherto only occupied by natives, although two previous but abortive attempts had been made to colonize it in 1688 and 1721 by the Afrikander Dutch.

The first Kaffir War, in 1834, was the beginning of the prolonged struggle for supremacy betwixt the white and black races of South Africa. In the same year the Slave Emancipation Act was passed by the British Government, a measure that revolutionised the labour question throughout the Empire wherever the Sons of Ham were bought and sold. As one distinguished writer (Dr. Conan Doyle) aptly observes—[1]

> It was a noble national action, and one the morality of which was in advance of its time, that the British Parliament should vote the enormous sum of twenty million pounds to pay compensation to the slave holders, and so remove an evil with which the mother country had no immediate connection.

Except to the philosophical moralist, who has never seen his black brethren under ordinary conditions of life, this special measure might seem to be in advance of *all* time. It is a debatable question whether absolute freedom has not been responsible for greater demoralization of the negro race than was ever brought about in the old slavery days. Proselytism, or contact with civilization, may temporarily elevate him;

---

1. *The Great Boer War* by Arthur Conan Doyle is also published by Leonaur.

but, left to himself, his decline is rapid. Restriction of liberty appears essential to his well-being, though not the repugnant slavery of a bygone age. Not only did the Emancipation Act produce rapid impoverishment in our West Indian possessions, but its application to the Cape Colonies produced a movement that actually altered South African history. The utter futility of offering armed resistance to the law had already been made manifest to the Boers—nearly all of whom were slave owners—who saw in the act ominous signs of a ruinous future.

Notwithstanding that a liberal compensation was being paid them, the enforced loss of their slave labour was regarded as the last straw of British iniquities. Sweeping reforms are always viewed by those whom they adversely affect as an injustice, and the Boers were no exception to the rule. The crude ideas of government that had prevailed with them for generations, when each farmstead was a miniature republic and its owner a petty president, were sufficient extenuation for their obstinate belief that, when equitable and fundamental laws superseded their individual liberties, they were being oppressed. Migration, then, was the only remedy for the real or supposed evils that cession to England had brought upon them.

The Great Trek was resolved upon and carried into execution, the result of which was the founding, about 1840, of the Transvaal and Orange Free State Republics. The departure from the colony of the majority of the Dutch colonists, estimated at some 8000 families, was a stupendous movement. President Kruger has, when addressing his *burghers*, frequently likened this exodus of Boers to the Israelitish flight from Egypt—the children of Boerdom fleeing from the British Pharaoh. And a reasonable comparison it is, so far as the immense difficulties that beset their journey, from start to finish, are concerned. Fierce opposition from savage tribes, and attacks from wild beasts, greatly reduced their numbers, about a quarter of them perishing before they could peaceably settle in the conquered territories. The new States they created will for all time remain a standing tribute to the indomitable bravery, stamina, and resourcefulness of the Boer race. With the creation of these alien States began the interminable series of troubles which successive British statesmen and Cape Governors have had to face, until at last the solution was sought for in war.

Following the succession of main events which concern South Africa generally, we find a state of war in the newly fledged colony of Natal. The Boers had descended from the north, and had attempted to establish a republican government at Pietermaritzburg, but the Cape

Governor sent a military expedition against them, drove them north again, and in 1843 annexed Natal to Cape Colony.

A second Kaffir War, in 1847, proved how difficult it was to secure expansion of territory and enforce the recognition of civilised laws by uncivilised natives.

In 1848, owing to the turbulent condition into which the newly born Orange Free State had fallen, Sir Harry Smith, the Cape Governor, proclaimed the republic British territory. The Free Staters offered a brief resistance at Boomplaats, were defeated, and a British Garrison was established at Bloemfontein, the capital The Boer leaders had been unable to enforce their laws among the burghers, thus producing a chaotic condition of affairs within their own State. Their unsuccessful warfare with the native tribes had also greatly endangered the peace of South Africa, and gave ample excuse for British intervention.

In the Transvaal, whither the majority of the Boers had migrated, a certain stable form of government prevailed, though even there civil war was only narrowly averted. Settling their internal differences themselves, and desiring a recognition of their independence as a State by the British Government, they accepted an agreement in 1852, known as the Sand River Convention, which provided, under certain conditions, for their self-government

In 1853 representative government was granted by the Crown to the Cape Colony, which, notwithstanding the loss of a number of seceding Dutch colonists, was progressing rapidly in wealth and population.

The withdrawal of British troops from the occupancy of the Orange Free State in 1854, and restoration of its own government, restored this country to the rank of an independent State, with whom the British remained on the most amicable terms up to the present crisis.

Natal was proclaimed a Crown Colony in 1856, after having been associated with the mother colony for thirteen years. Except for the memorable Zulu War of 1879, when Cetewayo's power was destroyed and Zululand also became a Crown Colony, Natal has enjoyed a peaceful and prosperous career. So rapid became its progress, that responsible government was conceded to the colony in 1893, and the Zululand territory made over to it in 1897.

These, then, were the four principal Colonies and States (Cape Colony, Natal, the Transvaal, and Orange Free State Republics) involved in the contest in South Africa, whose territories became one vast theatre of war in the coming race struggle.

Responsible government was granted to Cape Colony in 1880, a concession which marked an important phase in this colony's history. The Dutch electors were still preponderant, and this fact had the effect of changing the constitution as it had existed under Crown Colony Government The colony practically reverted to Dutch methods of legislation, the Dutch language obtaining equal official recognition with English. The discoveries of gold and diamonds, coal and other minerals, had added new, and valuable industries which enabled the colony to hold continuously the paramount position in South Africa, commercially and politically. Cape Town, its capital, and seat of Government of the High Commissioner of the Cape, is the metropolis of South Africa. As a commercial port it ranks first, and the town itself is a model among modern cities.

Native troubles were again prevalent in the colony almost continuously from 1877 to 1881, *viz.* the Gaika and Gealeka rebellions, and the Basuto War. The Basutos, being a proud and warlike race, had occasioned considerable trouble during the thirteen years of their annexation to Cape Colony, which ended with their complete severance from it Basutoland from that time became an inland Crown Colony, with special laws restricting European settlement therein. During this period an important change was taking place, shading all other pages of South African history, since this is the particular time from which can be dated the growth of that Dutch ambition which involved the British Empire, eighteen years afterwards, in a vital struggle for supremacy in South Africa.

Owing to internal dissensions, financial embarrassment, and ill-luck with several native wars, a condition of affairs had been produced within the Transvaal Republic akin to chaos. The British intervened, saved them from a revengeful war which the powerful Zulu nation were planning to wage against them, and Sir Theophilus Shepstone, with the tacit approval of the *burghers*, annexed their country in 1877. British assistance, no doubt, was opportunely rendered and appreciated at the time; but progressive British rule was no more palatable to the unprogressive Boers than before. The Zulus did not forgive us our action in frustrating their design upon the Boers, and two years later we had the fateful Zulu War on our own hands as the first result of our intervention.

In December, 1880, the Transvaalers proclaimed the Second Transvaal Republic, and took the field against British occupation. The towns held by our troops were invested, and a state of war was ended, after the disastrous reverse to Sir George Colley's relieving force at Majuba Hill, by a second surrender of independence to the republic in March, 1881. This ultra-magnanimous policy of the British Government of the period was so little in accordance with our Imperial traditions, that it stands almost alone in the ranks of historical events which will puzzle posterity. Another convention was entered into between the British and Transvaal Governments, Paul Kruger becoming the first President of the rehabilitated republic. Fate decreed that he should also be the last.

The establishment of a German Protectorate, in 1884, over the western region north of the Orange River was the introduction of another European sovereignty into South Africa, with possibilities of future trouble.

Rhodesia, or Central South Africa, is an immense territory under British protectorate, but governed principally by a corporate body known as the Chartered Company, founded by Mr. Cecil Rhodes. Two powerful tribes—Mashonas and Matabeles—inhabit a large portion of the territory, with whom severe fighting took place before the order which now prevails there could be established. Salisbury and Buluwayo are the two principal centres of government and commerce, and the country, rich in mineral deposits and pastoral districts, is being highly developed. A railway from the Cape connects these towns with the outer world, and it is this route which the proposed Cape Town to Cairo line will take.

The Bechuanaland Protectorate, as a separate administration, is the last of the group of states, colonies, etc., national and political, which, prior to the war, accounted for the divisions of territory in the map of South Africa. This tract of country was added to Cape Colony in 1895, but is separately administered by the high commissioner, who is represented by resident commissioners.

Incorporation! annexation, and sovereign protectorates have practically extinguished or absorbed all the other petty native kingdoms and territories which have not been touched upon in this compressed history.

******

The Anglo-Boer conflict was, logically, the natural result of the great historical error of judgment of 1881, and of racial antagonism of many years' growth. The unmilitary, inglorious, and abrupt termination of war following the British disaster at Majuba Hill, together with the generous terms of peace which were then granted by us to the Boers, indicated a policy too magnanimous for their comprehension. The restoration of independence under such circumstances was suggestive to the Boers that they had gained by war a position of equality with us in South Africa—even if not of supremacy. This idea conceived by them at that time, and never subsequently eradicated, was at the bottom of all the trouble that followed.

The Transvaalers remained quiet for a brief period, but their later aggressions compelled the British, in 1884, to employ force to keep them within their defined territory. In seeking expansion, which could not possibly be necessary, they invaded British territory both east and west Their objective in Zululand was clearly perceptible, *viz.* an outlet to the sea. Becoming dissatisfied with the provisions contained in the Pretorian Convention of 1881, a deputation of Boer delegates, among whom was President Kruger, visited London to get it altered. The London Convention of 1884 was the result of their visit, and likewise the harbinger of much future trouble, especially in regard to the suzerainty question. Suzerainty signifies paramount authority, or power of veto over specified actions of vassal states or communities. The British claimed this authority of *suzerainty* over the Transvaal Republic; the Boers repudiated it The dispute arose from the fact that, while this term was distinctly specified in the preamble and articles of the Pretorian Convention, it was omitted from the corresponding documents concluded in London.

The British aver there was never any intention to abrogate the *suzerainty*, notwithstanding its omission from the London Convention; also that it was not, nor could have been, a question for controversial discussion. They say further, that the preamble of the Pretorian Convention, which constitutes the basis of relationship between the two Governments, was not repealed, and that the preamble of the London Convention explicitly affirms that the *articles* of that Convention be substituted for the *articles* embodied in the Pretorian Convention, thereby specifically indicating what changes were being made. The Boers, however, inconsistently asserted that the preamble as well as the articles of the London Convention displaces the document drafted in 1881. Nevertheless, the Boer delegates actually signed the 1884 Convention, fully cognizant that their direct request for abolition of suzerainty was refused. This may afford some explanation of the most supreme and vital of the many controversial questions at issue which brought about the war.

The discovery of rich goldfields on the Rand, about 1886, attracted a cosmopolitan congregation of wealth-seekers from most of the civilised nations. These people were designated by the Boers as *uitlanders*—or outlanders. Although gold was there in abundance, yet gold was required to obtain it. The Rand was no place for the adventurous nugget-seeker. Many companies were formed, principally British, and the capital thus raised was utilised in buying expensive mining machinery and plant with which only it was possible to secure the precious metal This gold fever created an undreamed of situation in this hitherto pastoral country. An impoverished State suddenly became an opulent and important country; an Eldorado had been unexpectedly discovered, and future prosperity appeared assured to the Transvaal. States, however, like individuals, are apt to succumb to the vanities that sudden acquisition of wealth places within their reach, and become intoxicated with the power associated with it.

Unfortunately, such a result overtook this State. The Pretorian Government imposed extraordinary and inconsistent taxation on the mines, and obtained an abnormal revenue from the various monopolies which they created. Within four years the taxation levied on the Rand industries had increased the revenue of the republic to twenty-five times its former amount.

The old instinctive fear of losing their nationality quickly supervened, and President Kruger, with his executive, assumed an arrogant attitude towards the *uitlander* population totally at variance with modern ideas of civilised government The Boers, who had themselves revolted against British laws that were impartially applied to all alike, were now refusing the ordinary rights of citizenship which are usually conceded to aliens in any well-ordered foreign country—the aliens, in this instance, providing about three-fourths of the State revenue. The common Boer populace were insulting, both in behaviour and speech, to the *uitlanders* generally, but to British subjects in particular, and the Boer police were equally intolerant and rancorous whenever possible. Redress could not be sought with any prospect of success in the law courts, where the magistrate (or *landdrost*), although known to be thoroughly conversant with English, would refuse to have it spoken in his presence, even making its use a punishable offence if persisted in. In many respects the land of the Inquisition would have seemed a paradise to British subjects on the Rand.

In Johannesburg itself, although a city of considerable external grandeur, the sanitary conditions were those of China, where the main street is also the main sewer. Water was a commodity obtainable only from water-carts, and, except to the well-to-do, was too expensive to use except for strictly necessary purposes. No vote or voice in, and no authority or control over, the municipal conduct of a town built by themselves was practically permitted them. Inequitable political privileges, a rigid press censorship, stringent regulations concerning public meetings, and numerous disabilities affecting their domestic and commercial life, were imposed upon all aliens, such as are not endured anywhere except under the most despotic of governments. Such was the condition of the *uitlanders*, enforced upon them in direct contravention of the solemn assurance contained in the proclamation issued by the Boer leaders when they reassumed the government of the republic in 1881, wherein it was stated:—

> To all inhabitants, without exception, we promise the protection of the law, and all the privileges attendant thereon. We repeat solemnly that our motto is, '*Unity and Reconciliation.*'

The gold that might have been a blessing to the State rapidly became its curse instead. It tainted the fingers of many high officials, whose, ideas of the morality that usually governs public life were somewhat analogous to those of a Chinese mandarin—very elastic. Bribery and corruption appear to have permeated every government department where gold could influence or obtain a concession. Greed of gold had taken the place of those tenets of Christianity hitherto sacredly handed down through each generation from the deeply religious pioneers of the Boer race.

With the development of the gold-mines came a rapid influx of foreigners to the Rand, which somewhat perturbed the timorous officialism of the republic, and tended to increase the severity of their infatuated policy. The State franchise, or privileges of citizenship, was raised, in 1890, from five to fourteen years of continuous residence within the republic, and so hedged round with distasteful conditions that even then its acceptance was a question of very doubtful advantage. This and other equally intolerable laws, political and economic, which were subsequently enacted, pressed heavily on those *uitlanders* who had enjoyed the privileges accorded by British or American institutions. Petitions were presented appealing against these laws, some of which directly contravened the articles of the London Convention, both in spirit and in fact, but without avail.

The arbitrary conduct of the Boer Executive provoked a feeling of repugnance to submitting to such a tyrannical oligarchy. The resulting effects were the Johannesburg revolt, and the Jameson Raid of 1895-96, which ended disastrously at Doornkop, near Pretoria. The Raid episode is of too recent a date to need recapitulation here; suffice it to say that the grit, if not the design, of those plucky five hundred men who rode from Mafeking to the relief of the *uitlanders* was generally admired at the time. Their act being contrary to the law of nations, the principal leaders of the Raid were sent to England under arrest, tried in London, and sentenced to various terms of imprisonment. The most prominent members of the Johannesburg Reform Committee were also arrested by the Boers, and tried at Pretoria for high treason against the republic.

Four of the principals were condemned to death, the others receiving imprisonment according to their degree of prominence and guilt, accompanied by the imposition of heavy fines. Owing to the outburst of adverse public sentiment the death penalties were commuted to a fine of £25,000 for each of the condemned leaders, and of £2000 as the price of freedom for each of the minor prisoners. At the request of the Imperial Government, the republic sent in an account for damages caused by the Raid, the Boers demanding indemnification under two heads: material damages, £677,938 3s. 3d.; moral or intellectual injury, £1,000,000, which unique claim was not entertained.

After the Raid, affairs went from bad to worse for the *uitlanders*, but especially for British subjects, who were now held in great detestation by the Boers. As a last resource, a monster petition, signed by over 21,000 *uitlanders*, was forwarded to the suzerain. Queen Victoria, early in 1899, praying for intervention and protection for British subjects. The serious attention of the Imperial Government was now arrested by this direct appeal, and the negotiations that ultimately ended with war were commenced.

Anticipating this procedure, the astute Boers had taken every advantage which the Raid had afforded them of strongly arming themselves. For so small a State, enormous sums were being spent annually for military purposes, and vast quantities of warlike material—guns, rifles, and ammunition—were imported direct from European arsenals into the republic. Ostensibly, these preparations were for internal protection and defence against future armed incursions of a buccaneering nature. In reality they were for quite a different object—the realisation of the fervent dream of the Afrikander Bond.

This Bond is composed of a political union of men belonging to each and all of the South African states and colonies, though the term is usually applied only to a certain political party of Dutch Cape colonists. The end and aim which they have in view is the expulsion of the British flag from South Africa, and the establishment of a united South Africa under Dutch supremacy.

In May, 1899, a conference between President Kruger and Sir Alfred Milner, the British High Commissioner, was held at Bloemfontein to discuss the main questions at issue. Impossible propositions were put forward as a solution of the *uitlander* grievances by the Machiavelian president, who also introduced into the conference difficult questions quite extraneous to the subjects intended for discussion. The historic meeting ended with futile results, the published despatches bearing on the conference showing that the situation had become sufficiently acute to demand decisive action from the Imperial Government The high commissioner stated therein: "The case for intervention is overwhelming;" and he emphasised the necessity for "some striking proof of the intention of her Majesty's Government not to be ousted from its position in South Africa."

The tone of the despatches which subsequently passed between the Imperial and Transvaal Governments became less and less conciliatory, although the British made a few ineffectual attempts to arrive at an amicable understanding with the republic.

Early in September an uncompromising despatch was received from the Transvaal Government, in which they withdrew what few concessions they had previously offered, and repudiated the existence of British suzerainty in emphatic terms.

A concise but very temperate reply was thereupon despatched to the bellicose republic, offering final conditions for a peaceful settlement The concluding paragraph of this extremely important despatch was full of significance. It ran as follows:—

> If, however, as they most anxiously hope not to be the case, the reply of the South African Republic should be negative or inconclusive, I am to state that her Majesty's Government must reserve to themselves the right to reconsider the situation *de novo*, and to formulate their own proposals for a final settlement.

Such were the words used by Mr. Chamberlain, the Colonial Secretary, who was conducting these delicate negotiations, and which admitted of only one interpretation. The reply "Yes" or "No," in substance, was only now required as the decision for either peace or war.

The Transvaal answer to this despatch was a substantive rejection of the collective proposals put forward.

On September 22nd the Imperial Government drafted another despatch, and sent it to the Transvaal, its purport being an expression of regret that the proposals submitted for the consideration of the Pretorian Government had met with disfavour, and that, in accordance with the declaration previously made, they would shortly put the same into execution.

The political position in South Africa was now *in statu quo* prior to the conference. Statesmanship and diplomacy had nearly got beyond the stage of argument and despatch writing, and the worst arbiter of all international disputes—War—was even now appearing above the horizon.

The situation was considerably aggravated owing to the very unfriendly attitude of the Orange Free State, with whom the British had no political differences, dormant or existent, but who pledged themselves to fulfil their treaty obligations to the sister republic. President Steyn had openly declared this hostile policy by a resolution which had received the approval of the Free State Raad; shortly afterwards emphasizing his avowed intentions by making military preparations. In the Transvaal also, ominous signs of the coming storm were everywhere conspicuous, such as the massing of armed *burghers* and of military stores near the Natal border which had followed the last British despatch.

The climax of the negotiations was reached on October 9th, when the Transvaal Government forwarded the memorable despatch—or ultimatum—containing demands of such a nature, and worded in such a bellicose tone, that instant rejection was the only treatment it could receive from the British Government. Besides submitting wholly impossible propositions for acceptance, President Kruger demanded—

> That the British troops on the frontiers be withdrawn; that all reinforcements which had arrived in South Africa since June should be removed from the country; and that all British troops then on the high seas, outward bound, should not land in any South African port.

The British Government were to offer compliance within forty-eight hours, *viz*, by 5 p.m., October 11th, failing which, the despatch affirmed, the Transvaal Government—

. . . . to their deep regret, would be constrained to consider such action as a formal declaration of war, and that any further movements of troops towards the frontiers within the specified period would also be considered a formal declaration of war.

On October 10th, the British Government telegraphed to the high commissioner the reply message as follows:—

Her Majesty's Government acknowledges with deep regret the receipt of the peremptory demands of the South African Republic. In reply thereto, will you be pleased to inform the Government of the South African Republic that the conditions put forward by them are such as Her Majesty's Government is unable to discuss.

The British representative in Pretoria was also instructed to demand his passports coincidently with the handing in of the British reply. Thus ended diplomacy.

On October 11th, 1899, the Boers commenced hostilities, the forces of the Transvaal and Orange Free State republics invading the British colony of Natal the following day. And thus the bayonet supplanted the pen.

CHAPTER 4

Naval Brigade in South Africa: Anglo-Boer War 1899-1900

From October 14th to November 2nd, 1899

Simons Bay, the headquarters of the British Cape Squadron, had become the scene of great activity. Rear-Admiral Sir Robert Harris took prompt precautionary measures to guard the ships of his squadron and royal dockyard against any contemplated machinations of the enemy, and also from seditionary acts of disloyalists with whom Cape Colony was known to be impregnated. Armed picket-boats patrolled round the ships by night, strong guards were posted at the dockyard and magazines, and proclamations were posted up informing the populace of the restrictions that were being necessarily imposed upon them. The crews of the squadron were also organised ready to land should any rebellious risings occur in the vicinity of Simonstown. Great disaffection among the Dutch-speaking colonists was known to exist, and the impulsive action of the dual republics—amounting almost to a *coup d'ètat*—had called for the vigorous policy of vigilance.

The *Terrible* and *Powerful* (cruisers, 1st class), *Doris* (cruiser, 2nd class—flagship), *Monarch* (battleship), the gunboat *Thrush*, and a few small types of torpedo craft comprised the naval strength in port; the other ships of the squadron being now at Durban and Delagoa Bay and at important points around the coast

Fleet routines were suspended, and a special daily programme was substituted, which chiefly took the form of field operations and other instructions which would be useful should the landing of a naval force become necessary.

The military position in South Africa during the early stage of hostilities will be briefly recapitulated, in order to place the subject under narration more clearly before the reader.

The armies of the two republics, then estimated at about 60,000 men, had been partially mobilised and concentrated near the borders of the colonies prior to the despatch of the Ultimatum. The Orange Free State forces were near the passes of the Drakensberg, while those of the Transvaal had assumed positions threatening the northern angle of Natal, which colony both forces—some 20,000 strong—simultaneously invaded under the supreme command of Commandant General Joubert One detached force of Transvaalers, about 7000 strong, proceeded westward, under the famous General Cronje, to seize Mafeking, with its supplies and railway rolling stock. Another force of Free Staters, nearly 5000 strong, under Commandant Wessels, were attracted to Kimberley, with its alluring diamond mines; while certain detached commandoes threatened the principle strategic positions in northern Cape Colony and along the western borders.

Nearly two-thirds of the republican forces were thus ready for war, the principal movement being directed against Natal. The objective of the Boer plans, as emphasised by their sudden stroke of policy in forcing on war, was to crumple up our scattered forces, and seize the whole of South Africa before reinforcements could arrive. Possessed with the vast military resources since known to have been at their disposal, and the golden opportunities within their grasp, there was no earthly reason why their avowed intentions and aspirations should not have been crowned with success, or something like it But the Shakespearian maxim—

There is a tide in the affairs of men.
Which, taken at the flood, leads on to fortune,

—was not heeded—providentially for us. Otherwise, Mafeking, Kimberley, and Ladysmith, with their lines of communication severed, and all hope of retreat barred, would have been kept in isolation pending the fortunes of war. Nothing but the white ensign could then have kept the Boers from the goals of their ambition—Capetown and Durban—though the coast towns themselves the Boers could not have occupied, nor could even have approached within the range limit of the British squadron's guns. What might have then followed nobody could possibly foresee, for the whole of the Dutch colonists would by that time have made the struggle a common causey thus at least doubling the Boer strength and creating an insoluble military

The remnant of the "Terrible's" 115-cwt. anchor, after having experienced a heavy southern gale at Durban

problem. Perhaps a complete mobilisation of the British Fleet and Army, and a general call to arms to fight for Imperial existence, might have been the final outcome—who knows?

But as the Boers did not execute this bold stroke, there is no further need to expatiate. Yet, the ambitious project of first taking those three towns, and thereby dealing a vital blow at our prestige, undoubtedly changed the Boer plan of campaign and saved the British forces from a task of infinitely greater magnitude—great even though the task was that did exist So much for the Boer aspect; the position, as it concerns the British, follows.

It will be remembered that a force of about 6000 British troops were despatched from India in September, and proceeded direct to Natal, the ministry of that colony being justly alarmed at its undefensive condition in view of apparent possibilities. About 2000 reinforcements also left England to strengthen the defence of Cape Colony, besides the battalion of infantry brought from Mauritius in the *Powerful*, which ship, and the *Terrible* had joined the Cape squadron, thus adding two large cruisers with 106 guns and 2000 men to the naval strength of the station. The military additions had now augmented the Imperial forces in South Africa to about 22,000 men when war broke out, *viz.* 15,000 in Natal under General Sir George White, and 7000 in Cape Colony under General Sir Forestier Walker.

The position in Natal, where it had been correctly surmised that the heaviest blow would be struck, had made it a military necessity to place the bulk of the troops in that colony. For urgent political and strategical reasons, Sir George White chose Ladysmith for his headquarters and defensible base, the concentration of an immense quantity of military material there, besides the junction at that point of the Free State branch line with the Natal trunk line, having given supreme importance to the town. Dundee, forty miles further north, the centre of the Natal coalfields, was held by General Penn-Symons with some 5000 troops, and was the most advanced position held in the colony, the other important towns further north having been reluctantly but judiciously abandoned to the enemy, though the railway was unfortunately left intact

To leave Cape Colony and our western possessions to run the hazard as the situation developed was all the general could do with the limited force at his disposal. The Rhodesian regiment, about 450 men, held Fort Tuli near the Limpopo drifts north of the Transvaal. The Bechuanaland Protectorate regiment, and police, together with the town guard, about 1000 strong, were holding Mafeking on the western border. Kimberley was defended by about 600 regular troops in conjunction with Cape police, local volunteer forces, and the town guard, a total of just over 3500 men. Orange River station, an important strategical point, was held by a force of about 2500 regulars and a few Colonials. De Aar junction, where considerable military stores had been accumulated, was occupied by 1000 troops. Naauwport junction on the Port Elizabeth line, and Stormberg junction on the East London line, were each held by some 500 men. The bulk of the remaining troops were established on the railway midway between De Aar and Naauwport, the rest being stationed on the lines of communication from Capetown northwards.

A glance at the map of South Africa will confirm the statement, that British troops never had a more arduous task than that which confronted them at this early period of the war. To hold the enemy in check, and prevent invasion as much as possible, until the reinforcements then outward bound could arrive, was their object, and all they could hope to do.

Napoleon's generals with their unique fighting experiences, could not have accomplished their task with better results than did the British commanders upon whom fell the shock of the enemy's premeditated onslaught The gallant Baden-Powell, with a humorous obstinacy, successfully held Mafeking against vastly superior forces, the town being rigorously besieged for seven months. The pertinacious resistance of Colonel Kekewich kept Kimberley intact, until relieved by French's brilliant cavalry dash, after some four months' investment The historical defence of Ladysmith by Sir George White is a brilliant episode in British military history, as the capture or surrender of the place would probably have produced disastrous consequences not easily gauged.

The enemy had obviously underrated the quality of their Imperial and Colonial adversaries, a peremptory summons to surrender, or a vigorous bombardment of each for a few days, being the only necessary preliminaries in Boer opinion to the possession of these three towns. They had arrested their forward movements in both colonies, bent on enforcing their submission; the delay that this change of plan entailed was as fatal to their scheme as it was entirely in favour of the British. Kruger had appealed to the God of battles—a euphemism for foreign intervention—to assist the republican armies against the hereditary British foe, but the strategy of his generals was certainly due to a mistaken view of the situation. His fervent appeal was being ignored or refused, for the British side had received the supplicated favours instead—a counterpoise to the sentimental policy which had placed our South African dominions at the mercy of the enemy.

This brief prologue may afford a fair conception of the military position from the Ultimatum up to the investment of Ladysmith. The principal events of the war, but those affecting the *Terrible* in particular, will now be followed in their order of sequence.

Reinforcements being urgently needed at every strategic point threatened by the Boers, a naval brigade was despatched from the ships at Simonstown on October 20th, to co-operate with the troops holding Stormberg junction, whither they proceeded *via* De Aar. Commander Ethelston (*Powerful*) was in command, Major Plumbe (*Doris*) senior marine officer, Captain Mullins (*Terrible*) the quartermaster of the marine force, and Fleet-Surgeon Porter (*Doris*) the senior medical officer. The brigade consisted of 300 marines, fifty bluejackets, with two Q.F. field guns. The *Terrible* contributed eighty marines, under Lieutenant Lawrie, and one medical steward and eight stokers for ambulance party.

The detachments received a hearty send-off from their respective ships, and on landing were inspected by the admiral, who delivered a brief and inspiring speech, reminding the brigade what the navy expected from those who had the enviable honour to represent it on such momentous occasions as this. Preceded by the squadron's massed bands playing "Soldiers of the Queen," they marched to the station, and entrained for the front, where they hoped "to fight for England's glory," as the words of the tune to which they marched encouraged them to do. Thus commenced the navy's active participation in the war.

The same evening a signal was made to the squadron announcing a British victory at Talana Hill, near Dundee. General Penn-Symons had received the first shock of the Boer armies, and had temporarily stemmed the swift current of invasion. This tactical victory cost our side the gallant general, who was mortally wounded, besides nearly 450 killed, wounded, and prisoners. The enemy had also lost heavily. The check, and gain of time, were the only results of the fight, except an object lesson in what British pluck can accomplish under capable leaders. This war has certainly proved that no hill is too high for the Boer to climb, or too high for a British soldier to dislodge his foe from. Two days after the battle the British abandoned Dundee, the Boer artillery having rendered the position untenable, the situation besides being too dangerous for a detached force to be placed in. The troops and necessary transport were hurriedly withdrawn to Ladysmith, the force being piloted through a wild and broken country by Colonel Dartnell, of the Natal Police, who was compelled to adopt a circuitous route to avoid undesirable collision with the enemy.

A distance of nearly 70 miles was traversed in four days, 30 of which were covered by a forced march on the last day—a military exploit that must almost rank with a victory. Meanwhile, Sir George White was affording the retreating column invaluable assistance by creating diversions in their favour elsewhere. On the 21st, a force was despatched from Ladysmith under General French northwards. The enemy was met with at Elandslaagte and defeated with heavy loss; 200 Boers, including the wounded general who commanded them, and two machine guns, being captured. The main object of the British having been accomplished, the force was withdrawn to Ladysmith next day. Again, on the 24th, while the Dundee column were executing the most critical part of their hazardous march, the Ladysmith troops sallied forth and delivered another check to the enemy at Rietfontein, seven miles N.E. of the town. The safety of the column having been assured, the force retired, elated with their successes.

The brief details of the Natal fighting received from the front had clearly demonstrated that the Boers were pre-eminently superior in artillery, both as regards power and range.

They had in the field large mobile guns throwing a 94-lb. shell with an effective range of 12,000 yards. The British had only light field artillery, firing a 15-lb. shell, with a range of not more than 6000 yards. This disparity in artillery placed Sir George White in a very serious position, and necessitated his appealing to the navy for assistance. The story of this appeal and the lightning response made to it is, perhaps, best related in the form of an extract from a speech, delivered by Admiral Harris at the public reception accorded him at Devonport in May, 1901. He said:

> On October 25th, General Sir George White telegraphed—'The Boer guns are greatly outranging my guns. Can you let me have a few naval guns?' He replied in the affirmative, but found that there were no field mountings. Then he sent for Captain Scott, of the *Terrible,* and asked him when he could give him plans for mountings of 4.7-inch guns. Captain Scott replied, the evening he saw him, 'Tomorrow morning, at eight o'clock.' The

plans were produced, and, by dint of hard work in the dockyard, the guns on their extemporised carriages were, by 5 p.m. on the 26th, on board the *Powerful, en route* to Ladysmith.

These few words spoken by Admiral Harris give the reason why long-range guns were asked for. The fact that they would be required had, however, been anticipated by our captain, and *some guns were actually mounted and ready* for service on shore prior to the receipt of Sir George White's telegram.

The following extract from a paper read by Captain Scott, at Hong Kong, bearing on this subject, may be found interesting:—

> On October 14th the *Terrible* arrived at the Cape and found the campaign commenced, the Boers already across the Frontier, the British with insufficient troops to resist them, and their base 6000 miles from the scene of operations.
>
> Under these circumstances it was apparent that the Boers might invest Mafeking, Kimberley, and Ladysmith, and then, having their base open, bring down from Pretoria long-range guns, against which field guns would be powerless.
>
> I therefore took steps to see whether a mounting could be made which would enable the *Terrible's* long-range 12-pounders to be used on shore to keep the Boer siege guns at a respectable distance. By the 21st a mounting was made, tried, and found satisfactory. It consisted of a log of wood to form a trail, mounted on an axletree with a pair of ordinary Cape-waggon wheels. On to this was placed the ship carriage, bolted down and secured in such a manner as not to interfere with its being put back on board, should circumstances have required it; the necessity of this of course added to the difficulty in designing the mounting, a fact which perhaps my critics overlooked when they condemned it as clumsy.
>
> On Wednesday, October 25th, General White, in Ladysmith, finding that he had no artillery capable of keeping the Boer siege guns in check, wired to know if it were possible for the navy to send him some long-range 4.7 guns.
>
> The admiral asked me if I could design a mounting for a 4.7 and get two finished by the following afternoon. It was rather a rush; but they were ready by 5 p.m., put on board the *Powerful*, and she started with them, and four 12-pounders for Durban. Immediately on arrival, Captain Lambton, with great promp-

4.7 GUN, AND LONG RANGE 12-POUNDERS, MOUNTED ON CAPTAIN SCOTT'S IMPROVED MOUNTINGS, UNDERGOING EXPERIMENTAL TRIALS AT SIMONSTOWN. Similarly mounted guns to these were taken by the Powerfuls to Ladysmith

titude, took the guns to Ladysmith. He arrived in the nick of time, and his brigade played a most important part in the defence of Ladysmith. Forty-eight hours after his arrival the door was closed, and the garrison remained beleaguered for 119 days. The mounting consisted of four pieces of timber, 14 feet long by 12 inches, placed in the form of a cross. On to the centre of this was placed the ordinary ship mounting, bolted through to a plate underneath. The pedestal and timbers were thus all securely bolted together. Next, the gun-carriage was dropped over the spindle, and secured down by its clip-plate. Subsequent experiments with a platform of this description showed that it was not even necessary to fill in round the timbers with earth; on firing, a slight jump of the platform, of course, took place, but this in itself was advantageous, as it relieved the strain.

Having explained how the guns were despatched, a description of their rapid transformation from immobility to that of complete mobility for field service may also be of interest. Prior to the war, the 4.7 gun came under the category of heavy ordnance, being used exclusively on board ships, where the mountings are secured to the iron decks, and in forts, where they are concreted down.

As no suitable mounting existed, one had to be extemporised, and Admiral Harris has tersely explained how promptly Captain Scott solved a problem upon which perhaps the fate of Ladysmith depended.

At 9 p.m. on the 25th, Captain Scott landed, to see the admiral with reference to opening up communication with Kimberley by searchlight. On his return, at 10 p.m., his earnest conversation in the gangway with the principal officers denoted that something of more import than this was on the *tapis*.

Rumours that guns were to be landed somewhere, and somehow, soon gained credence, but lacked confirmation. This, however, was forthcoming by midnight when the purport of the captain's mission became known, also that Sir George White's problem of how to checkmate the Boer long-range guns had even then been solved. A few lines on a sheet of drawing-paper (the rough sketch of a gun mounting) was the result of a long conference between the captain and the commander, and represented the solution, which was at once handed to an engineer officer for a fair copy to be reproduced to scale to facilitate the construction of the designed mounting. Minutes were proverbially golden; but, through some unfortunate misinterpretation of instructions, the drawing, which should have been completed by daylight, was not even commenced.

This *contretemps* was not allowed to retard the urgent matter in hand, and the upshot was the sending of the rough sketch to the dockyard, where the mountings were constructed under the personal supervision of Captain Scott

That evening, the 26th, the *Powerful* sailed for Durban with all available specially mounted guns, a performance which elicited the following eulogium in Sir George White's despatches:—

> Captain the Hon. H. Lambton, R.N., commanding the Naval Brigade, reached Ladysmith in the nick of time, when it became evident that I was not strong enough to meet the enemy in the open field. He brought with him two 4.7 and four 12-pounder guns, which proved to be the only ordnance in my possession capable of equalling in range the enemy's heavy guns. Although the ammunition available was very limited, Captain Lambton so economised it that it lasted out till the end of the siege, and under his direction the naval guns succeeded in keeping at a distance the enemy's siege guns, a service which was of the utmost importance.

À *propos* of their departure Captain Scott signalled to Captain Lambton—

> I shall be disappointed if your two 4.7's are not mounted in Ladysmith in less than four days, and the Boers sent to *Hades* with lyddite. Hope to see you soon with some more guns.

The signal was appreciatively replied to, and was a true forecast of events. The guns got there in the time specified, and the *Terrible's* guns subsequently entered Ladysmith when relieved some four months later. The distance from Simonstown to Ladysmith by sea and rail was nearly 1000 miles. Such, then, is the true story of the famous incident of the despatch to Ladysmith of the naval guns.

Captain Scott, with laudable persistency, did not remain content with having produced a stationary or platform mounting for the 4.7 gun, but resolutely aimed at establishing practical mobility for it, so that the gun could accompany troops in the field. Success again rewarded his effort to confound the enemy and destroy their "corner" in heavy field artillery. Moreover, the British 4.7 gun easily outranged the Boer "Long Tom"—with a few thousand yards to spare.

Under his personal direction, which thus exemplified that he was no mere theorist; the mobile carriage was hastily constructed in the dockyard, scientific procedure being in this instance reversed; for, instead of the carriage being built to the design, the said design was reduced or enlarged to meet the resources of available dockyard material. (The bluejackets facetiously described it as the scrap-heap carriage.) When this extempore-built carriage was completed, proper drawings of it were *then* made, and several more carriages were soon afterwards constructed. By its employment throughout the whole Natal operations under General Buller, the original carriage received ample attestation of its stability and utility.

On board the ship, the construction of 12-pounder mountings and carriages proceeded apace, the ship's mechanical ratings blending day with night without intermission. This department of the *Terrible's* "arsenal" was entrusted to Lieutenant Ogilvy, and Mr. Johns, the ship's carpenter.

The next item deserving notice was the installation of a searchlight on a railway truck. The admiral's instructions required it to be ready by the evening of the 27th, the order being received late the previous night. The necessary fittings were prepared during the night, and the task of fixing the apparatus, to which was attached one of Captain Scott's "flashers," was commenced at daylight Just as darkness was setting in, signals were being exchanged with the ship. This creditable evolution, performed by the ship's artificers and electrical staff under Lieutenant Ogilvy, was highly commended. The military authorities had requisitioned this signalling apparatus to enable them to reply to beleaguered Kimberley's messages, which were being nightly flashed by the De Beers searchlight

On October 31st, the following general signal was made to the squadron:—

> Owing to the concentration of some 20,000 Boers upon Ladysmith, our force moved out three miles yesterday morning. Boers opened with 40-pounder. Naval Brigade doing splendid work. British object was to check Boer advance, which was accomplished. British gradually withdrew. Losses not yet received.

This signal implied that the *Powerful's* guns had been in action, a circumstance of great interest to those who had identified themselves with their opportune despatch.

An important phase of the war is now reached

With the return of the Dundee column on October 26th, Sir George White had concentrated his whole force at Ladysmith, and was perfecting his defences to withstand the inevitable siege that loomed ahead. Before accepting investment, however, the general determined to give the enemy battle to prevent their converging too close upon the town, and perhaps delaying or smashing up the encircling movement going on. Circumstances ripened this decision on the 29th, when a *coup de main* was decided upon for the morrow. The general was fully aware that success, now that the Transvaal and Free State forces had united, was of doubtful issue; but, whatever the result, the Boers must disclose their strength, which would furnish useful knowledge in determining future action. Reputations are often sacrificed for want of pluck; but the bold and difficult enterprise Sir George White had planned proved him the possessor of that necessary quality to an unlimited extent

About midnight, he sent an Infantry column 1100 strong, under Colonel Carleton, to seize Nicholsons Nek—a ridge six miles northwards of the town, in order to cover the British left flank and secure the northern approaches to Ladysmith. Later, General French, with a strong mounted force, took an easterly direction over Lombards Nek, Bulwana, to cover the right flank. The attacking force was divided into two commands. Colonel Grimwood commanded the right wing, which moved off during the darkness, taking a north-easterly direction towards Long Hill, about four miles distant. The left wing, under Colonel Ian Hamilton, proceeded to take up a concealed position under cover of Limit Hill, ready to storm the main Boer position beyond, on Pepworth Hill, should Grimwood's Brigade be successful on the right. By daybreak the assigned positions had been occupied, and the British designs clearly exposed to the enemy's view. The artillery of both sides opened the battle, the six British batteries being stationed between the two wings to support Grimwood's attack, and then cover the main movement against Pepworth.

Until towards 8 a.m. a hot contest ensued between the opposing artillery, the Boer guns on the right, which were assailing Grimwood's exposed flank, being quickly silenced. The range to Pepworth being too far for effective shrapnel fire, two batteries were ordered to move forward, when a sharp duel, in which the fire on both sides was delivered with marked precision, was waged for half an hour, resulting in the Boer gunners being driven from their guns into shelter. On the

Working model of the original 4.7 gun as mounted by Captain Scott
Made by Chief Armourer Burke, of the Terrible,

right, the Boers, having frustrated French's flanking plans, developed a movement that seriously menaced the safety of the right wing. Severe fighting now followed, the Boers making strenuous efforts to turn both of Grimwood's flanks. These tactics proving futile, the enemy, now strongly reinforced, tried to dislodge the brigade from the forward position they occupied.

Supports and reserves were then pressed forward into the British firing line, and reinforcements drafted eastward from Hamilton's unengaged brigade; the position, effectively covered with two batteries, being thereafter maintained with little difficulty, though no advance was possible against the intense fire opposed to them. Towards noon ominous information had reached Sir George White that his plans elsewhere had met with disastrous and irretrievable failure, and that the town itself, bombarded by "Long Tom," was perilously exposed to the enemy. These facts, together with the knowledge gained that the Boers were greatly superior in numbers, gun power, and mobility, made a withdrawal to the town defences a strategic necessity. Already, two cavalry regiments and two batteries of artillery had been diverted to reinforce French, who was closely pressed near Lombards Kop, but was now enabled to withstand the enemy's vigorous attack as long as the battle was likely to last The retirement of the fighting line was the signal for a furious fusillade of rifle and gun fire into their retreating ranks, creating a critical situation for a brief period which called for exceptional generalship to control.

The covering field batteries (13th and 53rd) performed brilliant service in extricating Grimwood's wing from the perilous position which the retirement had created, fighting their guns at close range with stoical bravery, until the infantry had got into a safer zone. The fighting line of a position which an enemy is using all his available strength to push back or capture is not a cheery place, even for war-seasoned soldiers. But to face about—not knowing why—and be pursued at close range with pom-pom explosives that send a thrill shooting through the spinal column, bullets that whizz by with an enraged hissing noise, and shells that burst all round with loud exultant explosions, is a far more trying ordeal. A retirement in such circumstances may tax all a general's powers to prevent it from becoming a disorderly retreat

The *Powerful's* brigade had arrived in Ladysmith early that forenoon, the mobile 12-pounder guns being promptly detrained and taken out towards Limit Hill; but, before they could get into action, the retiring movement, then in progress, occasioned a reluctant retreat During their return journey the gunners of the omnipotent "Long Tom" espying their processional retreat, greeted the battery with a succession of 94-lb. shells, one of which burst under the leading gun, capsizing it and wounding all the gun's crew, besides stampeding the draught oxen and native drivers. The disabled gun was subsequently remounted and brought in.

Meanwhile the other 12-pounders took up a position and opened fire on the Pepworth battery at about 7000 yards' range. Their precision of fire quickly enforced the complete silence of the Boer guns, including "Long Tom," for the rest of the day, thereby infinitely relieving the situation and enabling the hitherto hasty retirement to be conducted in a comparatively leisurely style back to camp. The propitious and opportune arrival of the naval guns had produced a great moral effect on both sides. They had dismayed the Boer artillerists, who found they no longer enjoyed "long-range monopoly;" had restored confidence to the troops, inasmuch as they now saw the dominating Boer guns dominated in their turn; and had also allayed the semi-panic prevalent among the populace, which "Long Tom's" intermittent shelling of the town had created.

General French, as before stated, had not met with the success anticipated at Lombards Kop, and had finally to give way before ever-increasing numbers and take up a defensive attitude, finally retiring upon the town in accordance with orders. But the predominant slice of ill-luck of the day befell the Nicholsons Nek column, which had, in the blackness of night, nearly reached their destination when a disastrous incident occurred A sudden commotion at the head of the column had the effect of stampeding the mules of the Mountain Battery, which bolted pell-mell through the compact troops to the rear, with the sections of guns and ammunition on their backs. Fortunately, most of the animals careered back to camp with their warlike cargoes intact, but some fell down deep *dongas* to be eventually captured by the enemy, who thus secured three of the six guns.

Although premature discovery had undoubtedly taken place, the instructions to occupy the Nek were effected without molestation from the astute Boers, and protective works commenced, all the more necessary now the battery of guns was gone, and most of the reserve ammunition likewise lost The remainder may be told in few words. At daylight, the Boers, who swarmed the adjacent hills which dominated the Nek, directed a furious converging fire upon the now isolated column, who fought tenaciously to stave off what was an inevitable issue, unless opportune relief arrived. No relief was forthcoming; Fate had willed otherwise. The hazardous position of the column could not even be made known to General White, as the heliograph had also vanished in the stampede; nor could contact be made with them from the general, though his safety was jeopardised by their misfortune. The alternatives had to be faced sooner or later—-surrender or annihilation. So when their munitions became exhausted the former of these two evils was chosen, though not until a brilliant stand had been made, and further fighting had become hopeless.[1]

Though the actual surrender was deeply humiliating to our prestige at this early period of the war, yet the fact of having Carleton's column the less to feed somewhat lessened the difficulties of maintaining the protracted siege which followed It was, in fact, a blessing in disguise, if it could be possible to view it solely from that standpoint, which, of course, is out of the question. The total losses for the day were 1285 in killed, wounded, and prisoners.

By November 2nd, the investment of Ladysmith was completed by the enemy, and a rigorous siege commenced, which lasted for 119 days. The force thus invested totalled 13,500 of all ranks (Imperial and Colonial), besides a civilian population (white and coloured) of some 7500 souls; the presence of these non-combatants, owing to the limited sustenance supplies, immensely increasing the military difficulties of the situation.

The Natal Field Force being now hemmed in by the enemy, the safety of the colony south of Ladysmith became a subject for grave consideration. The province of Sir George White had been to protect the colony from invasion, and he had voluntarily accepted his present position as being, both from the political and strategical points of view, the best to adopt. The precipitate action of the enemy had enforced the general to make prompt decisions, with little time for forethought, or leisure to examine probable or possible consequences. This final decision to hold Ladysmith in preference to falling back south of the Tugela, was, as subsequent events proved, the act of a skilled strategist and a political pilot of sound judgment.

---

1. The surrender was prematurely made about 2 p.m. through the act of a subordinate—not by Colonel Carleton's orders—who commanded an isolated detachment, then nearly all placed *hors de combat*, or killed; though this result could hardly have been postponed much longer, as ammunition was nearly spent, and any attempt at charging through the enemy must have been a disastrous and futile effort.

CHAPTER 5

Arrival of Sir Redver's Buller in Natal

November, 1899

Captain Percy Scott having received from the High Commissioner the appointment of Military Governor and Commandant of Durban, the *Terrible* left Simonstown, November 3rd, for the purpose of placing Natal's important seaport in a defensive condition. Previous to leaving, the officers and men on passage to China were distributed among the Cape Squadron to supplement the ship's depleted crews. Guards of this ship were relieved from the posts they had been occupying, one of which, under Lieutenant England, had been keeping watch over captured Boer prisoners temporarily incarcerated in the prison ship *Penelope*.

Military equipment for landing-parties and campaigning stores had been obtained, and the ship's voracious bunkers had considerably lessened the size of the dockyard coal-heap. While on passage, the men about to comprise the defence force were organised, and final shape was given to the incompleted gun-mountings and carriages.

Arriving at Durban early on the 6th, the landing of guns, ammunition, etc., immediately began. This work was attended with great difficulty, owing to the heavy swell then, and nearly always, prevailing there. The draught of water on the bar was too shallow to permit of the ships entering the snug and spacious harbour, which would otherwise have saved much anxious and laborious work on this and several future occasions during our stay there. Next day, Captain Scott, accompanied by Major H.R.H. Prince Christian Victor of Schleswig-Holstein and Major Bousfield (Natal Volunteers), inspected the ap-

DEFENCE OF DURBAN
Commander Limpus, and staff of the Durban Defence Force

proaches to the town, settled for the disposition of the guns, and made arrangements for carrying the defence scheme into execution, the brigade being ordered to land next morning. Commander Limpus, and a few members of his staff, landed in the evening to arrange the details for the disembarkation of the force and guns from the surf-lighters. One huge iron shed, about 400 feet by 80 feet, was requisitioned on the wharf as a base for landing all naval supplies, and a guard of bluejackets, under a warrant officer, was permanently stationed here on transport service, a duty which proved no sinecure.

At daybreak on the 8th, the defence force landed, the journey from the ship into harbour, and the debarkation of men and material, occupying the early forenoon. Officers and men were dressed alike—all khaki clad—the former only wearing shoulder-straps, and the latter their distinctive badges to denote rank and rating. Except for the khaki-painted naval straw hats worn, and the piquant naval lingo used, little else remained to associate the brigade with their nautical calling. Thirty guns—two 4.7's, and sixteen ship's 12-pounders (on extemporised carriages); two 12-pounders, one 9-pounder, and one 7-pounder light field guns; two 3-pounder Hotchkiss, two Nordenfeldt machine guns, and four Maxims—manned by 450 officers and men, comprised the strength landed for the defence. The guns' crews of the field and machine guns were the only means of traction for those guns, but spans of oxen and some sixty horses had been requisitioned to transport the 4.7's, long-range 12-pounders, ammunition waggons, and *impedimenta*. By 10 a.m. the force was in motion and proceeding through the town *en route* to their assigned positions—a march of several hours' duration.

Durban's main street forms part of an imposing thoroughfare extending the whole length of the town—some six miles of road and street—the principal section being adorned with many fine buildings on either side. The splendid Town Hall faces the public botanical gardens, a majestic statue of Queen Victoria standing at the spacious entrance. It was on passing this central spot that the nautical brigade received quite an ovation from the vast assemblage of loyal colonists congregated here, and also from the thousands of *uitlander* refugees who had opportunely assembled under the shadow of their *suzerain's* statue. Durban's mayor and other civic dignitaries were officially present on the Town Hall colonnade, and before them the defence force passed by in something approaching review style, while the ship's band, which halted opposite the mayoral party, discoursed patriotic marches and airs to lend colour to the stirring scene. Such an exhibition of strength must have greatly impressed (as the imposing display of force was intended to do) the loyal burgesses with a sense of confidence and safety, and have also banished all hope from disloyal minds of ever seeing the *Vierkleur* hoisted over Durban Town Hall—a common boast of the Boers before the war.

On clearing the town the brigade divided into three detached commands, proceeding by different routes to their respective positions. Commander Limpus, Lieutenant England, and staff of the force, with one 4.7, six 12-pounders, and two Maxims, took up a position on the Berea Heights, overlooking the town in rear and commanding the Maritzburg road and other inland approaches, the position being connected by telephone with the outlying batteries. A battery of six 12-pounders, under Lieutenant Richards, proceeded westward to Claremont, about six miles distant, and entrenched. Their province was to guard the western road approaches and railway. Lieutenant Wilde commanded a similar battery which performed a like function on the eastern side of the town, their position being termed "Fort Denison."

To support the *Terrible's* main defence, a detachment from the *Thetis* manned the Bluff Fort guns, which commanded the harbour entrance and western routes; another from the *Tartar* supplied the crew of the armoured train; while detachments of *Fortes* and *Philomels*, with the light field and machine guns, occupied a flank position in the Umgeni Valley, between "Fort Denison" and the sea. A corps of mounted local gentlemen undertook all the scouting beyond the town, and the district rifle associations were ready to co-operate with the defence force if required This colony well deserves the title of "Loyal Natal."

By 4 p.m. the respective batteries were in position, guns entrenched, and camps formed, which fact enabled Captain Scott to telegraph to the admiral at Simonstown, and report to the Mayor of Durban, that the town was in a complete state of defence. The details of the organisation had been well considered, and so enabled the evolution—for such it was—to be so creditably executed. The rapid manner in which the hitherto unprotected town had been placed in a state of defence evoked the highest commendation from the responsible government officials.

An opportunity here occurs to place on record a grateful sense of the hospitality which Durban all through extended to all ranks and ratings of the defence force. "Colonial hospitality" is no mere phrase,

DEFENCE OF DURBAN
Lieutenant England, and crew of the 4.7 gun on the Berea

but signifies much more than the term implies to the ear, or may convey in print, and is highly appreciated by those of the navy who have become familiar with its real meaning when visiting our several colonies. The names of Messrs. Hartley and Denison, in whose private grounds the central and eastern naval batteries were respectively entrenched, are especially deserving of a place in these pages in recognition of their practical loyalty at a critical time, and of the hospitality shown to the officers and men attached to the guns. The mayor and many other prominent citizens were also in the front rank in both respects. Few British troops passing through Durban on their way to the front, or wounded men returning from the battlefield, but did not receive some mark of the town's hospitable favours. The Terribles cherish their recollections of Durban.

Captain Scott now assumed the duties of his dual office as Commandant of Durban and Senior Naval Officer, the town having been placed under martial law. Major Bousfield, a colonial officer and member of the legal profession, was appointed commandant's adviser, and Assistant-Paymaster Cullinan secretary; Messrs. Laycock and Blanchflower, naval clerks, and Chief-writer Elliott forming the secretarial staff. Telegrams arriving in quick succession both day and night, and the mass of naval, military, and civil correspondence that flowed interminably through the Commandant's office for the next five months, imposed a continuous duty upon this staff of an onerous and important nature.

Martial law in superseding the civil law, confers great discretionary power upon those who administer it, and affords facilities for coping with emergencies which the ordinary law is slow to deal with. Those born under such institutions as are enjoyed by the Anglo-Saxon race find martial law very inconvenient—which it undoubtedly is, even in its mildest form—and are apt to resent its application. But for dealing with treason or sedition in war time, or for the suppression of civil commotion, extraordinary powers are essential to the ruling authorities, not only for dealing effectively with traitorous individuals or lawless mobs, but for giving protection to loyal and law-abiding persons. Martial law provides that power, its severity, of course, varying with the situation it has to contend with. In Durban the loyal inhabitants did not suffer much inconvenience beyond being restricted to the confines of the district, and subjected to a sort of curfew routine that curtailed freedom abroad at night.

In addition to knowing how to handle and fight his ship, a na-

R. A. Laycock, F. H. Brooke, R. Alexander, T. O. Fraser, F. C. Blanchflower,
Clerk R.N. Sergt. N.P. Supt. Boro' Police. Press Censor. Clerk R.N.

Major H. R. Bousfield, Capt. Percy Scott, W. F. Cullnan,
D.L.I., R.N., Asst.-Paymr. R.N.,
Staff Officer. Commandant. Secretary.

COMMANDANT AND STAFF. DURBAN, 1899–1900

val captain must also be a practical diplomatist, always prepared to conduct delicate negotiations of a political nature all over the world where duly accredited officials do not reside, and when guns may have eventually to settle the disputes at issue. Admiral Sir Gerald Noel, during the Cretan *imbroglio*, and Admiral Sir Edward Seymour, lately in China, have recently shown how diplomacy of the highest order can be displayed by naval officers in view of international entanglements.

The most prominent among the many important subjects dealt with by Captain Scott during his tenure of office will be briefly sketched, as being interesting topics of the period.

The great influx of criminals, spies, and suspects, who had crossed over the borders of the two republics into Natal, required close supervision. In the person of Superintendent Alexander, of the Durban Police, was found an officer to whom the task of keeping this motley throng under proper surveillance was safely entrusted. A few notorious characters the commandant actually imprisoned for safe custody, where they were at liberty to think out nefarious schemes—but unable to execute them. The most notable suspect dealt with was a certain Mr. Marks, who was arrested on suspicion of being in the employ of the Transvaal Secret Service. His case attracted much attention at the time, owing to the threat of the Pretorian Government to shoot six British officers by way of retaliation should capital punishment be the result of his seizure. This threat—strictly against the usages of civilised warfare—was both premature and unnecessary, as the chaise of espionage preferred against him was never proved The Imperial Government, however, informed the Boers of the dire consequences that such a proposed violation of the recognised customs of warfare would entail should it ever be carried into execution.

The commandant, in conjunction with Mr. Fraser (the official censor), had to deal with the examination of letters, and suspicious or irregular telegrams, detained under martial law procedure. When one is aware of the number of fabulous accounts which have emanated from pens propelled at the will of imaginative brains, has read the unjust—and often malicious—criticisms and accusations glibly directed against men and matters which are intended for dissemination among a credulous public, and knows the means employed to furnish the enemy with desirable information, the much traduced censorship is seen to be an indispensable institution in war time. The questions arising from the detention of goods, etc., and prevention of trade with the enemy from the port, were matters involving great discretion and tact

The refusal to allow the ambulance and its staff, sent from England by Sir James Seivewright, to proceed through Natal for the use of the Boers, was an action of Captain Scott's that received almost universal approval It is worthy of notice that President Kruger also rejected this sympathetic donation when it was afterwards landed at Delagoa Bay in order to proceed from that direction—a significant rebuke to the would-be donor.

As a protection for the *burgesses* and their property, and also to limit the opportunities of suspicious persons for doing possible mischief, public bars were closed at 9 p.m. (under penalty of cancellation of licence), and a system of night passes was introduced, without which no person could remain abroad from his habitation between the hours of 11 p.m. and 5 a.m. Infringement of this latter regulation meant prompt arrest and detention until satisfactory evidence of identity was forthcoming. The commandant himself was twice arrested for being unable to produce his "permit"—once when out to test the vigilance of the police, the other occasion being an inconveniently legitimate occurrence one night when unexpected urgent duty compelled his detention abroad, and his "permanent permit" had inadvertently been left at the office. The constable, not personally knowing Captain Scott, and refusing to believe his apparently fantastic story about being Commandant of Durban, promptly locked him up until he was identified some few hours later by his secretary, who had been telephoned for from the "Commandancy." The constable naturally felt that he must tender an apology even for doing his plain duty; but the captain warmly commended him for his sensible prudence. Martial law had ambushed its administrator.

The detention of the German mail steamer *Bundesrath* for having on board suspected persons bound for Delagoa Bay was an episode which caused diplomatic representations between the British and German Governments. Satisfactory explanations resulted in the vessel being freed from arrest shortly afterwards, and the owners subsequently indemnified. Such incidents will always be responsible for some of the international issues which result from war, acts of this kind, whether right or wrong, invariably arousing national sentiment, as appears to have happened in the present case.

The prompt suppression of a journal styled the *Review and Critic*, which had transgressed the limits of fair reviewing and reasonable criticism, and had published diatribes reflecting on the conduct of our generals and troops in the field, exemplified the necessity of applying

Defence of Durban.
"Terrible's" cyclist section of Durban Defence Force.

martial law when acts to the prejudice of good order required immediate restriction.

Trials of offenders for martial-law offences, and interviews with all sorts and conditions of men—and women—formed the daily forenoon routine. The variety of subjects dealt with, including the examination of suggestions and schemes—impossible mostly—submitted by enthusiastic loyalists, transformed the commandant's office at times into a sort of King Solomon's Court. One eccentric old gentleman, and a certain lady of doubtful age but unquestionable self-possession, who styled herself the "Queen of South Africa," were both possessed of phenomenal brain-power—the lady especially so. The former had an occult scheme for producing discomfiture to the enemy by firing at their entrenched positions chemically filled shells, which, on bursting, were to induce temporary inertia and envelop the foe with an impenetrable black fog, whereupon our troops would advance and capture their positions at leisure. But, as he could not state by what process the said shells could be manufactured, nor guarantee exemption from inertia and fog to our own troops during the operations, his alchemic scheme was pigeon-holed in the waste-paper basket.

The pseudo "queen's" rocket scheme was a sublime idea—for seineing parties, perhaps, but not for war. Six or more giant rockets, with a huge net attached to their tails, were to be simultaneously fired towards the enemy's position, when, upon the rockets falling beyond the foe (which they *must* do), the net would entrap a shoal of Boers. Our troops would then serenely pull the net into camp with the haul of captured prisoners of war inside! But the sending up of a sort of flying-machine was her pet fantastic project. She submitted a written statement of what this marvellous contrivance should do, but had no machine, design of one, or even reasonable notion of one. She herself was to be the aeronaut, taking up a huge stock of miniature flags of all nations and scriptural monitions, and scattering them broadcast into all the Boer camps. This inept proposition, she contended, would so confound the enemy that they would assume the world was wrath against their iniquities, and cause them to flee to their homes demoralised. (What a saving in war loans and income-tax demands if it had!)

Failing to impress anyone with her wild suggestions, she at last donned a sailor's old straw hat, with a *Terrible's* ribbon attached to it, and proclaimed herself as commanding all forces at the Cape. Her strange conduct, of course, amused the brigade, with whom she became a general favourite, and who listened with mock attention to her passionate addresses of mixed jargon, and thus humoured her hallucinatory ideas. Few will forget this quaint personage, who seldom missed paying a daily visit to the office and town camp near by. This was one form of diversion that wormed its way into the serious business of war.

With many people, of course, the war was unpopular, but instead of trying to promote British defeats, they resorted to the bloodless method of sending anonymous letters vilifying Captain Scott's official conduct, and threatening him with various pains and penalties if he did not seek refuge on board his ship. These missives adorned the pages of a scrapbook, and provided some amusement for visitors while awaiting their turn for interviews. Ridicule can do much good when properly applied, as it did in this instance, for this form of rancour soon ceased.

The capacity for administering an office so environed with political and economic responsibilities was well exemplified in the person of Captain Scott, as the following eulogistic reference[2] to his five months' tenure of office cogently affirms:—

> The officer responsible at this time for the administration of martial law in Durban was Captain Scott, R.N., . . . who has left behind him a reputation for spotless integrity, practical common sense, tact, and inflexible justice, of which the service he so worthily represents may well be proud. . . .

A brief summary of current events again becomes necessary to elucidate the course of the war.

General Sir Redvers Buller, who had been selected by the Imperial Government for the supreme command at the Cape, arrived at Cape Town on October 31st. Three days afterwards Ladysmith was invested, thereby causing the temporary loss of the services of nearly the whole Natal Field Force. Estcourt, 30 miles south of Ladysmith, was now the most advanced British post north of Pietermaritzburg. The military and political situation thus created in Natal caused General Buller to alter his original plan of campaign, and order the bulk of the troops intended for Cape Colony to be diverted to the sorely pressed sister colony. Although Cape Colony was still in considerable danger, the knowledge that transports with succouring troops were quickly nearing the Cape, and that the enemy's attention was still

---

1. *Life in Natal under Martial Law*, South Africa, May 10th. 1902.

firmly fixed on Mafeking and Kimberley, was largely responsible for the general's change of plan. Indeed, the pressing exigencies of Natal's situation, the obligations due to this ultra-loyal colony, and the natural expectations of the beleaguered garrison, obviously appeared to the general to be of paramount importance. Altered circumstances had demanded altered action, and a second British general was compelled to embark on a policy involving considerable personal responsibility, owing to unexpected issues and developments which had been at no time subject to his control, and which have no precedent in modern military history.

Following closely the Investment of Ladysmith, the enemy became particularly active in northern Cape Colony, threatening the garrisons of Colesberg, Naauwpoort, and Stormberg. The troops holding the two first-named towns concentrated upon De Aar, those of the latter, with whom were associated the Naval Brigade retired south on Queenstown, the railway junction at Sterkstroom between these two positions, being held by Colonials as an advanced post. Shortly afterwards General Sir William Gatacre arrived with reinforcements from England, thus rendering Queenstown a safe position. The Naval Brigade, now released from defensive duty, were ordered to rejoin their ships, and were sent by rail to East London for embarkation. The Simonstown contingent proceeded there in the s.s. *Roslin Castle*, the *Terrible's* detachment embarking in the s.s. *Moor* for Durban.

By November 19th, Lord Methuen had concentrated his Kimberley Relief Column of 10,000 men at the Orange River. On the same date a second Naval Brigade left Simonstown under Flag-Captain Prothero (*Doris*) to join Methuen's column. Arriving at Orange River on the 22nd, they detrained and marched onward, in time to take an effective part with their guns in the Battle of Belmont next day. The losses here were 53 killed and 275 wounded.

Two days later the Battle of Graspan was fought, the most memorable day throughout the war for the navy, owing to the severe losses sustained by the Naval Brigade in this action. As at Belmont a strongly entrenched position was carried by direct frontal assault This being the only occasion during the campaign that a Naval Brigade were specially employed as infantry, a description of their gallantry, vividly portrayed by an eminent historian [2] of the war, is given as being eminently worthy of record.

---

2. Arthur Conan Doyle, *The Great Boer War*, (also published by Leonaur.)

... Here a single large *kopje* formed the key to the position, and a considerable time was expended upon preparing it for the British assault, by directing upon it a fire which swept the face of it and searched, as was hoped, every corner in which a rifleman might lurk. One of the two batteries engaged fired no less than 500 rounds. Then the infantry advance was ordered, the Guards being held in reserve on account of their exertions at Belmont.... The honours of the assault, however, must be awarded to the sailors and marines of the Naval Brigade, who underwent such an ordeal as men have seldom faced and yet come out as victors. To them fell the task of carrying that formidable hill which had been so scourged by our artillery. With a grand rush they swept up the slope, but were met by a horrible fire. Every rock spurted flame, and the front ranks withered away before the storm of the Mausers. An eye-witness has recorded that the brigade was hardly visible amid the sand knocked up by the bullets.

For an instant they fell back into cover, and then, having taken their breath, up they went again, with a deep-chested roar. There were but 400 in all, 200 seamen and 200 marines, and the losses in that rapid rush were *terrible*. Yet they swarmed up, their gallant officers, some of them little boy-middies, cheering them on. Ethelston, the commander of the *Powerful,* was struck down. Plumbe and Senior of the Marines were killed. Captain Prothero, of the *Doris*, dropped while still yelling to his seamen to 'take that *kopje* and be hanged to it!' Little Huddart, the middy, died a death which is worth many inglorious years. Jones, of the Marines, fell wounded, but rose again and rushed on with his men. It was on these gallant marines, the men who are ready to fight anywhere and any how, moist or dry, that the heaviest losses fell.

When at last they made good their foothold upon the crest of that murderous hill they had left behind them three officers and 88 men out of a total of 206—a loss within a few minutes of nearly 50 *per cent*. The bluejackets, helped by the curve of the hill, got off with a toll of eighteen of their number. Half the total British losses of the action fell upon this little body of men, who upheld most gloriously the honour and reputation of the service from which they were drawn. With such men under the white ensign we leave our island home in safety behind us.

On the 28th, General Lord Methuen again advanced and fought the Battle of Modder River, which resulted in a hardly contested victory for our troops, whose casualties amounted to 450 killed and wounded.

Three actions within a week, and a loss of nearly 1000 men, had brought Methuen's force to the Modder River, but also to a standstill condition to await reinforcements, with an ever increasing enemy between them and Kimberley—twenty-five miles away. General Gatacre was still at Queenstown preparing an offensive movement, and General French had reoccupied Naauwpoort, his force guarding the right flank of the Kimberley column.

In Natal the enemy were steadily advancing southwards, but the bulk of them were held by centripetal force around Ladysmith. On November 15th, an armoured train that made daily scouting expeditions northwards from Estcourt, came to grief near Frere on its return journey. The train was composed of an engine and tender and five waggons, manned by about 120 naval, military, and civilians, the latter mostly railway employees borne for repairing the line. The enemy had prepared the inevitable ambush of almost daily expectation by detaching a rail and placing large boulders on the line. They had with them three field guns and a pom-pom, mounted on a *kopje* about 1300 yards distant from the ruptured section of the line, besides numerous riflemen posted so as to command the same spot. The train had first to round a curve, and descend a steep incline before it reached the derailing obstacles, its downgrade run being involuntarily made at full speed in consequence of the enemy's guns beginning to act their part in the *ruse de guerre* by shelling it.

Running the gauntlet of shell fire onwards to supposed safety, the train quickly reached the spot marked out for the catastrophe, with disastrous and fatal results. Three trucks—those in front of the engine—went crash, two overturning, and the rest of the train came to a dead stop, fortunately, especially in the case of the engine and tender, keeping on the rails. By dint of almost superhuman effort the line was cleared of debris, which allowed the engine and tender to pass and escape loaded with wounded and civilians, a slice of ill-luck preventing the two uninjured trucks in rear from being taken on without a hazardous delay.

Meanwhile the enemy kept up a murderous cannonade and rifle fire, to which the heroic defenders as vigorously replied while covering the task of extricating the engine. This completed, and further resistance or escape for the remainder being quite hopeless, an honourable surrender was the sequel of this brilliant stand against insuperable odds. This episode might be termed a semi-naval affair as a 7-pounder gun and crew of five men belonging to the *Tartar* formed part of the train's mixed complement

> The bluejackets, bravely commanded by their petty officer—who was the incarnation of coolness—got their 7-pounder into action. They sent two, if not three, well-aimed shells at the Boers, several hundred of whom lined the hills. But just then a shot from the enemy's 3-pounder, or field gun, hit the small naval 7-pounder, knocked gun and carriage on to the *veldt*, and wounded several of the seamen. But the men were not a whit beaten.

Thus Mr. Bennett Burleigh (*Daily Telegraph* correspondent) describes how the naval gun got knocked out of action.

The unlucky disaster caused a loss of about 80 men—killed, wounded, and prisoners; among the latter was Mr. Winston Churchill (*Morning Post* correspondent), who exhibited the traditional courage of his race while controlling the operations that resulted in the escape of the engine with the wounded, a service which merited the highest recognition. Armoured trains have their vocation, but it certainly was not here on this circuitous switchback railway, unless to court disaster and give the enemy an ill-afforded success.

> *At full speed, at full speed,*
> *At full speed, onward!*
> *Down to Frere's fated plain*
> *Rushed forth the armoured train.*
> *Meeting death with disdain—*
> *This Score and One Hundred.*
>
> *'Krupps' to the right of them;*
> *'Mausers' to the left of them;*
> *Line blocked in front of them—*
> *Shells screeched and thundered.*
>
> *Theirs not to reason why.*
> *But with orders to comply.*
> *Theirs was to do or die—*
> *Bravest of deeds!—the world wondered.*

The opportune arrival of General Hildyard's Infantry Brigade from

Defence of Durban "Terrible's"
12-pounder battery ensconced on the Berea

England and their rapid despatch to Estcourt, somewhat allayed the excitement hitherto existing in the colony as the result of the report that the Boers were moving south in force.

Lieutenant James (*Tartar*) was also sent north with two long-range 12-pounders to augment the artillery strength, their arrival at Estcourt being described as a "welcome acquisition," since the town had been exposed to serious danger for some time. Its safety was now practically assured, the garrison consisting of over 6000 men, fairly well supplied with mounted troops and guns. Later, at Mooi River, a small township thirty miles further south, another force of 5000 troops, with two batteries of Royal Artillery, had assembled under General Barton.

On November 21st the enemy struck the railway between Estcourt and Mooi River, severing connection and isolating the former position. Their main object, so it was averred, was to seize Natal's capital, Maritzburg, and then hold the colony from there northwards. One strong force of Transvaalers threatened Estcourt, while another of Free States menaced the Mooi River garrison.

But General Hildyard objected to being surrounded at Estcourt without a fight; besides, the situation generally had become much too serious to continue a strictly defensive policy. A night attack was therefore, planned.

On the afternoon of the 22nd Hildyard's force moved out towards the Boer positions. Before nightfall. Beacon Hill, eight miles distant, was reached, and up its boulder-strewn slopes the naval gun was dragged amidst a torrential storm of exceptional severity. But before the summit was attained discovery had taken place, and the difficulties of ascent were increased by a shelling from a Boer "Long Tom." Once the gun capsised, but was righted, and eventually hauled to the summit, having had several narrow escapes from being struck. A few rounds were now fired towards the Boer positions, whereupon silence was obtained for the night, the troops bivouacking on the storm-sodden ground, to await their first fight.

About 2 a.m. the attacking battalions (West Yorks and East Surreys) cautiously moved forward to the assault on Brynbella Ridge, which was carried with but trifling loss to either side, the enemy offering but slight resistance before fleeing to the protection of their main body.

At daylight the Boers began sweeping the captured ridge with their guns, and also brought an enfilading rifle fire to bear upon it The naval 12-pounder, still on Beacon Hill, strove hard to locate the enemy's guns, but without avail; no detective shell could unearth them.

DEFENCE OF DURBAN

"Terrible's" 12-pounder battery entrenched at Claremont

Having struck a moral blow at the enemy, a withdrawal of the British troops became a necessity. All that could be done had been done; so the untenable ridge was vacated, the greatest losses occurring while the troops were crossing the open ground to gain the flanks of Beacon Hill. The field guns had not, owing to the broken country, been able to offer much material aid except to cover the retirement. By noon the whole force were back at Estcourt, having suffered a loss of 86 casualties.

This spirited attack, known as the action of Willow Grange (owing to its proximity to that small place), had evidently arrested the invasion, although small marauding units of Boers succeeded in plundering a station about forty miles north of Maritzburg, causing a flutter of excitement in the defenceless capital. The Free Staters, who had closed on Mooi River, contenting themselves with a brief skirmish and an almost harmless shelling of the British camp, then withdrew, to join the Transvaalers, the whole of the invading enemy having retreated northwards by the 26th.

If the invaders had not succeeded with their military enterprise, they must have greatly exceeded expectation in the matter of looting of cattle, besides causing wanton and malicious injury to the private property of loyal colonists, many of whom were rendered homeless by these predatory acts. "Commandeering" of supplies may often find justification in war time, but no allowance can be claimed for a belligerent who gratuitously inflicts unnecessary suffering or injury upon peaceful non-combatants, and thus creates superfluous horrors of war and eternal enmity.

The sudden retreat of the enemy behind the Tugela marked an entirely new phase of the situation in Natal. The tide of invasion had turned. Hildyard's force was quickly pushed on to Frere, ten miles north of Estcourt, where a concentration camp for the Ladysmith Relief Force was to be formed; Barton's Brigade from Mooi River following shortly afterwards. This account of the situation has now brought the narrative back to Durban and current war events.

The cyclone of invasion having expended its force at Willow Grange, the feeling of apprehension of danger to either Maritzburg or Durban had given place to a normal consciousness of safety from organised attack. This result found expression in the withdrawal of the main Berea battery to a position near the Town Hall. The "Fort Denison" and Claremont batteries, however, still remained at their posts, which it was important to hold until even clandestine attacks

The "Terrible's" guns concentrated at the town camp, Durban, just previous to proceeding to the front

had become remote contingencies. The steady arrival of troops, and their rapid despatch up-country, was gradually but surely completing the barrier that would block another incursion south of the Tugela.

An equitable system of relief duties between the ship and defence force had been established; Lieutenant Bogle now commanded at "Fort Denison," Lieutenant Drummond at Claremont, and the subordinate officers were interchanged in the batteries to increase their experience. But a change of extreme import was impending. News had leaked out that the commander-in-chief had left Capetown for Durban, and great developments were therefore expected General Sir Francis Clery had already arrived, and had, during his brief stay at Durban, inspected the mobile 4.7 gun, which was manoeuvred at his request The smart evolutionary tactics performed elicited the highly favourable opinion that the gun would be a valuable asset in the field. So it proved to be.

On November 26th Sir Redvers Buller arrived, being received on landing by a bluejacket guard-of-honour of Terribles, under Commander Limpus and Lieutenant England His arrival was hailed with extreme satisfaction, his presence in the colony being described in the Press "as the needful factor that would completely restore tranquillity of mind to the colonists, and instil ultra-confidence in the troops—and more." Terse, but true.

On concluding the customary inspection of the naval guard, upon whom he bestowed a much appreciated eulogium in respect of their fit appearance, the general proceeded to scrutinise the mobile 4.7 gun, its working, etc., being explained by Captain Scott, who was in attendance as commandant. Little perception was required to convince the observant bluejackets that the gun had met with the general's approval, and that its destiny—the front—was practically assured. The wish, perhaps, may have impelled the thought, as it often does, for the brigade were well aware that unless their guns were required, the romance of war would be confined to the defence of Durban.

A certain official prejudice appeared to exist against sending these powerful guns to the front, and it might reasonably be asked why. The theory of the field gun had suddenly changed from the accepted idea. The advent of the 4.7 gun especially had been rapid—a creation since the war began—and an innovation as yet untried in the field. The Boers, however, had heavy long-range guns, and had used them to advantage; the British, therefore, could hardly submit to artillery inferiority with a remedial weapon, possessing even greater qualities than its rival, at the disposal of those responsible for the conduct of the war. Moreover, there is strong official reluctance, and for very excellent reasons, against employing a naval force on shore, except under urgent circumstances. Modern naval warfare has enforced an extensive technical and practical system of training, requiring years to perfect in the individual officer and man; and a plethora of trained personnel does not exist.

Moreover, the depletion of the crews of a squadron is always undesirable in this age of new diplomacy and sudden strokes of international policy. The duty assigned to the Naval Brigade at Graspan was unquestionably allotted by the general, and accepted by the brigade, as a coveted mark of distinction; but the exploit, if viewed solely from the standpoint of economics, was an error of judgment under the circumstances existing. A *Terrible* in action, manned with an untrained scratch crew, no matter how patriotic, would surely go to its doom. Efficiency in working the hydraulic and electric fittings of the guns, mastery of the intricacies of the mechanical torpedo, and knowledge of how to manipulate other scientific instruments of war, are the province of the twentieth-century seaman.

The press-gang system of the Nelsonian period has given place to a healthy patriotic volunteer movement, as this war has sufficed to show; but the science of war has reached such a high pitch in the navy, that it would fare badly if its *fighting personnel* became dependent on impulsive or spontaneous volunteering for supplying the demands of war. Individual resolution, white hot with the fire of patriotism, seems capable of performing anything; but science has demolished the prevalent idea and belief that there exists an arbitrary way by which any one can quickly adapt himself to every situation. Hence it is obvious why it is impolitic to employ a naval force outside its sphere of service, except in the last resort

General Buller proceeded to Maritzburg the same day, and at once assumed active control of the delicate war machinery. His activity was soon evidenced by the receipt of telegraphic instructions next day, wherein he requested Captain Scott to despatch to the front, without delay, a naval force with six guns.

The order received in the town camp on this quiet Sunday afternoon from the commandant was:

> Entrain two 4.7-inch guns and four 12-pounder guns, with full crews and necessary staff, a large supply of ammunition, stores,

and camp equipment, by 6 p.m. today, November 27th.

By five o'clock all arrangements had been completed, and the guns and warlike stores placed on board a special train.

The electrical order had been electrically responded to, and executed with a dogged determination that nothing less than a miracle should now step between the order and the object of the brigade's ambition—the front.

Captain Edward Pitcairn-Jones, C.B., who commanded the Naval Brigade in Natal.

CHAPTER 6

Relief of Ladysmith Operations

November 27th to December 14th, 1899

Captain Edward P. Jones (*Forte*) was appointed senior naval officer of all naval forces in Natal, north of Durban, about to be employed with the Ladysmith Relief Column. Captain Bearcroft (*Philomel*) received a similar appointment in Cape Colony, succeeding Flag-Captain Prothero (*Doris*), severely wounded at Graspan.

The contingent now under orders for the front consisted of 130 officers and men from the *Terrible* under Commander Limpus. The unit officers were: Lieutenant England, No. 1 4.7; Lieutenant Hunt, No. 2 4.7; Lieutenant Richards, two 12-pounders; Lieutenant Wilde, two 12-pounders. Also attached to each unit were Midshipmen Troupe, Sherrin, Down, and Ackland, respectively. The staff comprised Lieutenant Hunt (*Forte*), as staff-officer; Staff-Surgeon Lilley (*Forte*), in charge of ambulance section; Assistant-Engineer Roskruge, as engineer officer; and Midshipman Hutchinson, A.D.C. to Captain Jones.

Previous to entraining, the brigade was addressed by Captain Scott, whose animated speech partook somewhat of the nature of a lecture on artillery in the field. He especially enjoined the commanders of units and the captains of guns to remember the responsibilities vested in them as individuals, now vastly increased owing to the almost unique conditions the sudden change of field gun had enforced, and what a concentration of attention the heavy guns were certain of attracting from their critics. He laid great stress on the importance of straight and rapid shooting; the confidence it would instil into the troops when the guns were covering attacks on entrenched positions. Moreover, they were to excel the standard of mobility attained by the enemy, who at present were enjoying a heavy gun monopoly.

About 6 p.m., November 27th, the heavy special train steamed out of Durban central station amidst the cheers of the assemblage gathered on the platforms, *en route* for the Frere concentration camp. Up the steep gradients the engine snorted and puffed, the train at times only moving at a walking-race pace. Pietermaritzburg was reached at midnight, and here orders were received directing the four 12-pounders to remain in the capital to await further instructions. This unexpected order naturally caused intense disappointment to those whom it affected; but orders are orders, and—that's enough. The trucks containing the 12-pounders were quickly detached from the train, which proceeded again on its journey northwards.

Mooi River station was reached at 6 a.m., where a brief stoppage for breakfast was made, and a cursory glance obtained of the camp which had recently sustained a shelling from the Free Stater commandoes. Proceeding, Estcourt was reached four hours later, where it was found the traffic system had become so dislocated owing to the Boers having wrecked the span girder bridge adjoining Frere station, as to necessitate detention here for an indefinite period. Tents were pitched close to the station, the guns, etc, remaining on the trucks, ready to move forward as soon as the congestion of traffic was relieved.

A straggling but prettily situated township, Estcourt appears to the eye as a thriving centre of a pastoral district—which it really is. The enemy's recent incursions in the neighbourhood had forced in cattle in such numbers from outlying farmsteads, that they gave the place the appearance of a cattle market in full swing; the farmers not yet feeling the district sufficiently quiescent to return safely with their stock. It was tonight that details of the Graspan fight were obtained and read out on parade, the exceptionally heavy losses of the Naval Brigade naturally appealing to the sympathies of this brigade, many of whom had lost personal friends.

Urgency having passed with the destruction of Frere bridge, orders to proceed did not arrive until the 30th. The short run to Frere—about ten miles—was interesting, as being part of the mountainous stretch of route traversed by the ill-fated armoured train. Frere evidently expected the naval train, as the platform was thronged with a large party of troops, sent to assist in unloading the British "Long Toms," besides spans of oxen in readiness to haul them away. The railway staff officer appeared to view our warlike cargo with apprehensive misgivings, the tenor of his conversation implying that however useful a 4.7 gun might be in the field, it was certainly, from his point of view, something of a "white elephant" on a railway truck. This opinion was excusable, especially when a little delay spelt confusion of the railway system for hours.

The order to unload guns quickly sent the brigade to their previously allotted stations, and with the additional help of the troops present, the guns were soon trundling behind the spans of oxen on their way to camp, and the train steaming away south. Almost needless to add, the unloading evolution was appreciated by the hard-worked responsible railway officials, upon whom much anxious and arduous duty had devolved throughout the war; the genial general manager, Mr. David Hunter (since knighted), having carved out a name for himself in the railway world for his high administrative abilities.

Next morning the white ensign fluttered in the breeze above the tents, conspicuously denoting the naval contingent's position in the huge camp, and, until reality should supersede drill, the intervening time was spent manoeuvring the guns and getting the transport into a perfect condition.

On Sunday, December 3rd, instructions were received for the guns to co-operate in a reconnaissance taking place that night towards Chieveley. Moving off at 10 p.m., the brigade made excellent headway towards the rendezvous, until the ridges over which the guns must go were reached, when unlimited ill-luck beset all further movements. To ascend these rugged *kopjes* during daylight would have required great care; but the night was pitch dark, a heavy rain falling, and the track unknown to any one except the guide, whose capacity for his task was, like our further progress, extremely limited in range. Troubles followed each other in rapid succession. First we failed to make contact with the infantry escort sent to guard the guns—or they did with us.

Next the track—such as it was—disappeared and reappeared as if nature was playing tricks, while during the intervals the guns got into such difficulties that to extricate them it was necessary to multiply the traction power by employing all available manual and animal labour the brigade could provide; the pick and shovel also being much in evidence. Strenuous but futile efforts to carry out the instructions in time brought General Hildyard and his staff on the scene to ascertain the cause of detention; their presence increasing the already existent perturbation the misadventures had created This *contretemps*, however, was not a tangible test for the guns.

Their mobility, it must be confessed, did not produce a very favourable impression on this occasion, owing to their non-arrival at the rendezvous until near daybreak, the movement, in consequence, having to be abandoned, as darkness was very essential to success. *Experientia docet.* This nocturnal episode taught us enough to reduce to a minimum the danger of failure to perform a similar movement, and also the imprudence of placing implicit confidence in amateur night guides.

Two days afterwards, the mounted troops and two batteries of Field Artillery, under Lord Dundonald, penetrated the zone of the enemy's defence, drawing their fire, which, though well directed, did no damage.

Determined to obtain personal and topographical knowledge of routes likely to be traversed by the guns, Commander Limpus made daily expeditions abroad for that purpose. On one of these rambles the commander and Lieutenant Wilde proceeded unarmed towards Chieveley station, some good distance beyond our occupied lines, with the intention of surveying the Boer positions and obtaining certain bearings and distances, the writer accompanying them. When we were about two miles distant from the station, and nearing the place selected for the survey, several horsemen suddenly appeared, coming over a rise of ground well away to the right flank, causing a few anxious moments of guessing who they might be. General Clery, his staff and escort, they luckily proved to be, who were also viewing the enemy's positions. The general considerately informed us that to proceed further would probably mean a continuation of the journey as far as Pretoria, for the enemy were then in occupation of the station. A trip to the Boer capital being just then an undesirable excursion, a retreat was made to the friendly cover afforded by the picquets' rifles, and a survey on a smaller scale made from thence.

General Sir Redvers Buller's arrival at Frere on December 6th was evidenced by the stimulation discernible throughout the entire camp. In the early forenoon an impressive funeral service was read over the victims of the armoured train at the spot where the catastrophe occurred. Representatives from all branches of the force attended, among whom were a few Dublin Fusilier survivors who had escaped both capture and injury. From these some personal details of the episode were obtained, the wrecked, war-torn trucks grimly corroborating the story of a fight which pen could scarcely over-magnify. In the afternoon another strong cavalry reconnaissance, conducted by General Buller in person, was successfully accomplished. It extended beyond Chieveley to the ridge afterwards known as Gun Hill, overlooking the undulating stretch of veldt that slopes towards Colenso and the Tugela. A week of inactivity followed to-day's programme—for the force generally, but not for the generals and their staffs, who were fully occupied elaborating the machinery of war.

Meanwhile, the strength of the Naval Brigade was almost daily increasing, either in personnel, guns, or transport. Such proportions did the strength of the brigade eventually assume, that few would assert the navy had not received full recognition from General Buller for the various timely services already rendered elsewhere. The war, especially in Natal, had furnished a premonitory lesson on the value of long-range gunnery as a potent factor in this struggle, and naval guns were being largely requisitioned, *pro tempore*, so that nothing likely to assist in attaining the object of the relief force was being sentimentally withheld.

To follow closely the brigade's history, it will be necessary to revert for a time to Durban.

On the departure of the first contingent to the front, under Commander Limpus, the Claremont battery was withdrawn to the town camp (now styled the Town Hall Camp), Lieutenant Drummond commanding. Next day, November 28th, in response to a requisition for instructions as to any further dispositions necessary to be taken for the defence of the town, General Buller wired from Maritzburg to Captain Scott as follows:—

> I think you can now make yourself as snug as possible, parking your guns where most convenient for your men, and where giving them least duty. I cannot say for another week or ten days that Durban is absolutely safe, but it looks as if, at present, it was not in immediate danger.

Consequently, within the next few days, the "Fort Denison" battery and other outlying detachments were withdrawn into the town and reorganised. A plan was also drawn up for an emergency landing-party to be disembarked from the ships present in port, officers and men being detailed and held in readiness to comply with the confidential instructions issued on this subject.

Up to the present, news from Ladysmith was entirely conveyed by carrier pigeons, the birds having been patriotically lent by the Durban Homing Society to the military authorities. Messages were thus obtained from the beleaguered town, but none as yet could be transmitted back. The one-sidedness of this intercourse, however, was soon to be remedied, Captain Scott having submitted a scheme to General Buller whereby news of any description could, with impunity and safety, reach the invested garrison. This scheme was a searchlight with a "Scott's Flasher" attachment

Another evolution! The general wired his acceptance of the proffered apparatus, whereupon Lieutenant Ogilvy and Engineer Murray, with their respective electrical and artificer staffs, were landed, and directed to carry out the constructive work with all despatch. The searchlight was borrowed from the *Terrible*, a dynamo was commandeered from a dredging vessel, a locomotive boiler (requiring considerable overhauling) was requisitioned from the railway authorities, and connections were extemporised, some having to be manufactured. Three railways trucks were furnished, on which the machinery and apparatus were secured in position. About noon, November 30th, within 48 hours of receiving the general's telegram, the searchlight train steamed out of Durban in charge of the aforementioned officers, and, in spite of great official opposition along the line of route, Estcourt was reached at 9 p.m., and Frere by midnight, a cipher message being transmitted to Ladysmith an hour later.

This smart evolution could not have been so easily achieved had not Mr. David Hunter (general manager of the Natal Government Railway) placed his entire establishment and staff at the disposal of the commandant. Some of the methods adopted to break through (to use an hibernianism) the wire entanglements of military red tape on this journey north would, if seen in print, startle some of the higher authorities. The searchlight apparatus was also usefully employed to supply lighting power while damaged bridged were being repaired by night. Having concluded his mission, Lieutenant Ogilvy returned to Durban next day, leaving the train in charge of Sub-Lieutenant Newcome and Engineer Murray, with whom were Artificer Jones and Yeoman of Signals Arnold, as assistants.

À *propos* of the pigeon service, a few instances of their efficiency is worth recording. General White, wishing to send a plan of the situation at Ladysmith to General Buller, had it photographed down. Even then it was found too heavy, so it was cut into four sections, each of which was entrusted to a different bird. Presumably all four pigeons were despatched together, for they arrived at the commandant's office, Durban, with an interval of only 25 minutes between the first and last arrival. The distance was about 120 miles in direct line of flight; the time occupied during the passage averaged from six hours upwards.

Another bird brought the following message:—

> From General Sir George White to H.R.H the Prince of Wales.
>
> The General Officer Commanding and the garrison of Ladysmith beg to congratulate Your Royal Highness on the anniversary of your birthday. A royal salute of 21 shells will be fired at the enemy at noon in honour of the occasion.
>
> Ladysmith, November 9th, 1899.

Ladysmith, like Paris during the Franco-Prussian War, owed much to the carrier-pigeon service.

Early on December 8th, Lieutenant Ogilvy left Durban in command of a second contingent for the front, consisting of 100 officers and men, with eight 12-pounder guns, drawn from the remnant defence force. Lieutenant Melville (*Forte*), Lieutenants Burne and Deas (*Philomel*), were the unit commanders. Gunners Wright and Williams, Midshipmen Willoughby, Boldero, Hallwright, and Hodson, were also attached to the battery; and Surgeon Macmillan was in charge of the ambulance section. A special train conveyed them direct to Frere, where they joined the naval headquarter camp, under Captain Jones, the same night.

Two days previously, the four 12-pounders detained at Maritzburg had also arrived at the front, the Naval Brigade arrangements being now completed.

The numerical strength of men and guns with the Natal Field Force and Ladysmith Relief Column at this period of the operations was as follows. Inside Ladysmith, Captain Lambton had under his command 283 officers and men of the *Powerful,* two 4.7 platform-mounted guns, three 12-pounders mounted on extemporised carriages, one light 12-pounder field gun, and four Maxims. With the Relief Column under Captain Jones, actually at Frere, there were 285 officers and men, two mobile 4.7 guns, and fourteen long-range 12-pounders mounted on extemporised carriages. Of this number, 24 officers and 217 men belonged to the *Terrible,* who manned all the guns except two 12-pounders, the crews of which were *Tartars.*

In addition to the foregoing. Lieutenants Anderton and Chiazarri, with 53 petty officers and men of the Natal Naval Volunteers, a well-trained corps, had joined the brigade at Frere, being mainly attached throughout the relief operations to the 4.7 guns. On the lines of communication were four long-range 12-pounders: two at Estcourt,

"Terrible's" search-light train which flashed the night signals into beleaguered Ladysmith

manned by 26 officers and men of the *Philomel*. under Lieutenant Halsey; two at Mooi River, under Lieutenant Steele, manned by 25 officers and men of the *Forte*. These numbers give a grand total of 623 officers and men and 30 guns, landed to date for active service in northern Natal by the Royal Navy, exclusive of naval volunteers.

The naval transport with the Relief Column consisted of 10 colonial conductors, about 100 natives as drivers, etc, over 400 draught oxen for the guns and ammunition waggons, and 15 horses for the staff and unit commanders. More men and guns arrived at the front at a later period of the operations, which, of course, implied more transport; but these will receive due recognition in proper order later on.

The *"Per mare, per terram,"* contingent is next to receive attention. After their return from Cape Colony side, the Royal Marine detachment were employed in and around Durban until all war alarms which threatened the town had ceased. On November 21st, Captain Mullins, Sergeants Peck and Roper, with 28 rank and file, relieved the *Tartars* from the armoured train. Three days later, and in consequence of the Boer incursions south previously related, a strong outpost was established for the protection of the Umlass waterworks (the Durban supply), some fifteen miles distant in the country. Commanded by Captain Mullins, this force consisted of Sergeants Peck and Stanbridge and 30 men, supported by a 12-pounder field gun manned by 18 bluejackets under Sub-Lieutenant Newcome.

The position occupied was on an eminence about 200 feet high, overlooking the waterworks and ford across the Umlass River, three sides being precipitous, while an abattis was constructed to secure the fourth or open side from chance attack. To obtain water a thick tropical undergrowth, among which the python and other dangerous snakes abounded galore, had to be forced through to get at the river. On one water-carrying mission a bluejacket incautiously disturbed a huge python by treading on it. It showed no fight, but tried to glide off, when Sergeant Peck shot it in the head. Its length was exactly nineteen feet, its skin being preserved as a memento of a risky escapade. On November 30th, Sub-Lieutenant Newcome was recalled for service with the searchlight train, and Captain Mullins, then down with a severe dysentery attack, returned on board for treatment. Lieutenant Lawrie, who had previously relieved his captain in command of the armoured train, now replaced him as commanding officer at the waterworks.

On December 9th, no further danger being apprehended in that quarter, the Umlass post was withdrawn, and the armoured train also dispensed with. From now the detachment was distributed. Captain Mullins (now convalescent), with two sergeants and 28 men, the 12-pounder field gun and crew, formed the new main guard established at the Town Hall camp. This small force was conspicuously placed in the centre of the town as the outward and visible symbol of martial law, to perform the variable duties the commandant frequently found it necessary to have executed under its powers.

Sergeant Lester and nine men were detailed as guard for the hospital ship *Nubia*. Sergeant Roper, one corporal, and six men, manned one 12-pounder of Lieutenant Richard's unit at the front Lieutenant Lawrie and the remainder of the detachment returned on board the *Terrible* for duty. Later, in February, Captain Mullins was appointed recruiting officer for the Colonial Corps, some 500 recruits passing through his hands. This officer was also military adviser to the commandant.

Before reverting to the main subject—the front—a brief reference to current events which affect the situation as a whole appears necessary; in fact, it deals with two of those three memorable reverses to British arms which made so painful an impression throughout the Empire.

Early in December, General Gatacre moved from Queenstown with the bulk of his force to Sterkstroom, some 30 miles south of Stormberg. Principally for strategic reasons, *viz.* to create a diversion of the enemy's attention towards his force while the Kimberley and Ladysmith relief columns were advancing, and also to reoccupy Stormberg, the general decided to drive the enemy from his front Consequently, a force about 2700 strong were taken by rail as far as Molteno, where they detrained late on the 9th inst., and from thence made a night march over broken country towards the enemy's positions. The guides having blundered, dawn was breaking before the column reached their objective. Continuing the march, now greatly retarded through fruitless travelling in wrong directions, the British force suddenly became aware of the presence of the enemy from a heavy fusillade opened upon their advance.

Surprised perhaps, but nothing daunted, the intrepid general hurriedly made his dispositions for attacking the almost invulnerable Boer stronghold, bringing his field batteries into action to cover the advance. The travel-worn troops made a brave attempt to storm the position, which hopelessly failed—Nature had already enervated them for this their baptism of battle. Retreat followed the repulse, an evolution fraught with every conceivable difficulty, harassed as it was by a fresh and vigorous enemy flushed with success, the two British batteries playing an important and brilliant role during the retirement in preventing retreat becoming a rout. 89 killed and wounded and 633 missing and prisoners was the price of this misadventurous enterprise. Collecting the remnant of his force at Molteno, General Gatacre securely held that town for the present. The reverse, though a strategic failure, was insignificant in its effect upon the military situation elsewhere. Politically, however, it was a regrettable incident; occurring as it did in the most disaffected district of Cape Colony, now teeming with virulently disloyal Dutch colonists. The sequence of events now brings the Kimberley relief column to notice.

After the Battle of Modder River on November 28th, Lord Methuen, finding his force inadequate to follow up the enemy, entrenched near the river to await reinforcements. These arriving in due course, the general moved forward on December 10th to attack the enemy, who had strongly fortified the Magersfontein *kopjes*, a few miles north of the river. In the late afternoon, the artillery began the preparative sweeping of the position, the naval guns—one mobile 4.7 and four long-range 12-pounders—assisting the field batteries in the bombardment Shortly after midnight, Methuen sent the Highland brigade forward to carry out the preliminary plan of battle—a surprise attack; the Guards brigade and artillery following later. To obviate the danger of dividing his brigade in the dark wet night that prevailed. General Wauchope advanced in close formation, intending to deploy at a certain point on the march previous to delivering the assault.

Almost at the moment that the deployment was being effected, which was accidentally protracted until within a few score yards of the Boer trenches, premature disclosure occurred The consequences were indeed momentous. A hurricane of bullets instantly swept into the unsuspicious Highlanders with withering exactitude, creating irretrievable confusion among their ranks; the darkness rendering all attempts to regain military formation or disciplinary control utterly futile. Their brave brigadier was slain, and over 700 casualties had occurred within a few minutes. The mysterious night march—a disastrous surprisal—irreparable disorganisation—loss of leaders—and an unseen foe dealing forth annihilation at close range, had followed each other in swift succession. Amidst such infernal surroundings there was no alternative but to fall back in face of the pitiless bullets.

DEFENCE OF LADYSMITH

Armoured train manned by "Terrible's" Marines under Captain Mullins, R.M.L.I.

A panic had been averted, a fact which speaks volumes for the bravery of the Highlanders, whose indomitable pluck in battle is a cherished tradition. They had hastily retired, but with irrepressible clannishness had rallied round their regimental chieftains, had reformed, and were ready to retrieve their misfortune. But this could not done, for when dawn disclosed their location, the hurricane of lead burst forth afresh, compelling the eager brigade to observe the closest cover. With the arrival of the British batteries, succour to some extent was afforded them, but though compelled to abate its severity, the enemy never sufficiently slackened their fire to permit of any attempt to redeem the day. The field batteries went into action at close range, rendering exceptionally brilliant service throughout the fight; their own position at certain times becoming somewhat hazardous. The naval guns were also conspicuously in evidence for the amount of moral and material damage inflicted by them, and the suppression of fire they effected.

Meanwhile, the general advanced his whole force in hopes of penetrating the Boer position, the enemy making counter flanking movements requiring exceptional leading and severe fighting to repel. Circumstances finally compelled the sorely tried Highlanders to be withdrawn from the fighting line, where they had been perilously exposed for many hours to a deadly rifle fire, and a scorching sun which had blistered their prostrate bodies and produced an intense thirst that could not be assuaged Neither generalship or bravery, nor gun power, could depose the tenacious Boers from their rocky stronghold, which appeared to bristle everywhere with rifles. The enemy's position being thus unassailable in front, and a detour to outflank it being impossible with the resources available, Lord Methuen ordered the inevitable withdrawal beyond the range of the enemy's guns, which had been inexplicably silent throughout the fight until just prior to the retirement.

Thus ended the Battle of Magersfontein, the second of that trio of misfortunes which made December, 1899, a disastrously memorable month. Nevertheless, except for the moral and political benefits usually associated with victories, the Boers, as at Stormberg, had not gained the slightest military advantage. Both sides were in the peculiar position of check, the result of lack of strategical knowledge on the part of the Boer generals of how to make the most of the military situation, and absence of necessary strength to reassume the offensive on the part of the British. The enemy, however, did not enjoy complete immunity, for the ubiquitous General French was actively operating in the Colesberg district between the two British columns, keeping the enemy in a state of constant disquietude. His harassing operations prevented further invasion of the colony, and effectually checked any projected flanking designs directed against either British force.

Returning to Natal and the main subject. General Buller is found ready to strike his first blow for the relief of Ladysmith. The completion of the temporary trestle bridge at Frere had restored railway traffic towards the Tugela, thus providing the general with the desired mobility which would considerably lessen the difficulties of advance, and afford rapid communication with his base.

On December 12th Barton's Infantry Brigade moved from Frere and occupied Gun Hill, just beyond Chieveley station. Captain Jones, Commander Limpus, and the naval staff, with the two 4.7 guns and 12-pounder units of Lieutenants Richards, Burns, and Wilde, accompanied the advance.

Next day the naval guns heavily bombarded the Colenso positions at ranges varying from 7000 yards upwards to nearly double that distance. Much visible damage was done to the enemy's works, but little sign did the enemy vouchsafe that they were in strong tenancy of those rugged hills, among which the relief force were destined to wage so many a bitterly contested fight.

On the 14th the naval guns, protected by a strong escort, moved forward to a low *kopje* (Shooters Hill) west of the railway, about 2000 yards nearer the enemy's central positions. Fort Wylie, a *kopje* terraced with entrenchments and honeycombed safety shelters in its rear, was especially singled out for shell practice. This position stood conspicuously forth as effectually commanding the railway and road bridges over the Tugela, the village of Colenso,. and also overlooked the stretch of *veldt* country between the river and Chieveley. Although the 4.7 guns sent scores of shell crashing with thunderous force into their boulderous breastworks, and searched with lyddite all located trenches for quite two hours, the enemy maintained the exasperating equanimity of yesterday. The firing, however, was not altogether a futile expenditure of ammunition, for much verification of ranges, besides the location of hitherto unknown trenches and positions resulted, and the knowledge so obtained proved invaluable on the morrow.

An apt reminiscence of Fort Wylie, closely associated with our present comrades of the Natal Naval Volunteers, seems *à propos* to relate just here. On Ladysmith becoming invested, the Boers pressed south to secure this all-important position, then held by the Dublin Fusiliers and this particular detachment of naval volunteers. Supported by field guns, the Boers occupied the adjacent hills which dominated the British position, rendering it untenable, and necessitating a hasty retirement to avoid being cut off. The volunteers had two small prehistoric field guns with them, mounted on Fort Wylie's summit, and, when retreat became inevitably received orders to disable their guns and leave them behind.

Instead, however, of our sturdy colonial friends complying. Lieutenant Anderton held a hurried council of war with his merry men, whereat it was decided to take the venerated guns with them. Suiting their action to the decision arrived at, they first fired their ammunition at the advancing Boers as if stubborn resistance was intended. This stratagem had the desired effect, bringing the enemy to a standstill, and thus enabling the volunteers to carry out a successful manoeuvre. Over the hillside the guns were rolled, taken across the river, and dragged by hand over the *veldt* to the train in Colenso, which was only awaiting their arrival before steaming away south to safety. It was a fine evolution, which obtained high commendation for the performance, though official censure followed for the infraction of orders. Lieutenant Anderton was evidently emulating the Nelson incident at Copenhagen, when that naval hero applied the telescope to his blind eye, to avoid seeing the signal to cease the action.

The eve of battle had arrived. Towards the close of day the main body of the relief army had marched over from Frere camp. Lieutenant Ogilvy arrived with six 12-pounders, two having been left behind under Lieutenant Melville to support the military force remaining to guard Frere and the large reserve of military supplies collected there. That evening the General Orders were issued to the respective brigadiers and commanding officers of detached units for the planned attack on Colenso, which was to take place on the early morrow.

Assembling the brigade, Commander Limpus informed them of the main instructions received from headquarters and of the proposed methods for executing them, impressing on the officers and responsible individuals the necessity for implicitly following the orders he had carefully explained. Later, after dark, the guns were withdrawn from the top of the *kopje*, and, together with all our impedimenta, got ready for moving off at the appointed hour next morning, a few hours' rest occupying the brief space of time which intervened betwixt the calm of the camp and the storm of tomorrow's battle.

GENERAL SIR REDVERS BULLER, V.C, G.C.B., ETC.
Commanding British Forces in Natal during
operations for Relief of Ladysmith.

CHAPTER 7

Battle of Colenso

December 15th, 1899

General Sir Redvers Buller put his army in motion early on the morning of December 15th, while the pall of darkness still enshrouded the camp, so that the attacking brigades could arrive at their assigned positions before sunrise, ready for the general advance.

Briefly, the dispositions of the force, with the main objective of each brigade, were as follows:—

General Hildyard's (2nd) Infantry Brigade had the post of honour in the centre. This brigade was to march north at 4 a.m. towards the railway bridge, cross the Tugela at that point, and attempt the capture of the *kopjes* immediately opposite, Fort Wylie being the position demanding closest attention.

General Hart's (5th) Infantry Brigade was to advance at 4.30 a.m. to the left, force a passage across the Tugela at Bridle Drift, west of Colenso, and, after crossing, to wheel right and assault the central *kopjes* in flank, to facilitate the crossing of Hildyard's Brigade.

General Lyttleton's (4th) Infantry Brigade was to advance at 4.30 a.m. to a point west of the railway, between the aforementioned brigades, ready to support either.

General Barton's (6th) Infantry Brigade was to advance at 4 a.m. to a position east of the railway, from whence it could cover Hildyard's right flank, and, if necessary, support the main attack, or the force sent against Hlangwani Hill.

The Mounted Brigade, under Lord Dundonald, about 1000 strong, and one field battery, was to proceed at 4 a.m. in the direction of Hlangwani; if possible, secure that position, from whence the central *kopjes* could be enfiladed, and also to cover the right flank of the army.

Two small forces of mounted troops guarded the extreme right and left flanks. Four infantry brigades and the mounted force, representing over 16,000 troops, have now been disposed of.

The Royal Field Artillery and Naval Brigade guns were detailed to support the respective movements thus: Two batteries, under Colonel Long, were to advance at 3.30 a.m. east side of the railway, to prepare the crossing for and cover Hildyard's attack. Two batteries, under Colonel Parsons, to move forward at 4.30 a.m. west of the railway, and take up a position from whence the central *kopjes* could be shelled in flank. One battery, as previously mentioned, was attached to Lord Dundonald's command Consideration for the main subject calls for greater detail respecting the naval dispositions.

Six guns, two 4.7 and four 12-pounders (termed the central battery), under Commander Limpus, were to move forward at 3.30 a.m. and take up a position on a slight eminence about 3000 yards from the river, and some 800 yards west of the railway. These guns were to do all possible harm to the enemy's men and *matériel*, to engage any guns which disclosed themselves, and to follow the infantry, if successful, across the river. The unit commanders and captains of guns of this battery were:—Lieutenant England and C.P.O. Bate, No. 1 4.7; Lieutenant Hunt and C.P.O. Stephens, No. 2 4.7; Lieutenant Richards, P.O. Jeffrey and Sergeant Roper two 12-pounders; Lieutenant Wilde and P.O.s H. Mitchell and Metcalfe, two 12-pounders, Lieutenants Anderton and Chiazarri, and the naval volunteer detachment, were equally divided for duty with the 4.7 guns. Mr. Cole, gunner, and Chief Gunnery Instructor Baldwin were attached to the battery for general duties; the remainder of the naval staff, under Captain Jones, also took station at this position.

Ogilvy's 12-pounder battery was assigned to Colonel Long's command, and comprised the following units:—

Lieutenant James, P.O.s Epsley and Bird, with the *Tartarus* two 12-pounders; Lieutenant Deas, P.O.s Symons and Ward, two 12-pounders; Mr. Wright, Gunner, P.O.s Venness and Taylor, two 12-pounders. Surgeon Macmillan had command of the ambulance section, and C.P.O. Cornish, general battery duties. To assist in guarding the flanks, the unit of Lieutenant Burne remained on Shooters Hill—P.O.s Mullis and R. Mitchell, captains of guns.

The baggage and stores, all parked together, were to be left behind under a strong guard, the troops dispensing with all except their actual fighting kit

The General Orders stated:—

The enemy is entrenched in the *kopjes* north of Colenso Bridge. One large camp is reported to be near the Ladysmith Road, about five miles north-west of Colenso. Another large camp is reported in the hills which lie north of the Tugela in a northerly direction from Hlangwani Hill.

It is the intention of the General Officer Commanding to force the passage of the Tugela tomorrow.

Completion of these details—the synopsis of the Battle of Colenso—has placed some 17,000 British naval and military forces, and 44 guns, in battle array.

Without a sign of molestation the army quietly carried out the preliminary instructions. The central naval battery, having the least distance to traverse, arrived at its destination with strict punctuality. The guns were quickly unlimbered for action, ready to cover the general advance. The teams of oxen were outspanned and sent back to Shooters Hill for safety under the charge of our very timorous but well-paid chief conductor, who expostulated against coming so close to the enemy's lines, which he emphasised the terms of his contract did not include.

Meanwhile the various brigades could be observed nearing the respective points assigned to them in the General Orders. Ogilvy's guns, closely following Colonel Long's batteries, crossed the railway on the right of the central battery just as dawn broke over the scene, and rapidly closed towards the Fort Wylie *kopjes*. The clear summer morn enabled the Boers from their lofty vantage ground to obtain a full panoramic view of the several British movements during the advance across the *veldt* towards them. Our line of front presented an arc from six to seven miles in extent, so that the enemy could easily infer from the nature of the dispositions exhibited, which section of their defence was principally threatened, and elaborate their plans accordingly. It had been announced in orders that the commander-in-chief would be found near the 4.7 guns. The arrival there of Generals Buller and Clery with their staffs indicated that the respective brigades, whose advance the generals had supervised, had sufficiently progressed to warrant the preparative artillery sweeping to be commenced.

The Battle of Colenso begun at 5.30 a.m. with a salvo of shells from the naval guns. Up to this time no sign was elicited of the enemy's intention to resist the advance, save the sudden dashes here and there of a few horsemen evidently conveying messages; the tactical silence prevailing giving rise to all sorts of fanciful conjectures. Lyddite and shrapnel shell again searched trenches, *dongas*, and the fringe of the river bank with a murderous examination. Common shell crashed into all visible positions and defensive works, producing volcanic results, scattering debris skywards, and rending huge openings with nearly every round; the explosions reverberating among the encircling hills giving forth a weird continuity of roar. The firing, as such, was indeed a magnificent sight for an artillerist to witness, as, the ranges being known, the shells burst with fine precision.

For upwards of forty-five minutes a vigorous bombardment proceeded, the field batteries adding their quota of destructiveness upon arriving at their allotted stations. But not a single reply was drawn until the attacking brigades had got well within the enemy's zone of rifle fire. Then—then the alluring calm of subtle silence suddenly gave place to an assailing storm of shell and rifle fire that swept with disastrous effect into the advancing brigades from the whole arc of defence. A lurking insuppressible resistance from at least ten thousand rifles and two score guns, ranging from a "Long Tom" to the dreaded pom-pom, had been aroused from a cunning slumber. Where least expected defiance was always found. Even on the south side of the river, where "Intelligence" could not have expected or foreseen them, were Boer rifle pits containing Boer riflemen, invisible themselves, though the effect of their fire was very much in evidence.

The zone of shell fire even encircled the central naval battery's position, though luckily very few shells obtained the correct range, the majority pitching well clear of the battery before bursting. It was at this juncture that desperate fighting was taking place with Hildyard's and Hart's brigades. The fortunes—or misfortunes—of the central attack demand principal attention, as it was there that the most calamitous event of this fateful day occurred, and that Ogilvy's battery especially distinguished themselves. No better description of this memorable episode can be furnished than that given in Lieutenant Ogilvy's official report. He wrote:—

> Acting on orders received from Captain Jones, R.N., I reported myself to Colonel Long, C.R.A., who directed me to attach myself to him until the guns had been placed in a suitable position. I therefore directed Lieutenant James of *Tartar*, to lead the battery behind the Royal Artillery field guns, and told him

that we were to form up on the left of the Royal Artillery guns when they came into action. About 6 a.m., the guns being in column of route march with naval guns in the rear, I was riding in front with Colonel Long about 450 yards from Colenso station, when he directed Colonel Hunt to bring his guns into action just in front of a deep *donga* running across our front at right angles to the railway. He then told me to come into action on the left, and proceeded to arrange our different zones of fire, while the Royal Artillery guns were getting into position. In front of us was a line of trees up to which our skirmishers had advanced, also a few artillery outposts.

Just as I was about to direct my guns where to go, and as the Royal Artillery were unlimbering, the outposts turned sharply and a murderous fire, both rifle and shell, was opened on the guns and ammunition column. I immediately galloped back to my guns and found that the fire had caught them just as the two centre guns were going through a drift across another *donga* parallel to the before-mentioned one, but about 400 yards in the rear. When I arrived I found that all the native riders with the exception of those for Lieutenant James's gun teams had bolted.

These guns had just crossed the drift, so I directed him to take up a position on the left and opened fire on Fort Wylie, from which the majority of the shell fire appeared to come. About this time my horse was shot through the shoulder by a rifle bullet. The two rear guns under Lieutenant Deas of H.M.S. *Philomel*, not having crossed the drift, I directed him to take ground on the left and open fire also on Fort Wylie. The two centre guns under Mr. Wright, gunner of H.M.S. *Terrible*, were unfortunately jammed with their ammunition waggons in the drift, the wheels of the waggons being locked and the oxen turned round in their yokes. I managed by the aid of some artillery horses to extricate these guns from the drift and to bring them into action on each side of the drift to the rear of the *donga*, one of the horses being shot while doing this. I could not manage to move the ammunition waggons, as the rifle and shell fire was too severe at the time, a 1½-pounder Maxim-Nordenfeldt being particularly attentive, and sending three shells into the drift at every discharge.

Repeated messages for more men came back from the Royal

Commander Frederick Charles Ashley Ogilvy.

Artillery batteries, and these were sent to the front by a Royal Artillery sergeant in charge of the ammunition column. After about half an hour's firing, as I should judge, the Royal Artillery guns were silenced, nearly all the men being apparently killed or wounded. Soon after this the fire from Fort Wylie slackened considerably. The commander-in-chief now rode up and directed me to move our guns and ammunition as soon as I could. The guns were got away each by a team of artillery horses, who galloped them up the hill to the rear. The waggons were far more difficult, owing to their weight, the large circle they required to turn in, and to the fact that they had to be got out from the drift and turned round by the guns' crews before the horses could be put on.

About this time a most brilliant feat was performed by two teams of artillery, who galloped to the front, against a most murderous fire, limbered up, and rescued two guns; a similar attempt by one other team, at least, resulted in the entire team, as far as I could see, being destroyed.

The advance of the infantry on an open plain, with little or no cover against a most heavy rifle fire from entrenched positions was also a magnificent sight. The conduct of our men without exception was particularly fine, the day being a very hot one and the work hard. The way Nos. 1 and 2 guns' crews of the *Terrible* got their waggons out of the drift under heavy fire from shell and rifle was quite up to the standard expected of all seamen. I cannot conclude without mentioning the way Lieutenant James of the *Tartar* selected the best suitable position and opened fire with great effect. Lieutenant Deas, of the *Philomel*, unfortunately had a gun capsised as they were moving off to the left to come into action, but managed to mount it quickly and brought both guns into action.

After the first few minutes these two officers took entire charge of their respective guns, and brought them safely out of action; Lieutenant James coming again into action on the left under the direction of Captain Jones. Mr. Wright, gunner, worked his guns well, and was of great assistance in withdrawing them. Surgeon Macmillan, R.N., Lieutenant Palmer, R.A.M.C., were conspicuous in their attendance to the wounded. Our loss was very small, three wounded, one of them very slightly, and I attribute this to (1st) the Fort Wylie guns and rifle fire being directed principally on the R.A. guns, which were some 300 yards nearer than we were: (2nd) to the enemy directing most of their fire on our ox teams and waggons, they being so much more conspicuous than the guns. Twenty-eight oxen were killed, wounded, or lost.

With regard to this unforeseen disaster, General Buller, after concisely dealing with Hart's fiasco on the left, wrote:—

At the same time General Hildyard was advancing on the bridge, and as I was proceeding in that direction to superintend the attack, and also to ascertain what Colonel Long's Brigade Division, which was very heavily engaged on the right, was doing, I received a message that he had been driven from his guns by superior infantry fire.

I believed at the moment that the six naval guns had shared the same fate, and I at once decided that without guns it would be impossible for me to force the passage.

Fortunately the naval guns had not reached the position taken up by the 14th and 66th Batteries when fire was opened; their drivers however bolted, and their oxen were stampeded, or killed; but by dint of hard work all the guns and the ammunition waggons were hauled out of range. All worked well, and Lieutenant Ogilvy and Gunner Wright, Her Majesty's ship *Terrible*, particularly rendered excellent service. These guns, however, had been rendered immobile for the day.

Colonel Long, Royal Artillery, has been dangerously wounded, and I am unable to obtain his explanations. His orders were to come into action covered by the 6th Brigade, which brigade was not, as he knew, intended to advance on Colenso. I had personally explained to him where I wished him to come into action, and with the naval guns only, as the position was not within effective range for his field guns. Instead of this he advanced with his batteries so fast that he left both his Infantry escort and his oxen-drawn naval guns behind, and came into action under Fort Wylie, a commanding trebly entrenched hill, at a range of 1200 yards, and I believe within 300 yards of the enemy's rifle pits.

From the foregoing official accounts the cause of the central attack being rendered abortive may be easily deduced.

In the meantime, Hildyard's Brigade slowly advanced towards

Colenso village and the river; the success of his movement vitally depending on the support he expected to receive from Long's now disabled batteries. Further progress beyond the village was found impossible against the terrible fusillade which then assailed them, though this position was maintained until the withdrawal.

The description of a few interesting incidents concerning Long's batteries, and the attached naval guns, may very properly follow the official versions.

After crossing to the east side of the railway, the field batteries moved forward direct towards Fort Wylie, while the naval guns, limbered up behind the heavy ammunition waggons, were compelled to advance by devious routes owing to the broken ground frequently encountered. Hence the reason of Long's batteries having outpaced the naval guns. On coming into action, the range distance for Ogilvy's guns was 1550 yards from Fort Wylie, and about 650 yards from the nearest Boer rifle pits, or shelters, dug on the near side of the river. These ranges may somewhat serve to illustrate the toughness of the position; the field batteries being about 400 yards nearer.

With the exception of the *Tartar's* unit, Lieutenant Ogilvy omits to mention in his report that the guns again came into action after retiring from the untenable position first occupied, though twice afterwards the other two units ventured their luck against that of the enemy. The second position was some 500 yards in rear of the one vacated, each gun coming into action, independently, as it arrived back, in order to cover the withdrawal of the two ammunition waggons isolated at the *donga*; the other battery waggons having been already withdrawn with the surviving oxen. The enemy's gunners quickly responded to this second invitation to a duel, and again forced the guns to retire, though, until the said waggons were well under weigh towards the rear, they continued in action. They were then withdrawn well beyond rifle range to comparative safety, taking part in the covering of the general retirement which followed the loss of the field batteries.

The slow, irksome process of getting the heavy ammunition waggons out of danger was a perilous duty. With great difficulty they were reversed by manual labour; General Buller and the whole staff dismounting, and personally assisting to turn them. The near waggon was easily removed by one artillery team, the other, being on the offside of the *donga*, required skilful pilotage. A second team of eight horses was obtained, and with the aid of a plucky artillery driver, young Frank Hayles, ordinary seaman, transported it safely to the rear amid a hail of bullets. The first horse which Hayles mounted was killed, and the second one he bestrode was severely wounded. While in the middle of the *donga*, Hayles stopped the waggon to recover some rifles which had been jerked off, whereupon the general shouted, "Push on, Jack, or you'll lose the waggon and the whole lot for the sake of a few rifles," an order that was promptly obeyed.

Hayles appeared much more perturbed concerning the insignificant loss of a couple of rifles, than satisfied with his lucky enterprise, and cogitated as to what would be the official verdict—whether "lost by accident," or, "pay the estimated value." His unobtrusive courage was warmly appreciated by his battery comrades, as was also the nonchalant adventure of Seaman Campling. This youngster, when the guns were retired, remained on the field to succour his chum, Seaman White, who was lying dangerously wounded in the back from a piece of shell, and bleeding profusely. When the ambulance removed White to the rear. Campling, instead of also returning, advanced into the firing line with the Queens, and stayed with that battalion until the battle was over, being reported as missing. Though guilty of an infraction of discipline, for which he received an official rebuke, he acted under the influence of the stimulus of battle; the impetus being derived from the traditional examples set by the officers and captains of guns, who never forgot the obligations due from rank and rating.

Conspicuous always was the person of Lieutenant Ogilvy, who while hazardously exposing himself in his search for the hiding places of the omnipresent Boer guns, sent the guns' crews into the *donga* for shelter. As he located a gun position the crews would instantly respond to his call, and continue firing until the gun was either silenced or removed On one of these occasions was witnessed a contest of skill between Petty Officers Venness and Taylor, who, amidst these infernal surroundings, mutually challenged each other to try which could first silence a Boer gun just brought into action at Fort Wylie. Taylor—a noted heavy gunshot—won, having the double satisfaction of seeing his target topple over, and of raising a British cheer from the excited infantry supports, who, even in battle, admired sportive skill.

The next minute, however, the Boers retaliated by sending a shell into the battery, the one which wounded Seaman White dangerously, and Seamen Newstead and Webster severely. Although the guns, limbers, and waggons, were fairly splintered with shell, and riddled with bullets, besides nearly three dozen oxen being killed or disabled, the guns' crews miraculously escaped with only the three aforementioned casualties. The proverbial *"sweet little cherub which sits up aloft"* had indeed guarded the life of Jack, but sadly neglected to perform the same office for his military comrades.

Respecting Colonel Long's two abandoned batteries, General Buller laconically remarked in his despatch:—

The men fought their guns like heroes and silenced Fort Wylie; but the issue could never have been in doubt, and gradually they were all shot down. . . .

The heroically brilliant attempts to recover the guns were numerous; two only being successful. The enemy concentrated a murderous fire on the exposed and isolated cannon, which were now apparently regarded by them as legitimate spoils of battle, an opinion which found no favour on our side, for although the personnel and horses of both batteries were nearly all *hors de combat*, volunteer men and impressed horses took their places.

Generals Buller and Clery, with their staffs and mounted escorts, arrived on the scene, encountering the legion of common risks and perils the storm of bullets and shells exposed them to. Three of the Headquarter Staff (Captains Congreve, Schofield, and Lieutenant Roberts—son of Field-Marshal Lord Roberts) rode forth with volunteer rescue teams. Roberts was mortally wounded, and Congreve severely hit during their rides. Surgeon-Captain Hughes, also of the staff, was mortally wounded close to the side of General Buller, who was himself sharply grazed by a bullet; the whole staff having numerous hair-breadth escapes. As fast as horses could be procured officers and men were eager to mount them, and rode without hesitation across that 500 yards of *veldt* which a withering hail of death-dealing bullets was sweeping without intermission.

One feat of spontaneous pluck, and the final attempt permitted by the general, was that performed by Captain Reed and men of the 7th Field Battery, who rode over with three teams from Dundonald's command to render help. They started, rode swiftly on, but before the teams had got halfway to the guns, the officer and five men were severely wounded, and one man was killed out of the dozen who formed the ride, besides thirteen out of twenty-two horses being lost. So great was the severity of the fire which had burst upon each successive attempt, that nearly half of the men and horses were removals from the active muster roll It is the performance of such brilliant deeds as these, the heritage of the Anglo-Saxon race, that has created the British Empire of today—an empire without parallel.

Leaving the centre, Hart's Brigade on the left comes next in order for special notice. Here also a sad misfortune had befallen the advance. The brigade had failed to strike the Drift, and had marched into veritable "jaws of death" instead The river's course here diverged northwards for some distance, then, curving back, formed a salient loop, projecting towards the foot of the hills beyond. Into this natural death-trap the brigade had well advanced when a storm of shot and shell burst with cyclonic force upon their close marching formation. From their front came a hail of bullets from invisible trenches; into their flanks was poured a withering cross-fire; while from guns concealed among the inaccessible hills beyond the river shells thundered destruction into their ranks. A tactical movement into open formation was quickly executed, whereupon the brave Irishmen were led by their dauntless brigadier to the attack. The bewildered brigade, in spite of the havoc being wrought among them, fearlessly pushed forward towards the place where the drift was expected to be found.

But it never was found, because, the Boers having dammed the Tugela lower down, it did not then exist! Into such an inferno had the hapless brigade plunged, that General Buller personally went to the scene; but the orders he at once issued for retirement could not be complied with unless support was afforded. Consequently two battalions from Lyttleton's Brigade and Parson's Field Batteries were diverted to assist in extricating Hart from an extremely perilous position. Meanwhile, the enemy also strengthened their position, not only to frustrate all attempts at crossing, which had now become impossible, but to pinion there, if possible, the hard-pressed Irish Brigade. They brought several hitherto silent guns into action which outranged and severely castigated Parson's batteries, obliging them to retire beyond range, and leave the infantry to work out their own salvation. The Boer guns, from the summit of the Grobelar Range, were making effective shooting at 7000 yards to which the batteries could not retaliate, though they had previously exacted an involuntary respite from the Boer trenches and works which commanded the tongue of land containing Hart's force.

> ... During all this time, and throughout the day, the two 47-inch and four 12-pounder naval guns of the Naval Brigade, and Durban Naval Volunteers, under Captain E. P. Jones, Royal Navy, were being admirably served, and succeeded in silencing

"Terrible's" 4.7 gun at Battle of Colenso.
General Clery and his staff viewing the Boer position

every one of the enemy's guns they could locate. . . .

Such are the words culled from General Buller's Colenso despatch, when referring to Hart's operations. It was indeed during the most critical periods of the various attacks that the services of the naval guns—the 4.7's especially—were in demand all over the field. "Direct your fire on Hlangwani Hill"—"on Fort Wylie"—"on the *kopjes* beyond"— "at 'Long Tom' on Grobelar"—"on the hills to your left"— "the fringe of the river banks"—were but a few of the urgent messages received by Captain Jones in rapid succession. Each one must be attended to; each brigadier naturally thought of his own brigade; each brigade believed it was opposed to the enemy's strongest defence; so each order was responded to—in the spirit, if not the letter. The demand and supply problem was here very perplexing. Lyddite especially was in greatest demand, not by the enemy, but by those who requisitioned gun support.

Whatever damaging effect to the enemy it may have been responsible for—morally, physically, materially, or otherwise—lyddite certainly produced a desirable moral effect on our own troops. They felt assured as they saw the huge red clouds of debris caused by each shell explosion, that their semi-invisible foe were being no less severely handled than themselves. Principally, the central naval battery fire was governed by the orders which kept it busy from the Headquarter Staff. It was in compliance with General Buller's directions that the 4.7's took in hand the silencing of the Boer guns located on the hills dominating the British left, which had been mainly responsible for much damage to Hart's Brigade, and the bane of Parson's batteries. At a range of 11,400 yards, and cleverly concealed except when actually in a firing position, the Boer guns were vigorously assailed with alternate rounds of lyddite and common shell.

For upwards of an hour intermittent attention was given them, the 4.7's having occasionally to divert their direction, and hunt "Long Tom" on the northern end of Grobelars, whose belch of black-powder smoke always disclosed his whereabouts, but whose defective shells caused far more anxiety than real harm. The precision of fire of Chief Petty Officers Stephens and Bate of the 4.7's, who vied with each other in their efforts to silence the guns, was, as General Buller described it—admirable! Between them the Boer guns on the left were completely silenced, and not heard from in that direction for the rest of the day. Hart's attack, however, had been a disastrous failure;

irretrievably so. The brigade had been the victims of extreme ill-luck. It is morally certain that had the irrepressible Irish Brigade got across the river, a different story—a story of success, so far as was provided for in the General Orders—would have had to be chronicled. Hart here, like Hildyard in the centre, had found execution of instructions impossible, owing to extraneous circumstances over which neither general possessed control, *viz*. an unfordable river, and premature loss of essential artillery support respectively.

The four 12-pounders referred to in the despatch extract were also particularly active in suppressing the enemy's fire; the general's commendation was no mere expression of courteous phraseology. Numerous instances might be cited, if space permitted, where apparent demoralisation seized the enemy whenever a gun or trench position was disclosed or located. Violent storms of firing would suddenly be lulled as soon as location and range were obtained, enabling our troops, who were perhaps cornered somewhere, to extricate themselves, after they had made up their minds that their future course was already shaped for Paradise or Pretoria. Two instances, one from each 12-pounder unit, seem worth relating.

A strong reinforcement of Boers was observed by Lieutenant Wilde emerging from behind Fort Wylie, apparently intent on crossing the bridge. A strong impulse seized this officer and urged him to execute quickly the spirit of his orders—not the words, which forbade firing into mounted troops beyond the river without express orders from some one high in authority. But as there was no mistaking the identity of the motley-dressed cavalcade pressing towards the bridge, he sent a few well-directed shells among them, causing those who were bodily fit to return rapidly whence they came. "Authority" rebuked this diversion from orders, but too late, the damage—to the enemy—was done. The marine gun's crew of Lieutenant Richards' unit actually fired 317 rounds from their 12-pounder during the day. One round was responsible for the complete disablement of one Boer gun, which had, for several hours, been hurling good shrapnel and very bad segment shells at Lyttleton's reserve brigade close by.

Careful observation at last discovered the gun in the firing position, masked among the undergrowth of a clump of trees. Its position was pointed out to Sergeant Roper, who sent a range-finding shell at 4500 yards in splendid direction, short, however, by some 250 yards; but, rapidly loading, and raising his sights to rectify the error, he sent his second shot smash into the gun, giving it its *coup de grâce*.

The telescope disclosed the muzzle of the gun pointing skywards as if unshipped from its carriage, the gun's crew having disappeared—somewhither.

There now remains the attack on Hlangwani Hill to complete the account of events. Lord Dundonald's force had been very heavily engaged, but had likewise met with non-success. They had, however, effectively prevented certain flank movements of the enemy from being developed. During their gallant but futile attempt to capture the hill, they had also entered well within the cyclonic battle storm, and had been driven to seek shelter. Hlangwani Hill was an isolated position on the south side of the river, and it had been apparently assumed that it could not, without considerable risk, be held in very strong force by the Boers, and certainly not with guns. But it was—the unexpected had occurred. The Boers had constructed a military bridge over the river beyond all hostile observation and damage, and consequently were enabled to occupy strongly this all-important and strategic position, the key of Colenso. From its summit, which is fairly accessible for guns to ascend, the Fort Wylie group of *kopjes* could easily be enfiladed and rendered untenable. We knew this—so did the enemy, who were prepared to defend its possession. To effect its capture, a rigorous artillery sweep of its crests and slopes in preparation for an infantry assault would be necessary. It was now too late; the issue had already been decided by the misfortunes already related.

Before the abandonment of Long's batteries, artillery was none too plentiful for the task before it. Now the situation was infinitely worse. The naval guns had proved themselves sufficiently mobile for the duty assigned them as long-range guns, and had performed prominent and invaluable service throughout the day, but the general also required guns possessing tactical mobility to support infantry attacks, and closely follow up successes. No successful frontal attack was now either practicable or conceivable. The troops had suffered heavily in casualties, one-fifth of the guns were lost; the terrible heat and aggravated thirst had severely exhausted the whole force, considerably affecting their physical endurance; moreover, the superior mobility of the fresh and vigorous enemy placed our exposed flanks in danger, and threatened the severance of our communications. Therefore, to remain in possession of the ground won, was to court further disaster. Ill-fortune throughout had attended every movement; no superiority had been achieved anywhere, and the day was irretrievably lost. The third of the series of repulses to British arms previously referred to had now befallen General Buller at Colenso.

Vehement protests against the abandonment of the guns have been numerous, but such protestations can only emanate from critics who could not have been at Colenso, and knew little of the actual situation. They forget that delay in retiring seriously imperilled the whole force—and Natal.

It was ten guns weighed in the balance against the relief force. The guns were sacrificed; the force was saved. The loss was an infinitesimal one in comparison with the incalculable advantages secured by the retirement.

Dealing with the general retirement, Sir Redvers Buller's own words will best suffice.

After this (referring to the loss of the guns) I directed a withdrawal to our camps. It was accomplished in good order. There was no pursuit, and the shell fire was negligible and controlled by our naval guns. The day was fearfully hot, the sky cloudless, the atmosphere sultry and airless, and the country waterless in most parts. . . .

We were engaged for eight hours with an enemy occupying commanding, selected, and carefully prepared positions—positions so carefully prepared that it was almost impossible for infantry to see what to aim at, and I think the force opposed to us must altogether have equalled our own. We had closed on the enemy's works, our troops were in favourable position for an assault, and had I, at the critical moment, had at my disposition the artillery I had, as I believed, arranged for, I think we should have got in. But without the immediate support of guns, I considered that it would be a reckless waste of gallant lives to attempt the assault

Considering the intense heat, the conduct and bearing of the troops was excellent.

The day's casualty list was a heavy one, the total losses being: 147 killed, 762 wounded, and 197 missing and prisoners. The Irish Brigade had suffered by far the heaviest; Hildyard's Brigade and the Royal Artillery very severely.

The Battle of Colenso was a tactical repulse of the first attempt to relieve Ladysmith.

CHAPTER 8

Desperate Assault on Ladysmith

December 16th, 1899, to January 9th, 1900

The Naval Brigade, after the battle, received the honour of occupying with their guns the most advanced position facing Colenso during the somewhat monotonous wait for the advent of reinforcements. The Fifth Division, under Lieutenant-General Sir Charles Warren, had been ordered to proceed to Natal to augment General Buller's army there, and until this force arrived at the front, no further attempt to relieve Ladysmith was possible.

On Sunday morning, early, December 17th, during an eclipse of the moon, the two 4.7's and the 12-pounder units of Lieutenants Wilde, Richards, and Burne moved back from Shooters Hill to Gun Hill, where, having placed the guns in position, this portion of the Naval Brigade encamped until January 10th. Ogilvy's 12-pounder battery returned with the bulk of the relief army to Frere. Hildyard's and Barton's Infantry Brigades, Lord Dundonald's mounted troops, and a Field Battery, comprised the defensive force left behind at Chieveley Camp, besides the naval guns.

Except for an occasional skirmish between the outposts and scouting patrols, and the normal bombardment of the Boer works by the Naval Battery, much of which was of a spasmodic nature, nothing of much import occurred to call for comment.

Commander Limpus again prosecuted his scientific researches, the result of his labour being the completion of a telescopic survey of the surrounding country—a work of inestimable value. Always on the alert for any new movement, he observed that the road bridge over the Tugela was proving too serviceable to the Boers, and a very undesirable advantage for them to possess. General Buller said it must be destroyed. Accordingly, the fate of the bridge—a, fine iron structure supported by stone piers—was delivered over to the precision of fire of the 4.7 guns. At a range of 7660 yards, Lieutenant Hunt and C.F.O. Stephens undertook the work of demolition. Upwards of thirty projectiles were fired, and the bridge itself was struck several times; but its destruction proved a matter of difficulty, owing to the fact that the object was nearly in an alignment with the line of fire.

In this instance, a change of gun brought with it a change of luck; the other 4.7 was given a turn, and scored a splendid success. Lieutenant and captain of gun again competed, not exactly making a contest of it, but for other reasons easily understood by artillerists. C.P.O. Bate fired first—hit the bridge. Lieutenant England followed with the next round—also hit the bridge. Then Bate took deliberate aim as if his very existence was staked on his second shot. Bang went the gun, smash went a stone pier, down went the bridge with a run, and up went a ringing cheer—which is exactly what happened, despite the unintentional rhyme. The Boers, in large numbers, were actually seen taking a keen interest in the prize firing; the prize here being, the honour of having disconcerted the enemy, and of receiving the general's approbation. It would be woe indeed to an enemy's ship that by chance presented its broadside to such individual shooting as had been exhibited lately, even at these four-and-a-quarter-mile ranges.

This daily practice invariably attracted a large concourse of military spectators, who, on hearing the battery "piped to quarters," would make a bee-line for Gun Hill to witness the firing. Often unsuspecting groups of busy Boers, digging away in a trench, or fortifying a *kopje*, would suddenly cease operations on hearing the warning shriek of a shell, and scatter in all directions. Sadly ludicrous at times were their tactics, for occasionally the direction of the wind would cause a lyddite shell to take them unawares and explode within death distance; an ambulance testifying to the result

Nocturnal as well as daily practice was also carried out at irregular intervals, and at uncertain hours. Not unfrequently during a middle watch the sepulchral stillness of the *veldt* would be suddenly broken by the roar of the 4.7 guns, sending several rounds of lyddite shells into the enemy's positions, where, on bursting, they produced a sort of pyrotechnic display. The explosion would cause the surrounding hills to echo loudly with weird resonant war notes which were heard for a score or more miles around.

This intermittent day and night firing must have seriously disturbed the tranquillity of the Boer camps. The slumbers of our own troops were also much interfered with, though they, of course, knew the cause of the firing, and stood in no dread of its murderous effects.

Continuous firing having worn out one of the 4.7 guns, another one to replace it was wired for from Durban. Two were immediately forwarded by Captain Scott, into whose liberal interpretation of the demand it was easy to read a recommendation not to save the shell or the enemy, for want of new guns. They arrived late one afternoon. Without delay Commander Limpus issued brigade stations for "evolution." Within an hour the worn-out gun was down to the railway—half a mile away—and a new gun taken up the hill and mounted ready for service. No sheers or tripods were used, the guns being solely man-handled and parbuckled in and out of the trucks. Captain Jones said, "Well done!" and, remembering the weight of a 4.7 gun (over two tons) it was undoubtedly well done.

The men were always on their mettle whenever some special service required extraordinary exertion; but on their backs enjoying camp life when off duty. With no decks to holystone; no brightwork to polish; no routine of clockwork precision to worry about; campaigning is indeed a welcome diversion to the sailor. Changes agreeable to the inner man are no less welcome. The field ration was a perfect *table d'hôte* menu in comparison with the eternal sameness of a man-of-war bill of fare, which is officially seasonable in all climates, from "*Greenland's icy mountains*" to "*India's coral strands;*" indeed the romance of war was being aptly illustrated in all its phases, from fascinating fighting to festive feeding.

Christmas Day is usually associated with the latter item, and right royally was the brigade enabled to observe it, thanks to the many thoughtful and generous spirits left on board who had not quite forgotten their chums at the front Many were the hampers and cases marked "For the Naval Brigade, from Durban friends," that also reached the camp for the December 25th celebration, besides the over-sea packages that opportunely arrived from relatives and friends at home. In fact a steady flow of useful gifts—books, magazines, pipes, tobacco, socks, etc., continued to arrive for several weeks; delayed owing to the stupendous traffic dealt with on the single track railway. One thoughtful gentleman sent pipe-lighting lenses to the brigade, which proved a boon and were an excellent substitute for matches, these luciferous articles being noted for their scarceness and liability to be either begged, borrowed or purloined, with complete unconcern. It can do no harm casually to mention here, that, to the vast majority, nothing was prised so much as the illustrated magazine and weekly newspaper literature, *Navy and Army Illustrated, Tit Bits, Lloyds*, etc.; and the indispensable pipes and tobacco luxuries. Food of any description sent from over-sea was practically superfluous, and often arrived in an unconsumable state. Clothing, except socks and certain underwear, cannot be carried; and books are too cumbersome and too tedious to read, except for the very few.

Times have changed considerably. The present commissariat and supply departments of the British Army are not those of Crimean history, but are systems nearly approaching a state of perfection; at any rate, to the Naval element they appeared admirably organised institutions. The charges directed against Field Hospitals find no favour with those of the Naval Brigade who became reluctant guests for long and short periods of the "Red Cross Corps" (the R.A.M.C.). Obviously, the luxurious accommodation and comforts of Haslar or Netley Hospitals were not found in a Field Hospital, but such comfort and professional attention as were consistent with circumstances were certainly obtained Though the summit of perfection has not yet been reached, to expect much more than now exists from the members of this noble profession, to whom legions of men owe life and limb, is to indulge the Utopian dreams of unpractical individuals who do not know what war really is. Unsolvable problems must ever encompass any system for dealing with sick and wounded in either naval or military warfare, because the ever-changing conditions of war make war, *per se*, the sole arbiter of what can and what cannot be done.

Reverting to Christmas Day with its associations, a sort of mutual armistice seemed to exist, for neither Briton or Boer appeared anxious to disturb the Peace and Goodwill that are observed by Christian communities on this natal day. Church parties in the early morning—camp sports in the afternoon—open-air smoking concerts in the early evening—convivial tent parties later on, these were the occupations of the Chieveley and Frere camps this Christmas Day, 1899. On the glorious South African *veldt*, so often depicted in romance, the camp sports were held, taking in every variety of competition from steeplechasing to the inevitable obstacle race. The Naval Brigade, of course, entered zealously into all the fun, but could not forego the naval time-honoured copper-punt party, even at *terra firma* races; a gun-carriage in this instance supplying the place of the punt. Concerning these sports

Mr. Bennet Burleigh, the genial *Daily Telegraph's* war correspondent, to whom much of their success was due, wrote[1]:—

Christmas and Boxing Days, as I have indicated, were ushered in by the drums and fifes merrily making the rounds. There are those who prefer the gentler home waits; but there is that peculiarity about fife and drum, those irritant early awakers from sleep, that their martial pulsations catch the heart and set the blood aglow thumping through the veins to their rhythmic beating. 'Jack's the lad for work, and Jack's the lad for play,' and our Bluejackets were the boys who provided the lighter vein of amusement. Christmastide in South Africa, and Natal in particular, has been frizzling hot. Here the sun was over the yardarm.

A band of jolly Jack Tars made the round of the camp, capering and singing, preceded by a sailor on horseback bearing a Union Jack and followed by nearly half a score of messmates making ridiculously rough weather on muleback. The sailors seated on a gun-carriage were two. Of their number, one represented John Bull, the other, a marine, personated Oom Paul—whom the tars and soldiers generally prefer to call 'Ole Kroojer.' Kruger had his hat, pipe, and umbrella, and real good fun the sailors made of the business, John Bull giving 'Kroojer' no end of nasty knocks, and occasionally sitting upon his chest, whilst Fat and Sandy further fairly bedevilled the wretched one. The tars and soldiers sang bravely during the marchings, and at the sports 'Rule Britannia' set to new words, and all the popular catchy airs of the day, were laid under tribute to enable the men to describe with gusto what they had in store for Kruger.

During the next few days the words of the song "Jack's the lad for work" were fully exemplified in the deed, for some 2000 fathoms of six-inch rope were worked into mantlets for covering the engine of another armoured train, that was intended to run towards the Tugela as an auxiliary for assisting reconnaissances. The open country just here rather favoured its intended vocation, and in fact some good results afterwards rewarded its promoters. C.F.O. Baldwin had charge of preparing this work, which on completion, transformed the engine into a monstrosity resembling a French poodle.

Naturally after the fight, many of the fighters assumed the com-

---
1. *The Natal Campaign.*

mon role freely adopted by numerous versatile and irresponsible individuals, known as amateur generals or strategic experts. Yet, be it said, the presumptuous vapourings of some few pusillanimous strategists, who only fight in their imaginations, and who, with an affected gift of prescience, pen condemnatory or laudatory articles *after every battle* according to its results, were never once heard. No one, however, seemed prepared to combat the general regret that Hlangwani Hill was not made the main point first selected for general assault, for upon the seizure of this hill the whole issue of the battle appeared to depend. But subsequent experience also partly demonstrated that the subjugation of Hlangwani and the successful occupation of the Fort Wylie *kopjes* might have been a short-lived victory.

It is an open question, considering the number of troops at General Buller's disposal, and the stubborn and unrelenting tenacity afterwards displayed by the Boers among these hills and *kopjes*, if the frontal advance could have been persisted in, and an enforced withdrawal south of the river still have been a possible contingence. These positions only formed the lower tier of the series of hills which rose higher and higher until Grobelars and Pieters Hills were reached. This hypothesis seems as much to the point as some others that have been advanced; certainly not as ludicrous as many.

Stories, of course, spun round the camp-fires were innumerable. One instance will bear relating of how discipline of the highest order was exhibited by the personnel of an ammunition supply waggon of Colonel Long's batteries. When the shock of battle occurred, these waggons were quickly sent a short distance to the rear, to take up a position in front of the *donga* that was affording shelter to the wounded and cover for unemployed men. With courage of the ancient Spartans, the men stuck to this position in spite of the hail of shrapnel, pom-pom, and bullets that drummed around and among them, notwithstanding the fact that their presence there had, owing to the guns being placed out of action, become of no avail, Petty Officer Taylor called Lieutenant Ogilvy's attention to them, and he went to inquire for the officer in command.

"I am in charge," said a superior non-commissioned officer, "all my officers being either killed or wounded."

"Then why don't you get what men and horses you have intact under cover in the *donga?*" queried Lieutenant. Ogilvy.

"My orders, sir, are to remain here until I receive instructions to move elsewhere." respectfully replied the non-com.

Engine of armoured train covered with rope mantlets by "Terrible's" Naval brigade at Chieveley, 2,000 fathoms of 6-inch rope was used to produce this effect

"All right," the lieutenant answered, "I will assume the responsibility, and give you the necessary order to get under cover as quickly as possible."

The non-com. thanked the lieutenant, and immediately gave the orders which took his small command into the shelter of the *donga*.

Battle has also its amusing side—so at least thought the men of Ogilvy's battery, who laughed heartily when they witnessed a shell explode into the officers' food-basket and scatter its contents into space. Also the impromptu war-dance, performed by the few *kaffir* drivers who involuntarily remained behind, being too timorous to run away, was the cause of some occasional mirth. Every shell that burst near them caused each to spring in the air and yell, then finally grin when he found himself still alive. To avoid being shot, with childlike innocence, they wrapped their blankets around them, covered their faces with both hands, and shut their eyes, which act provoked not a few frolicsome Bluejackets slyly to throw pebbles at them, in order to get a repetition of their fantastic leap-yell-and-grin performance. Still, these sons of Ham were otherwise useful, and proved faithful fellows when properly treated; and the man who can provide humour on a battlefield is a valuable asset to his officers.

It was also difficult to suppress a smile at the antics performed by the oxen—poor devils—when a bullet entered their "sternwalk." They would then behave as if possessed with satanic imps, and tax the agility of a bull-fighter to steer clear of them. In the oxen, also, were embodied a most useful, patient, enduring, and absolutely necessary creature. Another true yarn showing the light side of nature under adverse conditions seems too piquant to be omitted. With a blood-bespattered face and a roguish grin, one of the Dublin Fusiliers, sauntering along from the waning contest, stopped and asked for a "dthrink of warter" from the naval water-cart, then half empty, with no hope of replenishment in view. He was told that only to wounded men could water be given, unless an officer gave express permission.

"Then, me sonny-boy, give me a dthrink quick, for I am both wounded and a commanding officer; all me officers and non-coms, are either kilt or wounded, and I'm the senior private of me battalion," naively asserted this son of Erin.

Needless almost to add, he got his drink, for he was really severely wounded in one arm, and slightly in the head—a fact difficult to reconcile with his good humour. After quenching his thirst—always an agonising torment with a wounded man—he was given a "chew of rale ship's," and then directed to his "command;" but before departing he said, "So long, navee chapsies; I'll be sorree for the Boors when Buller gets his back up"—a remark that produced a roar of laughter from dozens of parched throats.

Concerning the conduct of the wounded, the stoical behaviour of the vast majority deserves special recognition. Declining attention until others had received surgical succour, officers remained gentlemen to death. For the same reason, rank and file incurred grave risks and endured intense pains to allow a married comrade or company chum to have the benefit of science first. Callous indifference to wounds, and eagerness to learn of the progress of the battle, was no uncommon part played by both officers and men when balanced between life and death. Such was the testimony of Surgeon Macmillan and his trusty medical henchman, Walter Attree, who, after Ogilvy's battery had retired out of the danger zone, rendered professional help to their army colleagues, and assisted to pass several hundred wounded cases through the "first-aid" rendezvous at Platelayer's Hut to the field-hospitals in rear.

One other diverting incident seems worth reciting. While awaiting an oxen team to haul the last 12-pounder gun back to camp, a certain battery of artillery trundled across the *veldt* from Hlangwani direction, taking up a position near the solitary naval gun. "Action right!" shouted the battery commander, who then asked Petty Officer Taylor if his gun was beyond range of the enemy's artillery fire.

"Yes, sir; all right here," replied Taylor—words scarcely spoken before a 45-pound shell from a Boer "Long Tom" contradicted them by exploding among the new target that the battery, nicely wheeled into line, had offered.

"Confound your yarn!" yelled out the battery commander to Taylor. "What the devil do you mean by giving me such rotten information?"

"Well, sir "responded Taylor, who could not refrain from smirking at the incident, "'Long Tom' hadn't fired at my gun for a long time, so I thought he'd piped down."

But this typical captain of gun also remarked, *sotto voce*, to his No. 2, "I wonder if he expected me to stop the darned gun from firing into his blessed circus?"—a remark that, as no damage to either man, horse, or gun had occurred, produced a subdued spurt of grinning among the other volatile sailors.

À *propos* of these field batteries, they were galloped into action, the guns unlimbered, and fire opened with a precision that elicited the admiration of all who admire spontaneous courage. Saddles were emptied, men, horses, and guns disappeared in clouds of shell-dust, to re-emerge again and again, loading, laying, and firing as steadily as if at manoeuvres on Salisbury Plain. Few will forget also how the infantry stuck to their hot work. It was indeed a revelation which proved that British pluck and endurance have not yet been civilised away, and so long as such valorous troops exist, the bugbear of invasion need have no terrors for us; nor will British soil ever witness the horrors of war with its rigorously enforced martial laws.

But militia, yeomanry, and volunteers must not forget that their respective quota of the repellent force is necessary to preserve our "tight little island." The fleet will act its part; the regulars will, and must, bear the fighting heat of the day; but for the volunteer defensive force of the country is left a large share of the burden of patriotically defending our shores and historical liberties. To keep the Empire intact, Britain's insularity must be kept inviolate, and patriotism and disciplined pluck are the two essentials that together can preserve our Imperial greatness.

Not since 1815—Waterloo year—until the present war, (as at time of first publication), has the Empire had its vitality assailed, or endured such trials as followed those three successive reverses—Stormberg, Magersfontein, and Colenso. These misfortunes produced a gloomy picture for the whole Empire to contemplate. Following the investment of three British towns, three disasters had befallen British troops, nearly three thousand losses had resulted, and consequently the British Empire had become aroused to a sense of the magnitude of the South African struggle. Begun with an enthusiastic optimism, the war had suddenly and unexpectedly developed into a military and political problem which not even its most pessimistic opponent could claim to have foreseen.

The British people being agreeably unused to hearing of British reverses, those of Cape Colony had caused considerable consternation; but the Colenso repulse had produced a deep and depressing shock of mortification. Excessive consideration for alien opinions and the feelings of the Boer Republics had prevented timely and adequate war preparations from being made; and this had been mainly responsible for a series of humiliating reverses, loss of imperial prestige, and an exposure to grave disaster of our South African forces, which was averted principally through lack of military spirit and enterprise of the enemy—the interdict of Fate,

These calamities caused the Imperial Government to reverse their policy of fatal magnanimity and optimism, the country quickly becoming reassured by the decisive action which was immediately taken. The pick of British generals and the flower of the British army were requisitioned. Recognising that Natal with its military difficulties would seriously demand all General Buller's capacity and personal presence, Field Marshal Lord Roberts was sent out as Commander-in-Chief in South Africa; General Lord Kitchener (then *sirdar* of the Egyptian army) being appointed chief of the staff. The sixth division were even now at sea; the seventh division and large reinforcements of other branches of the army were soon after despatched with great promptitude; and another division was prepared to follow when ready. The militia were embodied, several battalions being ordered abroad to relieve the regulars; besides which, many units ot yeomanry and volunteers, who loyally offered their services, were sent to the seat of war. The British colonies, also, all offered to assume a share of Imperial responsibility; each sending its respective contingent to the Cape with healthy despatch. Those military misfortunes had aroused a wave of patriotism throughout the Empire that stands unparalleled in history. That depressing "Black Week" of December, 1899, was, the nativity of a solid and cohesive Imperialism.

Both the military and political situation in South Africa had become of the gravest intensity. The Cape Dutch became suspiciously restless. Wavering loyalists developed into avowed rebels; and rebels into outlawed enemies. Moreover, the natives gave cause for serious consideration. British rule was still favoured by the majority, but recent events might easily have caused the black races to transfer their allegiance to the apparently dominant Dutch. Abroad also, with few exceptions, the gravity of the crisis was regarded with a certain pessimistic view, the significance of which was very obvious.

The Imperial political barometer stood indeed very low just at this period, but it began to rise with the arrival of Lord Roberts at Cape Town on January 10th. For the present, however. Lord Roberts will be left concentrating his grand army at the Modder River, and preparing those strategic plans which took the British triumphantly into Pretoria. But before this culminating event was to happen considerable difficulties had to be overcome, and much severe fighting, especially in Natal, loomed ahead. Imperilled garrisons also had to be relieved to obviate further loss of military prestige. Between the British generals and the goal of success there lay military problems requiring consummate skill to solve. There was a numerous and well-appointed enemy to defeat, possessed of exceptional mobility, who, ignoring modern military tactics, yet possessed a special aptitude for defensive fighting; who had bases everywhere, and blood relations or compatriots in almost every habitation and farmstead throughout the whole field of operations. Such was the crisis that enveloped the Empire at the close of 1899.

✶✶✶✶✶✶

Ladysmith—the centre of gravity of the world's attention—was, on January 6th, again heavily but unsuccessfully assaulted by the enemy. This was the second attempt to capture the town since the investment; a previous effort having been made on November 9th.

On this occasion the Boer commandant-general seemed resolved on attempting a *coup de main* on the town, acting as he was on imperative instructions from the executive at Pretoria to capture Ladysmith at all costs. Contrary to their hitherto fighting traditions, the Boers devised a secret night attack that very nearly succeeded.

The main point for assault selected was a commanding ridge, situated about two and a half miles southward of the town, which it commanded. Near its two extremes are two elevated positions—Caesar's Camp on the eastern end and Waggon Hill on the western; both entrenched separate commands. General White (Desp. March 23rd, 1900), wrote—

> On January 6th the enemy made a most determined but fortunately unsuccessful attempt to carry Ladysmith by storm. Almost every part of my position was more or less heavily assailed, but the brunt of the attack fell upon Caesar's Camp and Waggon Hill....

Among the garrison of the first-named position was a detached party of the *Powerfuls* and Natal Naval Volunteers with a 12-pounder gun. On Waggon Hill, in addition to its proper occupants, other *Powerfuls* were, by chance, enabled to render some excellent service during the most critical portions of the fight. The general relates—

> Waggon Hill was held as usual by three companies 1st Battalion King's Royal Rifle Corps, and a squadron Imperial Light Horse. A detachment Natal Naval Volunteers, with a 3-pounder Hotchkiss gun, had been sent there on the evening of January 5th, and two naval guns, one a 4.7-inch and the other a

12-pounder, were in process of transfer to the hill during the night. These guns were accompanied by naval detachments and a working party of Royal Engineers and Gordon Highlanders, who were consequently on Waggon Hill when the attack commenced at 2.30 a.m. on the morning of January 6th.

The attack was suddenly launched with a fierce determination to rush this position—the key of Ladysmith. Completely surprised, the garrison fell back in great confusion before the onslaught of the stormers. The said gun-mounting party, however, swiftly realising the position, formed a rallying base and checked the stormers' onward rush. The Boers themselves, also surprised at the steadfastness of this unexpected defence, as swiftly retired back to the crest over which they had come. Some sixty or seventy yards only separated the rival forces; at certain places on the ridge the distance was even but thirty yards. It was half an hour later before the attack burst on Caesar's Camp, no doubt purposely delayed so that the British attention might be riveted to the fighting on the Waggon Hill end of the ridge. Here also the contest for some time was very desperate.

Strong reinforcements were hurried to these hard-pressed positions, and to other points along the ridge. Daylight also made it possible for the cavalry and artillery to act in their respective capacities; the latter opportunely covering and assisting the defending troops from end to end of the ridge, and successfully checking the enemy from assailing the flanks. The enemy's artillery were also vigorously employed, most of them raking with great intensity the plateau and British side of the ridge, while other guns—especially "Long Tom" on Bulwana—briskly shelled the field batteries and other defensive positions, and even the town itself.

At over 9000 yards the *Powerful's* other 4.7 at Cove Redoubt made a dead set at "Long Tom," it being stated that "it was mostly owing to Lieutenant Halsey's gun that the Boer 6-inch made such erratic and harmless shooting." A naval long 12-pounder was fortunate enough partially to silence a Boer 4.5 gun situated on Surprise Hill, by sending a shell direct into its embrasure at 4000 yards range.

After detailing the disposition of his troops, and relating the close and deadly nature of the fighting that had occurred up to 8 a.m., the general wrote:—

Meanwhile the 21st and 42nd Batteries, Royal Field Artillery, and the naval 12-pounder on Caesar's Camp, were in action against Mounted Infantry Hill and the scrub on either side of it, and were of great assistance in keeping down the violence of the enemy's fire.

Later, some ineffective charges were made to drive the enemy back over the crests, but the hail of shell and bullets kept the fighting stationary and indecisive for some two hours or more.

By middle forenoon, however, good progress was made; the Boers were driven from the most dangerously held vantage points to below the crest-line, the fighting in consequence lessening in severity. It was but a lull, for at high noon the enemy developed another resolute assault on Waggon Hill, the sudden and terrific hail of fire forcing the defenders again to give way. But before the enemy could reap the full advantage of their well-devised attempt to rerush the position, our troops were rallied, the crest again occupied, and the enemy driven back. Swiftly executed, courageously frustrated, this second onslaught was a critical phase of the battle.

With the Waggon Hill end in the enemy's possession, the rest of the ridge would have become perilously insecure. Caesar's Camp, on the opposite end, could hardly hope to have withstood the transverse and convergent fire that would have assailed them; and had this position also fallen, the town must assuredly have been captured. Other defensive positions around the town were also being severely assailed, but were gallantly held secure.

From now till late afternoon the fight was maintained by a deadly fire from resolutely handled rifles, when, at 3.30 p.m., a violent storm of wind and rain broke over the bloody conflict In the middle of this visitation, which lasted about three hours, and while it was at its very worst, a third attempt to rush Waggon Hill was made. For the third time our troops were driven off, but were a third time successfully rallied, and recaptured the lost crest-line.

At 5 p.m., Lieutenant-Colonel C. W. Park arrived at Waggon Hill with three companies 1st Battalion Devonshire Regiment, which I had ordered up as a reinforcement, and was at once directed by Colonel Hamilton to turn the enemy off the ridge with the bayonet. The Devons dashed forward and gained a position under cover within 50 yards of the enemy. Here a fire fight ensued; but the Devons were not to be denied, and, eventually, cheering as they pushed from point to point, they drove the enemy not only off the plateau, but cleared every

Boer out of the lower slopes and the *dongas* surrounding the position.... At last, after fifteen hours of stubborn resistance by our men, and of continual effort on the part of the Boers, the enemy were driven off at all points during the same storm in which Waggon Hill was also cleared, as already described, their retreat being hastened by the heavy fire poured on them as they retired.

Thus Sir George White describes the closing incident of the battle.

Skilled generalship, brilliant deeds of heroism, indomitable courage, splendid endurance, and a providential storm, all combined, had saved Ladysmith from capture, and the Union Jack from being hauled down from over a British town.

In Chieveley Camp the fight caused considerable anxiety, speculation, and a co-operative movement of the troops. The intermittent booming of heavy guns roused out the slumbering camp, who gazed with wistful eyes towards 'Bulwana, from whence the flashes of the Boer "Long Tom" were plainly visible. With sunrise, the heliograph flashed the direful news of what had taken and what was then taking place. Succeeding messages, however, became reassuring, one conveying that Sir George White was confident of holding his own. After midday, further news was unobtainable, owing to the sun having become obscured by clouds. The situation, with its dread uncertainties, was keenly realised, as seldom has the fate of a single town had such vastly important bearing on the issues of a war.

To create a diversion in favour of the Ladysmith garrison, the troops were moved out shortly after noon towards the Colenso positions under cover of the naval guns. Shell, furious and fast, swept along the Boer line of works, while the force moved quickly forward in widely extended lines of attack. When near enough, the field batteries also opened a heavy fire, which drew upon them a long-range rifle fusillade. Pressing onwards, the troops also got within the zone of fire, and still further forward went the artillery; but the attack was not permitted to proceed. It was simply a demonstration. Its object was, no doubt, quite obvious to the enemy, considerable numbers of whom, nevertheless, it must have contained at Colenso who otherwise would have reinforced the assault on Ladysmith.

With dusk approaching, General Clery ordered a withdrawal to camp. Nothing further could be done but await the morrow's sun, whose rays controlled the helio news.

Near Weenen, several miles away eastward of Chieveley, stands the lofty Umkolanda Mountain, upon whose pinnacle-shaped summit were entrenched a gallant band of army signallers, under Captain Cayser, R.E., alone in the air. From here it was that the helio messages were transmitted to and from the beleaguered town and the camp. A more thrilling message no signaller ever repeated than the one next morning, which assured the camp, the empire, and the world, that Ladysmith's garrison had saved the honour of the flag.

To the querulous critic, who probably assimilates the smooth slopes of Portsdown Hills to the rugged, precipitous Colenso *kopjes*, and still unconscionably seeks explanation of why General Buller did not actively move on this occasion, the answer seems a very simple one. It was physically impossible, unless an ignominious defeat was the object in view. Every imaginable military obstacle opposed the venture. The bulk of the relief force was at Frere, twelve miles away, too immobile to carry out a swift tactical movement against an enemy so vastly superior in mobility, who could easily, as before, have met any frontal assault on their Tugela stronghold with impunity. The enemy had two alternatives for enforcing the submission of Ladysmith—assault or starve out; the obvious only at Colenso. This position must be defended by force. Therefore a hostile attack on Colenso, in preference to an assault on Ladysmith, would have demanded the primary attention of the Boer forces, whose numerical strength and mobility allowed them such option. All that could be done to co-operate with the Ladysmith garrison was done, except the offering up of a Napoleonic sacrifice to the fetish god of war.

The Ladysmith casualties totalled 500, among whom were scions of England's noblest blood, many colonial "Sons of the Empire," and brave regulars; men who had voluntarily exposed their lives in obedience to the dictates of an inward martial spirit, which urged them to uphold a glorious tradition. The enemy also suffered heavily. Their conduct was that of a worthy foe. They had gallantly fought a good fight for a cause that, to them, was as holy as our own was just. Their losses were estimated at about 700.

Such is the price of Empire, and the cost of attempting its usurpation.

CHAPTER 9

Arrival of Buller's Army at Spearmans

From January 10th to 15th, 1900

The arrival of the Fifth Division at Frere by route march from Escourt, had apparently completed the headquarter plans for a second advance to the relief of Ladysmith.

On January 9th the rumoured flanking movements had received welcome confirmation by the issue of general orders for a flank march westward to the upper Tugela, After dusk the naval guns were withdrawn from Gun Hill, the two 4.7 being dismounted and placed in waggons to facilitate the brigade's mobility, and arrangements made for the morrow's advance. Early next morning, 10th, the general movement commenced, the confluence of the Chieveley contingent with the Frere main body taking place about noon near Pretorius' farm on the Springfield road, where Hart's Brigade had encamped to cover the movement. Before vacating our position, dummy guns, prepared by our artisan staff, had been placed overnight on Gun Hill, but how far this artifice succeeded in deluding our wily enemy was very questionable.

Remaining entrenched at Chieveley to contain the Boers in Colenso, were Barton's Brigade, a small mounted force, and the 12-pounder units of Lieutenants Richards and Wilde, At Frere, the base of supplies, a small force, with Melville's 12-pounder unit, remained to guard the place and railway track.

The objective of this new movement was to proceed, via Springfield, to Spearmans Hills, which overlook the Upper Tugela, situated some 28 miles by route march (though only about 15 miles directly westward) from Colenso, and from thence attempt to outflank the enemy.

Preceding the main army, a flying mounted column about 1000 strong, accompanied by a battery of field artillery under Lord Dundonald, went on ahead and seized the all-important road bridge over the tributary Little Tugela at Springfield, now swollen to about the size of the Thames at London Bridge. This strategic point captured, one-third of their number and two guns were left to guard the bridge, while the remainder boldly pushed on, thirsting for further spoil By nightfall this intrepid band of horsemen had secured the heights immediately overlooking Potgieters Drift, actually seizing the ferry pont the next morning under the very nose—and a smart rifle fire—of the enemy. Securing themselves on the heights so as to command the drift, this force remained unmolested in their jeopardous position for some 36 hours before being reinforced.

This dashing exploit infinitely decreased the responsibilities and difficulties of the movement—especially the transport—that otherwise would have beset the force with the Springfield bridge defunct, and an active enemy in opposition. They had, however, over-reached their orders by many, many miles, but *"nothing succeeds like success,"* especially in a naval or military enterprise, though failure seldom meets with condonation. The New Year had heralded a few minor successes on Cape Colony side, and with this exploit included, a reversal of the general ill-luck prevalent hitherto seemed in sight. The ubiquitous Mr. Winston Churchill had ridden in that gallant 28-mile ride; a personage seemingly possessing talismanic influence. From *Morning Post* war correspondent and armoured train fighter to prisoner of war; then a dramatic escape from a Pretorian gaol, to a lieutenant's commission in the South African Light Horse, within two months—this was, in truth, the kind of romance in real life which appeals to all lovers of adventure.

Incomprehensible strategy, or else the swift action of the cavalry, had left the Springfield bridge intact, but the flooding of the Tugela was the obvious cause of the Boers retiring north of the river to await the arrival of Sir Redvers Buller's relief force.

To behold *en route* this huge column of some 30,000 soldiers, sailors, civilian ambulance corps, native "accessories," and some 10,000 animals drawing several hundred waggons, etc., was a scene to baffle description and defy imagination. At least ten miles of transport in "single column line ahead" was being steered towards one destination.

Here was evidence in galore of why it had taken nearly a month for a second attempt to develop. To plan such an organisation on paper must require intimate knowledge of the subject—scarcely secondary to war itself. But to carry it into practical execution was the product of a fully trained master-mind. To move such a vast column through practically a hostile country, and keep up supplies of all descriptions, was a task so stupendous that Moses himself might have pardonably shrunk from the undertaking. Civilised armies require modern transport, equipment, and sustenance; a circumstance that has not lessened the burdens of generals. "*'Tis true, 'tis pity; and pity 'tis 'tis true*," that so much transport, which renders mobility immobile, should be necessary; or so at least the generals must have thought Yet, nevertheless, as an organisation, there was little to cavil about.

The flank march proceeded apace; a journey full of incident The track, after a little traffic had passed over it, became a long road of quagmire resembling a canal of mud, rendering haulage of the transport very burdensome. Many times the oxen were compelled to give in dead-beaten, and not a few horses and mules died in their endeavour to struggle onward. To allow a waggon to leave the track, which was, at any rate, fairly solid under the thick *stratum* of mud, and attempt to travel on the alluring green *veldt*, was invariably fraught with disastrous consequences. One experience was sufficient to convince the most sceptic individual, after having both arms stretched for an hour or two on a drag-rope trying to extricate a waggon which had gone off its course on to the spongy *veldt*, that keeping to the track was the safest policy. Recent torrential rains had brought this condition into existence, for otherwise the route had been truly described as "road fairly good, but very little water anywhere."

To reverse this account and say, road fearfully bad, but water everywhere, would now be the correct description. It is strange but true, that if the oxen cannot free their load by themselves, they, invariably, will stubbornly refuse to co-operate with a drag-rope party. An ordinary team of oxen consisted of sixteen animals, and sometimes two and even three such teams were necessary to remove a waggon from a stranded position. *Spruits* and drifts hitherto dry, or nearly so, were now found to be rushing torrents of yellow coloured water many feet deep, requiring careful pilotage to get the transport across them at the exact spot. The approaches and exits of these drifts have their counterpart in the mud flats of "Pompey Harbour." Here oxen and the heavy waggons would often sink so deep that the former had the appearance of legless beasts, and the latter of sleighs, necessitating both teams and waggons being forcibly hauled through to relieve the congestion of traffic that invariably accumulated at these places.

Drifts and delays—either word possessed the same meaning.

Long preventer drag-ropes proved invaluable and even indispensable at these stages of the journey. Why not traction engines ? No, certainly not!—at least, not in the montanic regions of Northern Natal, except to use them like armoured trains—occasionally. Valuable no doubt they might be on hard ground or on a *bonâ fide* road, but not in a *kopje* strewn country, on spongy *veldt*-tracks, or in morass-like drifts. The only engine (I believe) that attempted this cruise out west was passed reposing gracefully on its side, having floundered deep into a soft section of the track—helpless, awaiting excavation. One Bluejacket facetiously inquired of the forlorn looking driver "if he wanted a sky-pilot to read the burial service over it."

"There's plenty of life in the beggar yet," responded the driver; which was quite true. Plenty of life—or steam—but no more. One good old navy drag-rope and a hundred horny-handed sailors would—and often did—take a heavy ammunition waggon or a 4.7 gun where no traction engine under full steam with an open throttle-valve or a prize team of oxen could approach within a respectable distance. Besides, men can be easily controlled, but engines and oxen—both extremely useful in their proper spheres—either stop dead when they should be moving, or bolt away when they are required to stop, and both consume a quantity of water that would suffice for a hundred thirsty tars. Moral:—drag-ropes, and good long ones.

Still, in spite of all obstacles, natural and otherwise, the movement went on apace under the personal supervision of General Buller and his indefatigable staff, who were ever ready to circumvent every apparent difficulty.

With the Naval Brigade, a kind of tacit permission to let them cruise along, or "anchor as convenient," appeared to exist. Profited by former experiences, they had become practical trekkers on the warpath; thanks mainly to our colonial comrades in arms, many of whom were genuine South African travellers, who understood trekking in all its mysterious technicalities. Though often delayed ourselves, we never retarded the movements of any one else, but more frequently assisted to remove difficulties rather than made any.

The usual comprehensive nature of a naval brigade enables cir-

Some of the difficulties of trekking with 4.7 guns in South Africa

cumstances to be coped with which sometimes appear insuperable to others. Besides captains of guns and seaman gunners to fight the guns, and torpedo men to lay a mine or perform other electrical work, there was also a sprinkling of mechanical and artisan ratings—armourers, blacksmiths, shipwrights—under an experienced naval engineer officer. Our ambulance staff, too, was composed of brawny "mechanical stokers," who became excellent pioneers whenever necessity for such duty arose. Moreover, almost every appliance for dealing with expectant contingencies formed part of our cargo: from sheer-legs to a shackle, from an anvil to an adze; thus enabling the brigade to be wholly self-supporting. With such a combination of practical and mechanical skill lumped together, and so many material resources available, no other result than proficiency was to be expected.

On the march, also, the brigade were not a whit in arrear of each day's programme. The longest march performed was eighteen miles in six hours, which time included stoppages to give the escort a spell; and this in a tropical heat, although the travel at this particular stretch of route was very good as roads go in Northern Natal. This march also evidenced the ordinary endurance of the oxen, whose motive power is quite equal to that of troops, with whom they can keep pace for many hours; on good roads, of course. In mystic language these patient animals (each owning a name) are encouraged onward by their *kaffir* drivers. The most experienced and trusty ones are those pairs on the dessel-boom, and the leaders of the team, who follow the black leader-boy with marked intelligence. Shirking, or lagging, will draw forth a swish from a skilfully handled twenty-feet-long whip-lash, but as often the offending beast will bestir himself when hearing his name yelled out, accompanied by a few admonishing words.

"No excuse was taken for not hearing the pipe," for punishment was certain to follow inattention to orders.

The 4.7 battery spent the first night at Pretorius Drift—about fifteen miles' march from Chieveley—where it had been waiting "on ranko" for hours to cross a swollen *spruit*. Ogilvy's battery, having left Frere in good time and being well ahead, had been more fortunate, and had encamped some distance beyond. Darkness, and an order to clear the route to allow Sir Charles Warren's Division to pass, prohibited further passage of transport for the night, so the 4.7 Battery bivouacked on the spot—or in the mud, either statement being true. Tramp—tramp—tramp, hour after hour, through a pitiless rain, went battalion after battalion, brigade after brigade; the early dawn breaking before the division had crossed the *spruit*—many of whom were destined never to recross.

Similar experiences to those of the first day were met with on each of the two succeeding days that occupied the journey, the guns eventually arriving at Spearman's Camp about noon, January 13th. Before nightfall the 4.7 guns were in position on Mount Alice, and the camp pitched in an umbrageous spot on its reverse slope. Ogilvy's guns remained in the main camp awaiting orders. By the 15th the whole army and its transport had arrived. Burne's guns arrived with Hildyard's Brigade, which had been strategically operating on the right flank of the army during the movement

From Mount Alice, an eminence about 1000 feet above the river, a magnificent panoramic view of the Tugela valley and an immense tract of country all around was to be obtained. The remarkably clear atmosphere enabled far-distant objects to be intelligibly delineated with the telescope, which ordinarily cannot be brought within focus. Far away on our left, to the westward, rose the stately Drakensberg Range, whose lofty peaks and pinnacles, rising to 11,200 feet, were grandly outlined against the sky. To the eastward (our right), some twenty miles or so away, stood Mount 'Bulwana, dominating beleaguered Ladysmith with a 6-inch "Long Tom," whose familiar puffs of smoke were grim reminders to the spectator of his duty. Entrenchments, presumably those on Waggon Hill and Caesar's Camp, could be easily discerned, from whence a blinking heliograph was busily flashing and acknowledging official cipher despatches, and private Morse messages.

The view in our immediate front was a picturesque scene. There the historic Tugela was winding itself snake-like fashion through a rich valley, forming two distinctive loops, which were found to be serious natural obstacles in the respective operations that followed. The valley extended in a wide concave, whose furthest edge (Brakfontein Ridge) was between seven and eight thousand yards distant from the hills south of the river, the ground gradually rising from the river towards the surrounding hills, meeting the plain beyond where the roads which lead to Ladysmith converge. Directly beneath Mount Alice, on the north side, was a plateau extending almost to the river, and about 400 feet above its level. A main road from Spearman's Campingground wended round Mount Alice, across this plateau, then dipped sharply down to Potgieters Drift.

Both rear wheels of ammunition waggons had to be secured and skidded behind the oxen, and the naval 12-pounder guns eased down with the drag-ropes, owing to the steep declivity of the track just here, when the guns afterwards took this route. On our left front the Spion Kop Range towered some 500 feet higher than Mount Alice, the nearest firing range being about 5000 yards, and the farthest nearly 10,000 yards distant. Far away in the dim distance, beyond Brakfontein, the outline of the Biggarsberg Range was perceptible, on the other side of which is Dundee, standing in the centre of the Natal coalfields. The tops of our hills were park-like in their wealth of rich grass and sprinkling of trees. The northern sides were exceedingly steep, and thickly covered with mimosa and cactus trees, while the southern sides were scantily clothed, and approached by a gentle slope, with the exception of Zwaatz Kop, which was fairly precipitous on all sides. A sharp dip connected the trio of hills—Mount Alice, Signal Hill, Zwaatz Kop—in our occupation.

The enemy had quite anticipated our movement. The telescope disclosed much defensive work completed, and much more in progress. Entrenchments, gun redoubts, and *sangars* were being established everywhere which would protect or command any weak point, or places offering easy access to infantry. Indeed, they had prepared an east-to-west chain of defences, which must be broken wherever the passage of the Tugela could be attempted.

It was with an indefinite feeling that one gazed on the formidable-looking natural fortresses that stood between the relief army and Ladysmith. The summit of Spion Kop served as a watch-tower to the vigilant enemy, who could from thence perceive much of our intended movements, and prepare accordingly to defend the threatened points. The whole of the enemy's defence was again protected by an exterior line of hills masking their interior defences, which afforded security from all but direct infantry assault. The river, also, in certain places was not altogether unfavourable to them.

So without fear, or favour, the Britisher was again ready to meet the Boer in the deadly contest for supremacy.

CHAPTER 10

Spion Kop Operations

January 16th to 23rd, 1900

Five brigades of infantry, some 3000 mounted troops, eight batteries of artillery, and ten naval guns—about 24,000 fighting men and 60 guns—would give an imposing array if placed in review order. Such a large force, however, became surprisingly microscopic after they had been tactically divided up among the *kopjes* which intersected the respective routes of advance. But General Buller had appraised his force, and the force implicitly trusted their general—a reciprocal feeling which engendered a healthy vitality, imparted a unity of purpose, and added a tower of moral strength to the relief army, that mere numbers do not always produce. There is much that is true behind that popular phrase that *"our little British Army goes a darned long way."* Such generals of the past as Marlborough and Wellington, and in the present age, Wolseley, Roberts, and Buller, have, owing to their magnetic personalities, made it so, while such admirals as Drake and Nelson of glorious memory, and latterly Lyons of Black Sea fame, the Seymours of China and Egyptian history, and Beresford, have similarly sustained our best naval traditions.

The following instructional and inspiring field order, which had been read out to the whole army, had given the force a fresh impulse to achieve their objective:—

> The field force is now advancing to the relief of Ladysmith, where, surrounded by superior forces, our comrades have gallantly defended themselves for the past ten weeks. The general commanding knows that every one in this force feels, as he does, we must be successful. We shall be stoutly opposed by a clever, unscrupulous enemy. Let no man allow himself to be

deceived by them. If a white flag is displayed, it means nothing unless the force displaying it halt, throw down their arms, and throw up their hands at the same time. If they get a chance, the enemy will try and mislead us by false words of command and false bugle sounds. Everyone must guard against being deceived by such conduct. Above all, if any are ever surprised by a sudden volley at close quarters, let there be no hesitation; do not turn from it, but rush at it—that is the road to victory and safety. A retreat is fatal. The one thing the enemy cannot stand is our being at close quarters with them. We are fighting for the health and safety of our comrades; we are fighting in defence of our flag against an enemy who has forced war upon us for the worst and lowest motives, by treachery, conspiracy, and deceit Let us bear ourselves as our cause deserves.

Late on the 16th, Lyttleton's Brigade commenced to cross the Tugela at Potgieters, which movement inaugurated the Spion Kop operations. A portion of the force forded the river—now rather high—using their rifles as a connecting link between each man, very slow progress being made. The ferry-pont, by which it was intended to pass across the bulk of the brigade, for some cause became unworkable, a circumstance which was noticed from Mount Alice, whereupon Captain Jones despatched Lieutenant Chiazarri, N.N.V., Midshipman Sherrin, Chief Instructor Baldwin, and a party of Bluejackets to render nautical assistance if wanted. Prompt charge of the ferry having been given to them, it was speedily set in motion, and troops rapidly transported across, half-companies at a time. By early morn the whole four battalions, one battery of artillery, and the 5-inch howitzer battery, together with their horses, had been passed over to the northern bank to occupy the low chain of *kopjes* a short distance therefrom. This fine evolution elicited the warm appreciation of General Lyttleton, who sent a message to Captain Jones "that the naval detachment working the ferry-pont were worth their weight in gold," and requested the retention of their services until the pressure at the drift relaxed—a request which was readily assented to.

Meanwhile, Sir Charles Warren marched from Springfield camp during the night with some 15,000 troops, cavalry, artillery, infantry, etc., to Trichardts Drift, whither Dundonald's mounted force had already proceeded to operate under Warren's orders, Talbot-Coke's Brigade, Bethune's Horse, and Ogilvy's Battery occupied the plateau

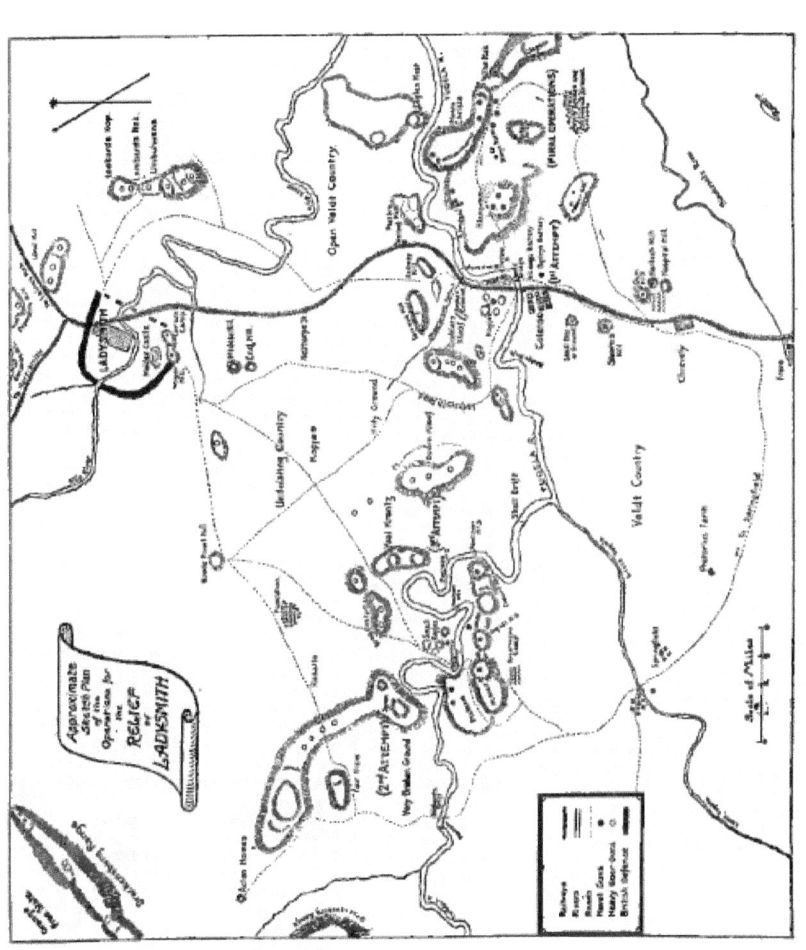

beneath Mount Alice, effectively masking Potgieters. A small force watched Skiet Drift, which was also commanded by a battery of artillery on Signal Hill—so called because the central signal station was established on its summit. Thus were the troops disposed.

The original plan of operations requires but little explanation. General Warren, with the whole force and transport at his disposal, was to cross at Trichardts, refuse his right, detour round by Acton Homes, from thence gain the open plain north of Spion Kop, force the Boers back from west to east, and effect a junction with the Potgieters force at Brakfontein. General Buller had evidently decided that the position facing Potgieters was too formidable for a direct frontal attack; a wide flanking movement was therefore adopted instead.

Early on the 17th, the naval guns opened a heavy bombardment on the Spion Kop and Brakfontein positions, being joined later on by the howitzer battery. A scattering of hitherto concealed bodies of Boers proved that the shelling was causing them serious disquietude. The searching effect of the howitzer lyddite shells, dropped with wonderful accuracy into entrenchments, gun-pits and redoubts, and behind the ridges, was responsible for much moral and physical damage; while the 4.7's, with common shell, contributed very largely to the material destruction. Far away defence works suffered considerable defacement, and were rendered untenable by their occupants, who appeared to find some difficulty in obtaining safe shelter.

Towards 9 a.m. Warren's force commenced crossing the pontoon bridge under cover of his batteries; the whole movement being well within view of Mount Alice, and about 8000 yards distant therefrom. A feeble resistance of long-range rifle fire was offered by the enemy; but whatever intention they might have had of opposing the crossing at that pointy most have vanished when the naval heavy guns were found to command every vantage point they could select from which to oppose. Apparently the Boers would not venture too close with their guns, or, feeling secure in their stronghold, were indifferent, and consequently the bulk of the force and impedimenta crossed over by nightfall.

Next day, while completing the movement Warren cautiously advanced his infantry, and sent Dundonald's mounted troops to find the finger-tips of the Boer right arm of defence. They found them, and moreover cut them off in a smart little action near Acton Homes, which cost the enemy a loss of 18 casualties and 24 prisoners before sundown; our losses were comparatively few, being 2 killed, 2 wounded.

To divert the enemy's attention from Warren's flanking movement, Lyttleton's force made a threatening demonstration against Brakfontein, all guns maintaining a brisk bombardment to lend colour to the feint advance. The wily foe, however, appeared little disconcerted by this manoeuvre, which merely drew a little sportive rifle fire, the force carrying out the prearranged retirement back to the *kopjes* before dusk. A close repetition of this day's programme engrossed the attention of Lyttleton's command during these protracted operations, their share of the fighting culminating in a brilliant affair which is related in its order of sequence.

On the 19th, Warren had deemed it necessary to abandon the original plan of operations—that of detouring round the Boer flanks by the Acton Homes route, and had, instead, so diverted his force that his fighting line was now extended in a north-west and south-east direction, his right being contiguous to the south-west spurs of Spion Kop. Having reconnoitred the roads, Warren had concluded that the Acton Homes route must be rejected as being too long, and occupying more time than circumstances would warrant. He had therefore adopted the alternative north-eastern route (*via* Fair View and Rosalie), which passage, though considerably shorter, was far more difficult to traverse, and also struck directly through the Boer right defences.

Certain progress towards executing this new plan was made on the 20th, the enemy having been compelled to vacate most of their outlying hillock defences, which Hart's Brigade, in face of stubborn opposition, had succeeded in capturing, assisted by the enterprising operation of Dundonald's horsemen, who had successfully wrested a dominating hill on the extreme left.

Retaining the ground won, the fighting recommenced at dawn next morning with a vigorous shelling of the Boer positions preparatory to another forward move. The task before Warren was extremely difficult and hazardous, having nearly resolved itself into a frontal advance, and in view of the fact four howitzer guns were despatched to assist him, Ogilvy's battery crossing Potgieters to replace them. Slowly onward pressed Warren's line, every yard of advance being hotly contested, but no obvious advantage was manifest.

During the 22nd a passive attitude prevailed, the troops tenaciously holding the captured ridges in face of a persistent bombarding from the Boer guns, which were situated on the exterior high ridges far beyond the effective range of Warren's batteries. To ensure success, Spion

Kop must change hands, further advance being next to impossible and quite impracticable while it remained in Boer tenancy. General Warren, with the reluctant acquiescence of Sir Redvers Buller, decided to settle the issue by a night attack on the fateful mountain. As, however, the ground to be traversed had not been reconnoitred, the venture was deferred until the following night.

Next day the troops endured another harassing shelling; but comparatively slight losses ensued, owing to the more intelligent disposal of the forces under cover. As Spion Kop stood in the direct line of fire of all guns on its eastern side, the 4.7's were directed to be fired over its summit at the ridges where the Boer guns were situated—but not located. Shelling invisible targets at uncertain ranges means usually futile practice, and an inordinate waste of ammunition, for the odds are indeed great against a lucky shell getting "home." Later in the day some changes in the dispositions of the troops took place. Lyttleton's command received two battalions which had arrived from Chieveley, while Talbot-Coke's Brigade, Bethune's Horse, and the newly raised Imperial Light Infantry, fresh from Durban, reinforced Warren.

The Boers had also received large reinforcements, evidently believing that the last two days of British inactivity was a presage of some bold stroke nearing maturity.

Arrangements having been completed, the venturous task of assaulting Spion Kop was entrusted to General Woodgate, who, with about half of his Lancashire Brigade, 200 of Thorneycroft's Mounted Infantry, and a half-company Royal Engineers (about 1600 troops), set out at dusk *en route* towards the south-western spurs of the mountain. The fate of the whole operations depended upon the success of this bold enterprise. By those who are conversant with the physical aspect of Gibraltar, looking at the Rock from the western side, some idea of this night attack may be formed.

The resemblance affords a tolerably close comparison, insomuch as Spion Kop was viewed from Mount Alice. In height both eminences nearly agree, and differ but slightly in length and breadth. To complete this mental picture, imagine that the ascent was made from the neutral ground end of the Rock, that the plateau (written of hereafter) reached as far as the signal station, and then dipped sharply a few score feet, forming a neck that gradually rose again to a conical peak at the opposite end.

Led by the intrepid Thorneycroft, the actual ascent of that 1500 feet of steep, rugged climbing commenced about 10 p.m. Cautiously

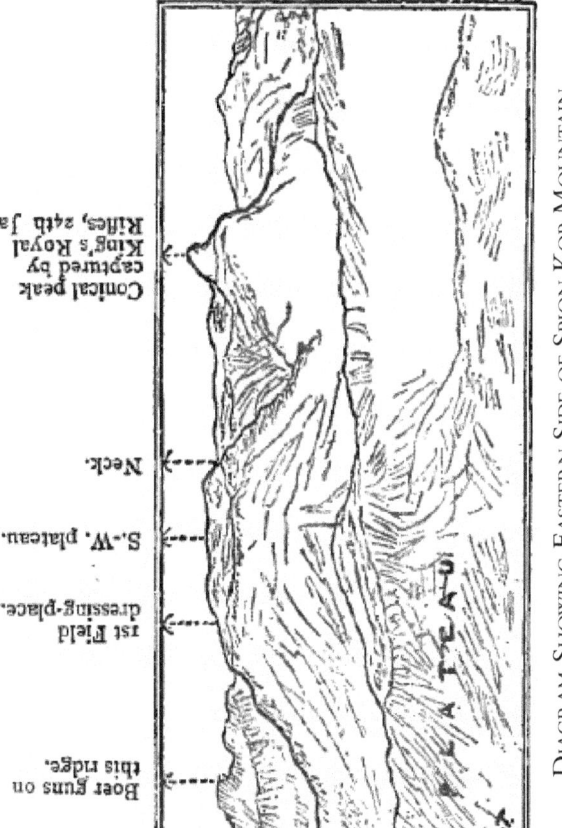

DIAGRAM SHOWING EASTERN SIDE OF SPION KOP MOUNTAIN.

trending their way upwards, the column nearly reached the southwestern crest by 4 a.m., unobserved, their formation then, owing to favourable ground, being in successive lines of attack as wide as the hill permitted. Presently, there came through the thick misty darkness the sentry's challenge of "*Wie kom dar*," ending further secrecy, followed by rapid firing from the surprised Boer picket, the assaulters sustaining only a trifling loss owing to their adopting "preparing to ram" tactics (lying flat down). The firing ceased directly their magazines were emptied, whereupon a bayonet charge, delivered with a loud British cheer, secured the south-west end of the plateau.

But Fate—that arbiter of futurity—unkindly decreed that their success was to end with costly disaster, and the captured summit thereafter became a scene of the bloodiest encounter of the war. The dense mist that prevailed, which had so far greatly favoured the enterprise, rendered further advance, now that discovery had occurred, extremely hazardous until it lifted. But for the persistence of this impenetrable fog, which, obviously, now favoured the alarmed Boers by screening their defences, a different story than what follows might have been related—a story of victory such as crowned Wolfe's exploit, when the heights of Abraham were scaled and Quebec captured.

Towards 7 a.m. (24th) the fog lifted, when the troops and the general position of Spion Kop became visible from Mount Alice, General Buller arrived shortly afterwards, and through the naval telescope gave his deliberate attention to what was taking place there. Realising the strategical success gained over them, and the vital necessity of recapturing the position, the Boers concentrated their utmost resources to undo the blunder of leaving the key of their whole position so utterly exposed to surprise. With shell, pom-pom, and rifle fire, the plateau was incessantly swept from now until dark, and successive attempts were made to envelop the British position. So scanty was the cover available, and so intense the raking fire, that a heavy casualty list was soon the resulting price gallant men were paying for the overnight success.

General Woodgate, while inspecting the frail defences, fell mortally wounded alongside Colonel Blomfield; the command, together with its unique anxieties and responsibilities which stand almost unparalleled in military history, eventually devolving upon the gallant Thorneycroft. The plateau appeared somewhat convex in shape, the neck being about 350 yards distant from the nearest British trenches, and the conical peak perhaps another 500 yards still further beyond the neck. It was from the neck that the Boers sallied forth, and crept round the sides of the plateau to enfilade the advance entrenchments, bayonet charges being necessary to drive them back. From the conical peak the enemy maintained a heavy fusillade, against which it was next to impossible to offer resistance where exposure was necessary, and from this point a machine-gun furrowed the plateau wherever a movement was attempted.

Warren's batteries vigorously shelled the western side of the mountain, while the naval guns endeavoured to subdue the fire on the eastern side—a storm of destruction which seemed to increase in severity as the day wore on. Shell after shell was rapidly hurled at the boulder-strewn neck, and also at the peak, nearly every round splintering huge rocks, which went hurtling down the sides at a terrific pace. As the enemy were in cover among them, distinctly visible from the naval guns, it must be presumed that they also were receiving severe punishment.

The following two messages, received on Mount Alice by Signalman Large of the *Terrible*, who, for the nonce, was attached to the army signallers staff, aptly describe the early forenoon position:—

> Am exposed to terrible cross fire, especially near first field dressing-station; can barely hold my own; water badly needed. Help us, Woodgate.

This message was from the wounded general; the heliograph being smashed by a shell during its transmission, which mishap necessitated the completion of it by flags, a method afterwards continued. The second message received was painfully brief.

> Reinforce at once or all is lost. General dead.

. . . . was the wording of the signal received, though it was afterwards asserted that the exact message should have read—

> General Woodgate killed. Reinforcements urgently required.

A message which more correctly expressed the situation than the one received. The signal, verbally stated to the signalman, had presumably been altered through pardonable inadvertency in the midst of such a scene of carnage. A reply message from General Warren, to whom the messages from Spion Kop had been retransmitted, was heliographed back to the summit as follows:—

> I am sending two battalions, and the Imperial Light Infantry are

on their way up. You must hold on to the last. No surrender.

The enemy also strongly reinforced their summit defences, and continually pressed forward with great gallantry under cover of their well-handled guns, only to be driven back by heroically led charges, each involving much sacrifice.

At noon the situation had indeed become very critical, as the enemy had at last established themselves on the plateau itself. One of Thorneycroft's officers, who was present, has vividly described the position at this period of the day,

> Only a stretch of some 150 yards now separated the men in the entrenchment from the Boers on the crest line. The raking fire from the guns on Green Hill and the belts of shells from the pom-poms, the rifle fire from the knoll, from Green Hill, from Brakfontein, and from the crest line itself, made it impossible for any man to live except under cover, and turned the little plateau into a terrific fire-zone of such density as has never been surpassed in the history of war. Only those who were on Spion Kop know how ferocious can be the fire of a numerous enemy entrenched in commanding and enveloping positions, equipped with an untouched artillery admirably served, on to an open space crowded with defenders who are within the most effective range—only those men know how nerve-shattering are the influences of such a fire when protracted hour after hour.... Moreover, to move forward and attack is less trying to a man than to lie still and try to stop wondering, not whether he can escape death, but for how many more seconds he can possibly live.[1]

The most crucial moment seems to have actually occurred about 1 p.m., when an isolated body of some two or three score of our troops, who were holding the eastern end of the British position, were observed in the act of surrendering themselves, as well as their section of defence. All their officers had succumbed, and apparently, after enduring the several hours of hellish fire which was rapidly decimating the defenders, their morale had finally deserted their exhausted bodies. But as such a proceeding, if permitted, might easily have imperilled the whole British position, the brave Thorneycroft rushed forward, prevented the surrender, and saved the situation by his plucky ac-

---
1. *The Nineteenth Century*, No. 287, January, 1901.

tion and conspicuous courage. Not only did he extricate these men from a forlorn predicament, but led them, together with some timely reinforcements, back to the position temporarily vacated, which was afterwards securely held with exemplary tenacity.

Meanwhile, to mitigate if possible the desperate position on the summit, the 4.7 guns again sent numerous rounds of shell over the top in accordance with signalled directions from Warren's camp. Lyttleton's force went forward early to threaten Brakfontein, but retired again by noon in consequence of the unfavourable turn events were taking on the fateful mountain-top. During middle forenoon the Boers contrived to place guns behind Brakfontein, and from thence began raking the plateau on its eastern side. Their reign of destructiveness, however, was short-lived, for the naval guns gave them such assiduous attention that, with the exception of a secreted pom-pom, their fire was reduced to nullity.

Shortly after noon several hundred Boer horsemen were observed approaching from the Ladysmith direction, escorting what appeared to be either covered-up guns or ambulances. Lieutenant England was ordered to try what effect a shell at an indeterminate range might have among them. The gun was given extreme elevation and directed from the foot of one of the Roodepoort *kopjes* they must presently pass. A lyddite shell was fired; a few riderless horses and a rapid dispersion of the unsuspecting enemy testified that a lucky result had been achieved—or, rather, an unlucky one for them. The distance was estimated at some 18,000 yards. Science meting out death at ten miles' range!

About 5 p.m. was witnessed a brilliant episode, which might justly be described as the silver lining of the cloud of calamity enshrouding our troops on Spion Kop. Two battalions from Lyttleton's command had been previously diverted to alleviate the pressure on the summit. The Scottish Rifles had already ascended the southern spurs, gained the plateau, and had behaved with great courage and energy in the firing line. The 3rd King's Royal Rifles had advanced to the northeastern base in order to assault the peak directly above them, and were now making the ascent covered by the naval guns. In many places the slopes were exceedingly steep, almost perpendicular at some spots, making the climb a slow process. Yet, in spite of obstacles and the severe rifle fire they were receiving from the crest line, the neck, from hidden snaky snipers, and from the Brakfontein trenches—a semicircle of fire—the upward advance went steadily on.

To clear out the nests of snipers, the supports fired over the heads of the leading line up among the overhead trees and rocks, and when the supports could no longer fire, the reserve line continued the covering, while the naval guns searched the crest lines, the neck, and trenches. As the assaulters approached the crest, the shell fire was directed solely at the peak and neck, the troops halting directly beneath their objective to enable them to freshen up for the *coup de main*.

The telescope for once saved a critical situation. By its powerful aid the Boers, who had taken advantage of the temporary inaction and diverted shell fire, were discovered lying in wait just over the crest line, ready to deliver the contents of their mausers into the troops as they clambered over the edge. It now seemed as if disastrous failure was again to be the reward of dauntless gallantry. To heliograph the danger lurking above them would occupy valuable time, besides informing the Boers (who understood Morse) that they were spotted, and possibly cause a premature collision and produce dire consequences that only a miracle appeared able to avert

While onlookers were watching and expressing propitious hopes. Lieutenant Hunt was deliberately laying his 4.7 at the covert enemy. *Bang!* A few seconds' suspense—a lyddite shell burst, not on the conical peak where the attacking party expected to see it, but on the crest line below among those stalking Boers, who cleared instanter. Seeming to interpret the cause of a friendly shell exploding where it did, Colonel Buchanan-Riddell at once gave such orders as took his men over the crest without further delay. The guns now ceased to fire, except at the neck. Forming up, the final charge up the peak took place, the enemy only retiring the other side of it just before the bayonets reached them. This brilliant achievement cost the battalion its gallant colonel, who was killed, and 70 other casualties. Only a temporary occupation of that end of the hill, which had fulfilled its purpose, being contemplated, the battalion was brought down after dusk, returning to the Potgieters *kopjes* about midnight

Meanwhile the heavy shelling of the plateau continued; the insuppressible Boer guns on the north-west ridges firing away at the British defenders, the British guns at the Boer attackers. The strong infantry reinforcements—four battalions—which had proceeded to the summit, though behaving with the utmost gallantry, had merely increased the density of the force—and the casualty list—on the limited confines of the plateau, their exertions being rendered utterly futile against the dominating shell-fire. As an instance of the intensity of the fire, Colonel Blomfield, of the Lancashire Fusiliers (whose son afterwards joined the *Terrible* as a midshipman), has related in the regimental *Annual* that—

> Nearly every shot they (the enemy) fired took its toll in killed or wounded. . . . Two shells passed through the thighs of one man, and on through the legs of the man next to him, leaving only the trunk of the first and carrying away one leg of the second man. A sergeant of the R.E. was lying on the near side of the two men killed, had also been hit by this shell, which had touched his spine and completely paralysed him.

The colonel himself was severely wounded in the forenoon, and was afterwards made prisoner when the position was vacated. During the time he was lying in the trench, trying to offer as little exposure of himself as was possible, his water-bottle was shot of his chest, he states:

> So heavy was the firing all day that carrying away of the wounded from the more forward and exposed trenches was impossible. Not till the welcome shades of night could their sufferings be alleviated, and in the darkness and confusion many were not found till morning. Many were killed as they left the trenches. Sergeant Lightfoot, who had so pluckily helped to bring me in, among them. . . . The Boer treatment of the wounded was kind and considerate. . . . The ordinary Boer seems to feel a good deal of sympathy for a wounded man, but not much for a sick man.

The injudicious dispositions of the British artillery were probably responsible for much of this devastating result. All the ten long-range naval guns were posted on Potgieter's side, unable to render real co-operative support or assistance either to Warren's force or the Spion Kop attack. Except for the incidents related, these powerful guns had done nothing beyond expending ammunition over noisy and futile bombardments, and trying to perform the impossible. One 4.7, and half the 12-pounders, at least, might easily have been spared and profitably employed out westward, where Warren's outranged batteries, all parked together on one hill within long-range rifle fire, were ineffectually but gallantly striving to be effective against the Boer guns.

As guns must invariably fight guns, it now became abundantly evident that if Spion Kop was ever to be wholly British, artillery must be more consistently employed, and that quickly. Hence it was that the *Tartar's* guns and the mountain battery were ordered to ascend the mountain.

Several assertions have been made that guns could not possibly have reached the summit unless a track was previously prepared for them. But to those who still adhere to that opinion, the writer respectfully points out that when naval field guns *cannot be wheeled* to where they may be required, they are either parbuckled, dragged, hoisted, or even carried there. Where men can walk, a field gun can be made to follow by one or other of the common methods just mentioned. As to whether the position on the summit was tenable for guns or not is, of course, a different and debatable question.

It was also proposed to place one 4.7 to the westward, so that it might have a direct line of fire at the Boers' dominating guns; General Buller and Commander Limpus proceeded towards Trichardts to select the position. Moreover, preparations were made to send fresh troops to the summit to relieve those who had dauntlessly withstood an intolerable strain of battle, such as few troops have ever faced for so long an unbroken period. The subsequent events which occurred on Spion Kop, however, negatived each of these inceptive movements. The "remedials" were too late.

Colonel Thorneycroft, in a despatch to General Warren, extracts of which are here given, tersely sums up the situation about nightfall. He stated—

> The troops which marched up here last night are quite done up (the Lancashire Fusiliers, Royal Lancashire Regiment, and Thorneycroft's Mounted Infantry). They have had no water, and ammunition is running short. I consider that even with the reinforcements which have arrived it is impossible to permanently hold this place so long as the enemy's guns can play on the hill. They have three long-range guns, three of shorter range, and several Maxim-Nordenfelts, which have swept the whole of the plateau since 8 a.m. I have not been able to ascertain the casualties, but they have been very heavy, especially in the regiments which came up last night. I request instructions as to what course I am to adopt The enemy are now (6.30) firing heavily from both flanks (rifle, shell, and Nordenfelt), while a heavy rifle fire is being kept up on the front. It Is all I can do to hold my own. If my casualties go on at the present rate, I shall barely hold out the night.

A large number of stretcher-bearers should be sent up, and also all the water possible.

The situation is critical. [2]

Owing to the signal apparatus being unworkable, night signals could not be transmitted, and written despatches naturally took considerable time to go to and fro. Therefore, in ignorance of what preparations were being made for holding the position, Thorneycroft gave the order, after a reasonable period of waiting for instructions had elapsed, for the total evacuation of Spion Kop. Towards midnight, Lieutenant Winston Churchill arrived on the summit on a mission from General Warren; but he was too late—the retrograde movement was then irrevocably decided upon.

It was early dawn when Lieutenant Lees (Naval A.-D.-C. to General Buller) arrived on Mount Alice and countermanded all movements of naval guns, the unexpected news of the evacuation having just been received at headquarters. With the sun's appearance the telescope confirmed the dire intelligence. The Boers were observed in full occupation of the summit, busily stripping the dead, dying, and wounded of their arms and accoutrements. Such was the disastrous ending of an enterprise which began with such brilliant anticipation of success. Nevertheless, the decision to retire, which produced the collapse of the whole plan of operations—if there was a plan!—and which act has since become the subject of a fierce controversy, received the unqualified approvement of General Buller in the following manner:—

General Buller's telegram, January 31st—

It is due to Colonel Thorneycroft to say that I believe his personal gallantry saved a difficult situation early on the 34th, and that under a loss of at least 40 *per cent* he directed the defence with conspicuous courage and ability throughout the day.

No blame whatever for the withdrawal is, in my opinion, attributable to him, and I think his conduct throughout was admirable.

Though Lord Roberts could not concur with General Buller that the evacuation was a politic course to have adopted, yet he fully endorsed the expressed encomium concerning Thorneycroft's gallant leadership. The following extracts from General Buller's despatches

---

2. *The Nineteenth Century*, No. 287, January, 1901.

(January 30th, 1900) furnish the sequel of a battle, which caused the nation a thrill both of sorrow and of triumph by the magnitude of misfortune and the valour of the troops it had revealed:—

On the morning of the 25th, finding that Spion Kop had been abandoned in the night, I decided to withdraw General Warren's force; the troops had been continuously engaged for a week, in circumstances entailing considerable hardships; there had been very heavy losses on Spion Kop. I consequently assumed the command, commenced the withdrawal of the ox and heavy mule transports on the 35th; this was completed by midday the 26th; by double spanning, the loaded ox waggons got over the drift at the rate of about eight per hour. The mule waggons went over the pontoon bridge, but all the mules had to be taken out and the vehicles passed over by hand. For about seven hours of the night the drift could not be used, as it was dangerous in the dark, but the use of the pontoon went on day and night

In addition to machine guns, six batteries of Royal Field Artillery, and four howitzers, the following vehicles were passed:—ox waggons, 232; 10-span mule waggons, 98; 6-span, 107; 4-span, 52;—total, 489 vehicles. In addition to these, the ambulances were working backwards and forwards, evacuating the sick and wounded.

By 2 p.m. the 26th, all the ox waggons were over, and by 11.30 p.m. all the mule transports were across and the bridge clear for the troops. By 4 a.m. the 37th, all the troops were over, and by 8 a.m. the pontoons were gone and all was clear. . . . Thus ended an expedition which I think ought to have succeeded. We have suffered very heavy losses, and lost many whom we can ill spare; but, on the other hand, we have inflicted as great or greater losses upon the enemy than they have upon us, and they are, by all accounts, thoroughly disheartened; while our troops are, I am glad and proud to say, in excellent fettle.

This second failure cost the relief army 324 killed, 1113 wounded, and 303 missing and prisoners—a total of 1740 officers and men.

CHAPTER 11

Retirement of Buller's Army to Chieveley

Situated between Spion Kop and Doom Kloof stand the Vaal Krantz ridges, within effective and dominating gun range from both those high eminences, as well as from Brakfontein. The objective of this next attempt was to capture Vaal Krantz, and then follow with an outflanking attack upon Brakfontein from its eastern end; a movement which must, if successful, cause the enemy to vacate the whole of his western positions, including Spion Kop. Such, then, was the plan, very simple in conception, and yet destined to fail.

The arrival of some 2400 reinforcements, which included half a regiment of cavalry, a battery of Royal Horse Artillery, and two army 5-inch guns, had more than counterbalanced the heavy losses sustained at the Spion Kop operations. The week's rest, coupled with General Buller's assurance to his troops that he had at last discovered the key of the Boer position, had produced a great recuperative effect upon the force, both physically and morally. Naturally the reverses had somewhat affected the martial spirit of the troops, but they had also made them fully realise the magnitude of the task before them—a task which the Empire was anxiously awaiting to see accomplished.

On Sunday night, February 4th, final orders were issued, troops and guns having been moving nearly all day, taking up their respective positions in readiness for the early morrow. The naval guns were now disposed as follows: the 4.7 were separated; No. 1 gun, Lieutenant England, was placed on Signal Hill; No. 2 gun. Lieutenant Hunt, remaining on Mount Alice, covering the whole left flank. Burn's two 12-pounders, with the two 5-inch guns, occupied a position immediately beneath Zwaart Kop. Ogilvy's six 12-pounders were placed on top of Zwaart Kop, also two R.F.A. guns, and the Mountain Battery. The evolution of getting the guns up this rugged precipitous mountain, previously reported upon as being an insuperable position for guns to ascend, is worth a brief description. There was no roadway up, but the R.E.'s had blasted away the worst rocky obstructions, and had otherwise prepared a sort of track, the general being anxious to place long-range guns on its commanding summit, if possible. The order was received at dusk on the previous Friday evening, the movement, which had to be secretly performed during the darkness, commencing that same night. While the battery was preparing to trek, Lieutenant Ogilvy reconnoitred the ground to be traversed, and a start was made at 9 p.m. Leaving the plateau beneath Mount Alice, whither the naval 12-pounders had been withdrawn, the battery, during a violent thunderstorm, descended the steep slippery track leading towards Potgieters, and then struck eastwards.

By midnight the neck connecting Signal Hill with Zwaart Kop was reached, over which it was imperative the battery should cross before dawn. With treble teams of oxen (48 animals, and every available man hauling with drag-ropes, each gun and waggon was separately transported over the rugged neck. Twice within 50 yards No. 4 gun toppled over the hillside during its transit, yet in spite of mishaps the six guns and ten heavy waggons were all transferred to the southern side and hidden from the Boer gaze in accordance with orders.

The men and oxen were then rested, to await the advent of dusk again before proceeding. Lieutenants Ogilvy and James ascending Zwaart Kop in the meantime, to select gun positions and inspect the track. To carry out their scheme, the balloon wire cable was requisitioned and obtained, an apparatus being rigged up with it during daylight. The ascent may be divided into three sections of route, each requiring a different method of haulage, (1) A rough track, with about 20 degrees of irregular slope, was traversed by the agency of men and oxen as on the previous night. (2) A rugged and crooked shoulder several score yards long, having an inclination of about 25 degrees, was surmounted by placing the Scottish Fusilier escort of 100 men on the drag-ropes, while the guns' crews pushed and man-handled the wheel-spokes. (3) The final and worst portion, some 300 feet in length, was covered with huge boulders, and had an inclination of about 40 degrees.

Some idea of the steepness just here can be imagined when it is considered that at an angle of 45 degrees it is difficult even to stand, let alone work. Here the wire hawser was used. It was first centred, the bight secured to the gun trail, and the ends led up through two leading blocks, one on each side of and at the top of the track; the hemp drag-ropes were then bent on to the ends to afford a suitable grip, and led down towards the gun, each rope being manned by 50 of the escort. Though "preventer guys" were used, a few capsizings occurred.

The *Tartar's* two guns were got up by midnight, by which hour both Bluejackets and military escort were so exhausted, many of the latter having bleeding and blistered hands, that a temporary cessation of the movement became necessary. Favoured by a dense mist, another start was made at 4 a.m., when all the guns, including the two R.F.A. guns, were safely landed on the summit before the mist cleared away.

Ammunition and supplies were carried up by the guns' escort as required. The northern fringe of the little plateau being thickly covered with trees, the guns were screened from hostile view among them. To obtain a clear range all obstructive trees were sawn nearly through, stayed with rope, then finally felled immediately before firing, thus preserving the ambushment until the action commenced. The evolution, performed in darkness, and in very unpropitious weather, was highly commended by the general in despatches, but its success was very largely due to the splendid co-operation of the Scottish Fusilier escort, who cheerfully responded to every order and worked like— what they were—real Britons. The Mountain Battery followed up later, the mules being carefully led to the summit at easy angles; one animal, however, with its section of gun, slipped and rolled for a good distance down the hillside. The piece of gun was again sent up, but the mule was defunct.

General Warren, commanding the British left, commenced operations at 7 a.m., Monday (5th), with a demonstration against Brakfontein. The Lancashire Brigade (now under General Wynne, *vice* Woodgate), actively supported by six Field Batteries, the Howitzer Battery, and the naval 4.7's, were thus to mask the real attack that was to follow against Vaal Krantz. Talbot-Coke's Brigade was held in reserve near Potgieters, one battalion guarding the main camp behind Mount Alice, and a small mounted detachment watched Trichardts Drift, now the extreme left

Constituting the right wing, and now concentrated near Zwaart Kop, was General Clery's Division (Hart's and Hildyard's Brigades), and also Lyttleton's Brigade, which was to lead the attack. The 1st Cavalry Brigade (regulars) and a battery of R.H.A, under Colonel

Burn-Murdock, were held in readiness to cross the pontoon and rush through the valley at the proper moment, to secure the right flank when Vaal Krantz should be wholly in British possession. The 2nd Cavalry Brigade (colonials and irregulars), under Lord Dundonald, was detailed to guard the right wing from any hostile flanking movements. Skiet Drift was held as the extreme British right. Such were the dispositions of the force; the operations to be personally directed by General Buller.

The feigned attack on Brakfontein was well sustained to absorb the Boers' attention, while the real movement had time to develop on the right. Covered by a heavy bombardment, the infantry closed to within about 1600 yards of the enemy's works, then halted, the field batteries remaining some 1000 yards further to the rear. Hitherto silent, the enemy now opened a heavy rifle fire on the troops, while three guns, situated on the northern spurs of the Spion Kop range, concentrated a well-directed fire on the batteries, and several concealed pom-poms divided their murderous attention between the two arms. For upwards of two hours an exciting artillery duel was waged between the exposed batteries and concealed Boer guns, the shooting from the latter today, for accuracy and rapidity, leaving no loophole for adverse criticism. Neither could pen over-praise the courageous conduct of our artillerymen, who stood forth in the open ground bravely serving their guns amidst a heavy drenching of shrapnel fire, and yet marvellously escaping with less than a score casualties.

Meanwhile, on the right, the Royal Engineers had, under severe fire, thrown No. 3 pontoon bridge across the river, east of Zwaart Kop, and, covered by Ogilvy's guns, Lyttleton's Brigade had crossed over by noon. The six field batteries were now withdrawn by single batteries from the Brakfontein ruse, crossing by No. 1 pontoon, and taking up another position inside the eastern river loop, joined in the general bombardment of Vaal Krantz. The battle now commenced in real earnest. On reaching the intervening space between the river and Krantz Kop, the attacking brigade was compelled to advance across the open ground. No sooner had they emerged from cover than three guns, posted on Doom Kloof, which for some time had been raking Ogilvy's guns on the summit of Zwaart Kop, gave the troops a brisk shelling, though doing them comparatively little damage. England's 4.7 on Signal Hill, and Ogilvy's 12-pounders, at 10,000 and 6000 yards ranges, respectively, attempted the silencing of these guns, while No. 2 4.7, and heavy army guns, divided their attention between the

Spion Kop and Brakfontein positions, also frequently assisting to rake the Vaal Krantz ridges.

By 4 p.m. Lyttleton had captured the southern portion of the ridges (Krantz Kop) by a dashing bayonet charge. The Boers now endeavoured to render its occupation a nugatory success, for all their guns were at once concentrated upon the victorious brigade, who found but scanty cover upon the isolated position they had so gallantly won. Fortunately the oncoming darkness was soon to bring some respite, though not rest, for throughout the night the brigade were busily employed building protective works, and otherwise securing themselves against possible counter-attacks.

Towards close of day, when the atmosphere, as at early mornings, becomes remarkably clear from mirage, the two 4.7's, owing to their favourable elevated position, were directed to use every effort to destroy or silence the Spion Kop guns. Every available telescope was focused at the ridge, each glass taking a certain section, and, by this scrutinising method, the gun positions were eventually located. The guns were only partially exposed when actually in the firing position, and recoiled back beyond the crest line on being fired. As the range was known, some tricky firing ensued. It was afterwards reported by a prisoner that two guns were seriously damaged by our fire; at any rate, it was a fact that they ceased firing altogether from that position.

Next morning, the 6th, a 94-lb. shell from a six-inch "Long Tom," which had been mounted during the night on Doorn Kloof's summit, was the surprising harbinger of dawn, and the precursor of a lively bombardment of the British position. Numerous invisible riflemen, with machine and field guns, had also been strongly posted among the hills, extending in an arc from north to south-east, from whence an incessant long-range fire was converging on Krantz Kop.

About 7 a.m., Lieutenant England's 4.7, while firing at "Long Tom," luckily exploded its magazine, a fact which was notified by a loud report and a huge column of smoke shooting skywards. This act suspended its freaky firing for a few hours, until its 'interior" could be replenished with more ammunition. All day long did our artillery vainly strive to silence the baffling Boer guns, and unearth their hidden riflemen, whose fire sorely harassed Lyttleton's force, compelling them to keep close cover, especially from the scathing shrapnel.

Nearly the whole of our position was dominated, shells falling everywhere, and generally where least expected. At one time all would be vigorously bombarding the captured ridge, then suddenly an indiscriminate shelling of the field batteries, the troops, and a raking fire at the Zwaart Kop guns would take place; even the general staff were not exempt from a visitation of Boer shell. One 6-inch shell struck the ground twenty yards in front of Lieutenant Burne's right 12-pounder, then ricocheted, unexploded, over their heads, covering the crew with dirt, and twice afterwards these two guns' crews had narrow escapes.

Luckily very few shells burst, other than shrapnel, while the practice of "Long Tom" was ludicrously erratic, as if he was hastily laid and fired. Every feasible device to silence him and the other guns utterly failed. It was only when a shell came whizzing along, or a puff of smoke was discerned, that their exposure could be determined—which also implied they had again vanished below the crest line beyond harm.

Late in the afternoon a determined attempt was made to recapture Krantz Kop, but the attack was easily repulsed with a bayonet charge, and the enemy cleared off the ridge. During the darkness, Hildyard's Brigade relieved Lyttleton's war-worn brigade, who recrossed at No. 2 pontoon for a well-earned rest from an almost untenable position which had cost them over 200 casualties to win and hold. About midnight the sudden crackling of musketry, and snappy barking of pom-poms, announced another counter-attack on the ridge, which, as before, was rendered futile with cold steel.

Dawn next morning, the 7th, revealed the fact that the Boers had reduced the radius of their defence, having, under cover of darkness, built *sangars* and dug fresh trenches nearer Vaal Krantz, besides increasing their artillery strength. The bombardment of the ridge recommenced, and though the severity of the fire was greater than yesterday's, its effect was much less felt, owing to the excellent shelters now constructed. Again the enemy frequently diverted their shelling in order to harass the reserve troops and guns, often compelling the guns' crews to seek shelter when the firing became too accurate. Lieutenant Ogilvy received a slight graze on the chest from a shell-splinter on one of these occasions. In the afternoon a balloon reconnaissance near the Vaal Krantz position disclosed the true nature of the Boer defence, and the impracticability of continuing the operations.

General Buller's telegram to Lord Roberts fully explains the situation—

> Having occupied Vaal Krantz, it was necessary to fortify the position, so as to make it a pivot for further operations. After

WITH THE LADYSMITH RELIEF COLUMN.
Naval encampment on the *veldt*

two days' work, I found the nature of the ground would not allow of this; besides which, we were exposed to the fire of heavy guns posted on heights dominating our artillery.

Once again the nature of the ground, more so than the enemy's power of defence, had impeded the advance.

Accordingly, after a conference of the generals, Hildyard's Brigade was withdrawn from Krantz Kop after dusk, and orders were issued for a general retirement back to Chieveley.

Beyond a desultory shelling, no attempt to interrupt the retirement was made, General Warren's Division covering the movement. The heavy guns on Mount Alice and Signal Hill also remained in position, replying to the enemy's fire till the front was entirely cleared of troops and transport. By dusk on the 9th, the naval guns were enabled to withdraw, having orders to follow the main column to Springfield, where they arrived at midnight; joining Ogilvy's battery, which had, on evacuating Zwaart Kop, proceeded there earlier in the day. During this journey a thunderstorm of unusual violence, accompanied by a torrential downpour of rain, was experienced, making the passage through the drifts a difficult matter. In such a mountainous region one hour's duration of heavy rain will often convert a dry drift into a roaring torrent, and prevent transit of waggons across for half a day.

The march was resumed at daylight, Pretorius' Farm being reached at 3 p.m., where the force encamped for the night At 4 a.m. next morning (Sunday, 11th), in company with those Natal veterans, the indomitable Irish Brigade, the journey was continued; Chieveley camp, eighteen miles distant, being reached at noon, when the guns were at once placed in their former positions on Gun Hill. By nightfall the whole force had arrived in camp, except an entrenched force of infantry, Burn-Murdoch's cavalry, a battery of R.H.A., and Lieutenant Burne's 12-pounder unit, which remained at Springfield Bridge to contain the enemy about that district

Owing to the handiwork of the Royal Engineers and communication troops, the return march had been performed with far less difficulty than was experienced during the outward journey. All along the route was evidence of their labour. Slushy drifts had been bridged over, dangerous gaps rendered safe, and huge boulders, which had almost capsised guns and transport, were now whitewashed landmarks on the track side. Indeed, a track that had demanded skilful pilotage to traverse even in daylight was now a respectable "king's highway," which could be safely trekked by night

Commenting upon the Vaal Krantz operations in his despatches of February 22nd, 1900, General Buller stated:—

> ... The Naval Brigade and the Royal Artillery, under Captain Jones and Lieutenant Ogilvy, R.N., and Colonel Parsons, R.A., did excellent work throughout the three days. ... I much regret my failure to pierce the enemy's line of defence, and the more so as I think we all of us thought at first the movement was going to be successful. I thought that it was no use pushing an attack which did not, if successful, promise a secure base for the next advance on Ladysmith, now still ten miles off, with Roodeport, a very strong, carefully prepared position, between us and it. I have every reason to believe, from what we saw, and from the report of deserters since, that the enemy's loss was much heavier than ours.

The total casualties during these operations amounted to 374, but seven *per cent* being killed. The third attempt to relieve Ladysmith had failed.

4.7 GUN MOUNTED ON A RAILWAY TRUCK BY CAPTAIN PERCY SCOTT

CHAPTER 12

Ladysmith Relieved!

February 12th to March 3rd, 1900

Field-Marshal Lord Roberts—the British Napoleon—in response to an interrogatory telegram from General Buller, inquiring whether his lordship thought that the chance of relieving Ladysmith at the cost of from two to three thousand men was worth such a risk, replied—

"Ladysmith must be relieved even at the loss you expect I should certainly persevere, and my hope is that the enemy will be so severely punished as to enable you to withdraw White's garrison without great difficulty. Let troops know that in their hands is the honour of the Empire, and that of their success I have no possible doubt."

Accordingly, a fresh plan was rapidly prepared for a fourth and supreme effort to relieve Ladysmith. It was now well-known to what a dire condition the beleaguered garrison was reduced, and that famine and disease, besides the acts of war, were rapidly decimating their numbers in their heroic struggle to uphold the honour of the flag.

Before proceeding to chronicle these operations, a brief reference to other relevant matters of minor import will be made. The following extract is culled from a lecture given by Captain Scott at Hong Kong in June, 1900:—

> While the main army was operating in the Spion Kop direction, General Barton was active at Chieveley, and wanted a 4.7 on a railway truck to shell a new position occupied by the Boers. There was no time to make a new mounting, so we put one of the platform mountings, similar to those sent to Ladysmith on a low truck, secured it down with chains, and cut off the ends of the transverse baulks so as to allow it to pass through the tunnels.

Owing to the amount of energy absorbed by the hydraulic cylinders and the general elasticity of the mounting, very little recoil was transmitted to the truck, and consequently the gun could be fired at right angles to the direction of the railway line.

As General Barton wished to have the alternative of using this gun off the truck if required, a little extra stability had to be given do compensate for the amount we had cut off the cross beams.

This was done by supplying a movable beam which could be bolted on when the mounting was *in situ*. This was found a great advantage, as the platforms could then be sent intact by train instead of in pieces, as was the case with those that went to Ladysmith.

Three more guns on this description of mounting were made and operated against the Boers at the final attack on Pieters Hill.

In this final attack, General Buller wanted still heavier ordnance, and wired to me, asking if I could possibly send him a 6-inch gun. The telegram arrived on a Wednesday, and the general expressed a wish to have it, if possible, by the following Monday, so there was not much time. A gun was taken out of the *Terrible*, and a design of a mounting prepared, the governing features of which were utility and a desire to comply with the general's wishes as regards time. It was finished on Sunday morning, and sent to the front. Some said that it was clumsy, others that it would fall to pieces the first round. It did not fall in pieces, but put upwards of 500 lyddite and common shell into the enemy's position, a fact which must have led them to regard it in more serious light than the view taken of it by a certain Member of Parliament, who referred to it as 'only picturesque.' A Boer prisoner, with whom I conversed, told me that they disliked this gun very much. The mounting was so very simple that I need not describe it.

After the occupation of Ladysmith, General Buller, anticipating going north over the Biggarsberg, asked if I could, now that there was more time, supply a lighter and more mobile mounting for the 4.7-inch gun; there was of course no difficulty in doing this. The heavy ship carriage was removed, and steel used instead of wood; a single wheel was placed in the rear between

6-INCH GUN ON EXTEMPORARY CARRIAGE ABOUT TO BE ENTRAINED FOR THE FRONT
Weight of gun, 7 tons; cradle and carriage, 4 tons. Taken out of "Terrible" at Durban.

the trails to facilitate transport. When the extreme elevation of 37 degrees was required, the rear wheel could be unshipped. When firing with the wheel shipped, a locking arrangement was provided for keeping it in a fore and aft line. It was very mobile and I believe answered well. Four of them were made and turned over to the Royal Artillery.

No limbers were provided for any of these guns. The 6-inch and 4.7-inch were travelled by a team of oxen, their ammunition coming along behind in an ordinary Cape waggon. The 12-pounders for a short travel were secured to the tail of the waggon which carried their ammunition: for a long travel the gun was lifted out of its trunnions and put on to its waggon with the ammunition, the whole not being an excessive weight for a team of oxen.

Lieutenant Drummond, Midshipman Skinner, Petty Officers Connor, Carey, Allen (captain of gun), 50 seamen and stokers, arrived from the *Terrible* with the 6-inch gun, which was placed on Gun Hill.

On February 12th, Lieutenant Dooner, Midshipman Kirby, Petty Officers Neil, Sparks, Bicker, another 50 seamen and stokers, left the *Terrible* with two field guns, and proceeded to Zululand. They travelled by the coast railway to the terminus, then crossed the mouth of the Tugela near by, and marched to Eshowe, 28 miles distant, there joining the composite force protecting the province from Boer incursions.

Although about one half of the complement of the *Terrible* was now at the front or landed in connection with the war, the ship was not by any means depleted of a sea-going crew. The supernumeraries brought out from England for ships in China, and 100 other men, who had formed part of a large draft sent out to reinforce the Cape Squadron, had together temporarily replaced those on active service. New guns from England had also been shipped, so that, except for a brief period, the ship still remained efficient as a first-class cruiser.

To resume the fighting narrative, the plan ordained—a wide turning movement—may be briefly explained thus:—Seize Hussar Hill, from whence expand eastwards, and take possession of the Cingolo (the Boer extreme left) and Monte Christo Hills. Success here would then render Green Hill and Hlangwani Hill, each in turn, untenable, or of easy capture. Upon the last-named position being occupied with our guns, the Fort Wylie group of *kopjes*, which were found impervious to attack on December 15th, would have to be resigned. Thereupon the enemy must retire to the northern *kopjes* which culminate at Pieters Hill, where a successful *coup de main* would break the strong barrier that encompassed Ladysmith.

The approximate strength of the force employed was 27,000 men and 80 guns.

Coincidently with the commencement of these operations, Lord Roberts began his memorable sweep through the Republics. Up to this time no important military movement had transpired on the Cape Colony side. Lord Methuen still faced Cronje's army at Magersfontein. Gatacre was also confronting the Boers occupying the Stormberg district, and keeping factious colonials in subjection. General French was just starting on his historic cavalry dash to Kimberley, which town was relieved by him on February 15th.

On February 12th a successful reconnaissance to Hussar Hill took place, and the next day general orders for an advance were issued.

Early on the 14th Hussar Hill was seized by Dundonald; Barton's Brigade, Ogilvy's Battery, and one field battery, quickly followed and secured the position. Later, General Warren, with the brigades of Wynne and Talbot-Coke, and divisional artillery, also occupied this slight eminence. General Lyttleton, with Hildyard's and Norcott's brigades, and artillery, occupied the thickly-wooded eastern slopes of Hussar Hill. The heavy guns on Gun Hill covered these movements, only a skirmishing resistance being offered to the respective operations. Hart's Irish Brigade remained at Gun Hill camp to guard the left flank. The Springfield observation force was there still.

The 15th and 16th were two excessively hot days, preventing any infantry operations being attempted. A series of artillery duels were waged; Hussar Hill, devoid of natural cover, being subjected to a fairly accurate shell fire. Ogilvy's guns were protected with an earth-bag redoubt, that unquestionably saved them serious losses, for numerous shells burst within a few feet short of and over their position, some even lacerating the earth-bags.

Evidently divining General Buller's intentions, the Boers had greatly prolonged their eastern defences, having guns placed in difficult locations as far as Cingolo Neck. On the 17th, the whole artillery opened up a vigorous bombardment on the Boer positions to mask Lyttleton's flanking march towards Cingolo. The enemy briskly replied, Hussar Hill again becoming a target for their well-directed shell fire. One shrapnel shell alone caused the loss of an entire gun's crew at one of the unprotected 5-inch guns near by, grimly demonstrating that to take sensible cover from the dominating fire of invisible guns is not a derogatory method of saving men and *matériel* from superfluous exposure to damage.

While Lyttleton's two brigades and Dundonald's mounted corps pushed through the difficult scrub-covered country eastward, another brigade and two field batteries advanced to threaten Green Hill. Before noon the flashing heliograph from the southern summit of Cingolo signified its successful occupation. The surprised enemy's brief resistance had been quickly overcome, and the enveloping movement thus auspiciously commenced. By nightfall the whole elongated hill was in British possession. The Boers, thrust off Cingolo, were seemingly dismayed at the changed tactics—from frontal to flanking attacks—and prepared a stubborn opposition for the morrow.

Artillery fire and dawn—synonymous indications that another day had commenced—brought both sides into activity. The enemy directed a heavy but ineffectual shelling at Hildyard's Brigade on Cingolo, which force was cautiously advancing towards the neck—a sharp, craggy dip connecting the hill with Monte Christo. Norcott's Brigade, and Dundonald's force, protected Hildyard's western and eastern flanks respectively, marching on either side of the hill correlatively with the brigade's movements on the top. Meanwhile, Barton's Brigade faced Green Hill to await the psychological moment at which to effect its capture.

One hostile gun, situated near Bloys' Farm, which was too accurately active, required silencing. The 6-inch on Gun Hill opened fire in that direction at 16,500 yards range. The proverbial three rounds silenced the gun, for it never fired from that locality again. Later, a few 100-pound lyddite shells, sent over Hlangwani in response to a signal, dispersed some bodies of active Boers. The general signalled an appreciative message, even though they were each lucky shots; for in this instance, though the direction was accurately given, the objects were invisible, and the range guessed at

Throughout the day the heavy guns harassed the enemy, compelling them frequently to shift their gun positions, besides rendering the passage of reinforcements to their left defences a difficult matter. Together with the field batteries, Ogilvy's guns were busily covering the Monte Christo attack, which by noon had developed into a successful assault, the crest having been brilliantly captured from a determined enemy. Now seriously threatened by Dundonald on their eastern flank, persistently shelled from the western side, and faced by a victorious brigade, the Boers very sensibly evacuated the whole Monte Christo position. Norcott's Brigade now advanced along the western spurs of the ridge to outflank and enfilade the other left defences, while Barton led his brigade direct upon Green Hill, which strongly entrenched position was carried with little loss by 4 p.m., the enemy retreating incontinently towards Hlangwani and the river, leaving camps and considerable stores intact behind them. Our day's losses, nearly 180, were insignificant in comparison to the great strategical advantages won—Cingolo, Monte Christo, and Green Hill, each in turn, having fallen into the enveloping net. General Buller stated (Despatches, March 14th, 1900)—

> Through this attack, which was made in echelon from the right, the naval guns, under Captain Jones, R.N., and royal artillery, under Colonel Parsons, R.A., rendered the greatest possible service, shelling the successive positions till the infantry closed on them.

The naval guns here referred to were those of Ogilvy's Battery.

That night Lieutenant Ogilvy with two guns, accompanied by a strong military escort, marched to Monte Christo, arriving there next morning at five o'clock. Assisted by the Devons, the guns were hauled to the summit, from whence a panoramic view of Ladysmith and the environing Boer *laagers* was visible some ten or twelve miles away. From this lofty concealment, three Boer 45-pounders were discerned about 5000 yards distant across the river, then actively shelling the British positions. A few common shell found the exact range, whereupon a rapid shrapnel fire was poured into the disconcerted enemy, compelling them to abandon their guns and seek shelter. During a storm which then unfortunately broke over the district, obscuring the range, the Boer guns were withdrawn to safety.

Early on the 19th, the 4.7 guns also proceeded eastward; some ten miles of the very worst country yet seen were traversed, and ten hours of broiling heat endured, before the guns reached their destination. Almost every form of natural obstacle was encountered nearly the whole journey beyond Hussar Hill. Enormous boulders were bounced over, trees were truncated by the sheer impetus of the guns, tough undergrowth was crushed through, and *dongas* were crossed with a "down and upward" rush. No recognised track existed, so a bee-line course was set for Cingolo Neck. When about two-thirds of the distance had been completed, the exhausted oxen teams refused to proceed further, and had to be outspanned. They had struck for water and rest; the latter was given them, but drink was unobtainable.

A serious dilemma was thus created, for without help of some sort, the guns could only be moved singly and slowly; the withdrawal of the naval volunteers at Gun Hill to man some platform-mounted 4.7's, had also reduced the guns' crews by 25 men each gun—exactly half of their former manual strength subtracted. Men and drag-ropes! Yes—that was the only solution. Accordingly, 100 men were courteously lent from the nearest battalion, and with their needful assistance the guns were hauled away and got into action beneath Ogilvy's gun position. The troops always cheerfully and readily responded to such requisitions for help, whenever manual haulage for the guns became necessary. This same journey, rough enough by daylight, was the route taken by Ogilvy's guns the previous night The 4.7's being exposed to shell fire from unseen guns across the river, and observation much interfered with, they were again moved after dusk, and ensconced in a better position before dawn.

The key of the Colenso position, Hlangwani Hill, was occupied on the 20th by Barton's Brigade, with guns, the enemy having been compelled to abandon it the previous evening. Hart's Brigade marched into Colenso from Chieveley, and some of Thorneycroft's Colonials swam the river to reconnoitre the Fort Wylie *kopjes* beyond, which were found weakly held by riflemen. The whole southern side of the Tugela River was again British. The vital point now to be considered was where the army should cross over and deliver the *coup de grâce*. Ladysmith's fate hung upon that momentous decision of strategy.

Skirmishing and desultory artillery contests is a fair summary of this day's fighting. One incident, however, is worth relating of how Petty Officer Ward, when firing at a located pom-pom, inadvertently aimed to the left of his object. His shot, instead of being wasted, luckily burst inside a *donga* in which a numerous body of the enemy was concealed, who, evidently thinking they were discovered, suddenly emerged therefrom and galloped wildly away. Both 12-pounders (Monte Christo guns) then went for this fresh target with shrapnel, and possibly made several hits.

Intelligence was received next morning, the 21st, that the Boers were retreating north; which news to some extent was true. It afterwards transpired that a few Free States Commandoes were leaving to protect their country against Lord Roberts's invasion, also that the

Boers were wisely removing their heaviest guns and superfluous baggage to a region of safety. That further fighting—if any—would partake of a rearguard action was the logical inference deduced from the report. Consequently the flanking movement was arrested, and a pontoon, nearly 100 yards long, was thrown across the river at Colenso, at a point a mile north of Fort Wylie, which offered many conveniences for crossing. Although this altered strategy eventually proved a fatal decision, yet, with such tangible evidence that the enemy were already retiring, the plan appeared to offer the easiest and swiftest method of success.

The bulk of the army was now moved westward towards the river. Ogilvy's battery was reunited, and with the 5-inch guns and Mountain battery, was posted on Hlangwani to cover the crossing. After shelling the retiring commandoes, the 4.7's vacated Monte Christo in the afternoon, and crossed over Hlangwani during the darkness, down to "A" pontoon, whither they had been preceded by the *Tartar's* guns.

By nightfall, the main Colenso positions had been wrested and secured by Talbot-Coke's and Wynne's Brigades. For the third time the Tugela had been crossed in force. But the occupation had been severely opposed, some 150 casualties having occurred, including General Wynne, the Lancashire's brigadier, who was wounded.

From early dawn next day, troops and guns continuously crossed the river, the enemy vigorously shelling the pontoon, its exposed approaches and exits, during their transit across, but doing comparatively little damage. The two 4.7's took up protected positions in close proximity to the pontoon, and with the Hlangwani guns, shelled Terrace Hill, principally, besides engaging any guns which could be located. The *Tartar's* guns crossed early, and were soon hotly engaged, Lieutenant James having his horse killed. The Boer generals had apparently grasped the new situation created by the reversal of our tactics, and probably realising the enormous advantages their singular defence had given them over previous frontal attacks, were venturing upon a final effort to bar the British advance. They still had with them much artillery—at least three 40-pounders, a dozen 12- and 15-pounders, several guns of smaller calibre, besides many pom-poms and other automatic guns—which together commanded the whole arena into which the British had now descended.

By noon, the 22nd, five infantry brigades and several field batteries had crossed; the general advance commencing soon afterwards. The Lancashire Brigade, now under their third brigadier, General Kitchener (a brother of Lord Kitchener), supported by Lyttleton's Division, advanced northwards, primarily to capture a prominent hill that commanded the whole valley between Onderbrook Spruit and the southern spurs of Terrace Hill. Progress was slow, the fighting for the interposed *kopjes* being severe, as they offered ample cover from which our field batteries could neither oust the enemy, nor suppress their fire. Occasionally artillery fire has been a peculiarly indeterminate factor; this was an instance of a searching shelling at a definite object proving quite innocuous when good results were confidently expected. However, the gallant Lancashire lads pressed onwards, alternating between successes and reverses, until finally, at dusk, they secured a strong footing on the coveted position, though they found its retention very difficult to sustain.

When darkness enveloped the scene, the Boers made a vigorous counter attack. So close did they press the position, that bayonet chaises were resorted to to relieve the pressure. Our casualties amounted to over 300, while the enemy also lost heavily. That night the Lancashires were relieved by Hildyard's Brigade, augmented by half of Barton's, who strengthened the improvised breastworks, to prepare for whatever danger might threaten with dawn's appearance.

> But, even then, the men had to lie crouched on the hillsides, sheltered by hastily piled stones, with an active keen-sighted enemy within 150 yards of one flank and 500 yards of the other. During the day the front line could scarcely move, for anyone who exposed himself was shot They were under constant fire, both rifle and artillery, both night and day, and they were three times heavily attacked; but for five days and nights they unflinchingly maintained this position. It was wonderful.

Thus General Buller describes their unenviable situation.

Early on the 23rd, the 4.7 guns, Melville's 12-pounder unit, and the 5-inch guns, crossed the pontoon, to occupy positions among the *kopjes* closely in rear of the field and howitzer batteries—then heavily engaged. Melville's guns were placed on a high *kopje* on the left of the 4.7's, the *Tartar's* guns being in action near by on the right. No sooner were the guns unavoidably disclosed to the enemy than they attracted a heavy shelling.

> During the whole day the enemy shelled very vigorously, and it is beyond my comprehension how so small an amount of damage was done, as they were shooting with great accuracy.

A dozen shells, mostly 40-pounders, fell within a radius of 20 yards round the 4.7-inch guns, and a great many passed over, while others fell a very little short.

I took the big glass up to the 12-pounders which were engaging on Grobler's side, to try to discover guns, and there I think it was even warmer, for we had a 'pom-pom' on us as well as two or three big guns. It was here that my coxswain, Thomas Tunbridge, who was sitting down on a stone, was struck by a shell, which tore away half his thigh. Fortunately the shell did not burst, as there was a little knot round the glass where an officer was pointing out the position of a gun to me. Only four men were wounded all day by shell, and one shot by a rifle bullet in the evening.

So soon as it was dark the enemy began to snipe our hills pretty freely; in fact, about nine o'clock it amounted to a considerable fire. We got the men under cover, and no damage was done. The firing continued till daylight.

These few lines, culled from Captain Jones's despatch, most aptly describe the situation at the naval guns. Seamen Weippart and Helman, and two naval volunteers, were the other wounded referred to, but Tunbridge and Helman only were taken to the field hospital as serious cases; the other three continuing to perform their duty after being dressed. Besides our own men, one of the gun escort was killed and nine wounded during the time the guns were at this position

Miraculous and hairbreadth escapes were of frequent occurrence, Midshipman Hutchinson, especially, receiving close attention from shells, for no less than three pitched and burst quite close to him, leaving him unscathed each time. Many times, too, the guns' crews were enveloped in debris when shells exploded on the ground in their front, but they were saved from severer losses by the earth-bag redoubts erected in front of the guns. Fire and dip, dip and fire, was often the method by which the guns were kept in action, directed by Commander Limpus, who sedulously searched for hostile guns, which, when found, were either driven away or silenced.

Shortly before noon, the *Tartars* and *Melville's* guns were withdrawn, and sent forward to assist the attack planned against Terrace Hill, where the defence proper was first to be bored into. This desperately perilous attack was entrusted to the gallant Irish Brigade, which moved off soon after noon. During their extremely difficult advance, the field batteries searched the broken ground ahead, while all the heavy and naval guns bombarded the main objective—Terrace Hill. Concerning this sanguinary assault, General Buller's own version (Desp., March 14th, 1900) seems the most consistent narrative to offer the reader. He states—

> It had been my intention that this attack should be made by five battalions, but the advance up the railway was necessarily slow, and, in some places, the enemy brought a heavy fire upon it, both rifle and Maxim-Nordenfelt, causing many casualties and checking the advance considerably. It was getting late, and General Hart attacked the hill when two battalions only were up, thinking his supports would follow. For the reason I have mentioned, the supports arrived but slowly, and the attack was made by two battalions, supported by a half battalion only—the Royal Inniskilling Fusiliers, the Connaught Rangers, and half the Royal Dublin Fusiliers.
>
> The attack was delivered with the utmost gallantry, but the men failed to reach the top of the hill. The regiments suffered severely, but their loss was not unproductive; their gallantry secured for us the lower *sangars* and a position at the foot of the hill, which ensured our ultimate success.

Two colonels, three majors, 28 other officers, and about 550 rank and file were Ireland's tribute this day to the flag—a tribute of blood which should ever haunt the consciences of those so-called representatives of the ancient Irish nation, who insensately cheered British reverses from their seats at Westminster. The ambulance corps collected as many wounded as the darkness permitted, but this humane work was abruptly stopped at daylight, as the Boers then renewed the battle, actually firing among the stretcher-bearers, which act, it is but fair to add, was the result of a misunderstanding. A large number were therefore reluctantly left on the hillside—indefinitely. During the night two fierce counter attacks were repulsed, the bayonet again proving its value at close quarters.

Yesterday's bloody encounter incontrovertibly indicated that no spirited rearguard action was being fought, but that the enemy were present in strong force, both in men and guns. Reinforcements from the Ladysmith investing force had undoubtedly replaced those Commandoes which had been observed trekking north. Thus, to pursue further with frontal tactics would obviously be to purchase success at a needlessly extravagant cost. The general, therefore, reverted to the original outflanking policy, and preparations for crossing the Tugela, further down stream, opposite the Boer left, were immediately commenced. Throughout the 24th a fierce artillery contest was waged, but no infantry movement took place for the reasons specified. The 4.7's received less attention than yesterday; but the howitzer battery in their front lost one killed, six wounded, and three horses incapacitated from one shell alone.

Occasional attempts to dislodge Hart's troops were made, but the front was preserved intact. That evening certain troops and artillery commenced recrossing the pontoon. The 4.7's were moved down to the river after dark, ready for crossing next morning, after which they were placed on Hlangwani Hill alongside Ogilvy's battery. The 12-pounder units of James and Melville had already proceeded to Monte Christo to strengthen the right flank. Wilde's unit was withdrawn from Frere to Gun Hill, relieving Burne, whose guns were now in Colenso attached to Talbot-Coke's Brigade. Every available man and gun was being requisitioned for the supreme effort now in preparation.

From dawn on the 25th until 8 p.m. a mutual cessation of hostilities was agreed upon to bury the dead and remove the wounded; for since Hart's abortive assault against Terrace Hill—some 40 hours past—our wounded had lain out on its glacis between the contending forces. It had been impossible to succour them previously, for the enemy instantly fired at anyone incautiously exposing himself to do so. Surgeon Macmillan proceeded there to assist the army staff. He afterwards related that within a certain area the ground was literally covered with dead, dying, and wounded intermingled together, their sufferings greatly intensified through the enforced neglect and the exposure to a torrid sun.

A Boer commandant was present, who courteously afforded the ambulance staff every assistance by directing them to spots where wounded men had crawled to cover. Indicating Colonel Thackery of the Inniskillings, who, with his drawn sword firmly grasped in death, lay nearest the Boer trenches, he asked what his rank was, and to what regiment he belonged. On being informed, he uttered a sigh of compassionate admiration for the brave dead colonel. On the completion of the ambulance work, Surgeon Macmillan casually strolled towards the base of the hill, but was sharply recalled by the commandant, who said, "Some of those slouch-hatted —— men sitting up there would have put a bullet through you if you had gone much further." Though extremely courteous himself, he evidently mistrusted his undisciplined subordinates. During this time the Boers were observed disposing of their own dead near their trenches, having also lost heavily from shell fire. The day itself was one to be remembered in connection with the relief operations.

As no proper armistice existed, but only a mutual truce respected on both sides while the victims of war were receiving a soldier's last honours, the Boers were busily engaged strengthening their defences, and the British likewise completing their dispositions of troops and guns, soon to furnish more work for the doctors and duty for the chaplains. Telescopic observations testified that the retro-movements across the pontoon were causing much speculation among the enemy, who were intently viewing the proceedings, and indeed were also producing no little chagrin among our own forces, who understood not the why or wherefore, but regarded the proceedings as another portentous event. Where the positions were in sufficiently close proximity to admit of it, soldiers and *burghers* spent much of the day judiciously fraternizing. Truly such an episode provides a luminous illustration of how civilised troops can banish all *animus* when the din of battle is hushed—even temporarily. *Pax in bello* is indeed a truism.

The termination of the truce was abruptly signalised at 8 p.m. by a terrible fusillade of rifle and machine gun fire along the whole Boer front, which was promptly returned by our troops. For about fifteen minutes the valley presented a scene in striking contrast with the peaceful quietude of this Sunday. The enemy were apparently ascertaining by this stratagem in what manner the movements of the day had affected our dispositions. Evidently satisfying themselves our front lines were still strongly held, the firing as suddenly ceased and a tranquil night was enjoyed. Coincidently with this fitful resumption of hostilities, the bluejacket section of the balloonists, under a Royal Engineer officer, pillaged the Boer searchlight while the firing was at its highest. The "Aeronautical" party had rushed the apparatus and secured the principal fittings before the enemy discovered them. The nine men who performed this service belonged to the *Forte*.

On the 26th, spasmodic shelling and a venomous sniping rifle fire were indulged in by the enemy; Petty Officer Symons and a white driver of Ogilvy's battery receiving slight bullet wounds. The naval guns combined the double duty of replying to the Boer fire and that of range finding. Every hill, valley, located trench, and *sangar*, was named, and the range recorded in view of tomorrow's task. The

Hlangwani position was an admirable observation station, and here General Buller established his headquarters for controlling the operations; the powerful naval glasses proving invaluable for observing both British and Boer movements. By nightfall all dispositions of troops and guns had been nearly completed.

> Two 4.7-inch guns with platform mountings came across from Chieveley. We mounted one on a hill to the right of Hlangwani, just finishing by 5 a.m. I left the other till night, not wishing to do it in daylight, as we were only 2300 yards from the enemy's highest position on the range. It was very heavy and tiresome work in the dark, and the glimmer of a lantern to the front always produced some sniping.
>
> On this, as on every other occasion, Baldwin, the senior Gunnery Instructor of H.M.S. *Terrible,* showed himself to be an invaluable man
>
> During the night we mounted the other platform gun, finishing by 3 a.m.
>
> Sniping was worse than ever all night, when the Engineers rigged a sand bag defence for them. I remained with these two guns during the fighting on that great day, 27th, and not only saw every detail of the fight from relatively quite close to, but also the finest shooting from one of them that I have ever seen in my life.
>
> Once mounted and at the ranges at which they were required to fire, the platform has a great advantage over the wheeled mounting.
>
> Having once got the range, of course you can put as many shots in as you like, and as quick as you like. A man from the *Philomel*, Patrick Casham, was the captain of the gun, and a born shot.

Thus Captain Jones refers to the two 4.7's manned by the Natal Naval Volunteers under Lieutenant Anderton, N.N.V., whose second officer, Lieutenant Chiazzari, was now commanding a party of Bluejackets who were transporting troops and stores across the river near the destroyed railway bridges. Colenso was now the rail-head.

Tuesday, February 27th, 1900.—A decisive battle, which decided Ladysmith's fate, was fought and won today—MAJUBA DAY!

About 7 a.m., Barton's Brigade began crossing the new pontoon "B" bridge, and the artillery had commenced a searching cannonade, nearly 80 guns being employed, whose combined roar would have drowned a violent thunderstorm. Kitchener's and Norcott's Brigades followed Barton's across, together comprising the attacking force, which, under General Warren, was detailed to assault those three formidable hills constituting the enemy's main defence. Pieters Hill (the Boer left) was Barton's objective. Next came the middle position, termed Railway Hill, which was assigned to Kitchener. Lastly, Terrace Hill, the strongest position, was the point where Norcott's Brigade, supported by Hart's valorous Irish, would eventually decide the momentous issue depending upon these respective assaults. These triple hills were partially connected with each other by entrenchments and stone *sangers*.

The British front was about five miles long. Talbot-Coke's Brigade, with artillery, secured the left flank near Fort Wylie. Hildyard's Brigade held the central low *kopjes* facing Grobelar, and Hart's Brigade still clung to the southern spurs of Terrace Hill. These three brigades were virtually commanded by General Lyttleton. The extreme right rested on Monte Christo, now held by the 12-pounder units of Melville and James and two mountain guns, while between them and Hlangwani crest were distributed Dundunnald's mounted force, and several field batteries.

Barton's Brigade, supported by the enfilading fire of the guns on Monte Christo, and the Hlangwani batteries which shelled in advance of them, successfully ascended the steep wooded slopes of Pieters Hill, though on gaining the crest they met with a severe rifle fire from both their flanks. But Pieters Hill—the key of the Boer positions—was won, and gallantly held throughout By this time, about 2 p.m.. Kitchener's Brigade deployed to the right along the railway, to assault Railway Hill, while Norcott also prolonged his force on Kitchener's left, preparatory to moving against Terrace Hill directly the Lancashires' success was assured. At this juncture, the whole artillery, being cognizant of all ranges, were vigorously bombarding the two hills, the trenches, and the *sangars* connecting them. From the Grobelar Range several Boer guns were retaliating, plying their shell dangerously among the brigades holding the central *kopjes*.

The 6-inch on Gun Hill did much to subdue their fire and clear the wooded slopes from snipers, but the 4.7's were responsible for their ultimate silencing. One of these guns, at a range of 9000 yards, placed three shells in rapid succession into the embrasure of a Boer gun-redoubt, absolutely silencing the gun, a feat distinctly affirmed through the telescope.

RELIEF OF LADYSMITH—BOERS' LAST STAND.

Platform gun, 4.7, commanded by Lieutenant Anderton, Natal Naval Volunteers, at the Battle of Pieters Hill

Resonant British cheers were just now reaching Hlangwani, and the general, who well understood their significant import, could not suppress his pleasure at the welcome sounds—sounds which seemed to augur approaching victory. Cronje's surrender to Lord Roberts at Paardeberg had been opportunely imparted to the attacking brigades, and this vociferous cheering had greeted the welcome tidings, which certainly imparted fresh inspiring force to their already insatiable desire to attack.

But desperate fighting was still ahead. Presently staff officers, mounted orderlies, and signallers were to be seen urgently executing rapidly given instructions. It had been noticed that Kitchener's advance had received a check. It appears that, in their eagerness to render the half-won battle a complete victory, the Lancashires had mistaken their objective—Railway Hill—and had moved across the open glacis towards Terrace Hill instead. A heavy fire from both hills and the numerous trenches had—perhaps luckily—stopped their advance. This *contretemps* produced some anxiety, for Barton was still in isolation on Pieters, his position there being somewhat insecure until each of the triple hills was won. Kitchener quickly corrected the tactical, but pardonable, error of his subordinate leaders. Meanwhile every gun that could bear was thundering away to its utmost capacity; a deadly storm of shrapnel, common, and lyddite shells was causing a volcanic commotion in and about the Boer trenches, and crashing along the crest-lines of the hills. Even then, not a few of those brave, tenacious, high-spirited Boers kept up an intermittent fire, their figures plainly visible dodging the shells.

About 5 p.m. Kitchener's skilful generalship had secured Railway Hill at the bayonet point. Flushed with success, the Lancashires, without hesitation, pressed onwards towards Terrace Hill, clearing the interposed trenches on their way, and finding time amidst the tumult of battle to cheer Norcott's men, who had timely arrived on their left Complying with instructions, all artillery now ceased firing at Terrace Hill, except the naval guns on Hlangwani crest—the two mobile 4.7's and Ogilvy's four 12-pounders. These guns continued to sweep the hillside and crest-line with common shell until the assaulting troops had climbed close to the breastworks, then fired over their heads, beyond the hill, to harass the Boer retreat which followed. There was no perceptible pause in the firing, hence no opportunity given the defenders to repel the assault. Loud and prolonged cheering, and helmets hoisted high on bayonets, announced the finale—victory at last!

Ladysmith relieved!!

The last few minutes preceding this grand result were minutes of extreme importance. Successful strategy and adroit tactics had paved the way for the delivery of the *coup de grâce*—that supreme effort which was to produce either a decisive victory or another disastrous repulse, and a few minutes would decide the issue—and Ladysmith's fate. No imagination could picture the scene just at this juncture of the battle—the most crucial and critical period of the whole fourteen days of continuous fighting. Near the six naval guns, which were firing with the utmost rapidity, stood General Buller and his staff, intently noting the effect of the shell fire, and anxiously watching the progress of the troops as they bravely ascended that formidably entrenched hill. As an example of the rapidity of fire attained on the extemporised mountings, one of Ogilvy's guns fired 190 rounds during the last fifty minutes of the fight, and the other guns also fired at a rate which would favourably compare with the results obtained on the most modern mountings.

The general was specially desirous of seeing the breastworks impierced before the infantry reached the summit Commander Limpus, from within his "conning tower," was directing the 4.7 gun fire, which guns brought about the desired result, the breastworks in places being nearly levelled. Besides rapidity of fire, accuracy was absolutely essential, as a few yards low would have certainly produced fatal results, and loss of confidence, among our own troops. Through the din of the firing could be heard the orders which ensured the precision of fire. "England—up ten yards—left three," or, "Hunt—down five yards—right two," were samples of the orders addressed to the lieutenants of the 4.7's, and repeated by them to signify each order had been correctly understood. In a similar manner Lieutenant Ogilvy controlled the 12-pounder fire, receiving valuable assistance from Lieutenant Lees, the naval A.D.C., who "spotted" for these guns.

Often did the firing appear so extremely hazardous to our own troops as to evoke monitory expressions from the staff, who, however, were positively assured by Lees that the fire control was safely invested in such experienced hands. It is doubtful if any such combination of artillery and infantry attack was ever before witnessed anywhere— certainly not during the relief operations—but such action undoubtedly assured success. Of the services rendered this day by the naval guns, General Buller wrote (Desp., March 14th, 1900)—

"The fire of the naval guns here was particularly valuable, their shooting was admirable, and they were able to keep up fire with common shell long after the Royal Field Artillery were obliged to cease their shrapnel. Indeed, Lieutenant Ogilvy, H.M. Ship *Terrible,* kept up fire on the largest *sangars* till the infantry were within fifteen yards of them. His guns must have saved us many casualties. No one who watched the operations can have the slightest doubt that artillery, co-operating with infantry in an attack on a prepared position, ought to have a considerable proportion of common shell."

Daylight, the 28th, disclosed the fact that the enemy had evacuated the whole position during the night. Cavalry and artillery were pushed on towards Ladysmith, and that evening Lord Dundonald entered the town with the mounted colonials of his brigade. The loss of the Colenso positions had caused the Boer commandant-general to raise the siege, the invading army having hurriedly retreated north to the Biggarsberg Range. In such a state of inanition was Sir George White's force that only a feeble attempt could be offered by the Ladysmith garrison to harass the enemy's retreat. They could only be pursued by good mounted troops and light artillery; but even their powers of damaging such a mobile foe in so difficult a country would have been extremely limited. The total losses, from all causes, sustained during this fourteen days' continuous fighting amounted to 2098 officers and men. The grand total of casualties, etc, according to official figures, during the relief operations, from the action at Willow Grange to the battle of Pieters Hill, was 5405 of all ranks. The casualties among the Ladysmith garrison during the 112 days of investment amounted to 894 of all ranks, exclusive of the heavy mortality from disease, which was responsible for the deaths of 541 officers and men.

At noon, the 28th, the 4.7's crossed B pontoon and bivouacked between Railway and Terrace Hills for the night. These positions naturally received considerable attention, and indeed offered most palpable evidence of the brilliant contest which had produced such far-reaching results. Next day the relief army moved in to bivouac at Nelthorpe, where, a short distance away, the Klip River provided the means of performing much-needed ablutions. Ogilvy's battery and most of the other 12-pounder units effected a junction with the naval headquarters at this encampment.

On March 3rd, Sir Redvers Buller rode at the head of his victorious army into Ladysmith. The lately besieged troops lined the streets, and the civilian inhabitants thronged around the Town Hall, where Sir George White, his staff, and civic authorities had assembled officially to welcome the relief force. The cadaverous appearance of the garrison fully testified to the hardships they had borne with an exemplary fortitude and courage which elicited the sympathetic admiration of the whole Empire. Their physical endurance and fighting qualities, together with the persistent and brilliant efforts of the relieving army, had saved Ladysmith from falling into alien hands, and kept unsullied the Union Jack.

CHAPTER 13

Return of the "Terribles" To Durban

Special Army Order.
Ladysmith, March 3rd, 1900.
Soldiers of Natal,—The relief of Ladysmith unites two forces, both of which have during the last few months striven with conspicuous gallantry and splendid determination to maintain the honour of their queen and country.

The garrison of Ladysmith have during four months held their position against every attack with complete success, and endured many privations with admirable fortitude.

The relieving force has had to force its way through an unknown country, across an unfordable river, and over almost inaccessible heights, in the face of a fully prepared, well-armed, and tenacious enemy.

By the exhibition of the truest courage, the courage that bums steadily, as well as flashes brilliantly, it has accomplished its object and added a glorious page to the history of the British Empire.

Ladysmith has been held and is relieved; sailors and soldiers, colonials and home-bred, have done this, united by one desire, inspired by one patriotism.

The General Commanding congratulates both forces upon the martial qualities they have shown. He thanks them for their determined efforts, and he desires to offer his sincere sympathy to the relatives and friends of those good soldiers and gallant comrades who have fallen in the fight.

Redvers Buller, General.

This inspiring "Order" was supplemented by the following gra-

LADYSMITH—LOMBARD'S KOP IN THE DISTANCE

LADYSMITH—MOUNT BULWANA IN THE DISTANCE

cious message to General Buller from the Queen-Empress.

Hope General White and his force are fairly well. Trust you and your troops not too done up after your exertions. Pray express my deep appreciation to the Naval Brigade for the valuable services they have rendered with their guns. V.R.I.

The foregoing order and message were read out to the combined forces at special parades, as were also, to the naval contingents, the following appreciative telegrams from the Admiralty and Sir Harry Rawson, the Vice-Admiral commanding Channel Squadron, respectively.

1. The Lords Commissioners of the Admiralty express to the Naval and Marine officers and Bluejackets and Marines who have been engaged in the successful operations in Natal and Cape Colony the sense of their great admiration of the splendid manner in which they have upheld the traditions of the service and added to its reputation for resourcefulness, courage, and devotion.

2. Very hearty congratulations from officers and men of Channel Squadron to Naval Brigade.

With the relief of Ladysmith the primary mission of the Natal Naval Brigade had ended. The *Terrible* had been sent from England to relieve the *Powerful,* but that the relief should have been effected in such a dramatic manner, was beyond the limits of human imagination. The episode stands unique.

Immediately following the relief the commands of General's Buller and White were broken up. A portion were transferred to the western theatre of war under Lord Roberts; the remainder were reorganised into one force under Sir Redvers Buller, who was to continue the operations in Natal.

Respecting the Naval Brigade, the *Terrible's* and *Powerful's* contingents received orders to rejoin their ships; Captain Jones, with the sections of the *Forte, Philomel,* and *Tartar,* was to be attached to the reconstituted Natal Field Force, to man two 4.7's and four 12-pounders; the remaining naval guns were transferred to the Royal Artillery.

The following information may serve to interest those whom it will mostly concern. Numbers of officers and men landed from the *Terrible* in South Africa—

	Officers.	Men.
Marine Battalion, Stormberg Defence Force (nearly one-fourth of the force)	2	88
Naval Brigade, with Ladysmith Relief Column (about five-sixths of the brigade)	24	220
6-inch gun's crew, with Ladysmith Relief Column	2	53
Field guns' crews, Zululand contingent	2	50
Employed at Durban, Commandant's Staff, Town Guard, Transport Service, etc.	6	77
Total, on continuous service =	36	488

(Note.—The Durban Defence Force was comprised of the majority of the above officers and men.)

Numbers of guns landed in South Africa on Captain Scott's mountings were—

1 6-inch on mobile mounting.
8 4.7's   "   "   "
26 12-pounders (12 cwt.) on mobile mounting.
5 4.7's on platform mounting.
1 4.7 mounted on railway truck.

___

41 guns.

Two searchlights, with Scott's flasher attachments, were fitted on railway trucks.

Nearly 20,000 rounds of shell were despatched to the front for the naval guns, more than three-fourths of which were expended by the guns of the relief column, about 4000 by the 4.7's, and the remainder by the 12-pounders; the 6-inch, at the final operations, fired nearly 500. Gun-carriages were manufactured, gun trials carried out, and much arduous work of a continuous nature was performed by those employed at the Durban base.

During the brief stay in Ladysmith camp, full advantage was taken of the permission accorded to visit the town defences and Boer investment works; visits which were interesting and instructive to the brigade. The town itself appeared practically impervious to assault, so methodically and scientifically were the defences arranged and constructed; so that, assuming that the works could have been fully manned, and that supplies were not lacking, the town's safety could not have been jeopardised, even if assailed by the whole Boer strength of Natal The perimeter of the defence—about thirteen miles in extent—was very large indeed for so small a garrison to defend, yet could not have been reduced without imperilling the whole position. All honour is due to the general and force for preserving such a vast line of defence intact, even when stricken with famine and disease, against a vastly more numerous, better equipped, and well-supplied foe.

An inspection of the Boer works was of equal interest to those of the town. Everywhere was evidence of a sound and scientific knowledge of military matters; the disposition of the investing works offering little opportunity for the Ladysmith garrison to co-operate with the relieving army, or to force a way through (even if such a venture had ever been contemplated). A view of Nicholsons Nek could provoke nothing but sympathy for Carleton's unfortunate column. Unless the most cogent reasons demanded the utmost of resistance, surrender was the inevitable outcome of that luckless enterprise. The alternative was annihilation. The Boer gun positions naturally offered the greatest attraction to the gunnery men. They were indeed object lessons, which real war only seems to provide, especially those on 'Bulwana, where the guns and magazines enjoyed absolute immunity from hostile shell fire, except, perchance, from a lucky shot fired with a miraculous precision of aim.

Nevertheless, the Boer artillery, being kept at respectable distances by the long-range naval guns, had not produced much visible disaster, for the straggling-built township did not present the appearance of a place which had been heavily bombarded for some four months past. The Boers may be termed a nomadic and unmilitary people, but their works here, as elsewhere, were the products of the higher military skill, even though the strategical ability of the Boer generals was certainly in inverse ratio to the tactical mobility of the forces they commanded. The strategy they displayed, especially during the early period of the war, when the military and political situations were all in their favour, and the inexplicable inactivity of their forces at the Spion Kop withdrawal, and on the occasion of other reverses to our side, confirm this judgment. Yet they were no mean adversaries.

A brief account of the main incidents of the now historical Siege of Ladysmith is here given. On November 2nd, three days after the abortive action of Lombards Kop, the town was isolated from the outside world, General French and his staff escaping south in the last train—the general who subsequently rendered very signal service under Lord Roberts, and who relieved Kimberley. The next day the mounted forces attempted to prevent the enemy from closing too near the southern side of the town, but their effort proved fruitless. During this day the bombardment of the defences was very heavy, numerous shells also falling inside the town, particularly about the public buildings and churches, which were then being largely used as military hospitals. This dire visitation of war to their very homesteads naturally alarmed the civilian inhabitants, who besought General White to obtain permission for them to pass the enemy's lines and proceed to Southern Natal, which request, for obvious reasons, the Boers refused to accede to. Many now bemoaned their ill-luck in not having cleared away when opportunity afforded

Dr. Conan Doyle writes:

> One example of that historical luck was ever before their eyes in the shape of those invaluable naval guns which had arrived so dramatically at the very crisis of the fight, in time to check the monster on Pepworth Hill and to cover the retreat of the army. But for them the besieged must have lain impotent under the muzzles of the Creusots . . . when every hill, north and south and east and west, flashed and smoked, and the great 96-pound shells groaned and screamed over the town, it was to the long thin 4.7's, and to the hearty bearded men who worked them, that soldiers and townsfolk looked for help. These guns of Lambton's, supplemented by two old-fashioned 6.3 howitzers, manned by survivors from No. 10 Mountain Battery, did all that was possible to keep down the fire of the heavy Boer guns. If they could not save, they could at least hit back, and punishment is not so bad to bear when one is giving as well as receiving.

On November 5th, by special arrangement with the Boer commandant-general, the sick, wounded, and such of the civilian population as elected to go, were sent to a neutral position, termed Intombi Camp, about four miles outside the town. As a prolonged siege appeared inevitable, all the provisions in the town were requisitioned by the military authorities and systematically issued as part of the government rations. On the 7th, a vigorous shelling of the British positions took place, and a threatening movement was directed against Caesar's Camp, but beyond a long range rifle fire no actual attack occurred. At dawn on the 9th, the enemy's artillery opened forth as a sort of

4.7 GUN MOUNTED ON IMPROVED STEEL MOUNTING DESIGNED BY CAPTAIN PERCY SCOTT
Photo taken while gun was being actually fired at testing trial on Durban beach

prelude to another attempt to oust the British from the Caesar's Camp defences; the Boers, on this occasion, pressed the position more closely, but were held off without very great effort, and driven back.

To ascertain the enemy's strength to the westward, and attempt the capture of some convoys observed on trek in that direction, a strong cavalry reconnaissance was made on the 14th, but the enemy being found too strongly posted on the intermediate *kopjes* which must have been left in the rear, the movement altogether failed. That night the enemy bombarded the camps and town at midnight for a brief period; a practice which they indulged in for about a week, after which they ceased altogether with their nocturnal gunnery. Until the 20th little of import occurred, but on this date many casualties were caused from shell fire.

The next day one of the most regrettable incidents of the siege took place, the enemy on this occasion deliberately shelling the Town Hall, which building was then being used as an auxiliary to the neutral hospitals at Intombi Camp, the Red Cross flag flying upon its tower being visible evidence of the use to which it had been put. On the evening of the 23rd, an old engine was sent under full pressure of steam along the Harrismith line to try and wreck the only engine the enemy possessed on that branch to the Free State. But the astute enemy, expecting that such an attempt was likely to be made, had blown up a culvert near the town where the evil-intentioned engine came to grief. On the 27th, the Boers unmasked a 6-inch gun on Middle Hill, south of the town, about 4500 yards distant from Caesar's Camp. An extract from General White's despatch of March 23rd, 1900, seems *à propos* to insert just here.

> On November 28th, two 6.3-inch howitzers were sent to occupy emplacements which had been prepared for them on the reverse slope of Waggon Hill; a naval 12-pounder was also placed on Caesar's Camp. From this position they opened fire next day, and proved able to quite keep down the fire from the enemy's 6-inch gun on Middle Hill, which some days afterwards was withdrawn from that position. I arranged an attack on Rifleman's Ridge for the night of November 29th, but was compelled to abandon it, as just at sunset the enemy very strongly reinforced that portion of their line.
> There can, I think, be no doubt that my plan had been disclosed to them, and indeed throughout the siege I have been much

handicapped by the fact that every movement or preparation for movement which has taken place in Ladysmith, has been at once communicated to the Boers. The agents through whom news reached them, I have, unfortunately, failed to discover. I have sent away or locked up every person against whom reasonable grounds of suspicion could be alleged, but without effect. . . . On November 29th, also, we observed flashing signals on the clouds at night from Estcourt, and were able to read a portion of a message. At a later period of the siege no difficulty was experienced in reading such messages, but we were without means of replying in similar fashion.

On November 30th another 6-inch gun disclosed its presence from Gun Hill, about 7000 yards distant eastward from the town, and one of its shells entered the Town Hall, causing ten casualties. From this date the building was evacuated for hospital purposes, and its inmates were placed under canvas in a gorge where shell fire could scarcely penetrate.

Certain enterprises were planned and carried into effect on the night of December 7th. One of them, a sortie, was made with the object of destroying the 6-inch on Gun Hill. Six hundred men from the colonial regiments, and an explosive section, commanded by General Hunter, chief of the staffs sallied forth about 10 p.m. on their perilous mission, no one on starting, except the principal leaders, knowing whither they were bound or what was expected from them. Absolute secrecy was essential to ensure success. On arriving at the hill two-thirds of the force stayed at its base to support the movement, while the remainder scaled the hill-side in silence. When nearing the top the stormers were challenged by a suspicious Boer sentry, who, upon being answered in his own language, was content with the reply, but soon afterwards discovery of the plot took place and a heavy rifle fire ensued.

Too late, however! The explosive section rushing forward, placed the gun-cotton charge and ignited the fuse, when, after a few moments of intense suspense, the heavy gun was completely disabled. A 4.7 howitzer close by received similar treatment with the same result, and a Maxim gun was seized and carried off as a trophy of the successful venture. This brilliant exploit was performed at the small cost of eight wounded. Coincidently with the departure of the sortie force, three companies of the 1st Liverpools marched out and seized Limit

Hill, an enterprise which permitted a small cavalry force to penetrate some four miles northwards and destroy the enemy's telegraph wires, and also fire some of their encampments, without loss of any kind to our side. Early the next morning a strong cavalry force proceeded north again to reconnoitre, and, if possible, destroy the railway. The reconnaissance was successful, but the vigilance of the enemy prevented any demolition of the line.

The Rifle Brigade, having volunteered to destroy a 4.7 howitzer on Surprise Hill, north-west of the town, nearly 500 of that battalion, under Colonel Metcalfe, proceeded after dusk on the night of December 10th on what General White described as "an undertaking of very considerable risk." Skilful guidance took the force to within a few yards of the crest line before discovery occurred, the surprise being most complete, likewise the gun's destruction. While effecting the retirement the line of retreat was found barred by the exasperated enemy, who compelled the stormers to fight their way through to safety with the bayonet. Though success had rewarded the venture, the gallant Rifles lost in casualties about one-tenth of the number who went forth.

The inspiring feeling which these cheering episodes had created was soon to be marred by the dispiriting helio news received on December 16th, announcing General Bullet's reverse at Colenso. That *"hope deferred maketh the heart grow sick"* was bitterly realised by the disappointed garrison. The rapid increase in the number of sick, which had risen from 475 on November 30th to 1558 on December 31st, was, states General White, "a chief source of constant anxiety," as is easily understood, for each sick man was a unit lost to the defence.

The desperate assault on Ladysmith on January 6th having already been dealt with in a previous chapter, further description here would be superfluous, suffice it to say, that by the issue of that brilliant contest a crisis of immeasurable magnitude was averted. On the 8th a thanksgiving service was celebrated in commemoration of this invaluable victory to the British arms. From that date until the town was relieved on March 1st. To quote General White:

> The struggle became one against disease and starvation even more than against the enemy ... the supplies of drugs and suitable food for invalids being entirely insufficient for so many patients for so long a period. Even more important was the regulation and augmentation of the food supplies, as will be

realised from the simple statement that 21,000 mouths had to be fed for 120 days ... and that at the date of relief we still possessed resources capable of maintaining this great number on reduced rations for another 30 days.

The general's statement may be more fully appreciated when the fact is adduced that on November 30th only 70 days' rations were in stock for the garrison. Colonel Ward, C.B., was the military Moses who organised the system which supplied the multitude of oppressed warriors and townspeople with food. Towards the close of the siege the bill of fare became scanty and variable, every conceivable means of sustaining the defence to the last extremity being resorted to. Horseflesh was issued in various forms, such as meat joints, sausages, soup, and jelly; and those horses that were likely to die a natural death from exhaustion and weakness, following upon an insufficiency of food, were timely killed, and their flesh prepared into a reserve ration of "dried *biltong*."

Respecting the part taken by the navy in the defence, Sir George White wrote (Desp., March 23rd, 1900)—

> The Naval Brigade of H.M. Ship *Powerful,* under Captain the Honourable Hedworth Lambton, R.N., have rivalled the best of our troops in gallantry and endurance, and their long-range guns, though hampered by a most serious want of sufficient ammunition, have played a most prominent part in the defence, and have been most successful in keeping the enemy from bringing his guns to the ranges at which they would have been most efficient.

The amount of ammunition taken for the two 4.7's was 200 rounds each of lyddite, common, and shrapnel shells, with a corresponding supply of cartridges, and about 1150 rounds of assorted shell for the four 12-pounders. The casualties among the *Powerful*s during the siege included two officers and 25 men killed or died from wounds and disease. The gunnery officer. Lieutenant Egerton, lost his life on the first day of the siege. He was directing the fire of a 4.7 gun when a 6-inch shell from a Boer "Long Tom" entered the sand-bag redoubt and shattered both his legs. "This will put a stop to my cricket, I'm afraid," was all he said, after which he lit a cigarette, thus proving himself a born leader of his fellows. All his men idolised their "Gunnery Jack," and knew him for an officer and a gentleman, whose loss could never be made good to them.

When concluding his despatches (March 23rd, 1900) concerning the siege operations, Sir George White, after justly commending his forces for their respective quota of services, which will ever illuminate the pages of British military history, wrote as follows:—

> The civil inhabitants of Ladysmith, of all ages and both sexes have uncomplainingly borne the privations inseparable from a siege, and have endured the long-continued bombardment to which they have been exposed with a fortitude which does them honour.
>
> In conclusion, I trust I may be allowed to give expression to the deep sense of gratitude, felt not only by myself but by every soldier, sailor, and civilian who has been through the siege, to General Sir Redvers Buller and his gallant force, who, after such severe fighting, so many hardships, and notwithstanding very severe losses, have triumphantly carried out the relief of my beleaguered garrison.

Contrary to the general and hopeful anticipation that, with Kimberley and Ladysmith relieved, Cronje's army surrendered, and Blomfontein in British occupation by March 13th, the war would either end with the fall of Pretoria, or, in the meantime, collapse altogether, a bitterly protracted struggle was maintained for more than two years longer. The subjugation of the two republics taxed the utmost military resources of the nation, and demanded all the traditional fortitude and intrepidity of British troops during that lengthy period. In about five months, or by the end of March, 1900, over 166,000 troops left English ports for South Africa, exclusive of the Colonial contingents, troops drawn from India, and those forces already at the Cape when this war broke out. Few greater achievements have ever been successfully carried out than the transport of this enormous force, a feat the difficulties and importance of which have been well brought out by that distinguished historian, Captain Mahan,[1] U.S.N. He wrote—

> The transportation of the above immense body of soldiers, with all the equipment and supplies of war needed for a campaign, a distance of 6000 miles by sea, is an incident unprecedented, and in its success unsurpassed, in military history. The nature of the war, it is true, removed from the undertaking all military or naval risk; there was in it nothing corresponding to the anxious

---

1. Author of *Story of the War in South Africa*.

6-INCH GUN EXPERIMENTS ON DURBAN BEACH
Photo taken while gun was being actually fired

solicitude imposed upon the British generals, by the length of their thin railroad line and its exposure in numerous critical points to a mobile enemy. But as a triumph of organisation—of method, of system, and of sedulous competent attention to details—the performance has reflected the utmost credit not only on the Admiralty, to which, contrary to the rule of the United States, this matter is entrusted, and which is ultimately responsible both for the general system in force and for the results, but also upon the director of transports, Rear-Admiral Bouverie Clark,[2] to whose tenure of this office has fallen the weighty care of immediate supervision.

To success in so great an undertaking are needed both a good antecedent system and a good administrator; for administration under such exceptional conditions, precipitated also at the end by the rapid development of events, means not merely the steady running of a well-adjusted and well-oiled machine, but continual adaptation—flexibility and readiness as well as precision, the spirit as well as the letter. When a particular process has had so large a share in the general conduct of a war, a broad account of its greater details is indispensable to a complete history of the operations. The number and varied distribution, in place and in climate, of the Colonial or foreign posts occupied by the British Army at the present time, and the extensive character of its operations abroad, during war and peace, for two centuries have occasioned a gradual elaboration of regulation in the transport system, to which, by the necessity of frequent changes of troops, are added an extent and a continuity of practical experience that has no parallel in other nations.

These have vastly facilitated the unprecedented development demanded by the present war. A leaven of experimental familiarity, by previous personal contact with the various problems to be solved, suffices to permeate the very large lump of crude helplessness that may be unavoidably thrown upon the hands of regimental officers; and even where such personal experience has been wholly wanting to a particular ship's company, the minuteness of the regulations, if intelligently followed, gives a direction and precision to action, which will quickly result in the order and convenience essential to the crowded life afloat. Nowhere more than on board ship does man ever live face to

---

2. Received the honour of knighthood for his distinguished services.

face with the necessity of order and system, for there always the most has to be disposed in the least space.... When an embarkation is to take place, the position and arrangement of the ships at the docks, the number and regiments of men assigned to each, are arranged often many days before.

The system and manner are laid down by regulation, from the time the detachment leaves the post where it has been stationed until the ship is ready to cast off from the dock and go to sea. Each man takes with him in the car, from the starting-point, his sea kit and immediate personal equipment, from which he is not permitted to part until it is handed aboard for stowage in the precise place assigned to it in the vessel. The muskets, when carried by the men on the journey, are marked each with a label corresponding to the rack where it is to stand in the ship.

Upon arrival at the port, and during the operation of transferring, a naval officer is in charge so far as general direction on the dock and on board the ship is concerned, but without superseding the military ordering and management of the troops by their own officers. The same general arrangement continues at sea. That is, the discipline, routine, and supervision of the troops are in the hands of the military officers, as though in a garrison; but they can give no orders as to the management or movements of the ship to the sea captain who commands her.

On board, the mode of life is fixed by regulation—subject, of course, to the changes and interruptions inseparable from sea conditions. The hours for rising, for meals, for drills, for bed, and all the usual incidents of the common day are strictly prescribed..... The large number of seasoned sergeants and corporals, who had embarked and disembarked half a dozen times before, contributed immeasurably to the order and rapidity of the process in each shipload that went to make up the 166,000 that left England for South Africa.

But while so much falls naturally to the military element, and can best be discharged by them, because by their own self-helpfulness alone it can be carried out, the choice and equipment of ships, the entire preparation and internal arrangement of them, as well as the direction of their movements, coaling, etc., belong most fitly to the navy, for the simple reason that equipment and supervision of this character are merely a special phase of the general question of naval administration and management, and no specialty, in whatsoever profession, is so successfully practised as by a man who has a broad underlying knowledge of, and wide acquaintance with, the profession in its general aspect. To this unimpeachable generalisation the settled practice of the nation, whose experience in this matter transcends that of all others combined, gives incontrovertible support

A brief detail of the methods of the first departure, October 30th, 1899, will facilitate comprehension, and serve for all others. That day four transports lay at Southampton Docks, to take on board Major-General Hildyard, with the first brigade of the first division of the army to be commanded by Sir Redvers Buller. The trains ran down to the wharf near the ships, the troops remaining in them till the usual officers, alighting, had placed the markers to indicate the positions for each company. At the signal the companies fell in; the regiments in quarter column. The companies then advanced successively, forming in line abreast their ship, between two gangways—one forward and one aft—along each of which was stretched a chain of men, who thus sent on board, one set the rifles, the other the sea-kits and valises, which, passing from hand to hand, reached certainly, and without confusion, the spot where their owner knew to seek them. The company then moved off, clearing the ground for its successor, and was next divided into messes; which done, each mess, under charge of its own non-commissioned officer, went on board by a third gangway to the living or "troop" deck.

This unceasing, graduated process completed its results for the first ship by 2 p.m., when she cast off her lines and steamed out. The three others were then nearly ready, but were delayed a short space to receive a visit and inspection from the Commander-in-Chief of the Army, with a number of the distinguished higher staff-officers. Thus five thousand troops, who had slept inland the previous night, were before dark at sea on their way to South Africa. The same scene was repeated on the Saturday, Sunday, and Monday following. By the latter evening—October 23rd—21,672 men had sailed, the order for mobilization having been issued just a fortnight before. Of this number more than half were of the Army Reserve; men, that is, who had served their time, gone into civil life, and now rejoined the colours. . . . . In October, from the various ports of the United Kingdom, were despatched 28,763 officers and men; in November, 29,174; in December, 19,763; in January, 27,854.

In the short month of February the spur of the December disasters began to show its results, for then the figures rose to 33,591; in March, with which month my information ends, 27,348 went out The grand total, 166,277, may in its effects be summarised by saying that from October 20th to March 31st—162 days—an average of over one thousand men sailed daily from Great Britain or Ireland for the seat of war.

Some illustrations of the capacity of great ocean steamers for such service may also be interesting. Thus, the *Cymric* carried a brigade division of artillery, 18 guns, 36 waggons, 351 officers and men, 430 horses, with all the ammunition and impedimenta, besides a battalion of infantry; in all, nearly 1600 men. Another, the *Kildonan Castle*, took on an average 2700 officers and men on each of three voyages. The greatest number in any one trip was by the *Bavarian*—2893.

In effect, although embarkation was not wholly confined to the great shipping ports, the vast majority of the vessels sailed from Southampton, the Thames, and the Mersey. At each of these was stationed a captain on the active list of the navy, representing the Director of Transports at the Admiralty, and having under him a numerous staff of sea officers, engineers, and clerks, by whom the work of equipment, inspecting, and despatching was supervised. After sailing, the vigilant eye of the Transport Department still followed them by further provision of local officials at foreign and colonial ports, and by the network of submarine telegraphs, which has so singularly modified and centralised the operations of modern war.

From beginning to end of the war the number of troops despatched to South Africa reached nearly the enormous total of 400,000 men, who were transported, together with horses, guns, impedimenta, and other necessities of war, almost without incident or accident. Truly an undertaking, in magnitude, in conception and execution, which the Empire may contemplate with wholesome pride!

★★★★★★

On March 11th, the *Terrible'*s contingent left Ladysmith by special train for Durban, whither the *Powerfuls*, who were *en route* for Simonstown—homeward bound—had proceeded four days previously. General Sir Redvers Buller, his staff, and several distinguished officers of the relief column were present at the station to bid farewell; a high compliment much appreciated by the Terribles. "Goodbye, Terribles, and good luck to you all—hope you will have a pleasant commission in China," was the general's valediction as the train slowly steamed away, which received responsive British cheers, three times three, for the distinguished commander-in-chief who will ever retain the most profound respect and sincere admiration of his *Terrible* naval brigade. For Captain Jones, also, under whose command the contingent had found campaigning the most pleasurable of service, lusty cheers were spontaneously given. His genial personality at all times, under every condition, and the cheeringly optimistic attitude he aptly displayed even when the darkest clouds of military misfortune overhung the relief column, were just the qualities to make him a popular leader.

Early on the 12th, after some eighteen hours' passage on a much-congested line, the train steamed into Durban, and during the forenoon the Zululand contingent, which had also been recalled, arrived back from their bloodless but adventurous mission. A special mark of favour from this notoriously hospitable town was awaiting the combined contingents, for the townspeople had prepared a noonday banquet, which was well calculated to leave upon men fresh from campaigning fare a pleasant impression of the last few days spent in South Africa. On the 13th nearly the whole of the landing parties rejoined the ship, which had remained continuously in the roadstead off Durban, performing the duties of senior officer's ship under the command of Lieutenant Hughes-Onslow, the navigating officer. On the 27th, Captain Scott and his staff re-embarked. Colonel Morris, C.B., having relieved the captain as Commandant of Durban.

To conclude the narrative of events of Part 1, an extract from the speech (*Times*, June 6th, 1902) of Earl Spencer, delivered in the House of Lords on the "vote of thanks to the troops" at the expiration of the war, is here given as aptly ending the South African war history of H.M.S. *Terrible*. After delivering a well-merited panegyric upon the conduct of the military operations and the brilliant services rendered by the Army, British and Colonials, he said—

> Our thanks are due to all these forces. But I come to another force to whom I may perhaps be allowed to refer in somewhat partial terms—I mean the Royal Navy and the Marines. I say

I may refer to them in partial terms because I had the high honour, not many years ago, of presiding at the Board of Admiralty. Our thanks are specially due on this occasion to them, and I will recall some of the circumstances connected with the advent of the navy to South Africa.

When his Majesty's ship *Powerful* was returning home, nothing was known of what was going on in South Africa; but when the gallant captain who commanded her heard that war was declared, he at once put into port and placed himself at the disposal of the general commanding. He at once, although he had no orders from home, took action, which was no doubt highly appreciated at home. He proceeded to the Cape, and placed his forces at the disposal of the general commanding. His colleague, a very gallant officer, Captain Scott, of the *Terrible,* was also there, and he did very signal service by enabling the heavy guns of the navy—heavier, I believe, than any of those sent out with the army from England—to be put at once into the field.

The efforts of those two gallant men enabled a most powerful force to be added to the army, and in all the earlier battles that took place you will find prominent in action the sailors and marines. (*Cheers.*) With regard to Ladysmith, I would venture to say that the propitious and fortunate arrival there of Captain Lambton and the ship guns had an enormous and predominant effect on the possibility of resisting the great attack of the Boers on that place. The navy on that occasion proved, as they always have done, their valour, their desire to come to the front in war or whenever their services are required, and their power of adapting themselves to circumstances.

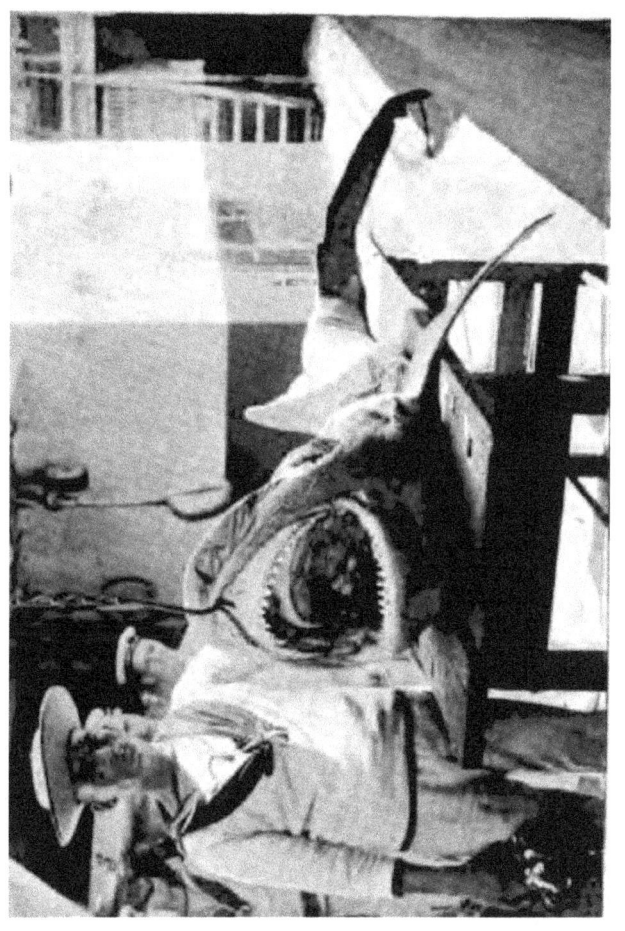

Monster shark caught at Durban by a "Terrible" angle

PART 2

CHAPTER 14

Colonial Appreciation of the Navy

March 27th to May 8th, 1900

The *Terrible* left Durban at noon March 27th for the China station, thus severing her connection with further history of the great Anglo-Boer War. The act of war had caused a certain shrinkage of the ship's complement. Commander Ogilvy (specially promoted to that rank for distinguished services in the field) and Engineer Roskruge had gone home, the latter invalided. Midshipmen Hodson and Boldero, and eighteen others, were left behind in hospital, and four men had died, all of whom had landed on active service.

Mauritius was reached at noon April 2nd. Next day the merchant ships in harbour "dressed ship" as a complimentary recognition of the war services rendered by the crew, and Captain Scott, when landing on an official visit to the governor, received quite an ovation from the large assemblage of colonists and natives. This favourable reception is worthy of note, because a considerable number of the inhabitants are well-educated descendants of former exiles of noble families and colonists of French extraction, and yet they, seemingly, had no inimical feeling concerning the war.

The island is picturesque in appearance, and thickly covered with tropical trees and vegetation, but it is situated within a cyclonic region, and subject to most devastating hurricanes between December and April One of these, in 1892, produced very dire results, and was responsible for some 1230 casualties. Mauritius was discovered by the Portuguese in 1505, was sparsely colonised by the Dutch from 1644 until 1712, when they abandoned the island. Thereupon the French established themselves there three years later, renaming it the Isle of France, when it became a prominent trade centre. During the Napoleonic wars between England and France the island was much used as a privateering base, from whence much damage was inflicted on British shipping.

It was eventually captured by a British force in 1810, since which time Mauritius has remained a colony of the Empire. Port Louis, the prettily situated capital, possesses an excellent harbour, to which is due much of the island's past greatness and present commercial value. Sugar production for export forms the chief source of employment for the population, which numbers about 400,000, two-thirds of whom are Indian subjects. The area of the island is 705 square miles, with minor dependencies attached thereto. After a visit of inspection from Governor Sir Charles Bruce, the ship sailed on the 8th inst for Colombo.

The seaport capital of Ceylon was entered at noon the 16th, a heat-wave of exceptional severity having been experienced during the passage. The roving Portuguese settled in Ceylon in 1507, but about 1650 they were ousted by the enterprising Dutch. In 1796 the British displaced the Dutch, took possession of their settlements, and annexed them to the Madras Presidency. In 1801 Ceylon was declared a Crown colony, and in 1815 the vassal King of Kandy was deposed and banished, and his kingdom in the interior was annexed to the colony. Here liberal leave was granted to officers and men, who took advantage of the privilege accorded of seeing the beauties of this paradise of the Indian Ocean.

In Colombo itself, a port of considerable importance, there is much of interest to occupy a passing visit, the public gardens, museum, and curio shops being well worthy a cursory view. The museum is contained in a splendid edifice, where much of the past and present history of this historical island may be gleaned from a studious ramble through the spacious rooms. Delightful drives may be taken in the vicinity through enchanting suburban and rural districts, where cocoa-nut plantations, cinnamon gardens, rice-fields, and other tropical products of the soil may be seen in a high state of cultivation, and a fair glimpse of Ceylonese village life may be obtained in its native picturesqueness. But a journey to Kandy by rail is the main attraction to most visitors, as the route passes through magnificently wild scenery, while the town's attractions, situated in a mountainous region comparatively cool and bracing, and in the middle of the tea-plantation district, offer a fair return for the time and money spent on the visit.

Here also charming and invigorating drives may be taken among the hill routes; one especially, termed the "Lady Horton," is worth traversing. The botanical gardens are among the finest and largest in the world, and through them it is necessary to drive if a full view of their wonderful extent is to be obtained. The Buddhist Temple in the town is a grand old structure of unusual historical interest to adherents of Buddhism, as it contains the famous shrine of ivory, precious metals, and stones, in which is deposited Buddha's tooth. The shrine, the ancient Sanscrit inscribed on the sacred palm-leaves, and the other interesting appanages of Buddhism are shown and explained to the visitor by the courteous yellow-garmented priesthood. One especially notable feature is the ghoulish pictures adorning the principal entrance, which pretend to portray the punishments inflicted hereafter on erring humanity for certain specific sins committed while in the flesh.

Still, each of them crudely depicts a scene which is not without a moral for the philosopher—not so common a character among seamen, since travel tends to capsize many of the conventional ideas on moral and spiritual subjects. There are other items of interest which lack of space forbids enumerating. The journey to Kandy occupies about four and a half hours; the fare, second class—good travel—is eight shillings return, and the various hotels are well appointed and the tariff very reasonable. Ceylon is about three-fourths in area, and in population nearly two-thirds the size of Ireland. The ancient Singhalese are largely predominant among the various races, the Europeans numbering nearly 10,000; and although the island is so near to the Equator, it is a salubrious and attractive place wherein to reside.

On April 22nd the ship sailed for Singapore. Early next morning a death occurred on board, the obsequies being performed in the evening—always an impressive ceremonial at sea. A brief account of how the final honours are accorded in the navy at sea may serve to interest those unfamiliar with the procedure. Directly after death has been certified by the surgeon, the body, after receiving the usual attention from the medical staff, is sewn up in a hammock by the sailmaker, then covered with the Union Jack and isolated, usually in a gun casemate, to await consignation. At the appointed time the ensign will be half-masted, the bell tolled, and the ship stopped. Just previously the crew are paraded, the firing party drawn up, all officers off duty assembled opposite the gangway where the last rites will be performed, and the ship's band stationed amidships.

Preceded by the chaplain, the body is slowly and reverently borne along the decks by former messmates of the deceased, followed by mourners—other messmates and representatives of his service rank—marching in unison to the strains of the "Dead March." On arrival at the gangway the body is placed on a grating, and the service is thereafter conducted in accordance with prescribed form for burial at sea. At the solemn words, "*We therefore commit his body to the deep*," the grating is canted overboard by the boatswain so that the body, weighted at the feet, may disappear unobserved, grating and flag being hauled up after the service is finished. A hymn, sung to band accompaniment by the crew, follows the Benediction, after which three volleys are fired, and salutes and "Last Post" sounded on the bugles.

Following the last bugle notes—the final honours—the band will play a lively march, while the divisions are being dispersed, and the most sombre ceremony observed upon the ocean is over. As soon after as convenient, the effects of the deceased (except private personal articles) are sold by public auction on board, and the proceeds therefrom credited to his account, to be disbursed by the Admiralty to the next-of-kin in due course. Should the deceased have left dependent relatives in indigent circumstances, the officers and men seldom fail to raise a subscription, the amount collected usually—though, unfortunately—depending largely upon the personality of the lost shipmate. *Requiescat in pace.*

The ship anchored in the Straits of Malacca, twenty miles from Singapore, at noon on the 27th to make preparations for carrying out heavy gun practice next day. The programme devised, was, however, cancelled, when the steamboat, on returning with the mails, brought the information that the civil and military authorities of Singapore had prepared a reception for the crew, and urgently requested the ship might proceed into harbour early on the morrow, as anticipated. Accordingly, targets were dismantled, and next forenoon the *Terrible* steamed into harbour, whence it was seen that the public and principal buildings were profusely adorned with flags and the streets gaily decorated. The next three days were entirely devoted to fulfilling a festive programme instead of firing. It was *en fête* routine—a pleasant *divertissement* indeed! Receptions and righteous revelling became daily indulgences.

But the principal event was the procession to the parade ground through streets densely packed with crowds of gaily bedizened and enthusiastic Orientals. A review was held before the governor, Sir J. A. Swettenham, and witnessed by a numerous company of European officials and residents, besides an innumerable throng of natives, the official ceremony being followed by a sumptuous banquet and theatricals. Almost needless to affirm that, after a lengthy existence on prehistoric salt sea rations, the dinner received ample justice, and the toast list was duly honoured, a pleasant duty which transported not a few to a temporary Elysium. The festivities were brought to an abrupt termination on the third day, owing to the death of seaman Gould from acute enteric contracted at the Cape. He was interred with full naval honours on shore, his funeral being attended by a large following of European and native sympathizers. The Reception Committee subsequently erected a handsome memorial tablet over his grave.

The Island of Singapore—the cardinal centre of the Straits Settlements—is about 26 miles long by 14 wide, containing an area, with the adjacent islets, of some 223 square miles, and a population of nearly 230,000. It was formally ceded to the British by the Sultan of Johore in 1824, but was actually acquired in 1819 by Sir Stamford Raffles, whose acumen in perceiving that to retain control of the ocean strategical and trade centres were needed, secured to the Empire this important place. It is extremely valuable in the capacities of a naval base and general coaling station, besides being among the greatest commercial emporiums of the world. It is said that nowhere is there to be seen such a mixture of the world's races as may be found here in the distinctive communities, each of which is engaged in a specific trade or calling, and intermingles with the rest only in keen trade enterprises. There are ample docks, wharfage, berthage, and necessary accommodation to meet the requirements of the enormous shipping trade which increases largely each year.

Though only 80 miles distant from the Equator, the climate is very salubrious, and Singapore is outside the cyclonic zone. The town, though not among model cities, makes a favourable impression, but offers few salient points of interest to the visitor—the botanical gardens at Tanglin, and the Raffles library and museum being the main show places. A visit of inspection from the governor signalised the conclusion of the stay, the ship leaving for Hong Kong on May 3rd, having received telegraphic instructions to arrive there on the afternoon of the 8th inst With strict punctuality the *Terrible* arrived at the "Gibraltarian" base of the China Squadron, and plunged once again into a whirlpool of festivities. The following is culled from the *Hong Kong Telegraph* reception pamphlet:—

The *Terrible* was signalled at 2.13 p.m., but, as she had been pre-

THE "TERRIBLE'S" NAVAL BRIGADE.
Reception at Singapore. Marching through the streets to be reviewed by the governor

viously ordered to reach her buoy at five o'clock, there was no need for haste, and the public had ample time to stroll on board the different craft provided, so as to be in time to meet the vessel as she entered the harbour and escort her to her buoy.

Hong Kong is renowned far and wide for its launches, and the crowd that went to greet the *Terrible* certainly did credit to the port, decked with flags as they were from stem to stern and containing all the beauty of the colony. The launches waited in two long lines on either side of the channel, extending from the line forming the harbour boundary to within a short distance of the Lyeemun Pass, and, as the *Terrible* entered between the two lines at about twenty minutes to five, deafening cheers were raised on all hands for Captain Scott, his officers and crew, accompanied by the waving of handkerchiefs, the tooting of whistles and the firing of crackers.

The *Terrible* steamed majestically ahead, and the two long lines of launches closed in and accompanied her to her buoy. At the Kowloon Dock the crew of H.M.S. *Orlando* were assembled on the dock head, and as the *Terrible* steamed by they raised a cheer which for the moment drowned even the tooting of the launches and the banging of the crackers. As she passed the various warships, the crews lined the rails and cheered, and the Terribles returned the compliment with interest. Then the salutes rang out, and the spectators in the launches were quite deafened by the reports, as the series of compliments customary *upon* the arrival of a new vessel on the station boomed out.

Soon after the ship had moored to the buoy an influential committee came on board to offer "an address of welcome." In presenting the document, Sir John Carrington, the Chief Justice of the Colony, said—

> Captain Scott, I have great pleasure in presenting you with this address, which, although in your name, yet of course is really addressed to all the officers and crew of this ship.
> The address reads as follows:—
> To Captain Percy Scott, R.N., C.B.,
> Captain of H.M.S. *Terrible*.
> Sir,—On behalf of the British Community of Hong Kong, we beg to offer to you and to your officers and to the crew of this magnificent vessel a very hearty welcome to this colony.

We congratulate you on the opportunity which was afforded to your ship by her appointment to this station in succession to H.M.S. *Powerful* of taking part with her in the operations in South Africa. How admirably this opportunity was used is known to all the world. We desire to acknowledge with the deepest gratitude, the devoted and invaluable services rendered to the Empire by the Naval Brigade in the advance towards Kimberley and in the defence and relief of Ladysmith. We are pleased to know that these services have been cordially recognised by the Queen and by the Empire, and in particular that Her Majesty has conferred upon you, sir, a Companionship of the Bath in recognition of that fortunate combination of scientific and practical ability in you, without which Ladysmith would have lacked her most effective weapons of defence. We learn that Her Majesty has just reviewed at Windsor the Naval Brigade from the *Powerful,* and we hope that the people of this colony will have an opportunity of witnessing a similar review of your ship's company on shore.

We agree with the late Mr. G. W. Steevens that '*the Royal Navy is salt of the sea and the salt of the earth also.*' We feel that we cannot do too much to show our appreciation of the navy, of the Naval Brigade, and of the services rendered by the *Terrible* in South Africa at a very critical period. In these circumstances we account it a great privilege to be able to extend this welcome to yourself, your officers, and crew, and to ask you to give us the pleasure of receiving you and them as guests at some entertainments which we have been arranging for your and their honour.

The address, after being read, was handed to Captain Scott, who, in a terse and pithy speech, accepted it on behalf of the Terribles.

The following afternoon the crew were reviewed on shore by Major-General Gascoigne, the acting-governor, the function being witnessed by a brilliant assemblage of naval, military, and colonial officials, besides a vast concourse of colonists and natives of this cosmopolitan colony. The review was followed by a banquet in *recherché* style, at which over 700 persons assembled in the City Hall to eat, drink, and be merry.

Among the many distinguished personages—colonial, military, and naval—who graced the festive board were Chief Justice Sir John

The "Terrible's" Naval Brigade being reviewed at Hong Kong by the Governor

Carrington, who presided, Major-General Gascoigne, and Commodore Powell, R.N., besides certain influential members of the colony and representatives from the American flagship *Baltimore*, whose presence bore witness to the fraternal relations which commonly exist between the British and American navies. The usual patriotic toasts were responded to with musical honours, and after the dinner stirring speeches *à propos* of the occasion were delivered by the gallant general and the Chief Justice. Of toasts, the one here given (reproduced from the *Hong Kong Telegraph*) may serve to amuse the reader.

A TERRIBLE TOAST.

The Terrible Toast
I have to propose
Of the Terrible s Terrible crew,
Who the Terrors of Hell, on the Terrible Veldt,
Spread to Boers and their allies too.

A Terrible lot are you, Terribles,
And a Terrible name you bear,
And a Terrible welcome well give to you.
When we think of your actions there.

You went to the front at a Terrible pace.
Took a Terrible four-inch gun.
Spread Terrible dead around the place.
Till the Boers were forced to run.

And Terrible shots we hear you made
O'er the Terrible Modder stream;
They were Terrible straight, so the Boers admit,
Who heard the shrapnel scream.

'Twas Terrible hard you Terribles worked
In that Terrible thirsty land.
And a Terrible harvest of death you brought.
Wherever you made a stand.

We'd have thought it Terrible, too, to see.
When a Terrible four-inch spoke.
The Terrible way the Boer collapsed.
In a smother of blood and smoke.

It wasn't superior force they feared.
But the Terrible, Terrible fire—
If what I relate isn't gospel truth,

I'm a Terrible handy liar.
We're Terrible proud of you, Terrible!
And Terrible glad are we
The crowd of you here to greet, my lads.
So, Terribles, here's to ye.
                    The Telegraph Terror.

A smoking concert, in the adjacent theatre, succeeded the repast, the conviviality being prolonged until midnight, when a memorable day of the commission all too prematurely ended.

On the 12th instant a successful gymkhana at the Happy Valley terminated four days of *fêtes* and functions in connection with the reception accorded the Terribles. The navy's service in South Africa had evoked unstinted appreciation, not only from those of British blood, but also from the Empire's colonial subjects of various castes, creeds, and colours, who apparently viewed the great war still proceeding as of vital Imperial import.

The welcome news of the relief of Mafeking, received on May 19th, was hailed with patriotic joy in the colony, and a telegram on the 23rd announcing the well-merited promotion of Commander Limpus to the rank of captain, gave extreme satisfaction in the ship.

The island of Hong Kong was ceded by the Chinese to the British Crown in 1841, but the cession was not finally ratified until the following year. It is a Crown Colony, about 11 miles long, from 2 to 5 miles wide, with a circumference of 27 miles in extent, consisting of a precipitous ridge of irregular shaped hills, formerly barren, but now with richly wooded slopes. Victoria Peak, the highest point, rises to over 1800 feet, and upon it, and in the vicinity of its summit, are erected many fine residential buildings and the military barracks. The aspect of the city of Victoria is impressive in the extreme, owing to the many public and commercial buildings, hotels, clubs, and banks, of imposing architecture which rise from the water side in terraced fashion to a height of nearly 500 feet on the sides of the peak. Viewed from the ships at night when lit up, the city offers a spectacle scarcely to be met with elsewhere.

Its institutions may fairly claim a rank creditable to any city, and its municipal "state and condition" would indeed be object lessons to the authorities of many British townships at home. Among its attractions must be reckoned an ascent up the peak by the cable tramway, but the first place is taken by the compact botanical gardens, which, with their aviaries, orchid houses, and ferneries, are grandly situated and justly command attention. In the far-famed Happy Valley are the racecourse, recreation grounds, and vast burial grounds of the respective communities, situated among sylvan scenery difficult to depict. The roads which intersect the colony are admirably made. Some constructed at a considerable height give access to the shady slopes which skirt the island, whence the view of Hong Kong harbour—among the finest in the world, having an area of ten square miles—with its diversified scenery and shipping presents an animated and imposing spectacle.

The various and mostly profitable industries of the colony are yearly increasing in importance. There is excellent and ample dock accommodation, where the largest ships can be received, and additional naval and private docks are being constructed on the island. The important peninsula of Kowloon, just across the harbour on the mainland, and the adjacent islands, are dependencies of Hong Kong. The modern town of Kowloon faces Victoria, and just beyond it the walled Chinese city stands alone in dirty dilapidation. At Kowloon also, important industries flourish; the extensive and well-equipped Kowloon docks offering every facility to trade. The population of the colony was over 283,000 in 1901, mostly Chinese; less than 10,000 being of European or other nationalities. The Chinese floating population numbered 40,100.

A convention, concluded in 1898, secured the hinterland behind Kowloon, termed the New Territory, which added an important stretch of country and another 102,000 Chinese subjects to Hong Kong. Its naval and military importance to the Empire is incalculable, as it affords an almost invulnerable base for the powerful China squadron; its snugly sheltered harbour being protected by powerfully constructed batteries and forts, which contain armament of the latest type. The climate was formerly notorious for its unhealthiness, but, owing to the careful attention given to afforestation and sanitation. Hong Kong is now as healthy as other places in the same latitude. Plagues and other endemic diseases of the East pay periodical visitations, but are scientifically and energetically coped with and soon got under. In 50 years of British rule an almost barren, rocky island has been transformed into a veritable Garden of Eden, a first-rate Imperial stronghold, and the greatest commercial emporium and shipping centre of the Far East.

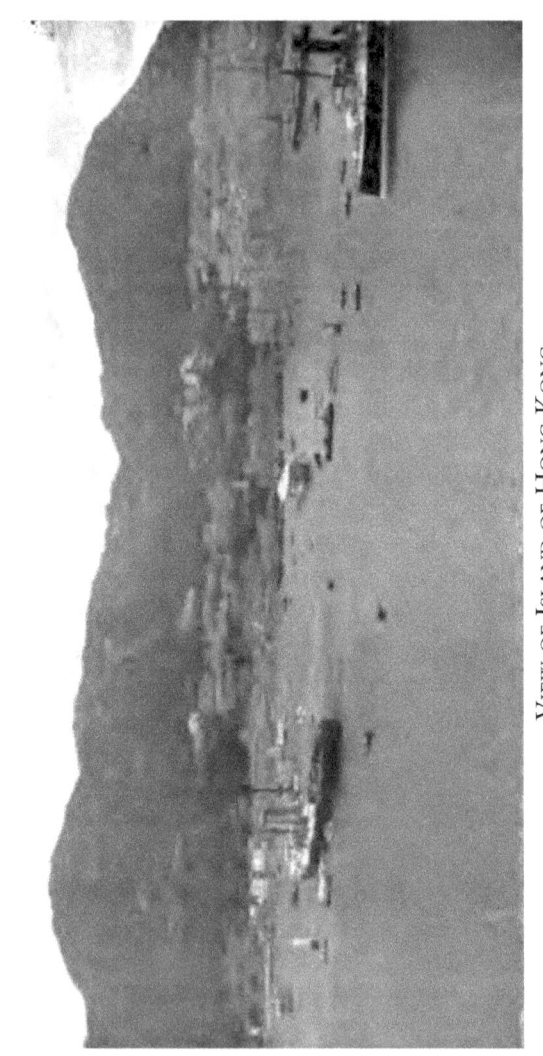

VIEW OF ISLAND OF HONG KONG

Victoria Peak is seen on the right, and the peak cable tramway is visible in the centre

CHAPTER 15

North China War

May 1st to June 17th, 1900

The Chinese Empire, so it is affirmed, is ruled by the most despotic form of government known in the history of nations. The reigning dynasty and principal officials are not Chinese, but Manchu Tartars, who govern the people with tyrannical laws, enforced by the sword of the executioner. China was obtained by conquest in the year 1213, and ruled by the Tartar invaders until 1366, when the usurping dynasty was overthrown by revolt, and the Chinese dynasty of Ming restored to the Celestial throne. In 1644 another successful invasion brought the Empire again under Tartar rule, under which it has remained ever since, the present Emperor of China, Kuang Sü, being the ninth sovereign of the Manchu dynasty of Ta-tsing. The two races are very dissimilar, physically and otherwise, and speak separate languages. The Tartars are described as being astute and treacherous, though possessing courage amounting to ferocity—inherent qualities of the Mongol tribes, all of which delight in atrocity and spoliation.

The Chinese, on the other hand, have tranquil, frugally industrious, and highly intellectual natures, but unprogressive ideas of government and national life; closely assimilating their mode of life to that which obtained with their forefathers. Much fabulous literature is published concerning China and other countries of the Far East. Nowhere do the traveller's preconceived ideas suffer a greater shock than in China. Instead of finding a land of exquisite enchantment, a picturesque people, and historical beauties, which for centuries have been lauded in poetry and depicted on porcelain, he views an eternal scene of national degradation. Beautiful bridges spanning healthy rivers, charming silvery lakes, gorgeously built mansions of mandarins, the love cottages and blissful bowery pathways, exist only in a fertile imagination.

Now for the bare reality. Rudely constructed bamboo trestle bridges cross turbid streams and rivers, slimy slush pools blot the landscape, gaudy-coloured barn-shaped residences with grotesque roofs represent the mansions, and filthy one-storied hovels house the indigent population. From the narrow undrained streets there constantly emanates a foul stench that would poison any other than a Chinese dog—the natural scavengers of China's polluted towns. Contiguous thereto, in the Foreign Concessions of the Treaty Ports, a state of civilization exists unsurpassed anywhere—a fact scarcely believable. The more glorious China's past may have been, the more signal has been her fall. To hold this prolific people in subjection to a hateful alien dynasty, Tartar officialism keeps them in ignorance and serfdom. The whole trend of their stultified education is especially adapted to ensure permanent hostility towards all reform, whether from within or without, it being the sole endeavour of impotent officialism to retain in every phase of Chinese national life the old morbid abhorrence of foreign contact Christian propaganda finds little favour with the Chinese, who bear a strong enmity towards a polemical Christianity whose teaching is in direct conflict with their more ancient and democratic Confucian religion. Native converts are regarded as criminals.

The Empire proper is divided into eighteen provinces, each governed by all-powerful governors, or viceroys. The principal dependencies are Manchuria and Mongolia, and Thibet is also a vassal State. The administration is conducted by seven boards of government—offices that correspond somewhat to those of western nations—each being supervised by a Minister of State, who together form the members of the Interior Council Chamber, or cabinet

The army is unreliably estimated at 800,000 troops; the Manchus, styled the Imperial Banner Corps, as being adherents of the reigning dynasty, form the major portion of it, and garrison nearly all the principal cities of the Empire. The navy, never powerful, is now insignificant, the French, in 1884, and the Japanese, in 1894-1895, having destroyed or captured the best ships. Their vessels are ill-found, indifferently manned, and, like the army, are wholly inefficient to withstand serious foreign attack, though possibly competent enough to enforce obedience internally.

The trade of China, however, is large, and capable of enormous, almost illimitable, expansion; that is if foreign capital and enterprise, national reforms and railways, be forcibly introduced. As nearly 70 *per cent* of the foreign trade is in British hands, as well as much administrative control, especially that of the customs, British interests are of paramount importance, and hence the object of Great Britain in assuming a prominent lead in suppressing the crisis of 1900. But proximity to China and Japan is affording rapid expansion to American trade, and seriously menacing British trade supremacy in the Far East, a situation much aggravated by the subsidised shipping services of Germany and France, which also threaten the home and European trading.

The purely commercial traveller (and sanitary inspector) has a wide field in China for his ingenuity, and will be the real pioneer of much needed secular reform among its dehumanised peoples. Enmeshed in a labyrinth of social and economic abuses, and existing between the narrow confines of poverty and famine, the Chinese ever look to an internal revolution for redemption. But their sublime ignorance afforded unscrupulous leaders the opportunity of diverting their attention from the true causes of their intolerable existence, and directing their rabid fury against foreigners, as the authors of the existent evils. Their intense patriotism is deeply wounded by continual foreign aggression and the seizure of some of their best ports, by the degradation of high officials at the demand of foreigners, and by the payment of extortionate indemnities, which together have accentuated that chronic hatred of the foreigner, which occasionally slumbers only to awake with a furious desire for vengeance. Therefore, an anti-foreign movement, now in a state of maturity, was an easy channel into which to pilot this periodical upheaval of the yellow race.

The Boxer sedition arose in the province of Shantung, the home of secret societies. The real name of the society was the *I-h-chüan*, or "Patriotic Harmony Fists," roughly rendered into English by the word "Boxers." These people had a ritual which was largely composed of gymnastic posturing; the initiated were said to be impervious to bullets; they could walk on sunbeams, arrest rivers, stop or create fires by their mere gesture. The society gathered to itself all the rascality of Shantung and the adjoining provinces, and its ambition was the extermination of the foreign missionaries and their converts, and of any other foreigners they came across. The new religion, which appealed to the ignorant peasantry, spread like wildfire, and when it assumed immense proportions, received the secret support of the officials, and of the empress-dowager herself The missionaries warned the ministers of the coming storm, and too late the fleets assembled at Taku.

A writer says:[1]

By this time the sedition was far beyond official control, and moreover, what did a Manchu official, who had never seen the sea, care for a naval demonstration? Their notion of a battleship is that of an exaggerated *sampan*. The Boxers swept up like a cyclone from Shantung, and gathered their strength at Paotingfu, the provincial capital of Chih-li. They began with railway destruction, making the business strictly compatible with the innate Chinese propensity for loot, and varying it with the murder of foreign missionaries and railway engineers.

In the neighbouring province of Shan-si the movement was taken under the direct auspices of U-hsien, the ex-governor of Shantung. This supreme villain asked some thirty-three Europeans, including many ladies and children, to his Yamen at Tai-yuan-fu for protection, and there and then let the Boxers loose on them to hack them to pieces with swords. He further supplemented this outrage on humanity by issuing most stringent orders throughout his province for the annihilation of all Christians, Europeans and Chinese alike. Next to the atrocity of Cawnpore in the Indian Mutiny, the story of the Shan-si massacre is the most appalling crime of the nineteenth century. The number of native Christians that have perished will now never be known, as the missions have lost their archives; pastors, members and premises have alike been exterminated.

A similar policy was followed by the Acting Viceroy of Chih-li at Paotingfu, and by some of the officials in Northern Honan, where, though many heartrending crimes and murders were committed, the story is mitigated by the fact that there were numerous escapes, and that many officials and gentry jeopardised their own lives in attempts to save the fugitives. The governors of Shantung and Shen-si especially distinguished themselves in their zeal for humanity. It was entirely due to their powerful protection of foreigners that the number of murders and outrages was restricted to its present figures—that is, to less than two hundred European lives; though there is still much doubt as to the fate of many Roman Catholic priests in remote districts. Sober estimates have been made that over 10,000 natives perished; most of these were Christians, or the kinsmen of

---

1. *Chronicle and Directory for China, Japan, etc.*, 1901. *Hong Kong Daily Press* Office.

Christians, but in vast numbers of cases greed and family feuds prompted the denouncing of pagans as Christians.

At the urgent request of the foreign ministers an international force of about 350 strong—nearly one-fourth being British Royal Marines—was despatched to Peking on May 31st to protect the Legations; another smaller force being sent to garrison the Tientsin Concession. Active foreign intervention was signalised by this act, which also precipitated the insurrectionary rising. The opportune arrival of the Legation guards proved the salvation of the foreign community in the capital, against whom the Boxers had matured a diabolical plot of massacre. A few days later railway communication was severed, outrages and murders of foreigners increased, and bodies of Boxers appeared in the vicinity of Tientsin. This last fact caused Intimate uneasiness, as a rumour had gained credence that the rebels intended repeating the appalling massacre of June, 1870. Reinforcements were therefore sent to Tientsin as a precautionary measure.

Anticipating serious trouble, some 25 foreign men-of-war assembled off Taku, Admiral Sir Edward Seymour being present in his flagship, *Centurion*, in company with seven other ships of his squadron. In consequence of the extreme gravity of the situation, greatly enhanced by the apathetic action of the Chinese Government, a conference of the allied commanders took place on June 9th, whereat it was determined to reopen access to the capital—by force if necessary. Later, during the day, a telegram from the British minister informed the admiral as follows—

> Situation extremely grave. Unless arrangements are made for immediate advance to Peking it will be too late.

That night, at 10.30 p.m., the flagship signalled—

> Have all landing-parties ready at short notice

And two hours later another signal to—

> Land all available men

—was flashed forth. The landing-parties were quickly sent into Taku to entrain for Tientsin, where, early next morning (10th), an international Naval Brigade had concentrated Prompt action being vital to success, the admiral left in the early forenoon with the vanguard of his command on his fateful expedition towards the capital, taking with him construction material and a line-repairing party. Later on two more trains followed in his wake with the bulk of the force, these closing on the admiral's train by nightfall, progress having been retarded because of much obstructive damage having occurred to the line. An incident of the despatch of the third train is worth recording. The viceroy, evidently anxious about his head's safety, issued orders to the railway authorities that no more trains were to depart for Peking without his sanction.

However, Captain Bayly (*Aurora*), now Commandant of Tientsin, determined otherwise, and forcibly procuring an engine with an armed guards he despatched the train in face of a strong mob opposition, whose feeble attempts to "rock" the line were frustrated by the firm action taken. This feeling against the allied authorities was displayed the next day when a fourth train containing French and Russians was being prepared for despatch, ending with exactly the same result—the train went. Early on the 11th, all the trains had reached Lofa Station, 30 miles distant.

The total number of the expeditionary force now with the admiral was 2066, of whom 915 were British, *viz*. 62 officers, 640 seamen, and 213 marines, under Flag-Captain Jellicoe and Major Johnstone. They had with them twelve guns—one 6-pounder Hotchkiss (Q.F.), three 9-pounder M.L., two Maxims, and six .45 Nordenfelts.

Proceeding further, Lang-Fang—halfway to Peking—was reached next day (12th), but not without a collision with the Boxers having taken place, in which the rebels were repulsed with severe losses. The railway was now found so seriously damaged that further advance was checked until extensive repairs could be effected. To minimize the destructive power of the Boxers, an advance guard of *Auroras* was sent to Anting, thirteen miles further ahead, to hold the station there. Meeting with opposition, which culminated in a determined attack whereby the rebels again lost severely, the detachment, getting short of ammunition, was compelled to rejoin the main body. A stronger party was then sent on the same mission, but they also were heavily attacked, and found the enemy too strong to risk isolation.

During the forenoon of the 14th a desperate attack on the trains took place, the Boxers rushing on the Allies with a fierce determination to overwhelm them. They were eventually repulsed with severe loss, but not until they had actually succeeded in charging close up to the trains. The assault having been made with surprising suddenness, the fight was a crucial test that the disciplinary cohesion of such a mixed force—a combination of eight nationalities—was very satisfac-

Admiral Sir Edward Hobart Seymour, G.C.B.
(First and Principal Naval A.D.C. to the King).
Admiral Commanding China Squadron
during North China War of 1900.

tory. The same day, the guard, left behind at Lofa station—some 60 men—were also fiercely attacked. A train with reinforcements was despatched to their assistance; but in the meantime the guard had successfully repelled the attack and routed the enemy. Some 200 Boxers were killed in both actions, and two small cannon captured, while the allies' losses were very slight

Meanwhile, the line was being prepared to continue the journey, the task being carried out under great difficulties. On the 16th, a train endeavoured to return to Tientsin to replenish supplies; but the track was found so badly damaged that it was forced to return to Lang-Fang. Reconnaissances next day established the fact that communication with Tientsin was effectually severed by rail, also that, with the resources available, no forward movement by the line was practicable. The admiral, now at Yang-tsun with one train of British and Americans, therefore decided to withdraw his command to that place to re-organise the expedition, preparatory to adopting the alternative river route, and sent messages for the other three trains to rejoin him.

At Lang-Fang another severe engagement took place in the afternoon (17th), the enemy suddenly attacking the two trains left there under Captain Von Usedom (Imperial German Navy). The assault was well devised, the trains being simultaneously attacked in their front and both flanks. The enemy were again repulsed with heavy loss; but when the allied force returned to the train, their assailants rallied and made another vigorous onslaught, and were a second time driven off leaving nearly 400 killed behind them. The fight cost the Allies six killed and 48 wounded. By nightfall of the 18th all the trains had safely returned to Yang-tsun.

Next day (19th) a conference of commanding officers considered the situation, now intensified by the hostile action of the Chinese Imperial troops, who had co-operated with their Boxer compatriots in the last fight, the captured Imperial Army banners being a sufficient verification. It was decided to desert the trains, abandon the present expedition, and retire on Tientsin by marching along the left bank of the Pei-ho River, the railway being hopelessly demolished. The wounded and necessary stores were placed in four captured *junks*, and a start was made the same afternoon. Early next forenoon (20th) the enemy commenced a harassing opposition to the retirement, rendering the march a slow movemen.t Each village along the line of route was found strongly occupied, and when rifle fire proved ineffectual in dislodging them, a cheering bayonet charge always produced the desired result Throughout this and the following day a stubborn resistance was met with, only some sixteen miles having been traversed in the two days.

Now near Peitsang, in which place the enemy were strongly posted with guns, and from whence they had not been dislodged by 6 p.m., the force was halted for a reconsideration of plans. A night march being resolved upon as the best tactical manoeuvre for outwitting the enemy and reaching Tientsin—still fifteen miles distant—the force moved off again shortly after midnight, all guns being placed in junks to expedite the movement. Secrecy being difficult to maintain, a galling rifle fire assailed them, at about 200 yards' range, from a village in the direct line of advance, and a shell from the opposite bank sunk the junk in which the guns were placed, the Maxims only being saved The British marines sprang forward and cleared the route with the bayonet, whereupon the march proceeded apace till near daybreak. About 4 a.m. (22nd), as the vanguard was marching past what proved to be the Imperial armoury, near Hsiku, on the opposite bank, a heavy rifle and shell fire was opened upon them at close range; but the guns, fortunately, having too much elevation, did little damage. Cover was immediately taken, and a heavy rifle fire directed on the enemy's semi-concealed guns, placing several of their crews *hors de combat*.

The desultoriness of the fire returned enabled storming parties to move out; 100 British seamen and marines moved up the riverbank, while a German detachment went down stream, both to cross the river and rush the position under the covering fire of the main force. Both movements met with great success. The crossing was unobserved, the positions were turned and the guns captured. The armoury grounds were then cleared of the enemy and occupied by the whole allied force. Later in the day a most determined but abortive attempt to recapture the place was made, the Chinese striving to carry it by assault covered by a bombardment from forts lower downstream. Their losses were very heavy, the Allies also suffering severely. In this fighting General Nieh's foreign-drilled troops took a prominent part. Couriers being still unable to reach Tientsin, a force of 100 British marines was despatched after dark to try and detour round the enemy; but the strong opposition met with made them reluctantly give up the attempt.

At dawn next morning (23rd) the enemy again heavily attacked the position, severe fighting ensuing until 8 a.m., when the enemy finally withdrew, severely repulsed. Several more casualties were also added to the Allies' list, the number of wounded now being 230. As the incapacitated wounded had to be carried from here on improvised stretchers, it was now next to impossible to reach Tientsin without assistance. But for the apt discovery of some fifteen tons of rice in the captured building, besides an immense quantity of warlike stores, guns, arms, and ammunition, the force would have been compelled to face the future with serious apprehension, as supplies of all descriptions were nearly exhausted. The guns were mounted, and the enemy bombarded with their own shell, while the armoury was placed in a defensive condition to await the much-hoped-for relief column. That night a native courier succeeded in getting through to Tientsin with a despatch.

On the 25th, early, a relief column arrived at Hsiku, and terminated the suspense and anxieties of a most hazardous expedition. Before dawn appeared next morning the combined forces were *en route* to Tientsin, arriving there at 9 a.m., the armoury, with its valuable contents, being blown up and destroyed.

The admiral (Despatch of June 27th, 1900) tersely sums up the cause of failure of his mission as follows:—

> The primary object of the expedition, *viz.* to reach Peking and succour the Foreign Legations, has failed. Success was only possible on the assumption that the Imperial troops, with whose government we were not at war, would at least be neutral; their turning their arms against us, and certainly conniving in the destruction of the railway (probably actually joining in it), made failure inevitable.
>
> For the undertakings of the expedition, for its conduct and its issue, I am responsible.
>
> The destruction of the valuable 'armoury,' near Hsiku, may be regarded as some object at least gained. . . .
>
> When the fact of the Chinese having beheaded anyone they got is considered, the conduct of such officers or men as risked themselves to such capture is to be praised far more than if against a civilised foe.

The British Naval Brigade lost 30 killed and 97 wounded, the total casualties for the whole force being 65 killed, 230 wounded.

Anent the expedition, the perilous position of the Peking foreign community, who were closely environed by a fanatical horde bent on massacre, had demanded urgent action. To have delayed the departure of the expedition, especially after the receipt of the supplicatory telegram from the capital, would have been a policy inconsistent with British traditions. Admiral Sir Edward Seymour courageously accepted a unique responsibility, and had personally led a venturesome enterprise in a manner characteristic of a chivalrous gentleman and British officer. The mission had failed, but the summons to duty had met with a ready response, and the expedition was but one more instance of how the navy meets those emergencies for which it exists.

During the period of the admiral's enforced isolation, highly important events had been enacted elsewhere in the sphere of trouble. To take them in their order of sequence appears the best method of dealing with them.

Following the departure of the expeditionary force on June 10th, the whole railway services became disorganised, owing to the provincial viceroy's perfidious action. Though ostensibly professing friendship for the Allies, and deprecating the action of the rebels, this paragon of Chinese officialdom was in reality the lurking spirit of mischief and intrigue. On one occasion he had the effrontery, knowing the fanatical state of the populace, to send his secretary to Captain Bayly requesting that 50 men might be sent for his personal protection. They were very properly refused, and an incisive answer to his request sent instead— his Excellency being referred *elsewhere* for protective guards!

The *Barfleur*, with RearAdmiral Bruce, arrived off Taku on the 11th, when 160 officers and men under Commander Beatty were sent from the ship to augment the Tientsin force. Next day the departure of many Chinese from their railway duties and foreign employers, besides the hurried transit by rail of a Chinese general with some 1000 troops that were abruptly detrained at Chun-hang-cheng, to proceed across country somewhere—probably to the Taku Forts—were ominous signs not to be neglected. The opportune arrival on the 13 th of a Russian force of about 1700 strong, including cavalry and four guns, brought up the garrison strength to 2700, including the Tientsin Volunteer Corp.

Early on the 14th Captain Burke (*Orlando*) arrived at Tientsin with a trainload of supplies for the admiral's column, intending to establish a base at Lofa Station. His train eventually reached Yang-tsun, but finding the line destroyed beyond that place he was obliged to return. Next day (15th) the Boxers displayed much wanton activity by firing several missions and houses in the native city, besides destroying telegraphic communications with Taku. Another attempt to take the supply train to Lofa failed, the line being more seriously damaged than the day before, and the woodwork of the bridges burnt; while the Boxers, with whom a brisk skirmish took place before returning, were met in force. That night the Roman Catholic Cathedral and other buildings in the native city were gutted with fire, and strong rumours of rebel attacks were rife among the foreign residents. Strict vigilance and strong defensive measures were adopted to prevent surprise attacks on the settlements, as Boxers were known to have closed on the city in considerable force.

Rumour became a fact during the moonlight hours of the 16th, the Boxers then attempting their first invasion of the settlements, and attacking the railway station; but at both places they were easily driven off with many losses. They, however, succeeded in firing several native houses in close proximity to the foreign quarter, presumably as necessary evidence of their much vaunted valour. The sudden disappearance on this day of all Chinese employees in every branch of industry and occupation, both at Tientsin and Taku, was inferentially a true indication of the coming storm. That night the armoured train, fitted with a searchlight for night patrol work, was shelled when approaching Tongku, and at once returned to Tientsin with news of the bombardment of the Taku Forts by the Allies—history repeating itself.

★★★★★★

Capture of the Taku Forts. Certain important facts becoming known to the senior commanders of the Allied Fleet, a conference was held early on June 16th to consider the situation, which was daily becoming more critical. The position now stood thus: Peking was entirely cut off; the whereabouts of Admiral Seymour's expedition was matter of grave uncertainty; Tientsin was threatened with isolation and exposed to serious danger; and the attempted blockading of the Pei-ho River by the laying of electrical mines at its entrance constituted a latent act of hostility. The result of the consultation was the despatch of an Ultimatum to the Chinese commandant of the forts, the purport of which was that all the forts were to be surrendered to the Allies by 2 a.m. on the 17th; non-compliance with such demand to be followed by their forcible occupation. Preparations for enforcing the mandate were accordingly made that afternoon by the despatch into Taku of 900 men from the fleet, 320 of whom were British, under Commander Cradock (*Alacrity*), for berthing on board the gunboats prior to occupying the forts.

It has since become a contentious question whether the Ultima-

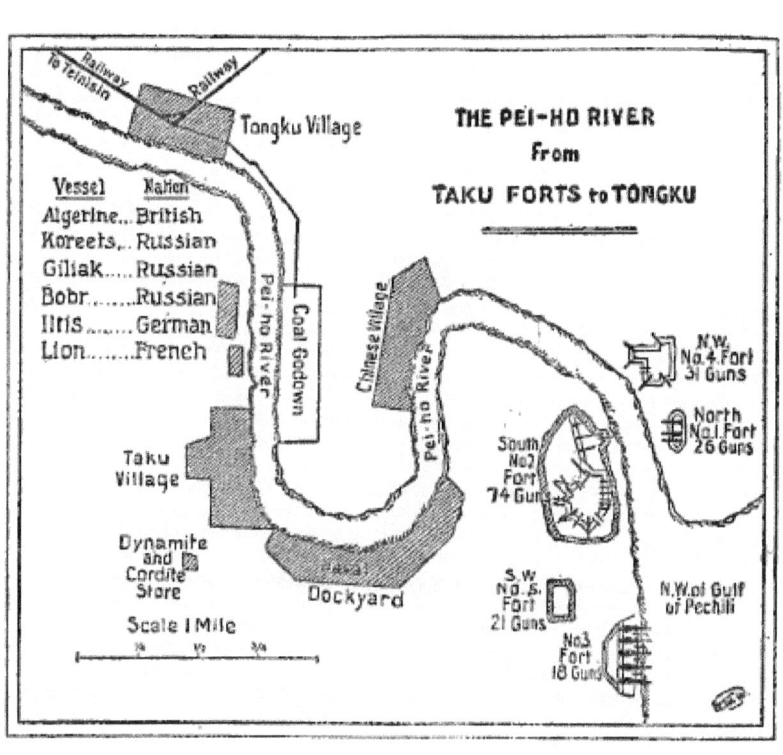

tum precipitated the crisis in Peking or not. Some authorities hold that it did, while others assert the contrary, affirming that the Chinese Government was already committed to the Boxer anti-foreign movement, and that the capture of the Taku Forts was the antidote which saved the extremely critical situation, and also impressed Chinese officialdom of the folly of their action. That the decision of the allied admirals was correct from the military point of view can scarcely be doubted.

The Taku Forts are situated on both sides of the entrance to the Pei-ho River, which waterway was the principal approach to Tientsin and Peking until the railway lessened its importance as a route. Two forts, termed the "North-west" and "North" Forts, are on the northern bank, and three, or the "South Forts," on the south side. They were formidably armed with numerous guns (170 in all), some of large calibre and of recent construction, these same forts having borne a prominent part in previous Chinese troubles with Great Britain.

In May, 1858, a British squadron under Sir Michael Seymour attacked and passed them, the famous Treaty of Tientsin being signed the following month. Again, in June, 1859, Admiral Sir James Hope was fatally unsuccessful when attacking them with gunboats; but in August the following year they fell before the combined assault of a British and French force, who afterwards made a victorious march to Peking. It may interest the reader to mention here that Admiral Sir Edward Seymour, commanding the China Squadron during these operations, was present as a midshipman in the *Calcutta* at the attack on these forts in 1858, and also served as a cadet in the old *Terrible* in the Black Sea throughout the Russian War.

As only vessels of shallow draught can cross the twelve-foot Taku Bar, the Allied Fleet lay moored off some twelve miles distant at sea, and therefore the ship's guns could take no active part against the forts. H.M.S. *Algerine* (Commander Stewart); H.M. Destroyers *Fame* (Lieutenant-Commander Keyes) and *Whiting* (Lieutenant-Commander Mackenzie); three Russians, one French, and one German, all gunboats, comprised the maritime strength of the Allies in the river upon whom the task of enforcing the ultimatum would devolve.[2] Captain Dobrovolski, Russian Navy, as senior officer, called a council-of-war

---

2. The American ship *Monocacy* took no active part in the battle as the ultimatum was not signed by the American admiral, and a Japanese gunboat, *Akaru*, was unable to do so because of disabled machinery. Many foreigners found refuge on the *Monocacy*, which, after receiving a shell through her bows, steamed out of range.

of commanding officers, at which a concerted plan of operations was arranged. The gunboats were to prepare the way with shell fire for the storming of the forts by the attacking column detailed for this object.

The Chinese replied to the mandate shortly after midnight (17th) by vigorously shelling those gunboats within range, which surreptitious act was the prelude to a fierce night battle. Fortunately the ships were "cleared for action" and ready for instant retaliation. The first shock fell upon the *Algerine* and Russian gunboats, then in their assigned stations, the French and German vessels joining their consorts soon afterwards. The position of the *Algerine* at this juncture—a small ship heavily engaged, with 320 extra men berthed about her decks, who had to be landed—will appeal to the naval reader as one demanding exceptional discrimination on the part of her commander, especially in the dark. That this body of men were all got off into boats, each man given a consumable ration of cocoa before leaving, and were at the appointed rendezvous on shore by 2.30 a.m., fit for fighting, is evidence sufficient that the embarkation was effected with marked coolness and promptitude.

For strategical reasons the two northern forts were selected as the first for attack, then the river was to be crossed and the South Forts captured after each had received an efficacious bombarding. Commander Cradock was chosen to command the shore operations of the Allies. The Russian ship *Giliak* was early unfortunate, having ill-luck throughout the action; one shell penetrated and burst near the stokehold, severing the main steam-pipes; another exploded the ammunition in one of the magazines, and within an hour she had been hulled below the water line. Yet with a loss of 8 killed and 47 wounded, and partially disabled, this ship gallantly fought what guns could be manned till the battle ended.

The *Fame* and *Whiting* weighed anchor as soon as the action commenced, and, acting on instructions, proceeded to capture four Chinese destroyers moored alongside the government dockyard. Steaming slowly towards their adversaries, each towing a whaler fully manned and armed, the British destroyers arrived unobserved abreast of their prey. The boats were then slipped, and were quietly pulled alongside to board, covered by the destroyers, which also closed in upon the Chinese vessels. When discovery occurred, the mystified celestials offered a feeble resistance, then bolted ashore, taking refuge in some outbuildings, from whence they opened up an erratic rifle fire. A few rounds of shell, followed by an armed attack, soon drove them off. The four captures were then unmoored and towed away beyond range of the forts' guns. It was whilst engaged in securing the prizes that the *Whiting* was struck by a 5-inch shell abreast of a coalbunker, which, though it failed to burst, caused much internal damage in the boiler-room, but happily none among the crew. A clever manoeuvre had realised an important capture, for had these hostile craft been manned by disciplined crews as resolute as their captors, they might have proved a source of immense danger and anxiety to the Allies.

Meantime the battle between the forts and ships had raged without cessation, the darkness favouring neither side. Towards 3 a.m. an advance towards the north-west fort was made by the storming-parties, but a reconnaissance proved that the fort had suffered so little from shell fire, no guns as yet having been silenced, that to press the attack meant exposing the force to a hazardous risk. A retirement to cover was, therefore, ordered until a better chance of success presented itself. This decision was communicated to the ships, whereupon the fort was again subjected to a rigorous shelling.

The Chinese had apparently reserved much of their energy until dawn appeared, for with its advent the ships were shelled with greater precision than heretofore. The Russian and German gunboats *Koreets* and *Iltis* received severe internal injuries, the former losing her gunnery officer killed, another lieutenant mortally wounded, and having a total of 31 casualties before the action ceased; while the *Iltis* had 20 casualties altogether, including one officer killed, and her gallant commander mortally wounded, both ships pluckily continuing in action throughout The *Algerine*, though struck several times, seemed impervious to other than slight damage and losses; the *Lion* (French), and the other Russian ship, the *Bobr*, being also extremely fortunate.

But for the fact that a large proportion of Chinese shells failed to explode, this miniature squadron might have found itself in a perilous position indeed. Even with badly fused shell, the complete destruction of the ships, with trained gunners behind the guns at such short ranges, would not have been a difficult feat to accomplish. Here were six gunboats engaged in an enterprise that, had the forts been properly manned, would have required the serious attention of at least a dozen modern battleships. But the tactical dispositions adopted and their excellent shooting, both in precision and distribution of fire, had prevailed against a wholly incapable enemy, possessing overwhelming means of destroying their fragile opponents.

By 4.30 a.m., the heavy guns of the north-west fort having been silenced, Commander Cradock led the Allies to the attack upon it The *Alacrity's*, *Endymion's*, and Russian contingents were leading, the *Barfleur's* remaining in rear of fighting line to reinforce it when the assault was launched, with the remainder of the Allies in close support. Observing the storming-party approach, the Chinese brought two field guns into action against them, but the tactical method of advance rendered their fire next to harmless. When about 300 yards off, the "advance at the double" was sounded. The gallant Japanese then doubled up from the nearest flank, and vied with the British as to which nation should gain the honour of first entering the fort. Both scaled the parapet together, the brave Japanese commander being killed at the moment of victory. The Chinese garrison then fled, declining further resistance to such an irrepressible assault. Two heavy guns of the fort were at once manned against the Southern Forts, which were then busily engaging the ships.

Attention was now directed to the North Fort, which was, however, occupied without resistance, being found deserted. Its guns were likewise directed against the active forts across the river.

About 5 a.m. the squadron weighed, with the exception of the *Giliak*, thus minimizing the risk of being hit, and engaging more closely the South Forts. The *Algerine* led the line down the river, having several narrow escapes of being hulled. About 6 o'clock the main magazine of No. 2 fort blew up with a tremendous explosion, only desultory firing issuing from there after the occurrence—a great relief, as this, the largest fort, contained 74 guns. There remained only the subjugation of the other two forts, which were still directing a heavy fire at the ships.

The storming-party, except the few guns' crews fighting the forts' guns, now re-embarked, and were towed across the river to carry them by assault. The Chinese garrisons saw in this movement a danger of being cut off from escape, so they, too, evacuated the forts and fled across country while the opportunity existed, their panic-stricken retreat being much harassed by a shelling from the very guns they had ignominiously deserted a few minutes before.

By 7 a.m. the national flags of five nations were floating above the captured forts, expressing the fact that victory was complete. The five forts were then occupied by the Allies, as arranged by a conference of commanding officers, and placed in a defensive condition, the British contingent occupying the North-west Fort. The total allied casualties in the ships and storming-parties together totalled 138, of whom only fourteen were British; the losses being insignificant in comparison to the magnitude of the task undertaken and successfully accomplished. The Chinese losses were heavy, 450 dead bodies being found in the forts.

Such was the fate of the famous Taku Forts, whose herculean power had miserably succumbed to a fleet, of comparatively pigmy dimensions.

CHAPTER 16

Story of the Six Days' Siege

From June 16th to 23rd, 1900

The *Terrible* left Hong Kong early on June 16th for Taku, with three companies of Royal Welsh Fusiliers and units of departmental corps on board, some 400 of all ranks. The previous day the Hong Kong regiment had sailed for the same destination, making a total of 950 troops *en route* for North China. These reinforcements were all that could be conveniently spared from the Chinese Colony, and sent in response to an urgent telegraphic requisition. During the passage north several ship's 12-pounder guns were mounted on extemporary field mountings—South African style, the guns' crews being detailed for landing on arrival if required.

The *Alacrity* was met off Chefoo on the 20th, and signalled brief particulars concerning current events. The position now stood thus: Following the capture of the Taku Forts the Tientsin Settlements became rigorously besieged; no news since the 13th had been received from Admiral Seymour's expeditionary force, nor could it be located; the dire situation in Peking was causing universal anxiety, its isolated position placing it beyond hope of near relief. Moreover, a considerable force of hostile Chinese Imperial troops, commanded by prominent princes and notable generals, was aiding the Boxer legions to resist the Allies.

A most critical situation was now in existence, rendered difficult of remedy by the inability to procure promptly sufficient reinforcements. Though the military resources of Japan were in available proximity, "political considerations" militated against their being too largely utilised, as each nation's interests and individual prestige demanded proportionate representation according to its degree of *locus standi* in

257

The "Terrible's" 12-pounders were again mounted on extemporary carriages in China, and landed for active service.

China. Peking's garrison must therefore wait, and depend upon its own power of resistance until the requirements of diplomacy were satisfied.

The redeeming feature, however, of the situation was the secure possession of the Taku Forts, whereby all future movements would be vastly facilitated. Besides which, the present neutral attitude of the influential General Yüan Shih-kai, viceroy of the neighbouring Shan-tung Province, who controlled many thousands of China's best troops, and also that of the other powerful provinces, was an important factor favouring an easy suppression of the rebellion—or war—when reinforcements should arrive. That the trouble did not spread further south was doubtless due to the powerful influence among his co-patriots of the Marquis Li Hung Chang, the greatest statesman of Chinese history, whose acumen and appreciative knowledge of the resources wherewith the Allies could mete out retribution, confined the crisis principally to the Imperial province of Chi-li.

So that no false impressions as to the intentions of the Allies should obtain credence among the Chinese, the following proclamation was promulgated:—

> The admirals and senior naval officers of the Allied Powers in China desire to make known to all viceroys and authorities of the coasts and rivers, cities and provinces of China, that they intend to use armed force only against Boxers and people who oppose them on their march to Peking for the rescue of their fellow-countrymen.

The *Terrible* arrived early on the 21st off Taku, where an imposing fleet of about 40 foreign men-of-war had now assembled. The previous night the following urgent message from the Consul at Tientsin had been brought by courier:—

> Reinforcements most urgently required. Casualties have been heavy. Supplies of ammunition insufficient. Machine-guns or field guns required. Beware ambuscade near Tientsin. Russians at railway station hard pressed. Chinese maintain incessant fire with large guns on European Concession, nearly all of which burnt.

The troops brought, and the field guns now ready for landing, had therefore opportunely arrived on the scene. The debarkation of the troops, who were urgently required to augment the Tientsin Relief

Column now preparing to advance, commenced at daylight By 8 a.m. they were *en route* for Taku. A strong Russian force and an American detachment had previously advanced with the object of breaking through the enemy's cordon, but were ambuscaded and repulsed with severe loss. After discharging the immense deck cargo of food supplies and war munitions into lighters, all available men and guns were prepared for an emergency landing order.

Early next morning (22nd) a signal to land 100 men and one 12-pounder was received, and by 7 a.m. this party, equally made up of Bluejackets and marines, was landed under Lieutenant Drummond. Captain Mullins, commanding marine detachment, Lieutenant Lawrie, R.M.L.I., Staff-Surgeon Andrews, Mr. Wright, gunner, and Midshipmen Sherrin and Dorling, were the other officers attached. Assistant-Paymaster Cullinan also landed for service as commissariat officer under Captain Sir George Warrender, who was commandant of the Taku district. Thus commenced the *Terrible's* active participation in the North China operations. Instructions were awaiting their arrival on shore for them to join the relief column then concentrating just beyond Ching-lang-chang under the Russian General Stessel, who had requisitioned all available men before starting for Tientsin.

Together with three companies of the Wei-hai-wei (Chinese) Regiment, and a troop of Russian Cossacks, the party entrained at Tongku at 4 p.m., railhead—only some twenty miles distant—not being reached until 11 p.m., in consequence of the "rocky" condition of the line. Here the party detrained and joined the British contingent under Commander Cradock, the relief column being under orders to start at daybreak. Rapidity being essential to success, the Bluejackets were chagrined to find that their gun could not proceed with the column, as no transport was available to carry ammunition.

At dawn (23rd) the relief force advanced, consisting of the following units: Russians, 1200; British, 550, *viz*. 300 Welsh Fusiliers, 150 Bluejackets, 100 marines, the latter forming two companies. No. 1, *Terrible,* Captain Mullins, No. 2, *Barfleur,* Lieutenant Lawrie; 30 Italians, who were attached for duty to the *Terrible's* company; and 150 American marines; total, about 1930, the whole under General Stessel. The column moved over a wide front on the northern side of the river, British on the left, Americans in the centre, Russians on the right. Nothing of any import occurred until Pei-yang Arsenal Creek was reached, when the Russians came under a hot fire, the Chinese also exploding some land mines, which, however, did no damage.

Landing of the "Terrible's" 12-pounder guns at Taku

The British and American contingents quickly crossed over the canal and advanced, extended in three lines, towards Tientsin, the *Terrible's* company guarding the rear of the column. The enemy were steadily driven back until near the settlements, when the Allies came under a heavy fire that caused several casualties. The Russians, supported by artillery, checked the Chinese attack on the right, which enabled the rest of the force to continue their advance, and eventually to cross over on a bridge of boats into the concessions. Thus was the relief of Tientsin effected, and by noon the city was in open communication with Taku.

The British losses were three killed, ten wounded, among the latter being Lieutenant Lawrie, slightly.

That afternoon Lieutenant Drummond's detached party, except the 12-pounder and its crew, left railhead camp for Tientsin, arriving there early next morning (24th), having marched along the railway track.

Sufficient transport having been procured for the ammunition, the gun also left at midday, in company with the Chinese regiment, a portion of whom were courteously lent by Colonel Bower to assist in dragging the gun and transport along the vile track. The settlements were reached at 9 p.m., the belated party arriving nearly dead-beat—but they were *there*. The British commandant, Captain Bayly, subsequently wrote of this journey and of the gun and crew thus:—

> The dragging of the gun during the last part of its journey here had been very trying, but its safe arrival was well worth the work. The 12-pounder was about the most welcome addition we could have had, as our 9-pounder gave away the position every round with its thick black smoke; its range was poor, and is about as heavy as the new 12-pounder, which is a most effective weapon, and the crew, fresh from South African experience, were thoroughly acquainted with its capabilities.

******

How the six days' siege was spent is now briefly related.

About the time the Allied flags were being hoisted above the captured Taku forts on June 17th, an armoured train with mixed detachments of Allies left Tientsin to reconnoitre towards Taku. Continual repairing of the line being necessary, progress was very slow. By 4 p.m. a large body of Chinese had assembled between the train and the city ostensibly to cut them off; but the train was reversed, and skirmished

The "Terrible's" contingent, under Lieutenant Drummond, waiting to entrain at Tongku to join the Tientsin Relief Force.

its way back to the station. Another train had also been sent in the opposite direction to disperse a crowd of rebel line-wreckers. Having driven them off, the train returned—so did the line-wreckers to their nefarious work, whereupon another train containing Russian infantry proceeded to the scene and again dispersed them, but a small detached party, sent to cut off some retreating Chinese, were, so it was reported, themselves overwhelmed and destroyed.

That afternoon an attack was planned against the Chinese military college, a large building containing war munitions and guns, situated across the river just opposite to and commanding the settlements. A force of 200 Allies, which included 50 British marines, was sent to effect its capture. As soon as the attack was launched, the first shells of the coming bombardment burst over the settlements. The college students, assisted by a number of Boxer compatriots and soldiers, made a determined stand, and for some time held the attack in check. After an entrance had been effected, a bayonet fight was carried on from room to room, the building being eventually captured in that fashion, when a sailor-marine climbed the roof and hauled down the Yellow Dragon ensign as a signal of victory. The college was then fired and its contents, except eight captured field guns, given to the flames. The Allies had but ten casualties, while the Chinese defenders lost 60 in killed alone. When darkness came on the enemy made a sort of demonstration at a safe distance, their position being easily located by the waving lanterns they carried and the tumult they created. At midnight tranquillity came with the moon's appearance, and so ended the first day of the siege.

With sunrise (18th) a bombardment of the concessions commenced in real earnest, the employment of artillery, which the Boxers did not possess, leaving no doubt that the Imperial troops had declared themselves definitely against the Allies. It was estimated that the enemy eventually brought at least 60 guns into action, 45 of which were in the city forts. On the Lutai Canal, about 3500 yards north of the railway station stood a battery of seven guns, and guns were also placed so that the Settlements were constantly exposed to irritating cross-fires, the Allies having nothing but "fifth of November" cannon to retaliate with! About 6 a.m. a train with 750 Russians, and a British 6-pounder and crew, left with the object of communicating with Ching-lang-chang.

For eight hours fighting and line repairing occupied most of the distance of the few miles traversed. Then the attempt was abandoned for want of more construction material, the train arriving back most opportunely to complete the defeat of the Chinese who had since 7 a.m. heavily engaged the Russians at the station. At 10 a.m. this position was so hard pressed that the Russian commander sent to inform Captain Bayly that unless reinforcements were quickly sent to his assistance the station would assuredly be lost. A company of *Orlandos* were immediately sent across the river, closely followed by three companies of Allies. From excellent and close cover the enemy were pouring in a heavy fusillade on its defenders, shells from the city forts and unseen field guns also constantly crashing into the buildings.

About noon, Commander Beatty arrived with a company of *Barfleurs* and a 9-pounder gun, that did excellent work in a position from which a Russian gun had just been withdrawn as untenable, after five of its crew had been shot in as many minutes. Still unable to subdue the severe rifle fire, an attack on their cover was determined upon, more reinforcements in the meantime having arrived on the scene. At 3 p.m. the British and Russians advanced direct upon the enemy's position, while the French and Japanese performed a flanking manoeuvre. For a brief time the Chinese clung doggedly to their cover, but were eventually driven out with the bayonet and utterly routed, the aforementioned train arriving at this juncture of the fight in time to inflict severe losses on the fleeing rabble.

The Allies had altogether 120 casualties, those of the British being four killed, 30 wounded. Besides the action at the station, several attempts were made to penetrate the settlements, each being easily repulsed. Nevertheless, the enemy were not found wanting in ignorant bravery, a fact which caused barricades to be erected across the several approaches as a preventive against rushes. The women and children were now quartered in the Gordon Hall for security.

With daylight (19th) the bombardment recommenced. To the eastward, across the river, two field guns were also brought into action against the Settlements with annoying effect. Lieutenant Wright (*Orlando*) being dangerously wounded in the head by a shell splinter while directing the 9-pounder fire from the Consulate roof. Thereafter Captain Bayly resolved upon their capture, directing Commander Beatty to lead three companies of Bluejackets on a surprise venture against them. They crossed the river, and manoeuvred to within 300 yards from the said guns, where they halted to await the development of a feint flank attack the Russians were now executing, after which it was intended to charge direct upon the guns.

But before the Russians could work round the position, a Chinese force had approached unobserved on the opposite flank, screened from view by the line embankment, and only disclosing their presence by a heavy fire, which wounded the commander, three other officers, and about twenty men. The surprise had therefore failed. To advance now through a galling enfilading rifle fire, and be also confronted with a shell fire from the guns themselves, was to court disaster or sacrifice many valuable men, so the party retired from a hazardous task. The hostile guns, too, were also withdrawn from their risky position. Desultory fighting had occurred at various other places around the Settlements, but the defence was preserved intact, notwithstanding the large perimeter to be maintained with such a small force.

That night a young English volunteer named Watts, accompanied by two Cossacks as escort, undertook the venturesome task of riding with important despatches to Taku, succeeding in his mission, for which gallant service he was subsequently rewarded with the decoration of "C.M.G." The previous day Captain Bayly had forwarded his despatches in a Customs steam-launch by a petty officer, and although the little craft came to grief through stranding in the mud, the party on board, deserting her, proceeded across country, and safely delivered the missives.

In consequence of the acute situation, a tentative proposal to evacuate Tientsin and establish a military base nearer Taku was put forward the same evening, but such an overture found no favour with the intrepid British commandant, who unhesitatingly affirmed his determination to await at all costs the relief column he knew would soon advance to their succour. Captain Bayly's prompt decision was characteristic of an officer who has very aptly been described by a war-correspondent as a:

> Bluff sailor, with a jest and a ringing laugh at the most anxious of moments, and a determination and vigour which carried his men irresistibly along with him.

On the 20th, sunrise and shelling announced the fourth day of the siege. During the day several clandestine attempts to pierce the allied lines took place, the enemy being repulsed at each point assailed. Severe refutations of the fallacy of Boxer invulnerableness against the bullets of the "foreign devils'" rifles were being vividly impressed upon them daily, but seemingly without effect "Want of genuine faith," was the reply given by the astute Boxer leaders to their sceptic compatriots

STREET IN FOREIGN CONCESSION OF TIENTSIN,
SHOWING EFFECT OF BOMBARDMENT.

when they shrunk from facing the music of the trigger.

Two Chinese, found with Boxer proclamations concealed upon them, were shot this day. Much misrepresentation resulted from this affair, certain eastern journals asserting that two native women were ruthlessly shot by the British, which, almost needless to affirm, was utter nonsense. If every belligerent treated women and children, whether hostile or friendly, coloured or white, in the same chivalrous manner as do the British, war would lose much of its horror.

Daylight, as usual, ushered in the routine bombarding of the settlements on the 21st About noon the wool mills, the roof of which was serving as an observation tower and signal station for the Allies, became the target for the Chinese gunners, whose good practice resulted in the premises being set on fire. By nightfall nothing except the bare walls remained as evidence of their former prosperous existence. Distant firing was heard in the evening from the north-west, presumably emanating from the admiral's column, then near Pietsang.

The gleams of a searchlight were observed early on the 22nd, which was the first sign of hope—or relief—vindicated to the besieged settlements. Later, a large body of troops was espied from the Gordon Hall tower approaching from Taku wards. These proved to be the Russian-American force aforementioned, that were pluckily trying to force their way through, but were driven back on Ching-langchang. During the enemy's indiscriminate shelling this day a large unexploded shell entered the hospital building, covering many of the wounded with debris, but otherwise doing no harm. A diversion was caused by the arrival of a native courier from Peking, bringing news, dated June 19th, that the ministers and all foreigners had been ordered to leave the capital within 24 hours, an ultimatum which was not, and could not be, complied with.

On the 23rd shelling and sniping announced the break of this the last day of the siege, for during the forenoon the head of the Relief Column marched into the settlements and ended the six days' siege of Tientsin.

CHAPTER 17

Fall of the Native City

From June 24th to July 14th, 1900

Communication with Taku had been restored, but the storm of fighting at Tientsin did not abate, but increased in violence, raging for yet another three weeks before the calm of tranquillity was secured by the fall of the native city. Many residents now seized the opportunity to send their families to the coast, a course they were wise to adopt.

With a force of about 4500 allied troops, offensive action now became possible within certain limits, the relief of the admiral's column being the first and foremost duty assigned to them. Accordingly, a composite force of 1900 men marched out at midnight to succour their comrades, then, as the reader is aware, anxiously awaiting assistance at Hsiku armoury. The force consisted of 1000 Russians and 900 of other nationalities, of whom 600 were British, *viz.* a naval brigade of 400 Bluejackets and marines under Commander Cradock and Major Luke—two companies of the brigade being Terribles, the seamen under Lieutenant Drummond, the marines under Captain Mullins—and two companies of the Welsh Fusiliers.

The whole force were commanded by Colonel Shirinsky, Russian Imperial Army, as senior officer. The respective units met at the appointed rendezvous and proceeded, led by a consulate guide, not direct towards their objective, but widely astray from it—as is the custom of most guides. Dispensing with the guide's stupid services—and he nearly so with his skin—the column reached the armoury early next morning (25th) with but trifling opposition, and, as previously related, relieved the admiral and the tension of suspense concerning the safety of his force, both columns returning to Tientsin next morning.

Early on the 25th, the bombardment of the settlements recom-

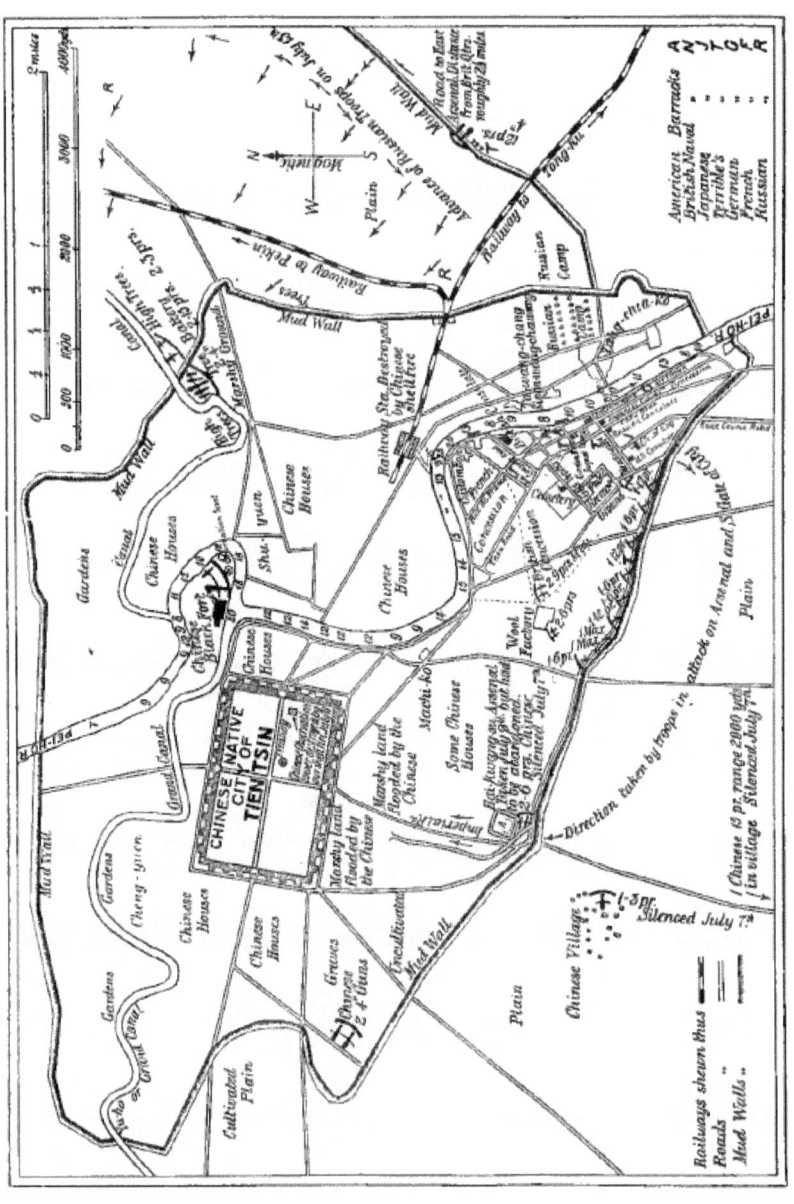

Plan of Tientsin, showing position of Allied armies

menced Suspecting that the western arsenal was full of war munitions, Captain Bayly decided to shell the buildings with the *Terrible's* 12-pounder, and so test its reputed merits. The gun was taken to the ruined wool mills, and got into action; a few well-directed rounds of shell soon starting fires that caused the partial destruction of the arsenal and its mischievous contents. As 12-pounder ammunition was not then too plentiful, the Chinese troops hovering around the burning buildings were consigned to a 6-pounder's attention, which gun thwarted all interference from the enemy. In the afternoon the 12-pounder was again in great activity; this time to shell the native city forts, which had hitherto enjoyed immunity from a retaliatory bombardment, a fact which had probably lulled the Chinese into a false sense of gun superiority. A few rounds at the Yamen Fort soon elicited a responsive fire from the Chinese guns. Concerning the result of this unequal combat the admiral wrote (Despatch, July 8th, 1900) as follows:—

On June 25th the *Terrible's* 12-pounder was placed in position, on the river bank, to shell the fort in the City which had been bombarding the settlement; the position of the gun (or guns) was not known, but by careful watching in the evening the flash was detected and the gun located. By directing the fire from the roof of some houses near, the direction and range was obtained, and after a few minutes the gun was silenced. This accounts for the return of the forces from Hsiku to Tientsin on the following day having been unmolested.

Captain Bayly, who had personally directed the firing, promptly congratulated Mr. Wright and his gun's crew on their scientific shooting; the line of sight being totally obscured. Consequently, after such results, Admiral Seymour sent for more of the *Terrible's* 12-pounder guns.

On the 26th, coincidently with the return of the admiral's column, Brigadier-General Dorward arrived from Wei-hai-wei to assume command of the British troops in North China. The united naval contingents were now reorganised into two forces, Captain Bayly being appointed Chief of Staff to Sir Edward Seymour (*vice* Captain Jellicoe, severely wounded), and to command the defence force, Captain Burke commanding the active field force of the Naval Brigade. The total number of all ranks of the navy now in Tientsin was about 1400. A general rest was observed today to recoup the Allies for the arduous marching, fighting, etc., which the respective forces had recently borne. To engross the enemy's attention, the 12-pounder was sent across the river to shell the Pei-yang (eastern) arsenal, and unmask the strength of its defence.

Early next day (27th) a Russian and German force attacked the arsenal, getting so heavily engaged that at 10 a.m. strong reinforcements were urgently requisitioned to assist them, as the position was found strongly occupied, and the enemy in a determined mood for fighting. With great promptitude a naval force, 700 strong, consisting of six companies of Bluejackets under Commander Cradock, and six companies of marines under Major Johnstone, and about 200 other Allies, were despatched across the river to support the hard-pressed Russo-German force. Meanwhile the 12-pounder was bombarding the place with excellent precision; every round finding some portion or other of the buildings. At 11 a.m. the main magazine was struck and exploded, debris and bursting shells being hurled with terrific violence upwards and outwards to inconceivable distances, while a huge column of smoke rapidly ascended into the clouds.

The effect of this explosion having subsided, the British support movement was converted into one of direct attack. An assault on the left face of the arsenal was decided upon, the Russo-German force undertaking the storming of the front and right sides. The British advanced parallel with their objective until the brigade and side of building had nearly assumed two lines of equal length, when they turned right, faced the position, and rapidly advanced to the attack. While crossing the flat open ground they were subjected to a severe flanking fusillade, and a harassing shrapnel fire from two guns near the left rear of the arsenal. Bayonets were fixed when some 250 yards distant, and a cheering charge was made, which cleared the enemy from that side of the buildings. They fled from its rear face across country, their rout being accelerated by the marine battalion, who, being on the left, were now nearest the fleeing enemy.

Similar success had crowned the assaults on the other sides, whereupon the arsenal was occupied by the allied forces. The Naval Brigade lost 7 killed, 21 wounded; the rapid movement and dashing charge saving the brigade a larger casualty list. In this fight Private Cooper, Bugler Carter, and Sergeant Roper were wounded, the sergeant being dangerously shot through the head, his subsequent recovery being a great tribute to the professional care and skill the wounded received.

This arsenal—the Woolwich of North China—contained much

valuable property, which included large factories equipped with modern machinery, many guns of various types, a considerable stock of ammunition, a proving ground, and a mint containing a large quantity of raw and coined silver. The British, having completed their mission, retired back to their quarters, receiving quite an ovation from their foreign comrades as a recognition of their timely services. The Russians removed much of the stores worth salving, then fired the buildings, and returned to their camp amid much rejoicing over their profitable victory. Meantime the city forts had made several fitful bombardments of the settlements, but little harm was done.

For a brief period next morning (28th) the Chinese tried to equalize somewhat for the previous day's severe physical and material losses by giving the settlements all their gun power, which brought the ubiquitous 12-pounder into action in reply. However, beyond the demolition of property, little damage was done to the Allies, though a sniping rifle fire was a daily annoyance; the admiral receiving a slight bullet wound, though he continued to do duty.

By piercing the Grand Canal the enemy contrived to flood the country near the western quarter of the native city; whether this act was intended for their own protection, or with a view of injuring the Allies, was not certain, for neither object was attained.

The arrival today of a native courier from Peking with a message, dated 8 a.m., June 24th—"Our case is desperate, come at once"—confirmed the worst fears that the situation in the capital was very critical. Three days later another message was received from Sir Robert Hart, stating—

> The Foreign Colony is besieged in the Legations. The situation is desperate. Make haste.

Which appears to have been sent as a duplicate or confirmatory message of the other. Though such urgent appeals elicited the sympathy of all, no advance to Peking was possible for the present, owing to lack of troops and transport Still, troops were daily arriving now—400 Germans, 800 Japanese, and 200 French troops having arrived by July 1st, while some thousands of Allies were at sea, *en route*. The Chinese had also received strong reinforcements within the last few days, which had been spent in comparative quietude. As, however, serious fighting was anticipated, orders were issued for the remainder of the women and children to leave the settlements as opportunities occurred; the sick and wounded being sent down to the ships by river route, as no trains were as yet able to run.

On July 1st a strong reconnaissance towards the native city was made by a British and Russian force, which proved that the enemy had gradually increased their artillery. Several lately mounted guns were unmasked by the movement, and many casualties occurred to the advanced Russians before the retirement took place. This was followed by a spirited attack by the Chinese on the station, which was repulsed by the station guards.

The next important item of interest occurred on the 3rd, when a shelling more vigorous than usual was directed on the settlements and station. The 12-pounder, with its marine escort, was ordered to the station to silence two guns then shelling the Russian guard from positions almost at right angles to each other. The guard were found in cover behind the platforms, sufficiently strong to prevent their position being rushed, but quite unable to subdue the heavy fusillade issuing from the burnt-out houses close by. As the gun could not be exposed without grave risk, it was taken back to a position on the French Bund, where it engaged the guns shelling the settlements, but with futile results, as the line of sight was wholly obscured by huge salt heaps. The enemy, however, got the precise range of the gun, one shell wounding A.B. Sherwin, while others of the crew had very narrow shaves.

Later, the situation at the station greatly changed, a battery of Japanese guns, supported by a strong force of their infantry, now being in action there, but sustaining numerous casualties before the Chinese rifle fire could be reduced. The 12-pounder was again ordered there to assist, a French gun taking the position vacated, but within a few minutes most of its crew were placed *hors de combat*. The heavier Chinese guns were eventually silenced, though a 3-pounder, which had kept up a venomous fire from the right flank, defied location. It had the range to a nicety, placing three shells in succession direct at the 12-pounder, two men being slightly hit. Just before dusk all the guns were withdrawn, an operation much retarded owing to two junks forming part of the temporary bridge being sunk by shell fire. Luckily Chinese snipers are not equal to Boer marksmen, for several were posted in cover along the bank a few hundred yards away, but only wounded one Japanese soldier.

At daybreak (July 4th) the Chinese commenced operations with a brisk bombardment The *Terrible's* marine detachment, one company Hong Kong regiment, with some French and Japanese troops, were

Railway station, Tientsin, the effects of the bombardment

detailed to guard the station, the Russians having declined to hold it any longer. The 12-pounder was sent to the mud wall, taking up a position about 3000 yards distant from the south face of the native city. Soon after noon a large force of the enemy moved out towards the ruined western arsenal, and from there across the plain, making a weird demonstration as if about to attack the settlements. A few shrapnel shells soon dispersed this body, who had presumably come out to divert attention from another movement preparing on the eastern side. About noon an expected attack was launched against the station, but it was quite 3 p.m. before the enemy actually pressed the position closely. Then commenced a fierce contest, the Chinese getting to within 100 yards of the buildings, evidently bent on rushing the place in force.

The 12-pounder endeavoured to help the station guards by shelling the fort near the *pagoda*, but a heavy deluge of rain coming on effectually obscured everything, and contrary to local expectation the Chinese did not stop fighting on account of the downpour. Strong reinforcements were hurried off to the station, their arrival soon enabling the enemy to be driven off, repulsed with great loss. Of the Terribles, Sergeant Peck and Private Walker were seriously wounded, and two more privates slightly hit, each man of the detachment having fired not less than 100 rounds during the fight. Many casualties occurred among the Allies assisting in the defence, and also to the supports who materially assisted to save an awkward position. Firing ceased at dusk, the station being secured against surprise during the night

During the afternoon two more 12-pounders with full crews arrived from the *Terrible,* under Lieutenant Wilde; Midshipmen Troup, Hutchinson, Reinold, Leir, Cargill, and Sumner being attached to these guns for duty. Petty-officers Symons and Metcalfe were the captains of Nos. 2 and 3 guns respectively. No. 2 gun was at once got into action alongside No. I gun on the mud wall. No. 3 joining them there the next morning—quite a powerful battery with which to oppose the Chinese artillery.

The *Times* correspondent stated:

> It was a grievous blunder not to send these guns up to Tientsin with the relief column in the first instance. Captain Scott had prepared four to land with the Welsh Fusiliers which he had brought up from Hong Kong, but for some occult reason he

was ordered to land only one, and H.M.S. *Terrible* was then sent to Chifu, where her guns were not wanted. This is the sort of thing that to the lay mind is utterly incomprehensible. The settlements at Tientsin were being bombarded, it was known that they had next to no guns, it was known that the Chinese had numbers of modern ones, and yet three fine pieces of artillery ready for the road are deliberately not sent with the relieving force. The one 12-pounder which was sent did yeoman's services.

During the ten days in which the settlements were subjected to a galling bombardment, the chief terror of the inhabitants was a big gun in the fort, which fired a 6-inch shell, and which was popularly known as the 'Empress Dowager.' When the relief column got into Tientsin, Admiral Seymour's expedition was imprisoned in the Hsiku Arsenal, situated above the fort on the river to the north, about as far from it as the settlements lie to the south. The 'Empress Dowager' was therefore in a position to divide her attention between the two places, and did so, shelling at one time the settlements and then slewing round and firing at Admiral Seymour's party at Hsiku. The gun also commanded the line of retreat to Tientsin. No small service was therefore rendered by the *Terrible*'s gun when it knocked out this formidable antagonist on the day after its arrival.

Again, in the attack on the arsenal it exploded the magazine there, and simplified the capture of the place considerably. If only four had been sent instead of one, the position today would have been assuredly less critical. . . . The lesson taught by it is the same as that which England has paid so much to learn in South Africa, the importance of heavy artillery. We are paralysed by lack of long-range guns.

A brief artillery duel and long-range rifle contest will express the fighting of the 5th.

On July 6th the enemy opened early with many guns, the 12-pounder battery replying and drawing much of the shelling to their position. During the forenoon an attempt was made to capture a quick-firing gun which was causing much annoyance from a hitherto concealed position, within fairly close range. The venture was nearly successful, the enemy being surprised, but the gun was found to be on the opposite bank of the river beyond capture, and the nearest

Lieutenant Wilde taking two 12-pounders from the "Terrible" to reinforce the British Naval Forces at Tienstin

bridge too exposed to risk crossing it Later, states Admiral Seymour's despatch—

> About noon a bombardment of forts in the native city, and of the arsenal, took place, the two 12-pounder guns of *Terrible* being assisted by the French and Japanese field guns. The guns in the Chinese forts were silenced by our guns, the French guns set fire to the viceroy's *yamên*, and the Japanese guns shelled the arsenal, where two guns were mounted, and kept them from firing at the 12-pounders while they were engaged with the forts in the city.

During this bombardment, two Chinese Krupp guns captured at Taku, manned by the *Terrible's* marines, were sent to assist the 12-pounder battery, but they had not been long in action before a serious mishap occurred at one gun, caused by a shell prematurely bursting while it was being loaded. Captain Mullins, Privates Jones and Rayner, and Gunner Wrangle (of the *Barfleur*) were wounded; the last named who was the loading number at the gun, had his arm blown completely off. In the afternoon another attempt either to dislodge or capture the aforementioned Chinese quick-firer was made by the Chinese regiment under Major Bruce, supported by a 9-pounder naval gun. Premature discovery of the force drew a heavy fire upon them, causing them to retire with several severe casualties, the major being among the wounded, and Midshipman Esdaile, who was with the gun, falling mortally hit.

That evening, at the special request of the Russian commander, Lieutenant Wilde took No. 3 12-pounder across the river for service with the Russian force. During the night the Japanese repelled an attempt of the Chinese to force the north-west corner of the settlements, the enemy afterwards firing several buildings on the outskirts to console themselves for their failure.

On the 7th fighting was commenced by the naval guns shelling large bodies of the enemy observed concentrating north of the settlements. The city forts responded at once, as did also two 40-pounders placed so as to rake the 12-pounder position on the wall from the westward. These guns soon got the exact range, dropping shells dangerously close. At last they were located and silenced, when the 12-pounders shelled Tree Battery, north of the station, and effected the same result there. Then attention was given to the city, a large *pagoda* being demolished that had given cover to riflemen. During the intermittent shelling that followed one shell entered the *Centurion's* quarters, killing two men and wounding three others. A reconnaissance towards the racecourse by Japanese cavalry in the afternoon unmasked a heavy fire from that direction, disclosing the fact that the enemy were trying to envelop the Allied positions and again cut communication with Taku.

Consequently, preparations were made next day (8th) to combat this dangerous movement and clear the Chinese from all positions south of the mud wall. This day the 12-pounders had the hottest time during all the fighting, their position being only rendered tenable by the gun pits and earth-bag protections, and A.B. Barrett was unlucky enough to have his right arm taken off by a shell fired from a gun placed at an angle that, till then, had been considered the rear of the position. No. 1 gun discovered its lair and shortly ended its mischief for the day. Two guns ensconced near the western arsenal then opened with shrapnel at the guns, and these, too, with the assistance of the Sikh battery, were quickly silenced, No. 2 gun smashing up one of their limbers. Next, four guns opened forth from among some ruined houses near the city walls, but their fire was ludicrously erratic and harmless. The 40-pounders also got into action near the transverse position they occupied the day before, a well-directed fire driving their crews into cover from the guns.

About 10 a.m. the Chinese guns ceased, but within half an hour renewed the contest with even greater vigour than before. Four small quick-firers, 3- and 6-pounders, opened up from the south-west near the racecourse and enfiladed the mud wall position, it taking nearly an hour to subdue their fairly accurate fire. (These guns were captured next day.) Several guns in the city, nearly opposite, then briskly bombarded the 12-pounder position, but ceased as soon as they were located, and so ended a lively forenoon. Had all the Chinese guns simultaneously concentrated their fire at the two 12-pounders some tangible result might have been achieved—by the enemy, as at various times the guns were subjected to frontal, cross, and enfilading fires. In the afternoon Black Fort and Tree Battery were shelled, No. 3 gun, with the Russians, adding its quota of help, though little appreciable damage was effected.

On July 9th a force of 1000 Japanese, 950 British (400 of whom were Bluejackets and marines), commanded by General Dorward, about 200 Americans, and 400 Russians, the whole force commanded by General Fukushima, Japanese Imperial Army, marched off at 3 a.m.

southwards along the Taku road. Proceeding for about three miles, the force then wheeled north-west, which brought them in front of the Chinese positions, the detour having been executed unobserved. The force now deployed for attack, British on the right, Japanese on the left, reserves close in rear, while the Japanese cavalry were sent away to the left front On discovering the movement, the enemy opened a heavy shrapnel fire on the Allies, which brought a responsive reply from the Japanese and Hong Kong (Sikh) batteries. Meantime the cavalry closed on the Chinese right flank, disclosing their presence by a brilliant chaise among them, whereupon the infantry advanced to support, but the enemy had already fled pell-mell towards the western arsenal and city, closely pursued by the cavalry, who accounted for at least 200 of those who had fallen. Six guns were captured, many rifles, and their whole reserve ammunition. The Allies then advanced northwards towards the arsenal, and at the same time a detached force of about 300 Americans and Japanese moved out at right angles along the mud wall to co-operate.

About 9 a.m. the Japanese rushed the arsenal, which had been evacuated but a few minutes before, the detached force entering almost at the same time. Two 9-pounders were captured here, the heavy guns having been wisely removed beforehand. The gallant Japanese then advanced towards the south gate of the native city, but meeting with severe opposition were compelled to return to cover. The close proximity of the arsenal to the city forts rendered it untenable for the Allies, so it was a second time fired and abandoned. Henceforth the southern side of Sankolinsins Folly (otherwise termed the mud wall, for shortness), was kept clear of the enemy. The Chinese losses were estimated at 400 in killed; the Allies had ten killed, 50 wounded Of the Terribles, Private Howard was killed.

Throughout this fighting the city forts vigorously shelled the 12-pounder position and settlements, the crews having an exceptionally hot time of it towards the finish. They made a direct hit at No. 2 gun, a shell splinter taking out the right eye of A.B. Brennan. The crew of a 9-pounder was withdrawn from the gun owing to the severe fire, a box of their ammunition being blown up. No. 1 gun had a shell put through its mounting, and the earth-bag protection of this gun was much mauled. By noon, fighting ceased for the day.

July 10th—That the victory of yesterday had somewhat demoralised the enemy was evident from the immunity the settlements en-

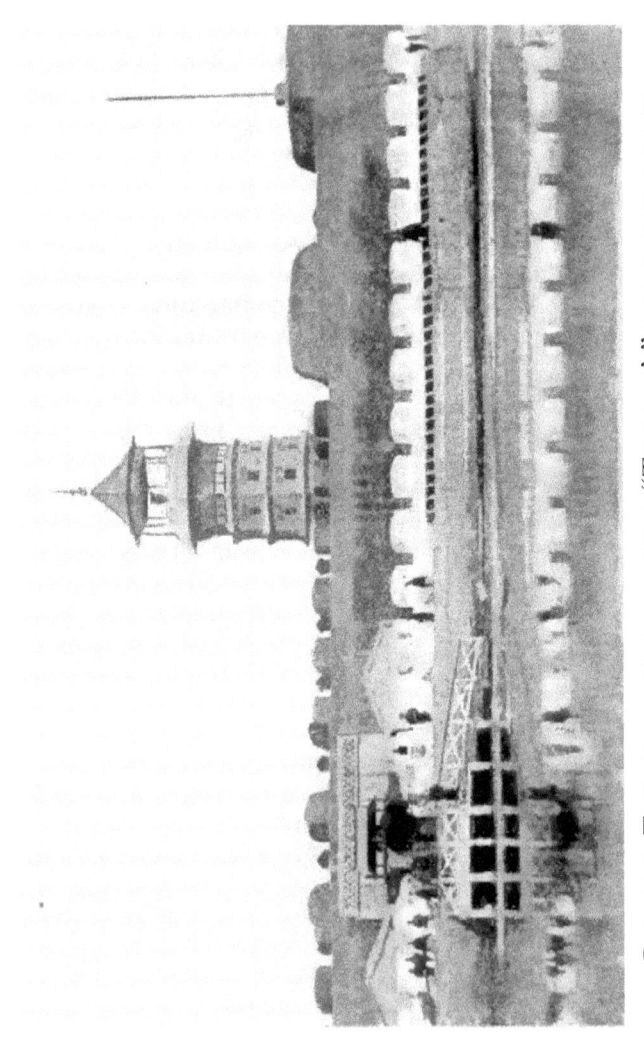

PAGODA IN TIENTSIN NATIVE CITY, *BEFORE* "TERRIBLE'S" GUN ATTENDED TO IT.

joyed today from the customary bombardment It was practically a day of peace, except for the sniping serenade that played its deadly music by day as well as by night Two 4-inch guns, sent from ships at Taku, were mounted today as position guns, manned by *Terrible's* Bluejackets. This addition of gun-power, together with the arrival of 2500 Russian and French troops in the afternoon, followed by the 9th Regiment American Infantry (about 600 strong) the next evening, allayed the uneasiness hitherto entertained by those in authority respecting the ability of the Allies to hold the whole of the concessions, owing to the constant flow of Chinese reinforcements and guns into the native city and the surrounding country.

At 5 p.m. the *Terrible's* marines relieved the *Aurora's* Bluejackets as British guard at the station—always a post of great expectancy. At midnight a strong force of Allies were assembled to attack a strong position—Tree Battery—containing several guns on the Chinese left flank, but finding that the pontoon bridge over which the troops must cross the river was wholly unreliable for the purpose, the movement was reluctantly abandoned for that night. Intelligence of this proposed attack having somehow reached the enemy, they, early next morning, made a most determined attempt to rush the railway station in force, evidently believing the troops were then absent on the venture aforementioned. Advancing in the darkness they actually succeeded in effecting an entrance into the station outbuildings and the trucks standing in close vicinity. The attack was well devised, for, knowing reinforcements would cross the river, they directed a severe shrapnel fire on to the bridge of boats over which the Allies usually crossed.

The fight was close and severe, Captain Mullins keeping his own detachment together so as to better withstand any direct onslaught. The same tactics were observed by the Hong Kong company and the French and Japanese units, who together formed the station guard. With daylight (11th) the Chinese shells began to crash into the buildings; at one period so severe was the shelling and rifle fire as to render the holding of the position a question of uncertainty. By the lucky arrival of a company of the Hong Kong regiment, coming as an ordinary relief, the tide of the fight was turned in favour of the Allies. Taking in the situation, these plucky Sikhs drove the enemy from the trucks, a task that proved a difficult and hazardous undertaking, the bravery of this British corps undoubtedly saving the position from disaster.

Strong reinforcements arriving shortly afterwards, the enemy were finally driven off, their losses being reasonably estimated at 500. The Allies lost in killed and wounded 150 men, principally among the French and Japanese, the Hong Kong relief company having sustained most of the British casualties.

At midday the whole Allied artillery bombarded the city forts, the Chinese guns replying with great vigour and precision. Over 400 shells were fired at No. 3 gun and one 4-inch, situated near the Russian camp under Lieutenants Wilde of the *Terrible* and Luard of the *Barfleur*, The 4-inch, after firing a few rounds, jumped its improvised mounting and became inactive. The other 4-inch, under Lieutenant Drummond's command, did good work throughout the afternoon, giving the enemy an impressive experience of lyddite. The general bombardment ceasing, Drummond's two 12-pounders engaged the two 40-pounders, which had been remounted in a new position 5000 yards distant, and were causing much mischief in the settlements. They were eventually silenced, when the 12-pounders again spurted forth at the city forts, demolishing a *pagoda* that had served the enemy as a watch-tower. The services of the guns received special recognition in despatches for their shooting today, Admiral Seymour stating—

> The *Terrible's* 12-pounders and one of the *Algerine's* 4-inch Q.F. did good work....

Petty-Officer Dear was severely wounded at the conclusion of the fight from a sniper's bullet.

This night a nest of treachery was casually discovered by AB. Stark, who, while on sentry duty, observed what he thought was—and what proved to be—some Morse signalling being made with a window blind at an isolated house not far from the 12-pounder position on the mud wall. On this being reported, the Welsh Fusilier picket near by received orders to raid the premises at once. As only three men could be spared from their post, A.B.'s Grady, Roman, and Dennis, of the gun's crews were sent to assist them. On arriving at the house, an entrance was forced, and as Grady entered, a Chinaman rushed at him, and was received upon Grady's bayonet, which somehow came unfastened, and remained in his opponent's body. He then clubbed another native over the head, breaking his rifle off from the stock with the blow.

A third native thereupon rushed at him with a war club, when Grady, then unarmed, darted upstairs to avoid a blow, his assailant following him up. Ere he reached him, however, Roman shot the Chinaman dead. Dennis now pushed inside in time to cover another

Engine house at Tientsin Railway Station, occupied by "Terrible's" Marines on 11th July

man armed with a revolver, whereupon the remaining miscreants surrendered. Treacherous dealings with the enemy were known to be rife, and here some seven blackguardly Europeans were entrapped and captured, their Chinese confederates escaping at the back into the darkness. Thus caught red-handed, they were imprisoned to await trial

A fourth 12-pounder and three Maxims with their crews arrived from the *Terrible* by river route today, commanded by Lieutenant Hutchinson, R.N.R., with whom were Midshipmen Willoughby, Down, and Ackland, and P.O. Mullis. captain of 12-pounder gun. The one lighter on which they had arrived presented a curious spectacle, somewhat resembling an "armed Noah's Ark," for besides the four guns mentioned, their ammunition, and 33 officers and men, there were also on deck an unmounted 4.7 gun, 16 tons of lyddite shells, over 300 head of cattle and sheep, many scores of live fowls, and heaps of vegetables. The whole was enclosed within a barricade formed with bags of potatoes, every inch of space being occupied by some one or something.

On the passage up they had come under a brisk rifle fire from rebels in the village of Shen-si-ku, near the bank; but as the Maxim guns were mounted in position and swiftly brought into action, the "Ark" and its occupants ran the gauntlet in safety without incurring any losses whatsoever. As all the cattle and sheep were loose on deck, the pandemonium that existed while the firing lasted can be more easily imagined than described. With the arrival of this party 231 officers and men with seven guns, four 12-pounders and three maxims, were now at the front from the *Terrible*.

Sufficient Allied forces having arrived to ensure the safety of the Settlements, Admiral Sir Edward Seymour, his staff, and the *Centurion's* contingent of the Naval Brigade, left Tientsin to rejoin the flagship lying off Taku. A few days after the admiral's return he issued the following "Fleet Order "to the crews of the Chinese squadron:—

> I desire to express to the officers, seamen, and marines comprising the late expeditionary forces towards Peking, my high sense of satisfaction with their general conduct therein, during a time which comprised much discomfort, hard work, and want of food and water, with little rest and decided anxiety, in addition to dangers of war.
>
> The above were encountered with zeal, patience, courage and

cheerfulness worthy of our noble service to which we belong. Similar trials may be before us, but will I know be borne as the above were.

At the same time I wish to express to the officers and men lately employed in the defence of Tientsin and to those in the operations about Taku, including the capture of those forts, my thorough satisfaction with all concerned.

The defence of Tientsin has been carried out with much risk and fatigue, constantly harassing those employed, but met with the true naval spirit

The capture of the Taku Forts was a brilliant affair, well planned, and well carried out, success, as not unusually, crowned very gallant and daring efforts: I congratulate all concerned therein.

It is my pleasing duty, and was that of the rear-admiral in my absence, to convey the above to their Lordships at the Admiralty, and will be known generally in England.

To me personally the fine conduct of these belonging to the British China Squadron is a matter of special pride and pleasure, and I have no misgiving but that whatever is before us, we shall if possible do better rather than otherwise, and uphold the traditions of the British Navy.

On July 12th the Allied commanders decided upon the capture of the native city, the number of Allies now present being about 12,000 men. Captain Bayly was again the senior naval officer commanding in Tientsin, and Captain Burke commanded the service companies of the Naval Brigade. All the naval guns, *viz*. two 4-inch, four 12-pounders, and several guns of smaller calibre, were manned by crews of the *Terrible*, who formed the artillery contingent of the naval force.

★★★★★★

Fall of Tientsin native city—July 13th, 14th. To allow the native city to remain in possession of the Chinese would mean a constant danger to the settlements, and also seriously prejudice another attempt to relieve the capital. A general bombardment, except at the forts and official buildings, had been deferred owing to the strong representations of the European merchants that such an act would involve them in heavy losses and impair future trade. But its retention by the enemy had become so intolerable that commercial considerations had to succumb to the stem necessities of war.

The official version of its capture is given to the reader as an unvarnished account of how the navy sustained its best traditions with gun and rifle in the field, besides being a most interesting story of a hard-fought battle.

From the general officer commanding British Forces, Tientsin, to the Secretary of State for War.

Tientsin, July 19th, 1900.

Sir,

On the afternoon of the 11th instant, I arranged with General Fukushima, commanding the Japanese forces, to carry out as soon as possible the capture of Tientsin city. Owing to our heavy losses during the daily bombardment of the Settlements we considered this movement necessary.

The Russian general was approached on the subject, and said he would co-operate in the movement by an attack on the Chinese batteries and forts to the north-east of the city. He desired to get his pontoon train in readiness, and said that as soon as he had done so he would give me notice of his readiness to move. His staff officer gave me that notice at 5 p.m. on the 12th instant, and it was arranged that the Russian forces, who had the longer march, should move in time to deliver their attack on the batteries about 10 a.m. on the following day, and that the Japanese-British force should deliver their attack on the city as early as possible, in order to attract the bulk of the Chinese troops to their side and so facilitate the capture of the batteries by the Russians.

I then called on Colonel de Pelacot, commanding the French forces, and Colonel Meade, commanding the American forces, and together with them visited General Fukushima to discuss the plan of operations.

It was decided that the Allied forces would parade at 3 a.m., and move in three columns, about 500 yards apart, on the western arsenal.

The French force, 900 strong, was to form the right column, and crossing the mud parapet in the British Extra Concession, was to move on the south side of it and under its cover direct on the arsenal, timing its movement to agree with that of the other columns. Two companies were detailed to advance from the French Settlement and clear the houses between it and the city of troops. They were unable, however, in the face of a heavy

Pagoda in the Tientsin native city as a lookout tower, *after* "Terrible's" gun had attended to it.

fire to make much headway.

The Japanese column, 1500 strong, under General Fukushima, was to move out from the settlement by the racecourse gate at 3 a.m., and move parallel to the mud parapet about 500 yards from it.

The left column, consisting of 800 British troops (500 military and 300 naval[1]), 900 Americans and 30 Austrians, moved out of the Taku gate at 3.30 a.m. under my command, and marched parallel to the Japanese column and about 500 yards from them. About 500 yards on the left column was the Japanese cavalry, 150 strong.

The left column was somewhat delayed in clearing villages of small parties of the enemy, and its head arrived at the road leading to the arsenal and south gate of the city, about a quarter of a mile behind the head of the Japanese column.

The French column suffered a check at a bridge in the mud parapet, about a quarter of a mile from the arsenal, and in crossing over which their troops were exposed to fire. The arsenal was cleared of the enemy principally through the agency of the Japanese troops.

The advanced British troops, consisting of the detachment and Battalion Royal Welsh Fusiliers, and the American Marines, moved forward and lined the mud parapet west of the arsenal, the 9th American Infantry being also brought forward under the parapet as support. The reserve, consisting of two companies Chinese Regiment and the *Naval Brigade*[2] were halted about 2500 yards from the city, and suffered some loss from long-range fire.

All the artillery of the combined force, consisting of mountain guns, with the exception of three 3.2-inch guns, belonging to the Americans, formed up a short distance south of the mud parapet and bombarded the city (5.30 a.m.).

One 4-inch gun, three 12-pounders, and a few 9-pounders and 6-pounders, worked by the navy from a position in the British Extra Concession, did excellent service in keeping down the fire from the city

---

1. The *Terrible's* marine detachment formed one of the three companies of Royal Marines included among the navals, having eight men wounded, *viz*. Sergeant Stanbridge, Privates Watts, Farley, Ellis, Rudgley, Cuell, Brown, and Edwards; A.B. Robertson was also wounded at the guns.—The Writer.

2. All reference to the Navy in this despatch has been printed in italics by the original publisher.

walls.

After about an hour's bombardment it was decided to attack. The French were to be on the right, the Japanese in the centre, and the British on the left, the centre of the attack being the south gate. Owing to the attack being pushed on somewhat too hurriedly in the centre, the Fusiliers and American Marines had to move forward rather too quickly under a heavy fire to get into their position on the Japanese left (7.15 a.m.).

General Fakushima had asked me to give some support to the left of his line during the attack, and the 9th American Infantry was directed by me to give this support, and also to support the attack of the Fusiliers and *Marines*.

"When the 9th Regiment had crossed the mud parapet, a body of men, estimated at 1500 strong, made up of cavalry and infantry, appeared about 2500 yards away from our extreme left. I directed the detachment of the Hong Kong regiment, who up to this time had been acting as escort to the guns, to take up a favourable position at a bend in the mud parapet about one mile from the arsenal to meet any attack. They had no difficulty in repulsing this threatened attack with the aid of two Maxim guns sent to assist them as soon as possible.

The Japanese attack extended considerably more to the left than had been intended, so that the Fusiliers and *Marines* were pushed more to the left than had been contemplated, and brought close to heavy enfilade fire from the suburbs south of the south-west corner of the city. They faced that fire in the steadiest way, taking up a position under fairly good cover, and during the whole day prevented a large body of the enemy from making any forward movement.

Meanwhile seven or eight guns of the enemy's artillery were replying to our artillery fire from a fort about 1¼ mile west of the West Gate of the city.

The reserves were ordered up to take cover under the mud parapet, and the whole of the artillery moved inside the parapet and took up the best positions obtainable to continue the bombardment.

Moving back from the Hong Kong regiment position I could see nothing of the 9th American Infantry; but when I reached the arsenal I saw that only a few Japanese troops were extended on the right of the road, and that the French troops were all in

Guard house on South Gate of native city, after being shelled by naval guns, July 13, 1900

compact bodies in the villages on the road leading to the south gate behind the Japanese, from which I judged that the fire on the right had been so heavy that the French attacking line could not be formed.

At the arsenal I met the acting adjutant of the 9th Regiment, who said he had been sent back with news that his regiment were in a very exposed position, which from his description I made out to be near the French settlement, and that they had lost heavily, their colonel, amongst others, being mortally wounded He said he had been ordered to ask for reinforcements, *and I directed 100 men of the Naval Brigade under Lieutenant Phillimore, R.N., to proceed to their assistance,*

I signalled in to Lieutenant-Colonel Bower, who was in command of the force left in the settlement, to send me out two more companies of the Chinese regiment with all the stretchers he could collect, and on their arrival sent the stretchers forward, carried by the men of the regiment under Major Pereira. Major Pereira made two trips out to the American position, and brought back many of their wounded under a very heavy fire, losing several men and being himself wounded. He told me on returning from his second trip that the Americans and *the men of the Naval Brigade* had got into a fairly safe position, so I decided to leave them there till nightfall. They detained a considerable body of the enemy in front of them, and prevented any attack being made on the right flank of the Japanese.

Major Pereira also informed me that the Americans were very badly off for ammunition, so I directed Captain Ollivant and a party of the Chinese Regiment to take a further supply to them. While performing this service I regret to say that Captain Ollivant was killed.

A Japanese staff officer afterwards told me that he had seen the 9th Regiment moving along the right rear of the Japanese attack in column of fours, and that he was afraid they must have suffered heavy

The naval guns were all this time making splendid practice, keeping down the fire from the city walls, and we were anxiously waiting for the sound of the explosion, which would tell that the Japanese sappers had reached the city gate and blown it in. Shortly after 1 p.m. I received the following note from the Japanese chief staff officer:—

Mon Général. Nos soldats sont déjà entrés dans la cité. Je vous prie donc de faire cesser le feu de vos canons immédiatement. [3]

Aski, Lieutenant-Colonel.

Orders were accordingly given for the cessation of all artillery fire and the advance of all our troops to support the assault on the city. The advancing troops were met with a very heavy fire from the walls, which continued to increase in intensity, and it soon became apparent that the Japanese troops had not entered the city. The troops were then forced to take cover close to the canal round the city. I shortly afterwards heard from the Japanese general that he had been misinformed, and that his troops had not entered the city.

Orders were sent for all guns to open fire again, and, owing to the beautiful practice of the naval guns, very little loss was suffered by the troops in the advanced trenches.

Towards evening the 1500 troops on the left flank again advanced, and began preparing a long line of shelter trenches. I received a request from General Fukushima asking me if I could undertake arrangements for the protection of his troops and the French, while in their advanced positions, from attack from the left flank or rear, as his cavalry had informed him that bodies of the enemy were threatening us from those directions.

The naval guns were then requested to direct their whole fire on the enemy facing the extreme left of our position, and undercover of that fire and of volleys from the detachment of the Hong Kong regiment, directed on the various points from which the enemy were harassing the retirement, the Fusiliers and American Marines were withdrawn with very slight loss and formed up behind the mud parapet. The movement reflected great credit on Colonel Meade, commanding the Marines, and Captain Gwynne, commanding the Fusiliers.

The more delicate manoeuvre of withdrawing the 9th American Infantry and the *company of the Naval Brigade* had to be undertaken. The naval guns were directed to sweep the barriers constructed along the fringe of houses between the French Settlement and the city from which the fire on the American troops proceeded. The American troops themselves were only about 300 yards from this fringe, and there was great danger of

---

3. Translation—Our soldiers have already entered the city. I beg you to cease the fire of your guns immediately.

Captain Edward Henry Bayly, C.B.

the fire from the *naval* guns injuring them as well as the enemy. The dead and wounded, of which the Americans had still a considerable number with them, were brought back with the assistance of the *company of the Naval Brigade*, and shortly afterwards the 9th Regiment arrived at the mud parapet in safety. I would specially bring to notice the conduct of Major Jesse Lee during the retirement; in him the regiment possesses an officer of exceptional merit.

The whole force is under the greatest obligation to Captain Bayly and Lieutenant Drummond, R.N., for their working of the naval guns.

After posting troops to secure our flank and rear from attack, the troops turned in for the night, during which there was some rain. News was then received that the Russian attack on the other side of the city had been delayed by unforeseen causes; but when made had proved very successful, resulting in the complete rout of the Chinese and the capture of eleven guns; the Russian loss was about 120 killed and wounded.

The Naval Brigade under Captain Burke, R.N., had their full share of the fighting in the centre and right of the position, and had the honour of being among the first troops to enter the city. The companies were splendidly led by Commander Beatty and Lieutenant Phillimore, and nothing could have been finer than their spirit and conduct. I have already brought to notice the exceptionally fine work done by Captain Bayly and Lieutenant Drummond, R.N., and the naval guns. I received at all times the most ready and unquestioning assistance from Captain Burke.

I have, etc.,

A. R. F. Dorward, Brigadier-General.

Co-operating with the Russians were No. 3 12-pounder, under Lieutenant Hutchinson, R.N.R., and a 4-inch position gun under Lieutenant Luard. These two guns performed conspicuous service in covering the Russian advance, and completely silenced the eastern Chinese batteries opposed to them, thus rendering the capture of the guns an easy matter.

Throughout the battle the naval gun fire was personally controlled by Captain Bayly by means of telephone from the signal tower of the Gordon Hall, some of the guns, from their fixed positions, having their line of sight totally obscured when firing at certain objects. He thus describes that incident of the fight which had nearly proved a costly error—

A most destructive fire was kept up by all the guns to the westward, under Lieutenant Drummond, of H.M.S. *Terrible*, on the south wall of the city as the attacking force approached from the south-west, with the view of keeping down the enemy's fire, which was poured heavily from the wall on either side of the south gate when our troops had once passed the western arsenal.

Large portions of the wall were swept away, and the fire was considerably subdued, when a signal reached me from the general to request that all guns might cease fire on the wall, as the Japanese had entered the city. This subsequently proved not to have been the case, and was due to some misunderstanding of a report

During the time the fire of the guns was taken off the south wall the Chinese remanned the battlements, and poured in a very heavy rifle fire, until the guns once more received permission to reopen on the wall, which they did with great effect.

The Chinese most gallantly stuck to their positions, keeping up a heavy rifle fire until literally swept away, wall and all.

The scene in and around the city after its capture was one of desolation and carnage. The work of the guns had indeed been effective, the numbers of dead Chinese being incalculable, as they were strewn all over the city. The losses of the Allies had also been very severe, nearly 800 casualties having occurred during the bombardment and assault

For administrative purposes the city was divided into four departments, the British assuming control of the north-west section. Numerous guns and large quantities of warlike stores were captured, and much treasure and valuables came Into possession of the Allies. The human propensity for looting was fully indulged as soon as the din of battle had hushed. Stern repressive measures, however, were adopted when the Allied authorities realised the enormity of the pillage which was proceeding, but the restraint came much too late to be effective.

The following congratulatory order, issued by the British general next day, cannot fail to be highly appreciated by the naval reader, particularly so by the Terribles, who, with their guns, had a second time greatly assisted in achieving another decisive victory:—

One of the "Terrible's" 12-pounders at Tientsin protected by earth-bag redoubts.

To Captain Burke, R.N., commanding Naval Brigade on 13th and 14th inst., from Brigadier-General Dorward, commanding British Forces, Tientsin.

Tientsin, July 15th, 1900.

Sir,

I wish to express my deep sense of the honour done to me by having under my command the officers and men of the Naval Brigade during the long and hard fighting of the 13th inst., which resulted in the capture of Tientsin city.

The success of the operations was lordly due to the manner in which the naval guns were worked by Lieutenant Drummond, R.N., the accuracy of their fire alone rendering steady fire on the part of the troops possible against the strong Chinese position, and largely reducing the number of casualties.

The delicate operation of withdrawing troops from advanced positions at nightfall to strengthen other parts of the line, and the bringing back of the wounded, could not have been effected without the aid of the well-directed fire of the guns.

I desire to place on record my appreciation of the gallantry and fine spirit of the men, and to join in their regret for the heavy loss in killed and wounded, and particularly with the Royal Marines in regret for the death of Captain Lloyd.

The Naval Brigade had their full share in the fighting at the centre and right of the position, and had the honour of being among the first troops to enter Tientsin. The succour they brought under a heavy fire to the hard-pressed American troops on the right was highly appreciated by the 9th Regiment United States Infantry, who found themselves unexpectedly under the heaviest fire of the day, and were much heartened by the arrival of Lieutenant Phillimore, R.N., and his men. It will be my honour to bring their conduct to the notice of the Secretary of State for War.

I join with them in their admiration for the gallantry, soldierly spirit, and organisation of our comrades of the Japanese Army.

I have the honour to thank you particularly for the ready and unquestioning assistance which you personally gave me at all times during the progress of the operations, and for the cheerful co-operation of your officers and men in instantly carrying out any duty assigned to them.

CHAPTER 18

Chefoo and Wei-Hai-Wei

From June 25th to July 30th, 1900

Preparations for the advance on Peking followed the fall of the native city, the future action of the Allies entirely depending upon the arrival of reinforcements and transport before the march to the relief of the capital could commence. The interspace of inaction will be filled in by following the movements of the *Terrible*.

Having discharged the troops and stores at Taku, besides landing Lieutenant Drummond's small contingent, the ship was ordered to Chefoo, arriving there June 25th. The place was found in a peaceful state, although the foreign community were somewhat uneasy regarding their personal safety should the rebellion reach that district. In conjunction with the captains of two American and one Japanese men-of-war then in harbour, arrangements were made with the respective Consuls to place the Foreign Quarter in a position of safety, should events render this course necessary. The town and roadstead are completely dominated by powerful forts, but no immediate danger was then apprehended that the Chinese troops would treacherously employ the guns, as the rebellious fever had not up to that time fired their ignorant brains. Nevertheless, precaution was necessary, as recent events elsewhere had proved. Commander Limpus privately surveyed places most suitable for landing men and guns, and Lieutenants Wilde and England made secret reconnaissances of the forts, obtaining much valuable information concerning them. Moreover, to prevent surprise, projectiles were placed in the guns, and the crews ordered to sleep near them by night. Landing parties were also organised.

Chefoo is in the Shantung Province, and is the principal treaty port of North China, attracting a considerable shipping, which increases

Wei-hai-wei

Showing the village of Liu-kung-tao, with the naval establishments on the right of the village, part of the China squadron at anchor, and the mainland opposite.

yearly. Except in the Foreign Quarter, which is well kept, the town is badly built and very dirty, but the inhabitants are orderly, industrious, and civilly disposed towards foreigners. It is a recognised coaling station for foreign men-of-war which frequently visit the port. The town is noted for its silk, and the fruit and vegetable raising industry in this district gives much profitable employment to the natives.

On June 30th, at 5 p.m., a signal was made by the consul to land an armed party at once. The crew were then at supper, but within fifteen minutes a strong party were on their way ashore, to find on arriving the disturbance at an end, and order being restored by the Chinese police. The trouble originated by some Japanese *coolies*, during a brawl, cutting off the pigtails of some of their Chinese brethren, the infuriated Celestials having retaliated by using knives against their assailants for ruthlessly shearing them of their sacred queues. So serious an aspect did the affair assume for a brief period that the foreigners gathered into their homes, and armed in case the brawl should develop into something worse. Peace being assured, the boats returned to the ship from their bloodless mission.

No revolutionary movement being anticipated, the ship left for Wei-hai-wei early on July 1st, taking there, as indulgence passengers, several refugee missionaries with their families, who had sensibly come in from the interior a few days previously. The ship arrived at noon, and that evening Lieutenant Wilde, and 90 officers and men, with two 12-pounder guns, embarked in the *Alacrity* for the front, arriving on the 4th of July in Tientsin, where the guns were then urgently needed.

Wei-hai-wei is situated on the south side of the Gulf of Pechili, 40 miles eastward of Chefoo, nearly facing Port Arthur on the north side, and about 115 miles distant from that Russian naval and military base of the Far East; the port of Kiao-chau, the German naval base, being about the same distance away on the southern side of the promontory. Formerly a strongly fortified Chinese naval station, it was captured by the Japanese in January, 1895, who held it until May, 1898, when it was then evacuated by them, and by an agreement with China was leased to Great Britain. The main object of the lease was to prevent the Gulf of Pechili falling under the exclusive domination of any one foreign power. The bay, surrounded by high hills, is nearly twenty miles in extent, sheltered to the northward by the island of Liu-kung-tao, upon which are situated the naval and military establishments, government buildings and commissioner's residence, and where the largest men-of-war can obtain good anchorage to within a few hundred yards from the shore.

On its seaward or north side rise steep rocky cliffs, three modern forts[1] having been built upon their highest summits. There are two entrances to the spacious harbour, the northern and eastern, but vessels of more than twenty-feet draught cannot enter the eastern channel Since its occupation by the British, the small Chinese town on the island has been remodelled, well drained, possesses a good hotel, officers' clubs, naval and military recreation rooms and ground; the pleasant climate rendering the place exceedingly healthy and invigorating. Opposite, on the mainland, is situated the ancient city of Wei-hai-wei, standing in squalid isolation, surrounded by high walls. About a mile therefrom new barracks have been built, wherein are quartered the Chinese regiment, a corps that, under its British officers, performed excellent service in the present war. A magnificent hotel, among the largest and best appointed in the East, has recently been erected in a commanding position overlooking the bay, and is much used as a sanatorium. A telegraph cable connects the island with the Eastern service, adding much to its importance.

The *Alacrity* arrived back from Taku on the 8th instant with wounded, a hospital rendezvous having been established on the island. She also brought orders for more guns to be forwarded. One 12-pounder and three Maxims, with 33 officers and men under Lieutenant Hutchinson, embarked that night, proceeding direct to Tientsin, where they arrived in good time to assist at the fall of the native city.

Early on the 10th, an urgent telegram was received from the consul requesting the ship to proceed to Chefoo at once. Leaving at noon, Chefoo was reached soon after 3 p.m.; the ship's company having been reorganised during the passage, as one-fourth of the crew were now at the front. Instead of the forts contesting our entrance to the harbour, or finding the town in imminent danger of attack from rebels, nothing occurred beyond the peaceful bumboat coming alongside laden with luscious fruit and other edibles which the Celestial purveyor was anxious to sell.

It transpired, however, that the consul had been appealed to by the Europeans to have the *Terrible* brought there, as a rumoured outbreak was expected to occur that night. Two signalmen were landed with a flashing lamp to signal off any signs of the expectant trouble, and the

---

1. Early in 1903 the British Government decided to abandon the arming of these forts, and to only utilise the place as a northern rendezvous for the China Fleet.

Wounded from Admiral Seymour's column at the improvised base hospital at Wei-hai-wei

crew slept with their accoutrements slung on their hammocks ready for any emergency. Next morning anxiety vanished with the sound of reveille—the continuity of peace had not been broken. The ship returned to Wei-hai-wei on the 12th.

On July 24th the *Centurion*, with Admiral Seymour on board, arrived with the *Terrible's* marine detachment, who had returned in the flagship to recruit their health and refit prior to the advance to Peking. That evening the *Centurion* departed for Shanghai, taking another *Terrible* 12-pounder gun, to which was attached Petty-officer Mitchell and four men as crew; Lieutenant Lawrie also embarking to fill the vacancy caused by the death of Captain Beyts, Royal Marines, killed at Hsiku. The foreign community at Shanghai—the commercial metropolis of China—were just now very restless, as reports of revolt in the Yangtse Valley were then rife, and the admiral was proceeding there in person, since British interests were of vital importance in that region.

Numerous transports conveying Indian native troops had proceeded westward to Taku within the past fortnight, calling at Wei-hai-wei *en route*, this place being now the base for the North China Field Force.

Notwithstanding the fact that a quarter of a million troops were now in South Africa, none of whom Lord Roberts could well spare, it was an achievement worthy of record that there were still ample resources of both men and material to enable the Empire to take its full share of responsibility, with the other interested powers, in suppressing the Chinese Rebellion. Partly to compensate them for their disappointment at not being actively employed in South Africa, the Imperial Government had decided to use the Indian Native Forces—one of the most valuable assets of the British Empire. Nor should it be forgotten that here, as well as in South Africa, the Australians were loyally supporting the Imperial flag, a naval contingent having been sent for service in North China.

On the 30th, the marine detachment left by transport for the front, their departure indicating that the preparations were nearing completion for the advance on Peking.

CHAPTER 19

Return of the Naval Brigades

From August 3rd to 15th, 1900

That portion of the Naval Brigade which advanced with the Peking Expeditionary Relief Force moved out of Tientsin with the *Terrible's* four 12-pounder guns during the afternoon of August 3rd, and proceeded to Hsiku, seven miles distant, where they bivouacked for the night Captain Callaghan, R.N. (*Endymion*), commanded the brigade, Lieutenant Wrey (*Barfleur*) second in command, Lieutenant Hulbert (*Endymion*) staff officer, Lieutenant Drummond (*Terrible*) gunnery officer; an accountant officer, one surgeon, one gunner, and six midshipmen were also attached to the brigade. Of the petty officers and men, 100 belonged to the *Terrible*, 35 to *Endymion,* and 5 to *Aurora*. 300 Marines formed a battalion under the command of Major Luke, R.M. (*Barfleur*); the *Terrible's* detachment being No. 4 Company.

The two 4-inch guns, under Commander Fraser (*Phoenix*), who had with him about 80 officers and men, mostly belonging to *Barfleur* and *Endymion*, were to remain in Tientsin and await orders. One of these guns afterwards went as far as Tungchow, but as Peking was then relieved, it was brought back.

The British force was commanded by General Gaselee, who had arrived from India to assume supreme command of all British Imperial troops in China, those taking part in this expedition being: Naval Brigade, 450 men, 4 guns; 12th Battery R.F.A., 6 guns; Hong Kong Asiatic Artillery, 2 guns, 4 Maxims; one detachment Royal Engineers; 1st Bengal Lancers, 400; Royal Welsh Fusiliers, 300; 7th Bengal Infantry, 500; 24th Punjaub Infantry, 300; 1st Sikhs, 500; Hong Kong Regiment, 100; Wei-hai-wei Regiment, 100; also units of departmental corps.

The Relief Army was composed of the following nationalities, and approximate numbers of men and guns: Japanese, 8500 men, 50 guns; Russians, 4500 men, 16 guns; British, 3000 men, 12 guns; Americans, 2500 men, 6 guns; French, 800 men, 12 guns; or a total of about 19,000 men and 96 guns.

It would be impossible to enumerate even approximately the numbers of the enemy opposing the advance. Some have estimated the Chinese troops at 70,000 men, about two-thirds of whom were regulars, commanded by Prince Ching and General Nieh; the Imperial Banner Corps and the Instructional Corps, under Prince Tüan and General Kang-Yi respectively, comprising the remainder of the Chinese Imperial forces. The horde of Boxers and their fanatical adherents might be estimated at anything between 50,000 and 100,000—or even more.

To provide transport—that indispensable component of a civilised army—had been a problem each general had found most difficult to solve; and in a country like China, where native locomotion and roads are only caricatures of the real articles generally understood by those terms, it was a task baffling description in few words. Men and animals must be fed, and reserve ammunition carried, without which no army can fight, or march very far away from its base. Even for the Naval Brigade, with their small number of men and guns, no less than twenty carts and twenty pack mules were necessary to carry a few days' provisions and ammunition, the officers and men alike carrying their own belongings and fighting equipment

The Japanese, by reason of the close proximity of their own country, were best provided for in this respect, but owing to the unexpected diversion of about half of the Indian troops to Shanghai, they had been obliged to double their original force, and, consequently, also had the transport conundrum to solve, which, however, they did with characteristic promptness.

At daybreak, the 4th, it was found that a few other troops had arrived in Hsiku during the night, and late in the afternoon, during a heavy downpour of rain, the British and American forces left Tientsin, arriving at dusk and bivouacking. General Gaselee and the Headquarter Staff took up their quarters in the mud village. In the order published today, it was stated that—

> The enemy is in position in the direction of Pei-tsang on both banks of the Pei-ho. The position is believed to be entrenched,

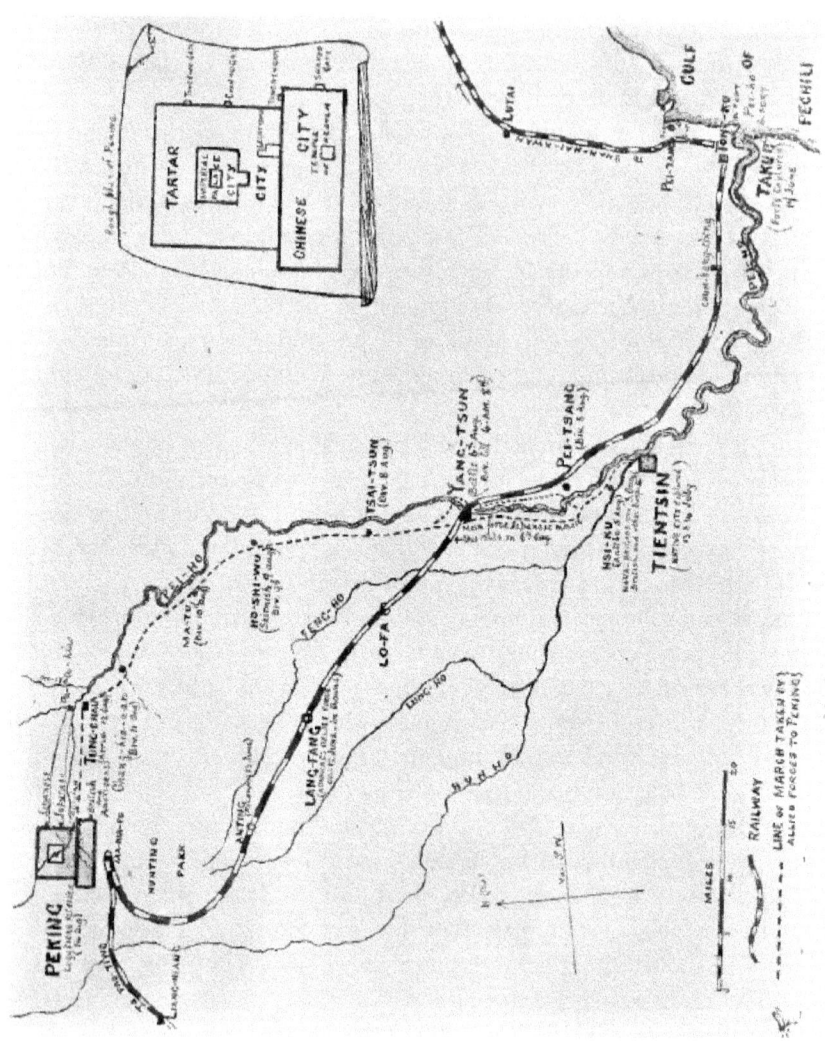

Map of Route, Taku to Peking

with outposts thrown forward.

Orders were issued for an early forward movement next morning, so darkness induced the force to lie down—no lights being permitted—and snatch a few hours' rest and sleep; muddy ground for mattress, and the uncertain canopy of heaven for a covering, since the rainy season—more feared than the enemy—had begun simultaneously with the start of the expedition. Certain troops began to move as early as 1.30 a.m. next morning (5th), and one hour afterwards the camp was fully astir, a hasty breakfast being partaken of—too hasty for those who had to struggle with navy biscuit, and owning only a limited number of grinders with which to crush them.

At 3 a.m., the brigade stood to arms, and manned the guns, firing having already occurred towards the front. The Japanese force, which had left Tientsin at midnight, had moved past the camp and had taken up a position nearer the enemy, with whom they had now come in contact.

The Chinese, estimated at 25,000 men, were found to be strongly entrenched in an extended position running northeast and south-west, cut through the centre by the Pei-ho, their right resting on an embankment which runs westwards from Hsiku village, their left extending as far as the railway near Pei-tsang. Both flanks were strongly held and protected. They had concentrated their main strength towards the centre, the defences here being skilfully planned, well concealed, and the position would have been difficult of capture if held by a resolute enemy. The plan of battle was for the Japanese to attack the enemy's right, supported by the British and Americans, while the Russians and French, supported by the British Naval Brigade, were to operate against their left. The cavalry and some of the field artillery were to assist on the flanks, and be prepared to harass a retreat. Shortly after 3 a.m. the whole force moved off towards the enemy's positions under cover of the embankment, on which the naval guns were afterwards placed, so as to give a clearer range of fire.

A Chinese battery, which had been well placed so as to enfilade any frontal assault on their centre, was the first object of attack.

This task was undertaken by the Japanese, who were not long before they made it change hands, also driving in the enemy's right for some distance towards their centre, with but trifling loss to themselves. With dawn, the allied guns opened on the enemy's position a fire which was vigorously but erratically returned, a smart artillery duel being waged for over an hour, when the enemy's guns ceased fire with surprising suddenness.

Meantime the infantry had successfully worked their way close to the enemy's central positions, and shortly after 5 a.m., the Japanese made a magnificent charge into the outlying trenches, cheering as they went. From a screened position on the opposite bank a galling cross fire was poured into them, which they gallantly withstood, clearing the lines of entrenchments in rapid succession. The Chinese—like the Boers—do not seem to fear long-range fire, but the bayonet they refuse to face, and, emulating Taku tactics, did not wait to oppose, but decamped in full retreat, with cavalry and shrapnel assisting them in this simple manoeuvre. A few bodies of detached Chinese troops, more courageous than the majority, made some show of resistance at respectable distances, but never permitted actual contact to take place. The whole force was now advanced, British on the left, Americans on the extreme left, to complete the victory, which was even now practically assured. Across the river, the Allies had not met with immediate success against the enemy's left, but the force opposing them did not wait long before they also followed the example set by those who had been defending the centre and right, and joined in the "all-comers race" for life now taking place. The rout was complete.

The capture of the Chinese main positions had led to the forced evacuation of their left, and had enabled the "Dual Alliance" to occupy it with only a loss of six wounded.

The Japanese had borne the brunt of the fighting, having suffered severely in casualties, their loss being quite 300 killed and wounded. The British had four killed and 21 wounded. The Chinese losses were estimated at about the same number as the total of the Allies, many being killed during the retreat. Three of the naval guns had been brought into action during the fight, making some excellent shooting, thereby greatly assisting to subdue the musketry fire during the advance.

On this occasion their fire was directed by an officer from the top of an improvised observatory, formed by two long bamboo ladders placed Λ fashion, which gave a wider field of vision.

By 9 a.m., the whole of the positions were occupied, the actual fighting having been short and severe, yet brilliantly carried out.

The whole allied force afterwards advanced on Pei-tsang, where the main road to Peking crossing the Pei-ho River, the Anglo-American forces crossing over on a bridge of boats early next morning (6th), and effecting a junction with the Russo-French forces.

The advance was continued towards Yangtsun, but owing to the execrable state of the roads, the naval guns had to be placed in *junks* and towed up the river, which would heavily handicap the chances of their being on the spot at the next expected stand made by the enemy. The main body of the Japanese proceeded along the right bank, but owing to inundations were eventually compelled to cross over; the rest of the Allies and detached Japanese moved along the left bank, the British who proceeded by a more direct route, getting in front of the other forces and coming within sight of Yangtsun about 8 a.m., with the American troops then on their right flank. The Chinese had taken up a strong position in some mud villages lying in the angle formed by the railway and the river which cross at Yangtsun, where the remains of the destroyed trains previously used by Admiral Seymour's force were now standing—grim evidence of a brilliant if unsuccessful expedition. The enemy's presence and position had been discovered and their fire drawn by a troop of Cossacks who had been ahead reconnoitring.

This information being reported to the British general, it was decided, in order to save time, which was important, to commence the attack at once by bombarding the enemy's positions. While the guns were paving the way, the Allies arrived on the scene, and, the plan of attack having already been decided upon, the troops were set in motion, British in the centre, Americans on the right, which flank was protected by the Bengal Lancers and American Artillery; Russians on the left next to the river; the Japanese held in reserve. Under cover of the guns the advance slowly proceeded, the troops having to march through nearly three miles of high-growing maize crops to reach the enemy's positions. When about halfway, they came under a severe shell and rifle fire, when the advance was made more rapidly; little damage, however, was done to them, owing to their widely extended formation.

The British led the direct assault on the positions, the 1st Sikhs in front, closely supported by the Welsh Fusiliers, with the Punjaubs and the 12th Field Battery admirably covering the movement. When close enough, the Sikhs made a brilliant dash upon the entrenchments, being received by a heavy discharge of musketry, but they never wavered for an instant, carrying the position with a rush, the fusiliers close at their heels. Again the enemy refused to face the bayonet and fled, making over the railway embankment, from the top of which they subjected the Americans, who were then marching towards the Chinese positions from the other side, to a very severe rifle fire for several minutes.

By 11 a.m., just two hours from starting the advance to attack, the Sikhs occupied the last position belonging to the enemy, who were now racing towards the town of Yangtsun and villages near it. The Russians advanced and shelled the enemy from their places of refuge, the Bengal Lancers meantime doing admirable work in outflanking them and eventually clearing the surrounding country of their presence.

By midday all fighting had ceased, Yangtsun was occupied by the Allied forces, and another victory recorded; the Chinese having shown throughout the fight that the moral of yesterday's battle had not been wasted. The Americans had suffered the heaviest in casualties, whilst the British losses were very small in comparison to the duty assigned them, being 45 killed and wounded (the Sikhs, who had led the charge, contributing 34 of this number). The Russians had 27 casualties, the Japanese none, having paid a heavy war-tax the previous day. As anticipated, the naval guns did not take any part in this battle, as, owing to the slow method of advance by river, although it would have been even worse by road, they did not arrive at Yangtsun till after dark, very much to their annoyance at being out of it. The whole force, men and animals alike, were thoroughly exhausted after their two days' fighting and heavy marching in the excessive heat, much difficulty having been experienced in obtaining good water to drink.

Orders were therefore issued that the whole of next day would be devoted to much-needed rest.

The general advance commenced at 7 a.m. on the 8th, the cavalry and field artillery having moved off at 4 a.m., the force much refreshed by the day's rest The naval guns, still in the junks, were sent forward, protected by a guard, the rest of the Naval Brigade moving with the troops, and bivouacking at Tsitsun for the night. Next day at 4 a.m. (9th), the march was resumed, the rear guard remaining till noon, then following on. The Bengal Lancers, who were well ahead screening the advance, came upon the retiring enemy near Hohsiwu, and had a brilliant little fight of their own, inflicting severe loss on the Tartar Cavalry, who were covering the retreat. The force arrived and bivouacked near the town for the night; the rear guard marching in about 8 p.m. The heat throughout the last two days had been intense, causing many cases of sunstroke and distressing fatigue, principally among the Indian Infantry, whom it appeared to affect the most; yet among the

Naval Brigade only two men were compelled to fall out, being probably more used to sudden climatic changes.

Captain Mullins (*Terrible*), was appointed Commandant of Hohsiwu next day, having detachments of Allies, about 500 strong, to guard the lines of communication.

The relief column moved forward again at 6 a.m. (10th), except the British contingent, which did not advance until 4 p.m.; Matou, the next rendezvous, being reached late that night after a cool march, and the Allies found there in snug bivouac. The naval guns and most of the brigade continued the journey by river route, while the remainder escorted the naval transport by road, the men being changed at intervals as convenient. During the evening, about 6.30 p.m., a well-stocked Chinese magazine was blown up by the Royal Engineers, the force of the explosion being felt within a radius of nearly half a score miles, and causing no small surprise among those forces which were unaware of its existence.

Nothing of notable incident occurred during the rest of the journey towards Tung-chao, which place was occupied without opposition on the 12th. The enemy had taken up a position south of the town, but thinking it prudent not to oppose the irresistible advance of the Allies, had again judiciously retired. The Naval Brigade did not arrive with their small fleet of junks until midnight, securing them to the bank until daylight, when the guns were disembarked and got ready again for field service.

Peking was now but thirteen miles off, and a conference of the allied generals had already met and decided on the plans for its capture, which was to be effected by four separate columns moving upon it and attacking it simultaneously on its east face, the British taking the extreme left of the assigned positions agreed upon.

During the forenoon (13th), the Allies sent out strong reconnoitring forces towards the capital, with instructions to concentrate at a certain rendezvous about five miles therefrom and await the rest of their respective columns, when a grand combined movement was to take place early on the 15th.

In the afternoon the allied forces left for the same direction, the Naval Brigade with their guns moving off with them. Strong detachments of Allies were left behind to hold Tung-chao under Captain White, R.A.

Marching, especially with guns, even now fairly heavy, was made infinitely worse by a thunderstorm, accompanied with heavy rain, which increased in violence as night advanced; so much so that at 9 p.m. further progress became impossible, the men not only dragging the guns along, but also the horses with them, which were now dead beat The brigade took sanctuary in a large *joss*-house from the infuriated elements, mooring the guns and horses outside. The rest of the force, being without encumbrance, moved ahead and bivouacked some distance further on.

A sad incident occurred directly after the brigade took shelter, a sergeant of marines, who had been somewhat seedy, suddenly became seriously ill, dying within a few minutes of the seizure. He was buried early next morning before daylight, with what military honours could be accorded him, the chaplain of the *Barfleur* reading the funeral service with the aid of a lantern; truly a pathetic ending of a plucky attempt to perform martial duty. The brigade again pushed on at 4 a.m., marching till 11 o'clock, when a halt was made until 5 p.m., and afterwards continuing the march until they ploughed their way through the turbid track to within one hour's march from the Celestial City. Then darkness—and the necessity of further instructions—brought them to another standstill and much-desired rest.

Here information was obtained that the Allies had already entered the capital, which news produced a mixed feeling of pleasure and chagrin in the weary Tars, who had hoped to assist in winning the grand finale, causing them to imprecate the Chinese, their roads, and the poor devils of horses which were not so much interested in swift military movements. For some mysterious reason the plans agreed upon at the conference for its capture had not been observed, at least not by some of the Allies, the concentration compact having been abandoned and a sort of international race for the Celestial City taken place between them since leaving Tung-chao. It will be seen by reading the British general's official despatches how Peking was captured, and which contingent won the race:—

> Our forces, on the night of the 13th, were concentrated on the river south-east of Tung-chao, about fifteen miles from Peking, with two guns, the 1st Bengal Lancers, and the 7th Bengal Infantry about nine miles in advance as an observation force. At 3.30 a.m., on the 14th, hearing heavy firing in the direction of Peking, I caused the "rouse" to be sounded, and marched without delay towards the supposed scene of action. About 7 a.m. I reached the point held by my advanced force, and at once

pushed on with the troops there available, directing the main body to follow after an hour's rest. About noon I got into touch with the Americans, who were on the south bank of the canal, and as they and the French were preparing to assault the Tung Tien Gate, I decided to push straight on and assault the southeast gate of the Chinese city, Sea-chia-men.

Here I met with no opposition, and about 1 p.m. the British troops passed through the city wall. I then ordered the 1st Bengal Lancers and the 24th Punjab Infantry to march straight to the Temple of Heaven Park, which I wished to secure as a camping-ground, and also as a protection to my left and rear, while with the rest of my available troops I pushed on through streets and alleys towards the water gate of the Tartar city, a point which I had learnt from a cipher message from Sir C. Macdonald would probably be the most vulnerable. Our troops were much exhausted by the long march and intense heat, and were much scattered in groups, but they struggled gamely on without attempting to reply to the desultory and ineffective fire of the enemy.

At a few minutes before 3 p.m., I, with a few officers of my staff and about 70 men of the 1st Sikhs and 7th Bengal Infantry, reached a point opposite the water gate. The British flag was still flying on that portion of the Tartar wall which we knew the Legations had occupied, but an ominous silence made us fear that the worst had occurred, and that the flag was only a ruse to lure us on; when suddenly, to our great relief, we saw a flag signal being made, 'Come up sluice street by Watergate.' Our small party at once rushed across the almost dry canal, and entered into the Legation zone through the water gate under the Tartar wall. As we crossed, a hail of ill-aimed fire was directed on us from the Hata-Men gate, but not a man was touched, and at 3 p.m. Her Majesty's troops had the supreme gratification of finding they were the first to relieve the sorely pressed beleaguered garrison.

Our loss during these operations was quite insignificant, which may be attributed to the fact that the enemy had never expected attack from this quarter, and had concentrated their defence on the eastern wall of the Tartar city, where the resistance was, I understand, of a most obstinate description.

The operations I have described have, happily, not been attended with the loss that might have been expected; nevertheless, the troops engaged have been subjected to a severe strain on account of the intense heat, the want of good water, the heavy mud or dust which characterizes the roads in this country, and, above all, the want of sufficient rest. The patient endurance and ardour of troops has, however, more than compensated for these difficulties, and I am proud of the manner in which Her Majesty's British and Indian troops have acquitted themselves.

The Japanese had met with most determined opposition at the two gates they attacked. They were several hours before they finally succeeded, and had lost very heavily during the operations, having abandoned the first attempt until it was dark, when they were successful in blowing up the gates with gun-cotton, and effecting an entrance about 9 p.m.

The Russians had fared somewhat better, but had also lost heavily before they succeeded in forcing their gate, which occurred about 6 p.m. They did not, however, arrive at their Legation till 9 p.m., six hours after the British, and four hours behind the Americans, who eventually entered the city by the same route taken by our troops. Thus the old maxim, "*The first shall be last, and the last first,*" had once again been exemplified.

The Naval Brigade inarched into the city next morning (15th), proceeding to the Temple of Heaven Park; but they were not to remain long in that blissful place (not because they were sailors), for the guns were needed elsewhere. Returning to the south-east gate, the brigade encamped there, placing the guns in position ready to repel any hostile movement directed at that city entrance. This was the last service performed in the North China expedition by the Naval Brigade.

The legations had been relieved, the primary object of the relief force had been accomplished; but several days of guerilla fighting subsequently took place before the Chinese were finally driven out of Peking and order within the capital restored. On the approach of the Allies the Imperial family, court, and ministers had wisely fled, escorted by many regular troops, and had formed another capital at Hsianfu, 70 miles distant, whither it was hopeless to follow them, and from whence the Imperial power would still be exercised, and decrees issued to the faithful but deluded adherents.

The war game had been played between the armed forces of

civilization and those of superstitious ignorance, and the former had won—as was only to be expected. It has also now been demonstrated that if a combination and unity of action could always be relied upon whenever a serious danger threatened the progress of the world, or public opinion has been outraged, the "Yellow Race" bogey, which is periodically exploited, would for ever remain a harmless myth.

In Peking a handful of foreigners had been rigorously besieged for several weeks; had held out against all attempts to capture or annihilate them; and so long as munitions of war and sustenance were obtainable they had been absolute masters of the situation.

The following "complimentary order" was issued to the Naval Brigade upon the conclusion of the fighting in the city—

> The general officer commanding cannot allow the Naval Brigade to leave his command without expressing to Captain Callaghan his complete satisfaction with the way the Bluejackets and marines have performed their trying and arduous duties. Their discipline has been admirable, and, as ever, the sea services have maintained on land their high reputation.

From H.M. the Queen a message was received by General Gaselee as follows—

> Heartily congratulate you and all ranks of my troops under your command on the success which has attended your remarkable advance to Peking. Trust that the wounded are doing well.

Exclusive of those who had succumbed to disease, the naval casualties during the operations in North China amounted to 61 killed, 274 wounded.

On August 30th General Gaselee inspected the Naval Brigade, and on the following day they left Peking to rejoin their ships, arriving back at Tientsin on September 3rd. Staying there two days, the whole brigade and guns were embarked in lighters and towed down the river to Taku. The *Terrible's* contingent then proceeded by transport to Weihai-wei, arriving on board the ship on September 7th, having thus assisted at the raising of two historical sieges—Ladysmith and Peking.

★★★★★★

The principal events connected with the siege of Peking, the thrilling nature of which are practically a separate history in themselves, will be briefly summarised in order to place the connecting link in the chain of the narrative, and record the lustrous deeds of the Navy's

Royal Marines.

It will be remembered that shortly after the International Guards arrived in the capital on May 31st, all communication with the outside world was severed, except for a little scant news, carried by trusty messengers, that occasionally filtered through to and from the Allies.

The destruction of the railway by the Boxers could hardly be regarded by the official Chinese as a calamity, since it made the transit of more foreign troops into Peking a difficult matter, and thus considerably strengthened their position.

So serious became the situation, accentuated by the arrival of the foreign troops, that the respective legations were placed in a state of defence to guard against treacherous attacks, and most of the foreign residents and European-Chinese officials went there for protection, many of them having received private warning from their native friends to adopt that course.

By the appointment to the presidency of the *Tsung-li-Yamen* (Government) of Prince Tüan, who was a noted anti-foreigner, and also accredited with much responsibility for the Boxer outbreak, the last hope of a favourable turn in the situation was entirely destroyed.

The total strength of the combined Legation Guards consisted of about 18 officers and 390 men, of whom 76 were British marines, one armourer, one signalman, and one sick-berth steward, commanded by Captain Strouts (in command), and Captains Halliday and Wray. They had with them four guns, *viz.* an Italian 1-pounder, one American Colt gun, one Austrian machine gun, one British five-barrelled Nordenfeldt; and one old British smooth-bore gun was afterwards discovered and effectively utilised, its ammunition being manufactured by Armourer Thomas, R.N. In addition to the force mentioned, about 150 Volunteers were enrolled from among the foreign community, and performed invaluable military service on several occasions; Dr. Morrison (*Times* correspondent) was a conspicuous member of this extemporised corps until he got severely wounded. A rough census showed that, inclusive of the troops, nearly 1000 foreigners were then in Peking.

On June 9th the ministers, realising the gravity of their isolated position, sent an urgent telegram for reinforcements, a belated request which—though compliance proved an impossibility—was met by the International Squadron off Taku in the truly naval spirit already described. Two days later the Chancellor of the Japanese Legation was brutally murdered and mutilated by Chinese soldiers as he was riding

Return of "Terrible's" marine detachment to rejoin the ship at Wei-hai-wei, after Peking was relieved

alone through the streets on duty, which dastardly violation of the very *sanctum sanctorum* of International Law signalised the commencement of a planned policy of plunder, destruction, and massacre.

As darkness set in on the 12th a general slaughter of Chinese Christian converts took place. Their habitations were burnt, and, the fire getting beyond control, a great proportion of the Chinese city, besides several foreign buildings and some churches, was destroyed. The appalling scenes witnessed and the hideous cries of the tortured and murdered victims—men, women, and even children being hacked to pieces in scores—made this night the most memorable episode of the siege.

The climax was reached next day when the revolutionary mob entered the Tartar City and menaced the Legation Quarter, compelling the Guards to use force to keep them outside the cordon established round the foreign sphere, through which no unauthorised natives were now allowed to pass.

On the 14th the Boxers attacked the foreign pickets, but were easily repulsed. To stop the "Massacre of the Innocents," which in the meantime had proceeded with unabated fury. Captain Halliday led a party of British and German marines next day and pluckily rescued several hundred native Christians who had sought refuge in the Nantung Roman Catholic Mission, killing a number of their ruthless assailants. Nearly 2000 of these distracted refugees were eventually rescued and quartered in the palace grounds of Prince Sü, which were directly opposite the British Legation; the defence of this important position being entrusted to the Japanese contingent, who courageously held the place against the many attacks the Chinese persistently directed against it.

The firing of palaces, historical temples, churches, public buildings, and whole streets, the greatest conflagration ever known in the Chinese metropolis, causing irreparable damage, was of daily occurrence.

The capture and occupation of the Taku Forts was interpreted by the Chinese officials as tantamount to a declaration of war from the Allies, consequently the Foreign Ministers were notified that they must quit Peking within 24 hours, *viz.* by 4 p.m. on the 20th. With the railway destroyed, the ultimatum was of course found difficult to comply with, and even had it been practical or possible with safety to do so, their departure would have meant the certain extermination of all native Christians left behind. Although protection was promised, which was regarded as an insidious assurance, the ministers wisely decided to remain and, if necessary, defend the Legations, as it was certain, now that the Boxers were in complete domination of the city, that the Imperial authorities, even if honestly intentioned, had not the power to afford safe conduct.

On the 20th, Baron von Ketteler (the German minister) was murdered, and his secretary, narrowly escaping the same fate, was severely wounded while proceeding to the Yamen to convey the decision of the Foreign Ministers. A grossly impudent message was sent to the German Legation concerning the murder, and that afternoon an official despatch was received by the ministers which rescinded the ultimatum and invited them to remain under Imperial protection in the capital That afternoon all the women and children concentrated at the British Legation, which place was to be held, if needs be, as the last line of defence. During a thunderstorm in the evening an organised attack on the Legations took place, the Chinese being repulsed with severe losses. This was apparently the sort of protection to expect, and this openly hostile act finally obliterated all further faith in Chinese officialism.

The fortification of the British Legation was rapidly proceeded with, and an organised system of defence of the foreign quarter adopted. The Legation buildings and grounds were now thronged with people of all nationalities, which included the ministers, their families and principal officials, besides the missionaries and numerous native converts, all of whom ably assisted in the defence. Towards the close of the siege nearly 900 persons had congregated within the enclosure of the British Legation. At the request of the foreign ministers, Sir Claude Macdonald, the British minister, took supreme command of the Legation Settlement

Fierce fighting now became general and of night and day occurrence, every artifice that the subtle Chinese could invent to destroy the Legations being resorted to. Incendiary fires were constantly breaking out around the Legations, but were speedily extinguished before their intended design could result All non-combatants, women and capable children, were organised into a fire brigade, who instantly responded to the fire signal—the tolling of the church bell. Even the famous Hanlin College, with its sacred library, was consigned to the flames by the vandalish Chinese soldiery in hopes of burning out the Legations; but all these attempts luckily failed.

Fresh entrenchments and new positions had frequently to be constructed to repel new modes of attack, or as protection from the shell fire of guns which were mounted on the city walls. Whenever the enemy approached too close, sorties were made to drive them back, an expedient attended with great risk against such a foe. Peking had become an inferno indeed, the surrounding enemy being possessed with fanatical fury, and thirsting for the blood of the "foreign devils" like beasts of prey.

On June 24th Captain Halliday,[1] with some 30 marines, made a sortie and successfully drove back the encroaching Chinese, securing many arms and much ammunition. In this affair the gallant officer was dangerously wounded in a struggle, in which he succeeded in killing four out of five of his assailants with his revolver. During the day the Chinese made a determined attack on the palace grounds opposite, where the native converts had taken refuge; but the assault was gallantly repulsed by the Japanese, though the palace buildings were fired.

On the 28th the French Legation Quarter was heavily attacked, and although its heroical defenders were driven from their barricades by sheer force of numbers, they held a portion of the Legation throughout the siege in face of intense opposition. Next day no less than 70 shells were fired into the British Legation buildings, causing considerable damage and anxiety. Captain Wray led a combined force of British, German, and Russian marines and volunteers, to capture the gun which was the worst offender, but met with non-success, owing to the Chinese withdrawing the gun on seeing the force approach.

For the next fortnight or so, and almost without intermission, the struggle continued with unabated vigour on both sides. The spirited fortitude maintained by the besieged was ever buoyed by the knowledge that their relief must assuredly soon take place, if they could but sustain the defence; and also by the consciousness that surrender, with the inevitable consequences, was an issue not even to be contemplated. Deliverance by friends or destruction by foes, one or other, was the certain sequels of the siege. Assaults were repulsed, and sorties, which alternated between success and failure, were frequently made. The several attempts made by the enemy to undermine the Legation defences were frustrated by the countercheck of trench digging to great depths, though this diabolical method of effecting their purpose very nearly succeeded, for on the day of the relief a mine, almost in a state of maturity, was discovered, and only a few more hours' delay would have resulted in a catastrophe of incalculable extent.

---

1. This officer was awarded the Victoria Cross for his brilliant services during the siege of Peking.

In spite of the huge sums offered (as much as £1000 in certain cases), the numerous attempts of runners to reach Tientsin with messages proved futile—except in the few cases already recorded. Some one hundred were sent forth, but three only returned. Considering the innate tendency of the Chinese to succumb to corruptive influences, this difficulty of transmission of news was a most curious feature of the situation.

On July 1st Captain Wray was severely wounded while supervising the building of a barricade by a mixed force of marines, who showed great tenacity and courage under a heavy and accurate fire during its erection. After darkness set in on the 3rd, 25 British, 15 Russians, and 15 American marines, commanded by Captain Myers of the American Guard, gallantly rushed and occupied two Chinese barricades of importance. Captain Myers fell severely wounded in the first charge, whereupon Sergeant Murphy of the British section assumed command and pluckily led the assault on the second barricade.

On the 5th the enemy opened on the Legations with round shot from four smooth-bore guns, mounted on the Imperial City wall, causing much damage to the outer buildings and harassment to the defenders. On this day Signalman Swannel [2] (formerly of the *Terrible*) especially distinguished himself in saving Mr. Oliphant, a Consular officer, who fell mortally wounded, from falling into the enemy's hands. Finding the British Legation quite impervious to their attacks, the enemy desisted from making their most strenuous efforts at this portion of the settlement defences, and directed them to less resistive positions.

On July 11th the French carried a Chinese barricade with great gallantry, and shot more than twenty of its miscreant occupants. By the device of sapping, the enemy, two days later, contrived to blow up two large buildings in the French Legation grounds, which seemed a sort of retaliatory act.

The gallant Captain Strouts was mortally wounded on the 16th, while inspecting the outlying defences with Colonel Shiba, the Japanese commander, and Dr. Morrison of the *Times*; the latter was severely wounded in the leg, and incapacitated, and the colonel had a narrow shave with a bullet which pierced his coat. As Captain Strouts had been Chief of Staff to Sir Claude Macdonald, his death was keenly felt by all the defenders. That evening a message was received from

---

2. This petty officer received promotion, and the Conspicuous Gallantry Medal for his courageous conduct on this occasion.

the Chinese Government, stating that they desired to protect the besieged foreigners, and had given orders for all fighting to cease. From July 17th to August 4th a cessation of active hostilities was observed, but sniping took the place of organised attacks and shell fire. Still, the enemy's virtual inaction was deemed a welcome respite by the war-worn refugees, though strict vigilance on both sides was unrelaxed, and in the meantime the defences were strengthened.

The supplies mostly needed—food, ammunition, and medical necessaries—were now running very short indeed, causing an additional anxiety. The ration, even at this period, was barely sufficient to sustain life, and towards the close of the siege the diet issued just staved off actual starvation. But for the admirable organisation of the respective departments, the gravity of the position would have been much enhanced. During the truce the Chinese soldiers displayed a keen desire to fraternize with our men, offering presents of food, which were invariably rejected with a just suspicion of their purport With inimitable effrontery, the Chinese officials also endeavoured to decoy the ministers, with seductive messages, into surrendering themselves to Imperial protection, but these sinister proposals met with the proper response—a firm refusal. It afterwards transpired that this unexpected armistice was the outcome of the cowardly fear that had seized the responsible Chinese authorities when the news of the fall of Tientsin was received in Peking, and was intended as a diplomatic stroke to cloak their villainous conduct

On July 20th a cipher message from Washington was delivered to the American Minister by the Chinese, who, though permitting a reply to be returned thereto, refused the general request of the ministers for permission to send to their respective governments an official list of casualties.

On the 22nd the Chinese made a desperate but futile assault on the completely isolated northern Roman Catholic Cathedral, where some 3000 native converts had assembled under the protection of Bishop Favier and the Catholic Fathers, with whom were 50 French and Italian Marines. This place now became the especial objective of the Boxers, who used all their fanatical endeavour to capture it; but here also a bravely conducted defence was maintained, which elicited the highest praise.

On August 4th the enemy reopened hostilities against the Legations, and from this date, until the end, they exerted themselves to the utmost to subdue the sorely pressed garrison.

But the end of the heroic struggles of the besieged was in sight, for on August 10th letters from the British and Japanese generals were received by runners, which prophesied that relief might be expected by the 13th, or next day, as the Allies were nearing Peking. On August 14th the generals fulfilled their promises, and thus ended one of the most thrilling sieges that will be written in the pages of history.

CHAPTER 20

Reminiscences of China and Japan in H.M.S. "Terrible"

From July, 1900, to July, 1902

1900. The two years spent in the Far East, outside of the period directly associated with war, were not altogether devoid of unusual interest—at least, for the Terribles,—and will be recounted in their proper sequence.

The first incident of note occurred on July 30th, when news was received at Wei-hai-wei that the Japanese new destroyer *Nigi*, homeward bound from England, was wrecked near the south-east of the Shantung promontory—60 miles distant. This information was brought by a Japanese officer of the ill-fated vessel, who, having spent 36 hours in a native sampan without sustenance, fainted while reporting the circumstances to Captain Scott. A gunboat was promptly despatched with the *Terrible's* divers and diving apparatus to render possible aid, but found that a choppy sea had in the meantime caused the vessel to break up and become a total wreck. However, the guns and other valuable property were saved, for which service the Imperial Japanese Government sent a courteously worded letter of thanks to the captain.

During the shore operations previously narrated, many of the crew were employed on the naval works of the island of Liu-kung-tao. The dilapidated iron pier was renovated, a stone pier was rebuilt, a hospital for wounded was extemporised and installed with the Rontgen rays apparatus, the cemetery was intersected with pathways and otherwise given a Christianised appearance, moorings were lifted and examined, the remains of a sunken Chinese man-of-war were blown out

THE ARTISANS OF H.M.S. "TERRIBLE"
Manufacturing a 4.7 gun carriage at Wei-hai-wei. Bending the massive tyre.
The improved forge is seen in the background.

of the "fairway," and a residential house was partly rebuilt and tiled by the "handyman," which place was subsequently occupied by Captain Scott and Rear-Admiral Bruce, respectively, "Jack-of-all-trades" the "handyman" is often termed, which is an apt description of him, judging from the foregoing paragraph.

The departure for England early in August of Captain Limpus, who was being relieved on promotion by Commander Ogilvy, was the occasion of much genuine regret among the crew, for much of the ship's history is inseparable from his name.

On August 17th the destroyer *Fame* brought the news of the relief of Peking, which event was celebrated by "splicing the main brace "that night, and a dress ship ceremony next morning. This was the second occasion of "splicing," the other taking place at Durban to commemorate Cronje's surrender to Lord Roberts at Paardeberg—and thereby hangs a tale. A rumour had gained credence in the town five days previously to the actual event of surrender, and the canard was indiscreetly signalled off to the ship as a fact by a certain enthusiastic subordinate of the commandant's office. Result—"splice main brace" to toast the event, but next day the deluded one, much to his chagrin, was crossing the bar to rejoin his ship far and safely away from the madding crowd of rumourers.

Late on October 1st a telegram from the admiral ordered the ship to proceed to Shan-hai-kwan, where the Chinese were still in possession of some powerful forts. To obviate the necessity of going out of harbour at dusk on an ebbing tide, through a narrow channel, the ship was placed in tow of the *St. Enoch* dredger. Instead, however, of this method proving an expeditious plan, the ship was found beyond the dredger's towing capacity, and the *Terrible* found the mud bottom, where she remained, undamaged but helpless, until the flood tide lifted her off. Fortunately, in the meantime a second telegram cancelled the sailing orders.

A gloomy event occurred on October 11th, when Senior-Engineer Arthur died from enteric, the interment taken place the same evening, full naval honours being accorded. This officer served with the naval guns throughout the Natal operations, and, besides being very popular with his wardroom messmates, was highly respected by his lower-deck shipmates.

The first annual prize firing of the commission was carried out the last three days in October. Following the return of the contingents from the front a strict curriculum of practical and scientific gunnery had been imparted to the gun's crews, with the result that a brilliant record with 6-inch quick-firing guns was established. With the two 92 (25-ton guns) 60 *per cent* was obtained; and with the twelve 6-inch (7-ton guns), which fired 104 rounds and scored 80 hits on the targets, a percentage of 77 was recorded; the average per gun per minute being 4.3 of rounds and 3.33 of hits. An unprecedented performance, perhaps—indeed, the figures were generally received with excusable scepticism and suspicion owing to the fact that the best scores hitherto obtained with 6-inch guns had been some 20 *per cent* lower; but the achievement was not an unexpected one—the captain even asserting that, considering the persistent instruction given, a much higher result ought to have been forthcoming. Four captains of guns made "possibles," the targets being demolished several times beyond recognition. As the total time allowance for all the heavy guns was but 36 minutes, divided into six minutes for the 9.2's, and two minutes for the 6-inch runs, many hours were occupied each day in repairing damaged targets.

On concluding the last day's firing, just as the ship anchored for the night, the wind, hitherto of slight force, suddenly freshened and the sea began to billow. Two steamboats and a launch were out attending to repairing targets, recording shots, etc. The boats were got alongside to be hoisted in, but the sea rose so rapidly that all attempts at hoisting them had to be abandoned, as it had become positively dangerous for both boats and crews. The launch was eventually hoisted at the bows, and the two steamboats moored astern. Towards dusk the wind and sea increased with great force, and every few minutes huge waves would break over the two steamboats, their crews pluckily baling them out to keep them afloat.

Shortly before midnight the launch was washed away from the bows, and drifted quickly astern, but was caught by a grapnel being thrown into her, which luckily secured itself, a man from the picket-boat jumping into her, at great personal risk, and securing a hawser to her bows. The sea was still increasing in violence, and rain falling at intervals, the weather becoming intensely cold. The crews in the steamboats were already suffering from exposure, but to relieve them had become an impossibility, as the boats were compelled to ride at the extreme length of the hawsers for safety.

The searchlights were kept playing on them, which was a certain amount of relief to the crews, as darkness, added to their other misfortunes, would have made matters appear worse than they really were.

Thus the night was passed; the ship's crew working in sea-reliefs ready for any emergency, though fortunately not required to meet any during the night Next morning, however, the shrill sharp pipe, "Away lifeboat's crew!" brought all hands tumbling on deck to find that the picket-boat had sunk, and all her crew were struggling in the sea.

The commander had provided against this contingency by having drifted a lifebelt for every occupant of each boat, so that there was no danger of anyone sinking before rescue could reach him. Six out of the seven drifted towards the launch, which was astern of the sunken boat, and were pulled in, but the other man went floating away on a water breaker, gaily waving his hand to intimate he was all right. The lifeboat was quickly after him, and got him on board safely; but the sea was so rough and wind so strong, that the cutter could not fetch the ship, so was ordered to run for the eastern entrance of the harbour, which it reached safely.

The lowering and getting away of the lifeboat was a smart evolution. The pluck and endurance of Petty Officer Sparks, coxswain of the picket-boat, is worthy of special mention, as it was entirely owing to his personal exertion, after midnight—the rest of his crew being numbed with exposure—in constantly baling out his boat, that she did not founder much sooner than she did (For his conspicuous courage on this occasion, he having also saved one man, whose lifebelt became detached, the Royal Humane Society awarded him the Silver Medal.) As the ship afterwards commenced to drag towards a lee shore, the captain decided to weigh anchor and go into harbour, which, of course, was an easy matter for the ship herself. The other steamboat followed the cutter, and the launch was towed; this latter boat was as safe as possible the whole time.

The men who had been in the boats all night had met with an unusual experience, yet they were so well attended to after coming on board again, that in the evening they appeared none the worse for the practical seamanship lesson of the previous night. The position being buoyed where the picket-boat sank. Commander Ogilvy took out a salvage party next day, and quickly located the spot. Two attempts were made by the divers to reach the boat, each of which was unsuccessful owing to the strong tide, but at slack water they again descended and secured their prize. A wire hawser was shackled to the hoisting-slings, and the boat drawn to the surface by the *St. Enoch's* machinery, little the worse for its submersion on the bottom of the Gulf of Pechili.

On November 22nd the ship left Wei-hai-wei for Japan. During

"Terrible's" 4.7 gun carriage manufactured under difficulties at Wei-hai-wei.
The carriage completed and fit for service.

the passage a twenty-four hours' steam trial was performed, and highly satisfactory results were obtained from the boilers and machinery.

Yokohama, the principal port of Japan, was reached late on the 26th. Here three days' continuous leave was granted to the whole crew by watches, which liberal relaxation from duty was much appreciated after some five months of arduous and varied service.

Japan, "the Land of the Rising Sun," is most aptly designated the Great Britain of the Far East In much less than half a century Japan has made a rapid progress in modern civilization and adoption of Western usages unparalleled in the world's history, and risen from an insular insignificance to the position of a first-rate power among the world's great nations. Her regeneration began in 1868, when the present emperor, Mutsu-hito, the 121st monarch of an unbroken dynasty, founded 660 B.C, overthrew and abolished, after a short war, the power of the *shogunate* (or paramount military commander), and that of the great feudal nobles, who had, for nearly 700 years, grossly misgoverned the country. From this period the emperor, or *mikado*, became the absolute, instead of the nominal, ruler of the Japanese empire; his subsequent reign having been marked as that of a wise, judicious, and progressive sovereign.

In 1875, his majesty instituted certain important political and economic reforms, and in 1889 a new constitution was proclaimed, by which representative government was granted to the people. The following year the first Japanese Parliament was elected and assembled. Since the China-Japanese war of 1894-1895, a large scheme of expansion of her naval and military strength has been adopted, which has made Japan a powerful factor to be reckoned with in the Eastern problems of the future. Both fighting services have proved their title to the possession of an organisation and standard of efficiency of a high order, hardly surpassed by any other notable power, and probably unequalled by some. Truly the Anglo-Japanese understanding of recent creation is reciprocally beneficial to both peoples, and must conduce towards the preservation of the *status quo* of the Far East, which is so vitally essential to the interests of both nations.

Japan's population is nearly 45,000,000, exceeding that of the British Isles. The islands which comprise the empire are mountainous, eminently volcanic, and subject to a frequency of earthquakes, not very serious usually, though disastrous visitations have occurred, one as recently as 1891, which resulted in 30,000 casualties and the demolition of 130,000 houses. Later, in 1896, a tidal wave, the probable out-

Raising the dredger, "Canton River."
Photo showing the parbuckles, etc., in place.

come of volcanic disturbances, claimed another 52,000 victims, killed and injured, and also destroyed about 7500 habitations. The country is hot in the summer, and typhoons are prevalent during the autumn, so that the winter months are the best time of the year to visit this wonderful land. Japan is rapidly developing her internal resources, and is even now a competitor in the world's markets. She possesses an ample mercantile marine, has admirable railway systems, excellent civil services, up-to-date harbour works, factories and mineral industries galore, and, in some respects, is actually ahead of certain European and American States who have clung to old and worn-out traditions.

The Japanese have evidently studied the politics of the most advanced countries, and then prudently discriminated between what to adopt or reject, appropriating the good, and discarding the unwholesome. Indeed, few innovations have been introduced hastily. True, the picturesque is dying, but the practical is very much alive. What Japan's future may be no statesman or philosopher can possibly predict, but it may be safely averred that no foreign yoke would remain very long on the necks of this capable, brave and patriotic people of the Far East

Contact with civilization has altered Japan's political and commercial principles, as well as many of her internal economic institutions, but has practically left untouched the social and religious national life. The principal religions are the National faiths of Shinto and Buddhism, though a perfect toleration of all religions exists. Morality is distinguishable from religion—a fact which might be noted with advantage in our own country to the welfare of the nation. It is written here with pleasure that few of the vices and iniquities of Christendom are publicly met with in this un-Christianised country. The streets and public places are virtually pure—the impurity exists only in restricted zones. The missionary (and even the sanitary inspector) is an individual whose services are quite as much required in London and New York. Life and property are far safer anywhere in Japan than in either of those world's centres. *Satis verborum*—truth is ever unpleasant

On anchoring at Yokohama the visitor is face to face with sumptuously appointed hotels and clubs extending along the sea front. In the distance, standing in stately solitude, is the sacred Fujiyama Mountain, which is over 12,000 feet high. On landing, one can easily imagine one's self to be in an affluent British seaport. Along the wooded slopes, and on top of the bluff, are the stately homes of the foreign community and well-to-do Japanese. There are few, if any, real places of interest inside the town beyond the inevitable curio shops. But in the adjacent district, within two hours' ride by rail, there are many historical places well worth visiting. At Kamakura maybe seen the Great Bronze Buddha (Daibutsu), which is 50 feet high, and 97 feet in circumference; the whole cast in sections and deftly brazed together. The town was selected by the first usurping *shogun*, Yoritomo, as his capital in 1185, and contains many temples, shrines, and other objects, famous and sacred in Japanese history. Enoshima is a most delightful little island. It is one blended scene of temple piles, groves, terraces, stairways, and picturesque tea-houses, and possesses a cavern about 400 feet long containing shrines. Yokosuka, the principal dockyard and arsenal of Japan, will always be a pilgrimage for both English and Americans. It is associated with the name of Will Adams, who is recognised by some as the English founder of the Japanese navy, nearly 300 years ago, and with that of Commodore Perry, U.S.N., who, in July, 1853, opened up Japan to foreign commerce and intercourse. *Keeling's Guide* thus describes the British celebrity:—

> This celebrated pilot left the shores of England to join a fleet of ships fitting out in Holland for a voyage of trade with Japan. The enterprise proved most unfortunate. The ships had to contend with boisterous weather, and the crews suffered greatly. Only one vessel of the fleet, with Adams on board, reached its destination in the year 1607. On arriving at Japan the troubles of the survivors were not at an end, for they were treated by the natives with much cruelty. The authorities, however, finally relaxed their severities, and the unfortunates were afterwards treated with kindness. Adams, owing to his knowledge of mathematics and shipbuilding, became a great favourite of the *shogun*, who conferred upon him the annual revenue of 250 *koku* of rice and a tract of land at Hemimura. Adams, although treated with this respect and honour, nevertheless wished to return to England, where he had a wife and daughters.
> This not being allowed, he ultimately took to himself a Japanese wife, by whom he had a son and a daughter. He lived for many, years at Anjincho (Pilot Street), so named in honour of Adams, near Shimbashi, Tokyo. Before dying he chose the spot at Hemimura for his grave. It commands a good view of the surrounding hills and bay. The original expense of the tombs and stone lanterns was defrayed by his neighbours living at Anjincho. One of his countrymen had a stone walk and a flight of

steps constructed, by means of which the tombs were made of easy access. He left 2465 dollars to be equally divided between his English and Japanese family. A new tomb has been lately built. Many Japanese believe themselves to be his descendants. The people of Anjincho celebrate an annual festival in his honour on June 15th.

Within one hour by rail is Tokyo, the capital of Japan, a city beautiful for the products of nature, science, and art, and ranking among the ten greatest cities of the world, containing about 1,500,000 people. It has an area about the same as London, possesses many spacious and fine public parks, and numerous intersections of waterways. A whole chapter would be required even to sketch the interesting itinerary of Tokyo. The city is indeed full of interest to the foreigner. Prominent among the sights is the emperor's palace, which, with its magnificent environment, occupies the space covered by some cities. The government, public, and mercantile buildings are noble piles, and out westward of the Imperial *demesne* are the stately mansions of the nobles, and foreign legations. There are over 3000 temples, mostly Buddhist, some of which are of notable historic interest and of vast proportion; all in daily usance, for no seventh-day worship exists in the religions of the East.

The mortuary shrines of the *shoguns*, museums, markets, and bazaars, repay the time devoted to their inspection, while for the curio-hunter the numerous curiosity shops, old and new, afford sufficient scope for a lifetime of pursuit. Throughout the day and well into the night the animated scenes in the broad well-kept main thoroughfares resemble those of the British metropolis. Much of the city is built with wood, but as conflagrations occur, modern improvements are introduced into the reconstruction. Obviously, during the transition stage of such a city from a primitive condition to that of a modern municipality, anomalies must exist in its architecture as well as in its people. In close contiguity with a noble stone edifice may be seen a row of one-storied wooden shanties, and the human element is attired in a mixture of Western, semi-Western, and native costumes according to fancy. The city Press is represented by over 100 newspapers, several of which are dailies, and, like our own metropolitan issues, each claims "the largest circulation."

Situated 90 miles north of Tokyo—five hours by rail—is the alpine town of Nikko, 2000 feet above sea-level, from which place it

RAISING THE DREDGER, "CANTON RIVER."
Photo showing the dredger righted, ready for the final operation of raising.

is generally admitted that the finest scenic view in Japan is obtained. *"Do not use the word magnificent till you have seen Nikko,"* is a popular Japanese proverb. Mountains, cascades, and monumental forest trees are its striking glories of nature; it is also noted for its marvels of art. As the Canterbury of Japan its temples, mausoleums, and shrines are unequalled in the country for their decorative, structural, and historical features. The miles of towering cryptomeria avenues are unrivalled in the world. A few miles beyond is Lake Chuzenji, a beautiful expanse of water at a height of 4375 feet above sea-level.

Miyanoshita Baths, also about five hours' travel from Yokohama, is a great rendezvous for foreigners as a fashionable seaside resort and sanatorium. With only limited time at one's disposal, the aforementioned places offer special attractions, and each of them was visited by organised parties from the ship. It is doubtful if any other country can offer the visitor such a large return for the time and money spent as does Japan. Railway travel is very comfortable, proximate punctuality is observed, and the fares are the cheapest in the universe. The officials are extremely polite, and the porters are courteously willing to oblige, with or without "tips," and it is very noticeable that after handling dirty luggage or goods they will wash themselves at proper ablutionary places provided.

The carriages, moreover, are always swept clear of accumulated rubbish at each long stoppage. British directors please take notice—especially those who govern our prehistoric Southern lines! In fact, an air of civility and politeness pervades the whole country, and punctilio is observed everywhere. Even the telegraph messengers, when not cycling the messages for delivery, are always seen running—they know not the funereal pace of the British G.P.O. youth. No wonder the Prince of Wales, after his recent colonial tour, called upon the British nation to rouse itself from a lethargic conservatism. The welfare of any country depends almost as much upon its economic policy as it does on naval and military strength.

The ship left Yokohama on December 10th for Hong Kong, arriving there on the 17th. Soon after the ship's arrival Captain Scott offered to raise a sunken dredger which had foundered in a position near the Murray Pier landing-places, thereby causing much obstruction to navigation at that spot. The *modus operandi* can be best explained by inserting Captain Scott's official version as published:

The dredger *Canton River*, length 180 feet, beam 36 feet, and displacement 1000 tons, was got out from England by the contractors for work on the new Admiralty docks at Hong Kong. In November, 1900, during a typhoon, she foundered 380 feet from the sea-wall, and turned bottom up. Her position is shown on Plate 1. The first operation towards raising her was necessarily to right her, and various attempts to do this were made, but without success.

On December 17th H.M.S. *Terrible* arrived at Hong Kong, and, finding the dredger still bottom up, an offer was made to right her. The offer being accepted, work was commenced on January 2nd, and she was righted on the 18th. The turning of the dredger was effected mainly by parbuckling, but this was assisted by lifting her on the opposite side with 'lumps,' and by forcing air into her, which displaced a large amount of water and thereby lightened her. The parbuckles were four in number, three of them capable of giving a pull of 100 tons each, and the fourth 50 tons—total pull: 350 tons. The parbuckles were wire runners and tackles, with Manilla fivefold purchases, the hauling parts of which were taken to steam-winches ashore. The standing parts of the wires were taken to anchors buried in concrete.

In all eight anchors were used, varying in weight from 2½ tons to 15 hundredweight. In order not to bring too great a strain on any part of the sea-wall, they were distributed over a length of 100 feet. The parbuckle chains were three double and one single part of 1 5/8-inch cable: they were passed with a complete turn round the vessel, the bights of the double ones and the end of the single being secured by shackles or lashings to suitable places on the upper deck: the opposite ends were brought up over the bilge and on to a barge where the purchases were secured. Cradles were placed on the bilge of the dredger to distribute the strain and give leverage: the barge was raised upon to ensure an upward pull. (See Plate 1.)

The connection between the parbuckle chains and the purchases offered some slight difficulty, as it was found impossible to get any block which would stand a strain of 100 tons. It was got over by making extempory blocks out of the dredger's spare links, which had holes in them at both ends. Sheaves were cast and mounted between the links on a pin of the same diameter as the holes; at the other end a similar pin was put through

Floral tributes of sympathy placed on the statue of Queen Victoria by the navy and army, and the respective communities of Hong Kong, January, 1901.

with a sleeve-piece on it to prevent the two parts closing in. This sleeve had two thimbles on it, round which was passed a bale-sling strop, the bights being shackled to the ends of the parbuckle chain. This precaution was taken to ensure the chains bearing equal strains. (See Plate 1.)

Counter parbuckles were laid out to prevent the vessel coming bodily in instead of turning. A lift on the opposite side was obtained from the bow of a tank steamer, and from two 'lumps.' These were filled and hove down at low water, and pumped out during the operations as the tide rose. (See Plate 2.) Air was pumped in by H.M. destroyer *Handy*, and the water in the upper compartments of the vessel thus forced down to the level marked X on Plate 1, materially assisted.

All being in readiness, on January 18th the winches were hove round and the vessel turned over without a hitch. When a purchase became 'two blocks,' a carpenter's stopper was put on to take the strain, and the block shifted. These stoppers were invaluable, and in future I shall have no hesitation in trusting the heaviest strains to them. In the righted position the vessel's upper deck was nine feet below high water, and an examination of it by divers disclosed considerable damage. The bulwarks, being crushed in, had opened the deck where it joined the side, and several iron stays were forced through. The leaks were all mended, coffer dams raised above high water placed round each hatchway, and by March 1st she was ready for pumping up. Four pumps were stalled (12-inch, 9-inch, 8-inch and 6-inch); the vessel lightened, was turned round at right angles to the sea-wall, and dragged into shallower water. (See Plate 3.)

On the 2nd pumping was resumed, the idea being to drag her along the bottom into still shallower water. The stem purchase was hauled taut, the vessel rose slightly, and there was every appearance of her coming in, when, unfortunately, a bad leak developed on the port side which the pump failed to keep under. This caused an excess of buoyancy on the starboard side, giving the vessel a list: the great amount of top weight then came into play, and she turned over.

On March 11th operations were started to turn her back again. Nine anchors were laid out in a line at right angles to her keel, and three parbuckle tackles of 100 tons each were rigged from them to six chains passed round the dredger. The hauling parts

EXPLANATORY SKETCH OF THE OPERATIONS IN RIGHTING THE DREDGER "CANTON RIVER" BY H.M.S. TERRIBLE

PLATE I.

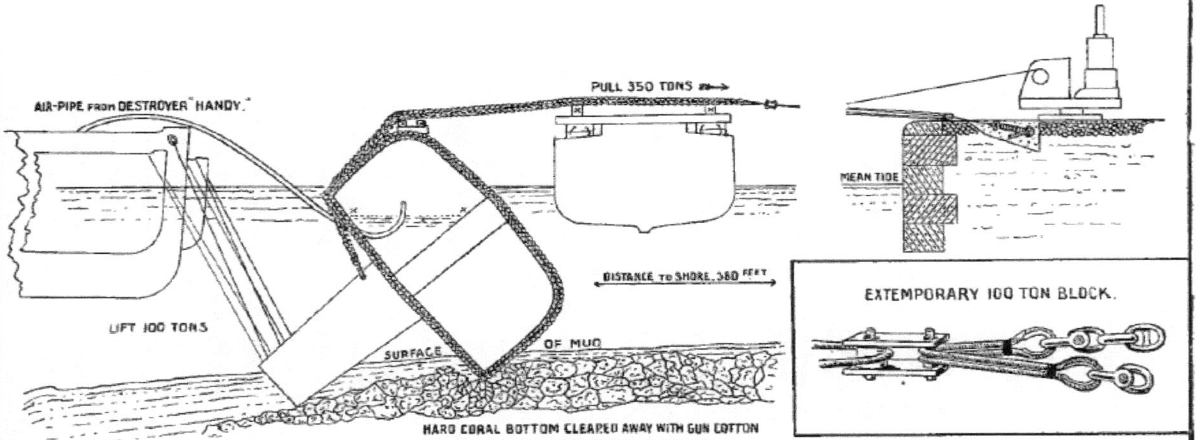

MEAN TIDE

EXTEMPORARY 100 TON BLOCK.

PULL 350 TONS →

DISTANCE TO SHORE, 380 FEET

SURFACE

OF MUD

HARD CORAL BOTTOM CLEARED AWAY WITH GUN COTTON IN ORDER TO GET THE CHAINS UNDERNEATH

AIR-PIPE FROM DESTROYER "HANDY."

LIFT 100 TONS

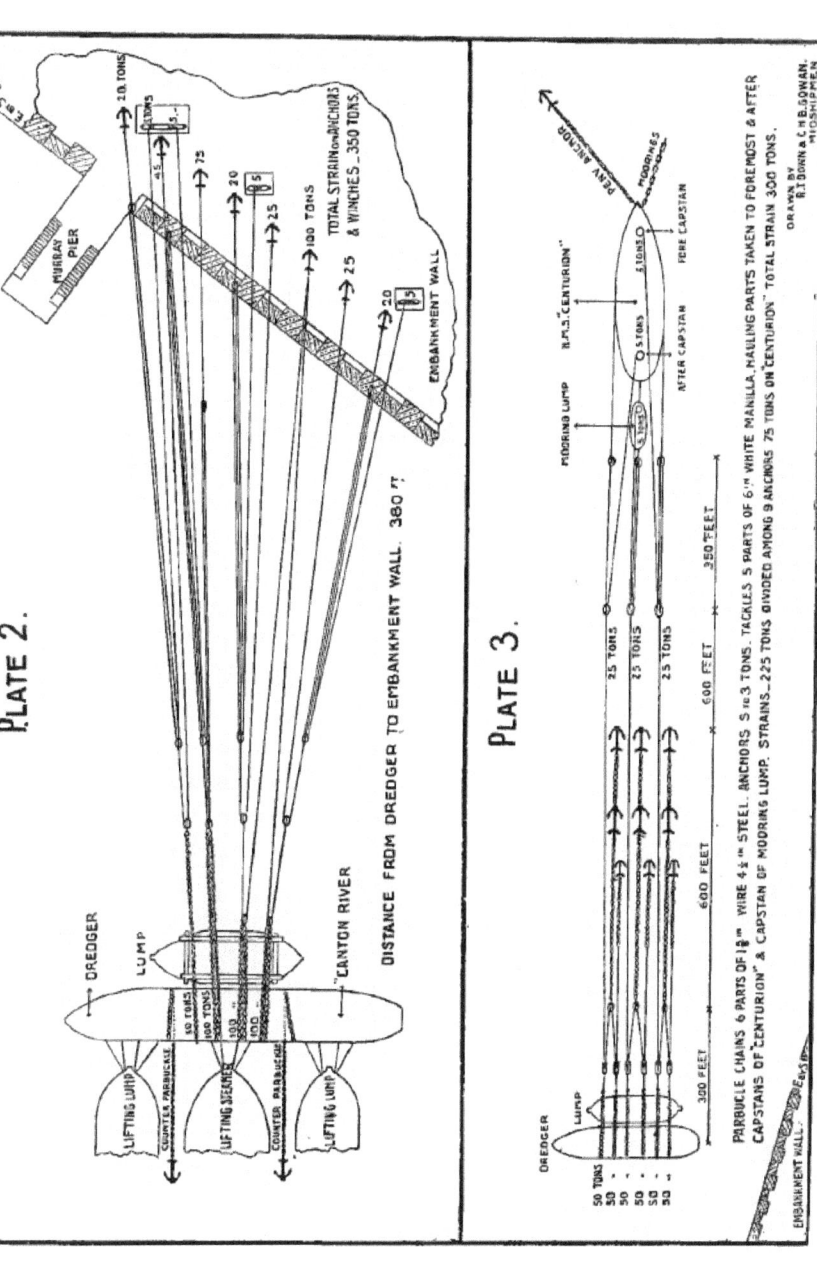

of two of the tackles were taken to the *Centurian's* foremost and after capstans; the third was taken to the capstan of the mooring-lump, which was secured to the Centurion's stem. The total strain on the *Centurian's* moorings was 75 tons. To assist, her port-bower anchor was laid out.

On the capstans being hove round, the vessel was turned to an upright position without any difficulty.

For plan of the arrangement of tackles, see Plate 3.

While the principal credit for raising the dredger must be accorded to Captain Scott, who devised the plans and demonstrated their feasibility by small working-models, the success of the operations was largely due to Commander Ogilvy, who supervised the undertaking; to Lieutenant Litchfield, who was responsible for the submerged section of the work; and to the indefatigable boatswain, Mr. Robert Ford, who, assisted by picked men of the crew, performed the seamanship work of rigging and placing the heavy tackle and other contrivances.

1901. The demise of her Majesty, the Queen-Empress Victoria, of blessed memory, who had for 63 years ruled over the vast British Empire, was signalled to the squadron at 9 a.m., January 22nd, whereupon all flags were half-masted. *La Reine est morte; vive le Roi!* and so the sorrowful tribute to the great queen was followed by the loyal acclamations which greeted King Edward VII. from millions of subjects throughout the Empire. On January 29th a naval brigade from all ships present landed and joined the military forces at a grand parade to hear the King's Proclamation read by Governor Sir Henry Blake.

Little of notable interest took place during the remainder of the stay at Hong Kong. The ship was docked, over 3000 tons of coal were shipped, and quarterly gunnery practice was carried out at Mirs Bay.

Early on March 20th the *Terrible* left for Amoy, arriving there next morning. Already in these pages have Chinese cities and characteristics been depicted as they present themselves. To enlarge further upon them here would therefore be repetition of matter. Any dissimilarity between Chinese towns is scarcely perceptible to the casual foreigner, for all, or nearly all of them, are walled-in spheres of demoralization with a complete uniformity in sombre architecture, maladministration, arid impoverished peoples. Officially, Amoy ranks as a third-class Chinese city, but is pre-eminent among the dirtiest, and its inhabitants are unusually squalid in their habits. The circuit of the city with its suburbs is about eight miles in extent, containing a population of about 300,000. Its harbour is one of the finest on the coast, and the natural scenery inside is most picturesque. There is a good foreign trade dealt with at this port. After staying here two days, telegraphic orders sent the ship to Wei-hai-wei, which familiar rendezvous was reached on March 27th.

Early in April, Commander Drummond, promoted to that rank for his war services, was relieved as gunnery officer of the ship by Lieutenant Woolcombe. On May 12th Vice-Admiral Sir Edward Seymour officially inspected the ship; and on the 28th inst. the gallant officer, whose name is so prominently associated with Anglo-Chinese history, hoisted his flag at the main of his flagship on promotion to full admiral's rank.

During the second week in June the Second Annual Prize Firing occupied the serious attention of the "man behind the gun." There was a reputation to maintain, and a result to achieve, which was either to substantiate the accuracy of or corroborate the prevalent scepticism concerning the unprecedented record of 1900. To promote rapidity of loading 6-inch guns, a contrivance had been devised by the captain and gunnery staff, termed a "loading teacher," at which innovation competitive drill was established between gun-crews which offered a combination of instructive and sportive practice. *Within one and a half minutes* a 100-pound projectile was passed clean through and a 55-pound dummy charge inserted and withdrawn, as if in action, *twenty times*; which represents a total weight handled of about 27 hundredweight! (One gun's crew subsequently reduced this time to 1 minute 13 seconds.)

Besides the five official umpires, the prize-firing was witnessed by Flag-Captain Jellicoe, C.B. (*Centurion*), and Captain Windham, M.V.O. (*Isis*), and certain invited military officers. Every expectation was realised, the previous record being broken both in rapidity of fire and hits made. The 9.2 guns fired 22 rounds, and scored 14 hits, which give 64 *per cent*; and the 6-inch guns fired 128 rounds, obtaining 102 hits, which produce a percentage of 80, with an average of 5.33 rounds and 4.25 hits per gun per minute. Several "possibles" were made. Petty Officer Grounds scoring 8 rounds 8 hits in his one-minute allowance, a performance which earned for him a world-wide reputation as a noted heavy-gun shot, and also inspired the following lines:—

If Britain's Fleet should chance to meet
A foe upon the ocean,

Its guns would greet that hostile fleet
And swiftly change their notion
That Nelson's Sons can't fight their guns;
Then picture the sensation!
When men like Grounds (eight hits, eight rounds)
Would blow them to—Damnation!"

On June 24th, in company with the *Barfleur*, a brief cruise to Chefoo took place, arriving back again at Wei-hai-wei on the 28th ins. In the meantime Vice-Admiral Sir Cyprian Bridge had arrived in the new flagship *Glory* in succession to Sir Edward Seymour and the *Centurion*, whose term of command and service on the station respectively had expired.

A second visit to Japan was made in July. Kobe was reached on the 6th inst. Next day three days' leave was given to all who could be spared without unduly depleting the ship of officers and men. Many availed themselves of the opportunity thus afforded to visit Kyoto and Osaka. Kyoto—the former Imperial capital of Japan—is a grand old city, famous for its trees and for its old and new world attractions; about two hours distant by rail. The city was founded 784 *A.D.* by the then emperor, and was thenceforward the residence of the Japanese Imperial family until the Restoration in 1868, when Tokyo was formally proclaimed the capital.

Kyoto is rich in historical associations, and was for many centuries the home of the art and literature of the Empire. The removal of the Imperial Court to Tokyo naturally exerted a depressing influence upon the city, both socially and commercially, though the industries of Kyoto are still able to support a population of 400,000. The celebrated Uji tea plantations are in the near vicinity. A visit to the Hodju Rapids, a few miles distant from Kyoto, is an agreeable excursion. The train conveys the visitor above the rapids to Kamioka, from which place the descent by boat, exciting but safe, is made over the troublous waters,

Kobe itself offers little of interest other than is associated with important maritime towns, but at the adjoining old town of Hyogo further gleanings of historic Japan may be obtained.

Osaka, one hour's ride distant, is the second city for size and commercial note in the Empire. Owing to its numerous intersections of canals, the town is aptly designated the Venice of the Far East The city is the centre of many Japanese industries, very compactly built, the streets being regular and clean, and with its half a million inhabitants

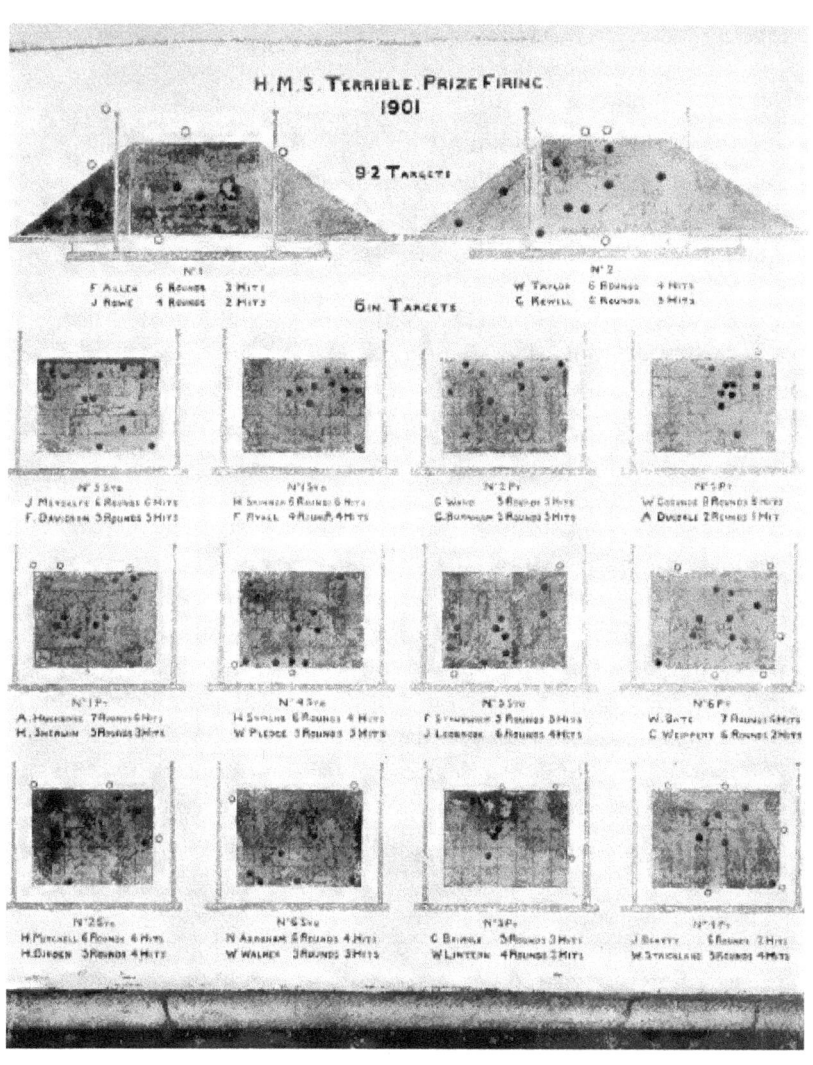

Photograph Showing results on each target.
Separate canvas for each heavy gun

always presents a scene of industrial animation. The principal object of interest is the imposing castle, erected by a famous *shogun* in 1583, which is said to be the second finest example of the ancient feudal castles of Japan. It is now the headquarters of one of the six great military districts.

The ship left Kobe on July 10th, and arrived at Yokohama early next day. Here leave for three more days was granted in watches, an indulgence which, almost needless to mention, was partaken of to the fullest extent. During the stay the Perry Memorial was unveiled with due pomp and ceremony at Kurihama, the spot where the noted American commodore landed 48 years previously and compelled Japan to abandon her policy of isolation. This act originated a new era for the Japanese, who now cherish the eventful and historic episode.

On July 26th the ship left to return to Wei-hai-wei. During the passage a steaming trial was carried out, four hours at full speed, the remainder at three-fifths power. Highly satisfactory results were again obtained, which seems to provide the logical inference that water-tube boilers, like modern guns, only require experienced manipulation to obtain from them the full measure of their capacity. Port was reached on the 29th.

After coaling, the ship proceeded to Shan-hai-kwan on August 3rd, arriving there early next morning. Nearly 3000 allies were still in possession of the forts, pending a pacific settlement of the country. Even for China, this town is shockingly dirty, and much requires its encircling wall to imprison the pollution contained therein. The "Great Wall" of China commences at this spot, and is well worth an inspection; its course being easily followed by telescopic aid for miles over the mountainous country. While here Commander Woolcombe left the ship on promotion to join the *Argonaut* as executive officer, he being relieved as gunnery officer by Lieutenant Grant. A Japanese evolutionary squadron arrived, stayed one night, and then departed on their cruise. Returned to Wei-hai-wei on August 25th.

The China Squadron Annual Regatta was held early in September, when the blue ribbon of the day, the Sir Thomas Jackson Challenge Cup, was won with easy honours by the captain's six-oared galley. The boat was temporarily fitted with outriggers to enable sixteen oars to be employed.

On September 20th Lieutenant Litchfield, the torpedo lieutenant, left the ship invalided home, having accidentally broken his knee-cap while at physical exercise on the poop. The night previous to his

"Terrible's" six-oared captain's galley pulling sixteen oars at the Annual Fleet regatta, 1901, winning the Sir Thomas Jackson Challenge Cup

departure a fraternal incident occurred after the farewell dinner was over in the wardroom, which he attended lying in a cot. On being hoisted through the hatchways to the poop cabin he was occupying, the hauling movement was performed in slow time by the officers, who sang, to the strains of the band, "He's a Jolly Good Fellow"—and so he was, too.

During September, quarterly target practice was carried out, after which nothing of noteworthy interest occurred beyond the usual routine until Christmastide, when the festive season was duly observed *à la* naval fashion—decorations, dinner, *divertissement*, and dyspepsia! On Christmas forenoon, in a temperature ten degrees below freezing-point, a football league match was played on shore, *Terrible* versus *Argonaut*, the latter team, after a swift exciting contest, scoring one goal to nil a few seconds before the whistle blew "time." As the *Argonaut* had only arrived late on December 23rd to relieve the *Terrible*, some 200 of her crew accepted invitations to dine, so that over 1000 men assembled at noon to witness the customary "rounds," and to eat, drink, and be merry.

As is usual on this occasion, there were many impromptu surprises, but deserving of special mention was the mutoscopic tableau. Standing in a recess made up of flags was a carved wooden model of the *Terrible* performing target practice at sea; so arranged that, while a supposititious run was being made, twelve shots were fired at a miniature target and a "possible" was obtained. Needless, perhaps, to add, this piece of ingenuity, so effectively manipulated, caused considerable fun, and indeed no little wonderment The final act that ended the ceremonial parade was the presentment of a significant lower-deck address, neatly written on a large blackboard with chalk as follows:—

> SEASON'S GREETINGS.
>
> *To the captain and officers from ship's company—*
> *Greetings true from all the crew—dissentients there are none—*
> *Also to Mrs. Percy Scott, and your bonny little son.*
> *To the commander and all officers sincere welcome is extended;*
> *But, Captain Scott, have "They" forgot, it's time our commission ended?*
> *Up at the main we look in vain to see if the pennant has descended.*
> *Nigh four years ago, "They" most well know—it admits of no denials—*
> *That up and down the Channel for months, the ship ran severe steam*

trials.
And afterwards, we, with our guns, bid goodbye to kin and kith;
At Colenso, Spion Kop, Vaal Krantz, at Pieter's Hill and Ladysmith,
Naval traditions we did uphold—and White relieved forthwith.
Queen Victoria (and their "Lordships") cabled a gracious congratulation.
Also telegraphic orders came—to sail for the China station.
Again "They" knew, our guns and crews were landed with expedition.
And with straight and rapid shooting sent the Boxers to perdition.
After all our arduous service, sir, will you chalk down a reply
As to when we may expect "Relief," and to China say "Goodbye"?

Taking the piece of suspended chalk, "I cannot tell you what I do not know myself," was the characteristic but hibernian reply the captain wrote; a sentence that did not fulfil the high hopes and eager expectations of the Terribles, who imagined the captain possessed the secret, and might disclose it on such an occasion as this.

On December 27th the *Terrible* left Wei-hai-wei, with its snow-clad hills and bitterly bleak Siberian winds, to the guardianship of the *Argonaut*, the officers handing over their sleighs, which had afforded them much sport, to their comrades of the relieving ship; but curiously to relate, a gradual thaw set in from this date, prohibiting further sleighing.

1902. Hong Kong was reached on January 4th. On Sunday, the 12th inst, after divine service, the "Seymour Heavy Gun Challenge Shield" was presented by Mrs. Percy Scott to the senior gunner, Mr. Wm. Mather, who accepted it on behalf of the assembled ship's company Captain Scott briefly expressed himself as to the honour attached to winning this fine trophy (instituted by Sir Edward Seymour before he vacated the China command), which, he stated, " represented that the ship holding it occupied the highest position among the China Squadron ships in that class of efficiency of most use to king and country."

During the month Rear-Admiral Grenfell, C.M.G., held the annual official inspection of the ship and crew. The official *Report of Inspection* promulgated, merits space in these pages.

The ship is very clean and well kept. The ship's company are a well-grown lot, and do their work silently, intelligently, and well.

H.M.S. "TERRIBLE" IN KOWLOON DOCK, HONG KONG, 1902.

For the last two years the *Terrible's* Heavy Gun Prize Firing for all natures of guns has been by far the best of any ship in the Service.

From the results noted in Torpedo Log, Whitehead practice is satisfactory. The engine-room department is clean and efficient.

The appearance of the marine detachment was very creditable.

Until April nothing but due observance of "fleet routine" occurred to chronicle, when the ship was again placed in Kowloon dock for a ten-days' overhaul of underwater fittings. The arrival of Captain Robinson, A.D.C., who had been appointed Commodore of Hong Kong Naval Establishments, was the occasion of a pleasant reunion; for officers, warrant and chief petty-officers, each in turn, were honoured with invitations to meet their former captain and Mrs. Robinson, who had accompanied him to the colony.

The next item to record was indeed a "record." As the ship's bunkers were much depleted of coal, a favourable chance presented itself to test the naval coaling arrangements of the port as regards rapidity of action; 2500 tons were required to complete the ship with coal, and work commenced at 7.20 a.m., the whole quantity being shipped and stowed by 5 p.m. Exclusive of intervals for meals, the actual time for the evolution was 9 hours 10 minutes. The mean average was 2727 tons per hour; but for eight consecutive hours the average was 300 tons. Thirty junks contained the coal, which was all placed alongside prior to starting. The coal was passed on board by some 600 Chinese *coolies*, carried to the banker shoots by the deck hands, and stowed by the sturdy stokers.

With a temperature of 83 degrees in the shade, and the bunkering difficulties of a modern man-of-war to take into consideration, this satisfactory achievement reflected no little credit on all connected therewith—from commodore to *coolie*, from captain to cadet, from boatswain to boy, all of whom took part in the evolution. The admiral's appreciation was signalled thus: "Average exceptionally high. Coal stowage must have been very well organised"—a high compliment for the commander and engineer officer. Thus was the blue ribbon for coaling won, but the irreducible minimum for coaling records—as for shooting—seems yet to belong to the distant future.

On April 26th, Sir Cyprian Bridge temporarily transferred his flag to the *Terrible,* on the occasion of an official visit to a British man-of-war of H.I.H. Prince Tsai Chen, cousin of the Chinese Emperor, who had been deputed as Special Envoy to attend King Edward VII's coronation, and was now *en route* to England. H.I.H. was received by the vice and rear-admirals, the commodore, and their respective staffs, the prince and suite making an inspectional tour of the ship, where every one was visibly impressed with their visit As only one clear day had intervened between the aforementioned coaling and the ceremonious visit, the admiral expressed his appreciation at the smart and clean appearance the ship and crew had so quickly assumed.

In May the Third Annual Prize Firing took place. On this occasion, owing to very unpropitious weather, and the fact of the cordite chaises having unsuspectingly increased some 30 degrees above the normal temperature for which the gun-sights are calibrated, a poor percentage, in comparison with the records established in 1900-1, had to be recorded. This great excess of temperature above the normal so increased the muzzle velocity that most erratic shooting was witnessed. Most of the shots went high over the target, the misty rain rendering "spotting" a difficult duty, consequently many shots were wasted, to the bitter chagrin of the firing numbers, who swore the target was under satanic influence.

It was not until the umpires had tested the ranges and found them accurate that the real fault was discovered. When the change in ballistics was computed, and the correct sighting announced, which necessitated the lowering of the sights 300 yards below the actual ranges given, the remaining twelve men who had to fire placed 51 hits on the target out of 62 rounds fired—a percentage of 82.2, though the mean percentage recorded was but 62. Petty Officer Grounds maintained his position as the best shot in the ship with nine' rounds seven hits, the tenth round being in the gun when his minute allowance expired, Captain Scott, after tersely explaining the technical causes of apparent failure in a notice to the crew—who, by the way, estimate success by the percentage obtained—concluded his remarks as follows:—

> The shooting was very much slower than last year, nineteen' rounds less having been fired, a fact that I attribute entirely to the misty and rainy state of the weather making the target very difficult' to see.
>
> The officers asked me to stop the practice, as they could hardly see the target from the casemates. I did not do so, as we have to bear in mind that we must be ready to fight an enemy in any

Commodore Robinson, A.D.C.　　Suite of the Prince.　　Capt. Percy Scott, C.V.O., C.B.
Admiral Sir Cyprian Bridge, K.C.B.　　H.I.H. Prince Tsai Chen.　　Rear-Admiral Grenfell, C.M.G.

VISIT OF H.I.H. PRINCE TSAI CHEN, THE CHINESE SPECIAL ENVOY TO ATTEND KING EDWARD VII.'S CORONATION, TO THE "TERRIBLE" AT HONG KONG.

weather.

Under these circumstances, I think the efficiency of the ship as regards shooting is as good as, if not better, than last year.

If we have to fight an action in the tropics, it is not our own constitutions we must think about, but the temperature of the cordite.

Ideal weather is, of course, much conducive towards producing exceptional results from well-trained gun-crews, but true efficiency can only be determined when heavy-gun firing is carried out by a ship under every atmospheric and climatic condition.

Had the firing been at unknown distances, the error in ballistics would not have appreciably affected the shooting, because, when the shots were observed going short or over, the sights would have been altered accordingly. When firing at definite ranges, inaccuracies, either in ballistics, the sights, or guns, are certain to be disclosed.

It might be here noted for the benefit of the querulous or pessimistic layman, that a fair percentage of shots which *miss a prize-firing target would hit an antagonist's ship.* A prize-firing target merely represents the "bull's-eye" of the target which an enemy's ship would offer in battle. No system or method of instruction is as yet infallible, but constant technical teaching and persistent practice are essential to ensure good gunnery, as with other scientific attainments.

On June 1st, "Peace proclaimed in Pretoria" was signalled from the commodore to the ships in harbour; news which was hailed with satisfaction—everywhere. An incident in connection therewith was the spontaneous official visit to the *Terrible* of Commander Gillmore, of the United States monitor *Monadnock*, to personally "congratulate the captain, officers, men, and British nation upon the conclusion of peace."

The following day Petty Officer Grounds, of 6-inch-gun fame, died suddenly from Asiatic cholera; his early decease from such a cause eliciting much sympathy from his shipmates and ardent admirers, many of whom sent sympathetic messages from afar.

The ship left on June 3rd to escort the destroyers *Fame, Hart,* and *Whiting* to Wei-hai-wei. Owing to rough weather being experienced, the shelter of Amoy harbour was sought. Another attempt to proceed north also proved futile, for the frail vessels could not withstand the continuous straining, and were ordered into Shanghai to renovate, the ship remaining at anchor off Saddle Island—many miles from any-

Condition below the water-line of the hull of H.M.S. "Terrible" when docked, greatly reducing the speed which should have been derived from the indicated horse-power

where. After three days of patient waiting, the *Hart* rejoined, her two consorts being indefinitely detained. Wei-hai-wei (since renamed Port Edward) was reached early on June 11th, when the discharge of the deck cargo of naval stores began. The ship left for Hong Kong the same evening, arriving back there June 14th.

A second voyage north with cargo, of such weight that the Plimsoll mark (water-line) was well submerged, took place in July; this time to Shan-hai-kwan, where the squadron out for evolutionary cruising was then staying. Leaving Hong Kong on the 10th, the ship arrived at her destination on the 16th, discharged stores, and returned south to await those "Orders" which would give a homeward-bound compass course. Before leaving, Admiral Sir Cyprian Bridge signalled:

> Though you are not yet under orders for home, I may not see the *Terrible* again. Wish all on board a happy return after an unusually interesting and important commission.

To which message a reply was made:

> We much appreciate kind signal made.

CHAPTER 21

Homeward Bound

July 29th to October 24th, 1902

"Orders for England," were received shortly after the ship arrived back at Hong Kong, and early on July 29th the *Terrible* steamed away from the China station—*homeward bound*. Except those who have served abroad for three years or more, far away from kith and kin, few can realise the true significance attached to those two words. For many they mean incomputable joy; for some they spell inexpressible sorrow.

Singapore was reached on August 3rd. During the passage south two deaths occurred. A petty officer was buried at sea the day after leaving, and a young seaman, who died the night previous to arriving in harbour, received interment on shore. Both were invalids from the station, who had expressed earnest desires to be sent home, which natural yearning was considerately acceded to by the authorities, even though little or no hope was entertained of either man ever reaching his native land.

The ship received 1500 tons of coal, which were placed on board within five hours—a coaling record for Singapore. On August 1st no less than 185,000 tons of coal were in storage here, all of which could be commandeered by the British Government if necessity arose for such procedure.

Leaving Singapore on the 4th, the ship arrived at Colombo on the 10th. Few will deny Ceylon the possession of natural and artistic glories, but none can deny that it also contains wily vendors of certain Brummagem manufactures, made for export, which are palmed off on the unwary and too credulous tars as genuine productions of native jewellery art, adorned with precious stones for which the island

H.M.S. "Terrible" at Hong Kong, 1902

In honour of King Edward VII's Coronation. The letters were formed by 210 men dressed in white clothing; the design of Commander Ogilvy.

is famous. Many purchasers found, upon their arrival in England, that *"all is not gold that glitters,"* or what will even stand the acid test, and that the stone settings were clever imitations of the real articles. Yet, in spite of admonitions, other homeward-bound crews will fall easy prey among the guileful land-sharks. True, the genuine is obtainable; but it is far safer to purchase expensive jewellery presents from trustworthy British makers at home, and then, if the conscience is elastic enough, present them to the fair one, with some imaginative story about their association with some place or other abroad, which would be partly true, seeing that gold and stones are imported.

After remaining five days, the ship continued the passage across the Indian Ocean in weather made agreeable by the invigorating south-west monsoons.

Anchoring at Aden at 6 p.m. August 23rd, coaling ship immediately commenced, the tiresome task lasting throughout the night, when, as dawn broke, the ship again proceeded. The Dublin Fusiliers, comrades in arms of the Terribles during the Natal operations, were found quartered at Aden, recuperating on this corner-piece of the Arabian desert after adding lustrous South African laurels to the annals of their regimental history.

Aden occupies the dual position of a strongly fortified coaling-station and that of a trade emporium of the Red Sea. It was occupied by the British in 1839, and became the centre of the British Protectorate assumed over the tribal districts of Southern Arabia. Though subordinate to the Bombay Government, its affairs are directly administered by a political Resident. Always of fluctuating importance, the Suez Canal route has considerably enhanced its position, commercially and politically, for it has become an important link, of much strategical value, in the Imperial chain of colonial possessions. Owing to the scanty annual rainfall, water storage has ever been a vital necessity here; hence the most interesting features of Aden are the famous reservoirs, which date from 1700 B.C.

The climate experienced in the Red Sea was virtually of a red-hot nature. Down below in the stokeholds the "man behind the shovel" was keeping his four hours' watch, feeding the furnaces in a temperature of 130 degrees! Yet, notwithstanding this fact, and that the canteen shelves were empty and the stokers existing on "bare navy," not more than three *per cent*, of them were placed *hors de combat*—a tribute indeed to their stamina. One case of heat apoplexy occurred; but the victim, though unconscious for many hours, recovered in the end.

On August 28th the ship arrived at Suez. The canal was entered early next afternoon, and Port Said reached at noon the following day, the 30th, the passage through having been performed, partially by night with searchlight aid, without incident or accident to record. The total length of the Suez Canal is 99 miles, with a uniform depth of 29 feet 6 inches throughout, but of insufficient width to permit of two vessels passing in opposite directions while both are in motion, one having to be hauled in at a gearing station to allow the other to go by. The canal was opened for traffic in 1869, the British Government acquiring £4,000,000 worth of its shares in 1875, their market value having risen nearly seven-fold, while their political worth is incapable of determination—a national legacy of that astute statesman, Earl Beaconsfield. A recognised convention exempts the canal from blockade in time of war; but it may be safely assumed that, in the event of a great maritime struggle, its neutrality would soon be violated. Vessels using this route to Australia and the East, though the canal dues appear large, effect a great economical saving both in time and money.

An erroneous opinion is often gleaned of Egypt by what is observed of the country during a passage through the canal. Much of the view on either side is of an arid description, and the people who live along its banks are seemingly in a state of mendicant poverty, giving the impression that the Israelitish flight from Egypt was a sound policy even viewed from a worldly standpoint. But Egypt with a Cromer at Cairo as the pilot of its fiscal and economic policies, if not of prolific resources and affluence, is a country that is capable of a greater development than it has hitherto enjoyed. Since the revolt of 1882, when the British Fleet under Sir Beauchamp Seymour bombarded Alexandria, and the power of Arabi Pasha was broken by Wolseley at Tel-el-Kebir, the country has been subjected to a British military occupation.

From that period an unabated era of comparative prosperity has set in. Since the *khalifa's* power was hopelessly destroyed by Kitchener at Omdurman in 1899, the reconquered Soudan provinces have again become an integral portion of Egypt. Nominally a tributary province of Turkey, it enjoys autonomy under its own hereditary *khedive*; but Egypt's separate existence and integrity as a state are vested in the goodwill of the Great Powers, of which England is the dominant factor. Port Said is a cosmopolitan town, entirely owing its prosperity to the canal venture.

On August 31st, after coaling, the ship anchored outside, well clear of the town, which was then shadowed with one of the endemic plagues of the East.

Leaving Port Said late on September 3rd, Malta was reached early on Sunday the 7th, when, owing to having had direct contact with an Egyptian port by coaling there, the ship was placed in strict quarantine.

As the combined Channel and Cruiser Squadrons, a total of seventeen battleships and cruisers commanded by Vice-Admiral Sir A. K. Wilson, V.C, K.C.B., were in occupation of the harbour, the ship was ordered to anchor off the entrance until after their departure next day. Early next forenoon the two squadrons proceeded eastwards to effect a junction with the Mediterranean Squadron; their processional departure from Valetta harbour in "Single Column Line Ahead," led by Rear-Admiral the Hon. A G. Curzon Howe, C.B,, C.M.G., evoking a feeling of pride in our first line of defence.

Proceeding inside the harbour, coaling at once commenced. The lighters were brought alongside and then abandoned the work being solely performed by the coal-worn crew, who, during the commission, have bunkered 67,717 tons!

The necessity for enforcing quarantine regulations is quite obvious to the average intelligence; but surely some consistent limit of stringency should be adopted to suit the circumstances of each case, and not a mere law of the Medes and Persians type. Here was the *Terrible,* without any infectious case, and with next to no sickness on board, placed under *twenty-one days' quarantine* by the civil authority, simply because she had coaled at an Egyptian port eight days previously. Ludicrously absurd were some of the restrictions imposed. The crew were not permitted to bathe, yet the sanitary pipes of the ship flushed directly into the harbour! A boat would come alongside, deliver its freight at the bottom of the ladder, then lie off, whereupon the goods, or whatever was brought, could be obtained. All monies or correspondence were received from the ship in collection-boxes secured to long poles—like offertory-boxes used in a church—and the articles disinfected with much genuine gravity by the uniformed José. Even the coal-lighters, after each was emptied, received the disinfecting process to purify the defilement with which they had been contaminated by the "handy-man."

One Bluejacket jocularly inquired if the smoke from the funnels was not going to be disinfected! Such "Prevention-is-better-than-cure" methods, if long persisted with, would soon produce a commercial calamity in a strictly mercantile port And even here the selfish quarantine policy was adversely affecting Maltese trade.

Coaling was completed by Monday midnight, when the ship steamed away *en route* for Gibraltar. During the passage the Japanese flagship *Asama* and cruiser *Takasoka* were passed, both exercising at towing targets. The admiral signalled to the *Terrible* by the international code, "Glad to see you. Congratulate you on your success. Wish you a pleasant voyage." To which polite signal the reply of, "Thank you very much," was made back.

Gibraltar was reached at noon, September 12th; but here, be it noted, the "Yellow Jack" was sensibly requested to be hauled down, and *pratique* at once granted by the courteous King's Harbour master. After completing with those goods so clearly defined in the Customs Notice as dutiable articles, the anchor was weighed and the ship's course set for Old England. The dream-like hope of years, months, and then weeks, was now within a few days of realisation!

Crossing the Bay of Biscay in weather which rendered the sea as smooth as the proverbial duck-pond, Plymouth Sound was entered at 2 p.m. September 16th. Did it rain upon our arrival? No!—therefore another record was established. Directly the ship was moored, Admiral Lord Charles Scott, K.C.B., the naval commander-in-chief, expressed a special mark of favour by his informal visit to the *Terrible* on her arrival.

All men whose homes were at Plymouth, or in the near vicinity, were considerately granted leave until the following midnight—an unheard of concession a very few years ago, but just the act of grace a subordinate cherishes.

Early on the 18th the *Terrible* was steaming up Channel, priming herself for the customary official trial of boilers and machinery, which final test was satisfactorily concluded. At 6 p.m. the ship anchored at Spithead, where, three years before, at about the same hour, the anchor was weighed, when the memorable cruise with its unique vicissitudes, that was now nearing an end, was being commenced. Among the many "messages of welcome home" received, one from Admiral Sir Edward Seymour, the other from Captain Bayly, C.B., of Tientsin history, specially struck the keynote of appreciation from the Terribles.

The ship proceeded up harbour early next forenoon. When passing the training-ship *St. Vincent*, her many hundreds of embryo handymen lustily cheered those whom they were being trained to emulate; such a scene probably adding a piquancy to their yearning for a simi-

The "Terrible" proceeding into Portsmouth harbour, on the termination of her eventful cruise, to pay off.

larly adventurous commission abroad.

By 10 a.m. the ship was secured to the South Railway jetty, after which several hundred friends and relatives of the crew trooped on board to effect the long-hoped-for reunion. Later, certain civic dignitaries arrived on board and officially welcomed the *Terrible* back to Portsmouth. From the Navy League a congratulatory address was sent, which read as follows:—

> To Capt. Percy M. Scott, R.N., C.B., His Majesty's ship *Terrible*.
>
> Sir,—The Executive Committee of the Navy League, on behalf of the members of this society, would beg to tender to you, the officers and crew of His Majesty's ship *Terrible,* their most cordial congratulations upon your safe return to this country.
>
> As citizens and taxpayers, we take this opportunity of conveying our thanks for the great services by sea and land which you and your ship's company have rendered to the Empire, and we would refer especially to the signal service performed by you in mounting heavy guns for use before Ladysmith and in the field, as also to the improvement in gunnery practice of the navy, which has largely been the result of the record firing by His Majesty's ship *Terrible*.
>
> We have the honour to be, sir,
> Your obedient servants,
> R. Yerburgh, President
> E. R. Fremantle, a Vice-president.
> H. S, Trower, Chairman of the
> Executive Committee.
> Wm, Caius Crutchley, Secretary.

On September 23rd the citizens of Portsmouth entertained Captain Scott, the officers, and crew, at a public banquet in the Connaught Drill Hall. At 6 p.m., preceded by the Royal Marine Artillery and H.M.S. *Excellent's* bands, the Terribles, to the number of 700, performed the processional march to the hall along a gaily decorated route, densely lined with enthusiastic crowds of Portsmouthians and visitors, the progress of the "Ladysmith-to-Pekin" brigade being attended by continuous popular acclamations throughout the line of march. Major Dupree, the Portsmouth mayor, assisted by the reception committee, received and marshalled them to their places at the profusely prepared tables. At the main guest table the mayor presided, having Captain Scott on his right, Rear-Admiral Henderson on his left, with the other prominent guests and officers placed according to precedence and service rank. In the galleries accommodation had been thoughtfully provided for some 400 ladies, about one-third of whom were close relatives of the officers and chief petty officers.

Throughout the repast instrumental and vocal selections were alternately rendered by the bands and a body of youthful tricolour-dressed choristers of both sexes from St. Luke's Schools, who gave intense pleasure when rendering their programme of patriotic melodies.

Upon the conclusion of dinner the Mayor proposed the toast of "The King," which having been duly honoured, the entire assemblage sang the National Anthem. The following telegram was then read:—

"The council and members of the Society of St. George offer a very hearty welcome to Captain Percy Scott and the officers and men of the *Terrible* upon their return to the shores of old England. They have proved that they did not forget (nor ever will) the imperishable signal of heroic Nelson, '*England expects every man will do his duty*.'"

After proposing in felicitous terms the toast of "Our Guests," the mayor delivered a brief summary of the *Terrible's* commission, in which he vividly enumerated the main incidents of the South African and North China Wars connected therewith, and tersely referred to the shooting records established in 1900-1901. In the course of his remarks he quoted the often-quoted aphorism, "*It is the unexpected that happens*," which he said "had been strikingly exemplified in the case of the *Terrible*," and concluded his speech as follows:—

> On behalf of my fellow-townsmen, I would say to yon, the officers, petty officers, and men of the *Terrible,* we feel that in tendering you our tribute of respect and esteem and our expression of heart-felt thanks, we are only acting as the mouthpiece of the nation at large. You have earned our deepest gratitude, and maintained nobly and well the grand traditions of our first line of defence.

Captain Scott, in reply, said:

> On behalf of the officers and men of the *Terrible* I beg to thank you very much for the magnificent reception that the inhabitants of Portsmouth have given us, and for the kind and hearty manner in which you have proposed the toast. The borough of Portsmouth has been for so many years and is so closely

connected with His Majesty's Navy, that a welcome from its citizens naturally finds full appreciation in the hearts of a ship's company, most of whom have residing in the neighbourhood all that is dear to them. I need hardly tell you how anxiously the order for our return was looked forward to, how eagerly all the home papers were scanned for some indication of our relief being commissioned, and how easily any rumour, no matter how unreliable the authority, was seized upon and believed, and it would be impossible for me to make you realise how hearty was the cheer which rang through the ship when I passed the word that orders had been received for our return to Portsmouth.

Much as we looked forward to our return, your welcome has entirely outdone anything that was dreamt of, and your reception of us will, I am sure, never be forgotten by any officer or man of the *Terrible*. With regard to the South African War, even before it commenced I realised that it was purely a soldiers' war. The Boers had no navy to fight, no seaports for us to secure, no commerce for us to attack, and the theatre of fighting was far too inland for a naval brigade to go. The small number of infantry that we could land would be inappreciable, and the only field service guns that we had to land were of the same pattern as the Royal Artillery. It, therefore, appeared obvious that it was a war in which the navy could take but a small part. A lucky chance, however, arose. The Boers had got long-range mobile guns, and our army had not.

This ill wind blew good to us. It was an easy matter to get a few Cape waggon wheels, put a bit of wood on the top of them, and on to that ship long-range 12-pounders; then one had a gun equal in range to those employed by the Boers. When heavier guns, such as 4.7 and 6-inch, were required, it only meant a little more wood and stronger wheels. These guns were found rather useful, and allowed the navy to work once more beside the sister service in the field. The manufacture of gun mountings, however, was not a very happy or fortunate event for me personally, as it meant my being left at the base to make more, and so precluded me from commanding my own officers and men.

However, they were fortunate enough to be commanded by Captain Jones, the present flag-captain here, an officer who by his capability, tact, and the cordial friendship which he extended to the Terribles made it a pleasure for them to work under him, and I was glad to hear from him that they had done well. You mention, Mr. Mayor, the services performed by Commander Ogilvy, Mr. Wright, and their guns' crews at the first Battle of Colenso. The saving of two 12-pounders by them on that occasion was a feat which all of us in the *Terrible* have been very proud of. When the native drivers had all bolted and the bullocks had all been shot, getting a couple of guns away was not an easy matter. I am extremely obliged to you, Mr. Mayor, for the kind way in which you have referred to my services as commandant of Durban.

Some of the duties I had to perform there in restricting civil rights would have been very irksome had I not been in such a loyal colony as Natal, where the aim and object of every one was to help, and I am glad to see that the valuable services rendered by Sir David Hunter and Major Bousfield have been recognised by the country. In North China the officers and men again had an opportunity of working ashore with the sister service, and eventually found themselves quartered in the forbidden city of Pekin, and I am very glad to see that one man who was shot through the brain there is well enough to enjoy your hospitality tonight. I have to thank you also for the very kind reference which you have made to the shooting of the ship. I feel sure that the captains of the guns and the officers who have taken so much care and trouble over their instruction will fully appreciate your remarks, and, further, that your public reference to it on this occasion will do much to stimulate a desire in others to follow their example.

As captain of the *Terrible* it has always been a great satisfaction to me to know that if we had to fight an enemy I could go into action with a perfect reliance on the man behind the gun. I beg, again, in the name of the officers and men to thank you and the citizens of Portsmouth for this magnificent reception, and to assure you that it is fully appreciated by us all, and at the same time to add that on board the *Terrible* we all appreciate our luck in coming in for the two campaigns, but we all know that we have done no better than any other of his Majesty's ships would have done under similar circumstances.

If in any little details the *Terrible* has been successful, I owe it all to the loyal co-operation of my officers and men.

MEDALLIONS AWARDED TO PRIZE GUNS' CREWS OF H.M.S. "TERRIBLE".
(Designed by a naval officer.)

After the cheers which greeted the gallant captain's speech had subsided. Miss Dupree (the mayor's daughter) presented to each of the Terribles a handsome silver souvenir of the occasion, suitably inscribed with "Naval Brigade, South Africa, 1899-1900. North China, 1900." During this ceremony a specially composed march, entitled "Welcome Home H.M.S. *Terrible*," was played with vocal accompaniment. The next item was the presentation of medallions to three 6-inch prize guns' crews, which trophies were the gift of the *Bluejacket and Coastguard Gazette*. For design and execution they were much admired. On the obverse side a bust of Nelson was depicted, with his famous signal inscribed around it, and on the reverse was portrayed a 6-inch gun's crew in action. Silver medallions were awarded to C P. O. Symons and P. O. Metcalfe, captains of 6-inch prize guns, and 21 bronze medallions to three prize guns' crews. (The silver medallion awarded to the late Petty-Officer Grounds was forwarded and presented to his father by the Lord Mayor of Birmingham.) The memorable proceedings terminated at ten o'clock.

On Thursday, the 25th, an animated scene was witnessed on board, when Captain Scott, the officers, and crew, were "At Home" to the wives, children, and relatives of those who had served at any period during the commission; over 1000 guests crossing the ship's gangway. An aerial railway, a shooting gallery, and the capstan converted into a merry-go-round, were prominent among the numerous attractions provided for amusing the younger generation; the ship's interior being gaily decorated with bunting. The next day a repetition of the festivities took place, when the choristers who had so largely contributed to the success of the banquet, together with their juvenile comrades of both sexes attending St Luke's Schools, about 800 altogether, were specially invited guests of officers and men. For four hours the youthful visitors indulged their frolicsome fancies at the variety shows, and later appeased their appetites with the toothsome dainties of the tea-tables. On both occasions the entire crew—captain, officers, and men—played the part of hosts in the proverbial nautical style.

By royal command Captain Scott visited the king at Balmoral early in October, and while there His Majesty invested him with the insignia of a "Commander of the Victorian Order," and with that of the "Companion of the Bath;" well-merited honours, which indicated that the services of the captain of H.M.S. *Terrible* were appreciated by the ruler of the Empire.

The presentation of the South African and China Medals by Cap-

"At home" to the children of St. Luke's schools on board the "Terrible" at Portsmouth.

tain Scott was the concluding function, and most vividly impressive ceremony, of the paying-off period. As each officer, or other notable subordinate, received their silver rewards of war, the captain handed them, with terse remarks, which aptly applied to each recipient, thus infusing much spirit into the proceedings. The valedictory speech which followed the issue was of a stirring nature. The captain briefly reviewed the principal events of the commission, and, in impressive language, enjoined the officers and crew, should similar lucky opportunities again occur, not to forget their obligations to King and Country.

Nothing of unusual interest apart from what is associated with a man-of-war's paying-off routine followed the interesting event just recorded.

On October 24th, 1902, the *Terrible* was paid off in Portsmouth Dockyard at the same place where, exactly four years and seven months previously, she commissioned for the eventful cruise the narrative of which is now ended.

Life and Routine in a Modern Man-of-War

Before proceeding with the subject proper, the constitution of the navy's personnel will be unveiled, and expression given to what is meant by routine.

Officers and men are officially divided into four branches, *viz*. military, engineer, medical, and a civil branch, the last-named comprising all officers and men not included in the other three branches, the military branch being usually termed the executive, and the remainder the non-executive. The Royal Marines are a distinct corps of the Royal Navy, detachments of whom are on board each commissioned ship borne for specific purposes.

Those officers who commence their service in the *Brtiannia* at Dartmouth as naval cadets, and who, should Fate favour them, may advance by degrees to admiral-of-the-fleet rank, and those bluejacket boys who enter a training-ship, whose careers, if fortunate, terminate with warrant rank, form the naval executive, or military branch. The cadet, on completing his studies in the *Britannia*, and after serving a specified period at sea as a midshipman, is promoted to acting sub-lieutenant at the age of nineteen years, and then completes his professional examinations at Greenwich and Portsmouth naval colleges before obtaining his commission. The bluejacket boy, on passing through his varied instructions in the training-ship, proceeds to sea, and is rated ordinary seaman at eighteen years of age.

The engineer officers graduate as engineer students at the Keyham Engineering College, Devonport Dockyard, before receiving the King's Commission as assistant engineers, while their subordinates—engine-room artificers and stokers—on joining, receive practical training at the respective naval depots. The stokers are a semi-military body, as they undergo a special course of military instruction, and perform the annual musketry practice.

Officers and men comprising the two other branches—medical and civil—are mainly entered direct from the shore.

Officers enter the navy by securing a place at Civil Service Examinations, and satisfactory tests, educationally or mechanically, according to the particular branch selected, admit aspiring recruits. A physical test is applied to all alike. The "Quarter-deck" is nominated from the classes, and the "Lower-deck" recruited from the miscellaneous masses. Officers and warrant officers serve to the retirement age of their respective ranks; all others complete a first engagement for twelve years' continuous service, but to obtain a life pension a total of twenty-two years must be served. The pension is indeed the "Grand Prix" of the navy—the allurement of second engagements. In the event of war, everyone in receipt of pensions may be called upon for active service until 55 years of age. Certain regulations, however, permit officers and men to sever their service careers under conditions to be adjudged of by the Admiralty.

The naval service offers a glorious and honourable career to those with an inborn desire for a roving and adventurous life. But it is no place for the fortune-hunter, for derivable income has its fixation in each degree of rank or rating. Nor for the aspirant for early fame, because there are limitation rules which govern advancement—except for war or other exceptional service performed. Neither for the drone, as every one in a man-of-war must each earn his "pound and pint." The scope for special talent and energy is unlimited, which attributes are mainly the open secrets of success in each degree while the respective ladders of promotion are being climbed. From ploughman to premier is a possibility in civil life; from private to general is already *un fait accompli* in the army; but an impassable gulf exists between the naval ranker and the admiral's list.

An admiral's flag forms no part of a sailor's kit same as the field-marshal's baton is popularly credited with being in the kit of each soldier recruit. Hence the gentleman ranker is an unknown species of mankind in the navy; unlike the army, wherein youthful scions of blue blood, plucked at college, and other defeated aspirants in the social world do not hesitate to join its attractive ranks for ulterior motives. In this respect the navy offers no analogy to any other profession or calling, for, besides the peculiar and prohibitory conditions of service forward, there also exists an inexplicable prejudice among naval rankers against being officered by those who emanate from their own social origin or standard of entry, even in this democratic age. Perhaps it is the comprehensive training given, and the worldly knowledge gained by travel, which better enables the sailor to appreciate the limitation of human capacity, and to recognise those essentials required for command. Nowhere is the old *axiom* that "*a little knowledge is dangerous*" more manifest than on board a man-of-war. Yet, on the other hand, exceptionally brilliant service or especial talent must, in the navy as elsewhere, receive due recognition in order to attract to its service the cream of the nation's youth. Patriotism and emulation have ever been strong qualities of the British seaman, but personal ambition is also as rampant in his nature, the same as with his civil and military compatriots.

Routine is the punctilious regimen of a man-of-war, without which life would be next to being intolerable. It provides for individual comfort, is essential to procure efficiency, and conduces towards the proper care and maintenance of the ship. An old naval proverb asserts that "*the stricter the routine, the more comfort for all*," which is a virtual truism; but its truth depends much on the *nature* of the prescribed routine.

In reality, routine furnishes the economic government for the navy, a squadron, and a ship, and may be classed under three heads, *viz*. service enactments, station orders, and a ship's regulations. The King's Regulations enact that certain observances, drills, practices, and various inspections shall take place at specified times, from daily to yearly periods for the personnel, and analogous instructions which apply to the *matériel* and ship. Station orders regulate the routine of a squadron, which are framed by the respective admirals commanding the naval stations. Ship's regulations provide for the internal economy of each ship as determined by the captain and executive officer. For enforcing precise and punctual recognition of routine discipline is absolutely necessary, which is sustained by the commandments contained in the Articles of War.

To fully elucidate the mystic life and routine in the navy would be tedious perusal to the naval reader, and mostly of an occult meaning to those unfamiliar with nautical nomenclature and sailor vocabulary, which requires experience afloat to appreciate. As instances—a commander of a ship is really the second in command; a fleet-engineer has nothing to do with a fleet; a master-at-arms does not officiate with arms; the guns are conspicuous by their absence in the gun-room—

Hands to bathe from the ship the bugle now sounding the "Advance."

which is a junior officers' mess; the ship's manger is not a trough for a horse or other animal; a dog-watch has no reference to dogs, nor the cat-head anything to do with cats, neither does to fish a spar concern the sport of fishing; and, lastly, the crew of the jolly-boat are no merrier than their shipmates.

Now follows a brief *résumé* of the *Terrible's* routine as carried out on the China Station.

Summer harbour routine:—At 4.45 a.m. the boatswain's mates with pipes, and the buglers sounding reveille, aroused the "Hands" with their shrill whistling and piercing blasts, accompanied by a continuous admonition to "Lash up and stow hammocks." From 5 o'clock clean decks and boats, then spread awnings, and afterwards hands to bathe lasted until 6.30, when breakfast was piped, and the crew performed their daily ablutions. At 6.50 the watch below cleaned the mess decks while the other watch completed the necessary work on deck. This sanitation and furbishing labour strictly ceased for the day at 7.35, when the bugle sounded "clean guns," during which duty the band played stimulating popular airs. At 8 o'clock the ceremony of hoisting the colours took place, when every one on deck faced aft and saluted while the National Anthem was being played. From 8.15 to 9 o'clock "Stand easy" and dress in the uniform of the day occupied this forty-five minutes of time, which was, in reality, the crews' proper breakfast-time.

At 9.10—after clearing up decks for executive officer's and first-lieutenant's inspections—-divisions and prayers, then both watches fall in, followed in succession, and at 9.30 drill and instruction classes commenced and working parties detailed for ship's work. Thus the forenoon was occupied till 11.30, when drills ceased. At 11.45 decks were cleared up, and at noon dinner was piped. The termination of the midday meal-time was announced at 1,15 p.m. by the bugle call "clean guns," during which formal occupation decks were cleared up. At 1.30 both watches were again fallen in and a repetition of the forenoon routine recommenced. All instruction classes finished with tuition at 3.30, at 3.45 all work ceased, decks were cleared up, and at 4 o'clock the whole crew were assembled at "evening quarters," which muster-roll took some five minutes to effect.

Then followed a watch evolution conducted by the officer of the watch, such as "Out fire engine"—"Up diving gear"—"Out collision mat," or whatever the flagship signalled, if present, or executive officer might order. When completed, this finished the day's duty, the crew being piped to tea at 4.45, from which time only certain absolutely necessary work or duty was performed j one watch going on leave. At 7.30 supper was piped, when, usually, the most substantial meal of the day was partaken of. Hammocks were piped down at 8 o'clock, mess-decks cleared up at 8.30, the executive-officer going the "Rounds" at 9 o'clock. "Pipe down" at ten o'clock closed an ordinary routine day.

Other routines:—Winter, Tropical, and Sea, were framed on very similar lines to suit climatic and other conditions. When at sea, as is the custom, the seamen are employed at drills and duty in two watches night and day, and the stokers divided into three steaming watches, but who, in harbour, all work stipulated hours to coincide as much as possible with the ship's regulations.

Throughout the service, on certain days, special events occur which temporarily interfere with the ordinary routine just described. One or more important evolutions are performed on Monday forenoons, but in the early mornings when within tropical limits. Nearly the whole crew are involved in such general exercises as "Out torpedo defence nets"—"Fire, or Collision stations"—"Man and arm boats," etc.—or the heavy drills of "Laying out a bower anchor," or, "Clearing ship for battle." On Tuesdays inspection of arms followed prayers. Wednesdays and Thursdays the marines and Bluejackets, respectively, landed for infantry and field drills whenever possible, or carried out the routine on board. The time-honoured custom of "Make and mend clothes" was piped with dinner at noon on Thursdays, an institution dating from the William IV. period, and which is regarded as being of such an inviolable privilege that to withhold, except for some especial reason, is to incur intense wrath.

Leave is also accorded for one watch from one o'clock, the afternoon being in reality a tacitly official relaxation from duties and drills. On Friday forenoons the whole crew were exercised at "General Quarters" (the fighting stations) which, with the "Abandon ship" evolution, requires the service of every soul on board—the latter one especially! In the afternoons the field guns' crews landed with the guns for drill. Boat-sailing exercise was performed when the weather was suitable, usually on Wednesdays. The whole day was devoted to cleaning ship, armament, etc., on Saturdays. Kit and bedding inspections were infrequent functions, but the habitually dirty and slovenly attired individuals were rigorously attended to!

The special Sunday observance is provided for by enactment; no unnecessary work being permitted or any form of punishment en-

"Terrible's" 6-inch guns' crews at physical training

The projectile, weighing 100 lbs., must be thrown 11 feet 6 inches to ensure it alighting on the rope mat.

forced on the Sabbath. The ordinary daily routine was observed until 9 o'clock, when the ship was prepared for the captain's weekly inspection. At 9.30 the entire crew assembled at divisions, were inspected by the captain, then dismissed; after which ceremony, accompanied by the chiefs of departments, the captain proceeded to scrutinize his command mainly from a sanitary and professional aspect. It is strange but true that a captain rarely fails to espy a dirty corner or a neglected piece of gun or other mechanism, and then "something" is said to the responsible chief, who in turn vents his displeasure in some form or other on the real offender for the dereliction of duty. Upon the conclusion of "rounds" the captain signs the departmental books presented to him for his weekly signature, and then proceeds to inspect junior officers' logs and work-books, when an unpleasant five minutes awaits the youthful middy whose results exhibit signs of inaptitude. At 10.30 Divine Service was held for Church of England adherents, those of other denominations attending their respective places of worship wherever occasion permitted.

By 11 o'clock the chaplain's more practical than theological ten minutes' sermon was verging on completion, the singing of the National Anthem announcing the finish of the service. Then followed the bugle call which assembled "Captain's Requestmen," who were individually dealt with according to King's Regulations or merit. From noon, when dinner and leave was piped, the rest of the day was leisurely spent Thus ended a week of ordinary life and routine, which cannot, of course, be fully depicted in a few pages, but sufficient is given for the purpose. Except, perhaps, the born caviller, few can complain of twentieth-century life in the Royal Navy. True, certain disabilities and disadvantages exist, much of which is of simple remediable nature, but difficult of removal owing to the innate distaste for change and almost fetish reverence for tradition which prevail in naval life. Nevertheless, the good derived greatly outweighs both real or apparent evils. Certain periodical drills are perhaps irksome and even of a laborious nature, but, usually, there is really little beyond coaling ship that comes within the category of hard manual labour as understood on shore. Therefore, as before stated, for those who desire a life on the ocean wave the naval service is nonpareil.

Many impressions, mostly erroneous have gained credence concerning the *Terrible's* particular *régime*. No "*callao*" whatever prevailed or indeed could exist when even a semblance of efficiency is obtained. Strict discipline was always enacted and due observance of routine continuously enforced throughout the long commission, but, perhaps, in many instances the method employed to achieve results were innovations in comparison to customary naval procedure. All instructions, drills, and evolutions were conducted under the personal supervision of the captain and direction of the commander. Each lieutenant, also, was allotted and profitably employed with certain instructional classes, and held responsible that precise and proper tuition was imparted. Vague technicalities were dispensed with, and the practical only taught. Besides conducting the men's instructions, the lieutenants, each in their own speciality, officiated at the professional curriculum of the junior officers in such subjects as construction, navigation, French, and signals, while an engineer officer taught the engineering subject. One lieutenant was appointed intelligence officer of the ship—a unique duty in other than a flagship.

One *Terrible* lieutenant, noted for his vivacious personality, once showed a remarkable aptitude for teaching. On one occasion he so correctly impersonated a certain French master of Hong Kong, that he went on board a newly arrived battleship on the station, instructed a class of midshipmen in the French language, and conducted the lessons to a finish without detection, much to the chagrin of his unsuspecting pupils, who much resented his affected punctilious manner towards them.

Target practice with heavy and light guns, torpedo running, and mining operations, are the principal quarterly evolutions, but the annual prize-firing and admiral's inspection are the two most important events of the year. Little need, or can judiciously, be detailed concerning gunnery. The principle of instruction was divided into five component parts—learning to (1) elevate, (2) train the gun, (3) note result of shot, (4) correct sighting errors, and (5) perform special loading drill; each being taught separately at specially devised contrivances and machines, then combined, and by constant practice the results previously related were achieved. Guns able to shoot straight have been constructed, telescopic sights of wonderful accuracy have been invented, mountings to allow the guns to be easily and quickly manipulated are provided, so that trained guns' crews are only needed to furnish the sequel.

The strain of maintaining efficiency is not great provided a continuity of instructions and drills are imparted and performed all the year round. Indifferent gunnery cannot wholly be ascribed to want of practice, as extraneous causes will occasionally vitiate against obtaining good results, however precise the guns or zealous the gunners. Science has produced almost perfect engines of war, but science will never produce infallible humanity.

When at prize-firing the ship steams up and down a base line marked off with buoys, and fires at canvas-rigged targets of specific dimensions laid off at variable distances from 1400 to 1600 yards' range for the heavy guns, to 600 yards for machine guns. The general conditions vary with the class of gun. At quarterly practice each gun has a limited allowance of ammunition, but when prize-firing an unlimited expenditure is permitted within the official time allowed for each run. The mechanically-worked 12- and 9.2-inch guns are allowed a 6-minutes' run at eight knots' speed, while the quick-firing man-handled 6-inch guns are only given a s-minutes' run at twelve knots' speed. As the base line buoys and targets resemble an inverted **T**, the targets being opposite to the central buoy, it follows that the distance changes during the run between the two outer buoys. Thus, at 1400 yards' range from the central buoy, the distance is increased to 1600 yards at the outer buoys. Efficiency, of course, depends upon rapidity of fire, and number of hits obtained; the umpires carefully noting that the prize-firing regulations are rigidly adhered to.

This annual prize-firing somewhat demonstrates what a captain may expect from his crew, or an admiral from his squadron, when in action. No mental pictures can be depicted of what a fight between modern naval opponents will resemble, for all scientific war inventions, theories, and systems of training, can only receive a true adjudication of their merits or demerits in the test of actual warfare. But it may be pertinently assumed that the advantage would assuredly rest with the belligerent, whose gunners were adepts at straight and rapid shooting. Prize-firing is not now the perfunctorily-performed functional event it formerly was, but has become the examination day of the year, by which a ship's efficiency is more or less gauged. A keen and healthy rivalry now exists to top the Prize-firing Return for the year, same as previously existed when "strike lower yards and topmast" was an evolution which earned enviable reputation to a ship which held the record for that thrilling but picturesque performance.

Nelson's famous strategy was much governed by the winds, his tantalising tactics depended upon adroit seamanship, and his decisive battles mainly won by personal valour—now supplanted by science, individual intelligence, and morale, respectively.

★★★★★★

Landing of a Naval Brigade.

Organisation.—In detailing the components of a naval brigade special points have to be considered, *viz.* nature of expedition, climatic conditions, transport, and whether a distinct or a co-operative force. For emergency landing, the ship's organisation is considered suitable, and was as follows: Each four parts of the ship formed a company under a lieutenant, to which was attached pioneers, ammunition, explosive, and ambulance sections, with bugler and signalman. The marines formed a distinct company, nearly 100 strong. The composition of each company was so arranged as to give it an independent position for a brief period of action, if detached. But for an expedition that may last for an indefinite period the above organisation is an invalid system. It is imperative that both men and *matériel* must be selected. Twice in the *Terrible* were special landing-parties organised at short notice for indefinite periods of active service in the field. The best men, physically and otherwise, were selected for the respective duties. The appendices show the organisation on both occasions.

Equipment.—The service uniform for those dressed as seamen, except underwear, is wholly unsuitable and unserviceable for active service on shore operations, as the writer has before experienced during the protracted Gordon Relief Expedition, 1884-5. Serge soon wears; when wet it takes a long time to dry, chafes the skin, and navy blue is a conspicuous colour to the enemy. Duck is cold and clammy, very uncomfortable when wet, and not a durable material. The straw hat, splendid for ordinary wear, quickly deteriorates, and if painted becomes too hard and heavy, causing sore heads. The cap affords no protection against the sun. The army boot was found more adaptable to the feet than the naval pattern, and the army sock, owing to the absence of the ribbed toe-seam, more congenial for wear and very durable. It might here be noted that none of the Naval Brigade ever complained of sore feet, though occasional long marches were made.

The khaki clothing, especially that supplied of woollen texture, is apparently the most suitable dress for field service, though the cotton material may be preferable for very hot climates. The military great coat was an infinite advantage over the blanket, which, when soaking wet, adds weight, and robs a man of cover when halted or on cold night duty. The service canvas gaiters, nice for drills or parades, do not compare with the army putties, either for wear, comfort, or service. Putties require a little experience to put on properly to get the best tension for supporting the leg, and are virtually watertight. By plastering mud round the front portion of the boot, a drift could be waded through dry-footed—a wrinkle learned from the old soldiers. Those who possessed the colonial felt-hats said it was an ideal headgear for day wear, and the woollen "balaclava" admirable for night use. The waterproof sheet was most useful, the military mess canteen indispensable, and cholera-belts a necessity. The compulsory and necessary accessories each man carried were one extra flannel shirt, one pair of drawers, two pairs of socks, one belt, patching and sewing material, a first-aid package, an emergency ration in sealed tin case, ablutionary gear, and an identification ticket whereon was stated the official number, name, rank or rating, and the inevitable sailor's clasp-knife.

Next-of-kin lists were compiled and left on board. Spare clothing was carried as stores and issued as necessary. The Natal Naval Volunteers had a commendable method of carrying their spare personal effects in small canvas holdalls. Slight modification in design and size, and if painted, would give its use great advantages over the system of carrying everything rolled inside the blanket. Any article could easily be procured, kept dry, the holdall could be carried alternately on the back secured by straps, by hand, or slung over the shoulder on the rifle, or used as a pillow, and, unlike the blanket, would not fall apart. With name of owner painted on, it could easily be claimed when transported as baggage.

There is also much room for improvement in the complexed accoutrement equipment. More simplicity for carrying ammunition is needed. The present style produces soreness of body, and hence unevenness of temper, permits loss of ammunition with the callous Tar, and allows it to get wet and in a *verdigris* condition. It has too many straps and separate parts for rough-and-ready service. The circular *bandolier* system might better distribute the weight, one to go round either shoulder, and another to girdle the body, fitted with flaps to guard against loss and rain, worn together or separately as required

Stores, implements, routine, etc.—Much of the success credited to naval brigades is largely due to the comprehensive nature of its composition and system, which invariably renders such forces self-supporting. Every appliance or instrument likely to be of use is taken on active service, mostly selected to meet expected contingencies. Commander Ogilvy, in a paper read at Hong Kong, when dealing with this subject, stated—

The "Terrible's" crew at bathing recreation while in Kowloon Dockyard, Hong Kong

The Wallace's spade on any ground is too small, and on soft and sandy ground only can it be used without breaking. The existing patterns of pioneer tools are unsuitable for practical work; every one of them is a compromise between efficiency and weight, and of a shape and size that the man is unaccustomed to work with. The pioneer should, on no account, be made to carry his tools, for, to enable him to do so, they have been so reduced in size and weight as to be practically little more than toys, and even so, the man arrives at his job tired out with carrying them.

One horse, mule, a couple of donkeys, or a few *coolies* will carry enough for a whole battalion, and these can nearly always be obtained where seamen are likely to land. As a matter of fact, we found our tools useless, and left them behind; or, perhaps more correctly, threw them away broken in less than a week. What we really used were good practical tools, *viz.* those used by the gaugers on the Natal Government Railway. Without these we should have been in a bad way.

The following tools were found essential for a battery of six 12-pounder guns—

    2 five-foot crowbars
    3 large picks
    2 large axes

(If guns are to be split up into pairs, one of each.)
And for each gun—

    1 small hand axe
    2 spades
    1 shovel
    2 small mattocks.

A shipwright went with each gun, and he had one large augur, two large coach-wrenches, one large saw, and a shipwright's donkey with smaller tools.

I should not care to carry less than the above with a battery of guns on detached service.

As examples of what can be done by naval shipwrights:—The shipwright attached to Lieutenant Burners battery, in the course of one night, dismantled two broken-down Boer waggons, fitted a pair of front wheels to the two guns forming Lieutenant Burne's section and was ready to march off next morning.

On another occasion, with another battery, the trail of one gun, which had a flaw in it, was broken short off when firing at a high angle. Within six hours of a rough baulk of timber arriving, the gun was again in action.

The 4.7 guns were also well provided with repairing outfit; but, fortunately, little repairs became necessary.

Regarding food, the field ration was of excellent quality and of ample quantity; the brigade as a body waxed fat on the liberal and luxurious fare provided—sufficient testimony of this statement. Anyone who ventured a grumble at his war food richly deserved to be punished with a long term of existence on salt sea rations! Cooking and messing utensils and implements were of the army pattern, which amply fulfilled all field requirements. Those landed with from the ship—the naval mess kettle soon burnt through, and the basins and plates, lasted the proverbial five minutes. Those Terribles who also landed on active service in China are excellent judges of army versus navy systems of field equipment, both for the outer and inner man. The marine equipment, except the deficiency of khaki uniform, is, of course, of the army pattern in most respects. ,

Camp routine was assimilated to that of the army in its military aspect, but to naval methods otherwise. Stringent rules regarding sanitation of the naval camps always prevailed, not carried out with spasmodic attention as was often noticed elsewhere when well-merited rebukes appeared in General Orders. Every possible precaution was taken for the preservation of health, which met with its reward, as a normal sick-list was the result. Water was always boiled whenever possible, and tea or coffee issued each meal, which the liberal ration, carefully used, permitted to be done. Though food was abundant, water was nearly always of very scarce supply.

There was, by the way, only one water-cart available for the Naval Brigade, mostly attached to the 4.7 battery, so that at times the detached 12-pounder units were badly off for water. But they managed as only sailors do manage, as the following incident tends to illustrate. One night on Hlangwani Hill, Ogilvy's battery were aroused from sleep by a man in charge of General Warren's water-cart inquiring the way. One trickish Tar readily grasped the situation and offered to show him the route. In less than a minute the cart was hopelessly jammed among the boulders that abounded, and the cart had to be *lightened* to extricate it The track was then speedily found, and it is assumed General Warren and his staff got the remainder of the water.

Commander Ogilvy's paper consistently asserts that one of the principal agents in spreading specific diseases was the dust, due to (1) shallowness of "convenience trenches;" (2) their proximity to cooking places; (3) and the dry nature of the climate and constantly recurring dust storms. It was not uncommon for the food to be covered in a few seconds with a thin layer of dust swept up from the whole camp by a whirlwind. He suggests the following remedies, but admits there are practical objections to them.

(1) To deepen the trenches; but the ground is often too hard. (3) Place them further off; but men when fagged out may discard them. Moreover, there is often no room unless the camp is spread out to unwieldy dimensions. (3) Cover them with a tent; but troops are often without baggage or tents for long periods.

Another method, he suggests, is to frequently disinfect the trenches, and states that two facts tend to substantiate the dust theory—(1) Sickness—enteric and dysentery—rarely occurred when troops were moving day by day. (2) Several men, down with dysentery, asserted they had drank none but boiled water. When it is considered that the health of an army is of as much vital moment as food or ammunition, it is evident this subject must be scientifically grappled with.

Fatigue parties were told off in rotation in equal proportions from the guns' crews when in camp, but all necessary non-military duty was performed by disengaged men when in action. One word will suffice to express the state of discipline—admirable. Discipline is as essential now as at any previous period, but scientific warfare has proved that individual genius is an indispensable factor in naval or military organisation to assure success. The quality or power of the individual to think and act for himself lessens the responsibilities and anxieties of his leaders, and enables them to concentrate their brainpower on the vital instead of dividing it among the subsidiary issues. The Boers have, on more than one occasion, proved the dictum that a force comprised of intelligent men, able to form sensible judgment and to act on it in a practical manner, may compel a superior body to succumb to its influences. Automatic discipline is pretty in peace, but often prejudicial in war.

The following extracts from Commander Ogilvy's paper is given as being of interesting matter to the naval reader, and, perhaps, not wholly without interest for general perusal.

Shell fire:—Most of us—I can answer for myself anyway—went

to the front with certain fixed ideas as to shell fire, such as—
(1) Shrapnel—no good over 4000 yards.
(2) Shrapnel should be burst some 200 yards in front of the object.
(3) The shattering effect of common shell.
(4) The impossibility of standing up before lyddite.
(5) How easy it would be to knock out a Boer gun.
6) How easy it would be to pick up a range; and many others.
Our opinions were rapidly altered. Our time fuses were marked up to only eighteen divisions, which, on the scale, gave 4500 yards; but owing to the rarefied atmosphere the composition burnt slower, and we could give effective shrapnel fire up to 5200 yards. How we prayed for a longer fuse! On one occasion a Boer 4.7 gun at 7000 yards with one shrapnel shell wiped out the entire crew of a 5-inch gun consisting of nine men; this shell burst less than twenty yards in front of the gun; for it passed over a naval gun which was only twenty yards in front and slightly lower than the 5-inch gun, and appeared to burst quite close to the 5-inch gun. This illustrates my second point, for if that shell had been burst 200 yards off, perhaps one or two bullets might have gone amongst the crew, but with such low velocity as to be not very dangerous. The method of adjustment of fuses we adopted was to increase the length of fuse until the shell did just not burst before hitting the ground, and then to come back one-fourth division.

Common shell in the open (I don't mean between decks), except at close ranges, when an extremely accurate fire can be maintained, has small effect on a well-protected gun and crew or a man under good cover, and, for that matter, has shrapnel under similar circumstances. Consider the size of the vertical target offered by a trench at 3000 yards which is only three feet wide and probably protected by a bank; the only danger, if a man is taking cover, is when the shell pitches in the trench. I never saw a Boer shell do this, though on some occasions I saw them explode in the earth bank, and the only damage they did was to temporarily bag the unfortunate man lying in the trench. On one occasion it was an Irishman—in the Dublin Fusiliers, I think—and all he said when we pulled him out was, 'Shure, yer honour, I thought I was killed and buried in once't.'

Another point that was soon discovered was the uselessness of the preparatory searching by artillery. The Boers simply sat in their trenches and had a good feed, as they knew that an attack would shortly be delivered, and reserved their energies for that. It also enabled the Boers to pick up our gun positions; but they would not give theirs away until the attack really commenced, and then it often took hours before all their guns were properly located—so cunningly did they conceal them.

The general idea of attack from a gun point of view was: (1) locate enemy's guns and trenches, etc., with powerful telescopes; (2) at night, place and conceal sufficient guns to hold the enemy's guns, protecting them with sand-bags, also sufficient guns to enfilade (when possible) and keep the rifles in enemy's trenches quiet; (3) attack with the infantry; (4) when enemy's guns open fire keep them quiet with heavy shrapnel fire during the attack, and prevent them being moved away if your attack is successful You cannot hope to disable them except by a lucky common shell, unless the range is very close; (5) as soon as you see the enemy's rifle barrels pop up out of the trenches, and hear the *pick puck* of the Mauser, you commence shelling with shrapnel, adjusting the rate of fire so as to keep the rifles down, but keeping it as low as possible to economise ammunition.

As the infantry get very near—say 300 yards at a 6000 yards' target—you shift to common shell, and open as rapid a fire as possible, only withdrawing, or rather changing this target to other trenches, as the final charge is made. The Boer prisoners said, that so long as they kept down in the trenches their casualties were practically *nil*, and it was only when they were compelled to stand up to repel the infantry attack that they suffered, and then it was awful.

Lyddite,—The extremely contradictory reports received from Boer sources on the efficacy of lyddite are due, in my opinion, to the fact that it frequently does not detonate. From long and continued watching through a powerful telescope, and also from the sound of the explosion, I think that quite 50 *per cent*, of lyddite only explode and do not detonate. An exploding lyddite shell has much the same effect as one of powder, and in addition produces a brownish-yellow smokes but should it detonate, there is a tremendous shattering effect, and the smoke of a thick greenish-yellow hue, and the effect on people in the neighbourhood, according to some of the prisoners, is a tremendous shock to the nervous system, causing temporary suspension of all bodily functions, and, of course, if too close, death. Those prisoners who said that the effect of lyddite was small, had, I believe, never experienced the detonation of a shell close to them, but only the explosion.

As I said before, the Boer guns were so cleverly concealed that it was often only possible to discover their position by a 'Sherlock Holmes' system applied through a telescope. On one occasion, for example, General Buller was very anxious about a certain high velocity Boer gun which was causing much damage to our infantry, who, forming the attack, were more or less exposed, and had been temporarily checked by rifle fire. He was told at once that the gun he referred to was behind a certain hill, and, though able to enfilade the attacking line at some 6000 yards' range, was perfectly protected from our artillery fire. 'How do you know a gun is there if you cannot see it?' was his query. Reply:

'Look through the glass. Do you see those six trees across the neck?'

'Yes.'

'Well, there were seven there last night, and if you look very carefully you will see that every effort to obliterate the evidences of the removal of the seventh has been made, such as removing all branches, putting earth on the fresh-cut stumps, etc. Further, if you watch very carefully you will notice a slight haze every now and then, and always, about sixteen seconds after, there will be a shrapnel bursting amongst the troops you refer to.'

He saw all this, and was quite convinced. On another occasion, a beautifully concealed gun position was discovered by the track through the dew-covered grass in the early morning, made by the gun's crew going down at night to get water.

Many methods were tried of concealing guns, but their position was generally given away by the dust thrown up by the rush of gas from the muzzle of the gun. Wetting the ground in front was effective, but rarely practicable on account of the scarcity of water and the smallness of our guns' crews (only ten men per gun), and the ammunition had sometimes to be carried some hundreds of yards. If there was considerable drop in the ground before the gun, matters were much better.

We sometimes placed our guns on the reverse slope of a hill, out of sight of the target, and directed the firing with the telescope; No. 1 of the gun laying on a visible object, say, for the crest of some high, distant hill, and working his deflection scale and sight as ordered by the observer, who noted the fall of the shots, the details being entered in a book by the midshipman of the gun when the range was found. Thus—'Pom-pom by Bloys' farm'—aim at top of right tree on Two Tree Hill—1000 yards, 10 knots right deflection—shrapnel, 17¼ divisions. Thus any gun of the battery could be instantly turned on a well-concealed position (actually out of sight of the gun), but even if in sight, only just discernible with the aid of a most powerful telescope.

Another difficulty which was occasionally at first felt by naval officers, as compared with the Royal Artillery, was the difficulty of ranging. It is so simple at sea. You see the splash, and raise or lower your sights accordingly; but on shore it is quite different. One example will suffice. To make this clear, imagine three hills rising up on the other side of the valley, all in line, the two nearer ones very steep to, and their crests level with your eye. The enemy's gun was on the crest of the middle hill; but we were not aware of this hill, but thought it a continuous slope back from the nearest one to the farthest. The smoke from all shells that missed the first hill and did not actually hit the middle one, or the farther one, could not be seen. This case actually occurred, and there were upwards of 3700 yards between the crest of the near hill to the visible part of the far one; the actual ranges being: crest of near hill, 3300 yards; middle hill, 4900 yards; visible part of far hill, 7000 yards. This, of course, was an exceptional case; but at any time ranging on shore, except in flat country, or when you have great command, is much more difficult than at sea.

Nearly all the firing with the 4.7 was done with a clinometer (the large ones supplied for adjusting torpedoes were those used), but considerable variations in the elevation when firing at the same object, with the same gun, and from the same place, was observed, according to time of day, temperature, etc., also whether using lyddite or common shell. This, I believe, led some people to disbelieve in the value of clinometer firing at first, but a little experience soon altered their opinion as to the accuracy of it. I see an officer here who, I was told, dropped a 6-inch shell into a farm at a range of 16,500 yards with his third shot. With the 12-pounder, we did not use clinometer firing for the very excellent reason that we had not got any. However, we improvised one for night work at positions selected in the daytime. We laid the gun for the object during daylight, then placed an ordinary spirit-level on the bar and drum, or telescopic sight, and brought the sight level; the range on the sight was then noted and small pickets put up for direction. All that had to be done at night was to set the sight at noted range, bring level horizontal by elevating gear, and lay for pickets—the gun was then properly laid.

At the same time, I consider this night firing at small targets useless, and worries your own crews more than the enemy. At one time we had to fire a certain number of shots every two hours throughout the night, and this after working all day, and never taking your eye from your glasses or telescope from daylight to dark. Two nights of this in succession were quite enough. Ammunition is so valuable, transport so huge without increasing it unnecessarily, that I am of opinion that not one round should be fired without a definite and sufficient target, and all promiscuous searching is worse than useless. A good telescope tells you far more, and leads to more damage being done in the end, and your gun positions are not given away sooner than absolutely necessary.

The value of command was most noticeable. Every one has heard of that from childhood almost, but I do not think many people really realised what a tremendous pull it gives you, at any rate it was quite an eye-opener to me. It benefits you in many ways,

1. It is so much easier to get your range, in the first place.
2. It enables you to see very readily where each shot pitches.
3. It is much harder for the enemy to get effective cover, and if they do they are forced to leave a great deal of dead ground in front of them.
4. You are yourself much safer than they are.
5. The accuracy of your fire is increased practically to an extent which I would not have credited, although, of course, I know it was theoretically.

Several examples of this could be quoted, but two will suffice.

1st. In the Vaal Kraz fight a 6-inch Boer gun using black powder opened from Doom Kloof having a good command of all our heavy guns. It became such a nuisance that at one time two 4.7 guns (naval), four 12-pounders long range (naval), and two 5-inch siege guns (military), and perhaps, but I am not sure, some howitzers were all firing at it at the same time, yet only three shots did any damage. One hit the gun and it took some hours to repair; one chance shot exploded a waggon full of ammunition somewhere in rear of the gun; and another disabled a second 6-inch gun which was coming up the reverse slope somewhere; thus there was only one hit out of, I should not like to say how many rounds.

The gun in rear that was damaged was one that had been damaged in a night attack from Ladysmith and had been to Pretoria and had some feet (I do not know how many) cut off its muzzle.

The second case the boot was on the other foot.

During the last flanking movement two 12-pounders were sent up Monte Christo, a very high hill. The first one that got up silenced in a very few rounds three Boer 4.7 guns (45 lbs.) and kept them absolutely quiet until a heavy thunderstorm gave the Boers a chance to shift these round a spur of a hill out of sight of Monte Christo.

About getting guns up high and steep hills, I think that it is perfectly safe to say that if it is possible to get a man up to the top it is comparatively easy to get guns up, provided always you have suitable wire rope and a few leading blocks and other rope gear. The ammunition column should, I think, always carry the necessary gear, as the occupation of some flanking hill which the enemy deems inaccessible for guns may easily mean the upsetting of his entire disposition and perhaps render untenable some most important point in his defence. Whilst talking of the ammunition column, I must tell you of the magnificent way in which the one that supplied us was worked.

Our movements were usually at night, especially towards the close of the operations leading to the relief of Ladysmith, and we never had an opportunity of communicating with them, yet next day I would see the familiar face of the sergeant of the column waiting for a slack moment to come to me and get the nature and quantity of ammunition that would probably be required. He would take back a rough chit to my friend Major Findlay, R.A., and that night it would be alongside of us no matter what difficulties arose, and the 4.7 guns had the same tale to tell. Never was there the slightest hitch. In getting guns up a steep slope it is always as well to remember that the road, or apology for it, should be, not absolutely a straight line, but the shortest between the two levels; by that I mean it should not run diagonally across the face of the hill, for, though that may mean a slighter angle, it is more difficult to prevent the guns from capsizing and slipping off the road, unless it is a properly laid and finished one, which you cannot expect.

Rapidity of Fire:—The tremendous advantage of a gun being able to fire rapidly was most marked. One 4.7 platform mounting was as good as two on the travelling mounting, the only disadvantages being its comparative immobility and the time it took to bring it into action; but, even as it was, two ox-waggons carried the gun, it could go anywhere that the others did go to, though perhaps the others might have gone to places where it would have been most difficult to get the platform mountings. With regard to the time it took to bring into action, *viz.* about one hour, that did not matter so much, as there was usually plenty of time. When dumped down on the ground without any anchors, it could be and was fired from the shoulder as fast as is possible on board ships, the slight jump of the mounting tending to relieve strain and not interfering with No. 1.

On several occasions many bodies of horse or artillery could easily have been severely handled had all our guns been similarly mounted. I am sure it would be quite simple to design a platform that could accompany an ordinary field gun like an ammunition waggon, and on which the field gun could be placed when the conditions were favourable.

With regard to communications, I feel that I am treading on very difficult ground, for though it is easy to criticise, I hardly think it fair to do so, unless one has some suggestions for improving the points criticised. Still, there is a grand opportunity for any one who can devise a system which will enable generals rapidly to communicate with their various units where all are on the move and extending over vast areas. I think the subject is too large to tackle here.

One of the most noticeable features in the campaign, as we

saw it, was the tremendous value of telescopes of high power. Without them, in that kind of warfare, guns are comparatively helpless to what they would be if they had them. We would far sooner have damaged or lost almost any guns than injured our big telescopes. Ours—we had three altogether with the Naval Brigade—were the large service size, mounted on tripods, and with a magnification of upwards of forty diameters.

In the early morning or late evening they were at their best, as there was then no haze or mirage, when a weaker glass is preferable. But even at midday, with a haze, if you placed the telescope so as to have no ground between you and the object, very near to the line of sight (for example, looking over a deep valley with the telescope on a big rock), the haze did not trouble yon very much. What is required is a powerful telescope magnifying, say, sixty diameters, with an adjustable eye-piece to vary the power according to the light and amount of haze. It would be on the same principle as the turret telescopic sights. Specially trained men are also required to use them; for, objects absolutely invisible to the untrained eye, even though the glass be pointed and focussed by an expert, can, not only be seen, but readily picked up by a trained observer.

As an example, on one occasion, it was perfectly easy for trained observers to see the leaf of the back sights of some Boers' rifles raised up and silhouetted against the skyline; they were firing at our troops, at right angles, or nearly so, to our line of sight, and this at a range of 2800 yards. Others tried to see them and laughed incredulously, saying that the Boers were firing at Hart's Brigade, who were only some 400 yards off; later we found that Hart's Brigade was out of sight of this trench, and that a relieving force, coming up some 2000 yards off, had been pretty severely handled. I may say that in a very short time those Boers were under cover, and the relief came up without further molestation. . . .

There is one thing, however, which we of the navy all noticed, and was, and is, the object of our highest admiration, and that is the courage, devotion, and skill of our comrades in the sister service, and it is my fervent hope that there will always be the same friendly feeling, and readiness with mutual help, whenever we are called upon to act together again, as there has been in both South Africa and China.

Appendices

List of All Commissioned, Warrant, and Subordinate Officers Who Have Served In H.M.S. "Terrible" During the Commission.

Name.	Rank.	Name.	Rank.
Anderson, Douglas M.	Lieut.	Campbell, Leveson G. B.	Midn.
Arthur, John F.	Engr.	Cole-Hamilton, Jno. C.	,,
Adams, Henry G. N.	Midn.	Cole, Edwin J.	Gunner
Andrews, Alex. G.	Staff-Surgeon	Coke, Erst. S.	Lieut. R.M.
		Chase, Jno. E.	Fleet Engr.
Ackland, Austin C.	Midn.	Coote, Bernard T.	Midn.
		Chichester, Ed. G.	,,
Baskerville, Henry S.	Fleet Payr.	Cargill, Geodfray	,,
Bennett, Wm. E.	Fleet Surgeon	Curtis, I.	Naval Inst.
		Candy, Geoffrey	Midn.
Bain, Dvd. H. W.	Asst. Engr.	Crichton	,,
Bland, Horatio S.	Midn.		
Bunbury, Evan C.	,,	Down, Richd. T.	Midn.
Barrow, Benj. W.	,,	Drummond, Jno. E.	Lieut.
Brown, Thos.	Lieut. R.N.R.	Darling, Hy. T.	Midn.
		Dooner, Jno. K. P.	Lieut.
Benson, Ar. W.	Midn.	Digby Ed. A.	Actg. Sub-Lieut.
Barr, Frs. T.	Commr. N.		
Benson, L. H.	Midn.		
Bogle, Robt. H.	Lieut.	England, Geo. P.	Lieut.
Bartlett, Erst. E.	Asst. Engr.	Ellaby, Joseph D.	Midn.
Boldero, Herbt. S. W.	Midn.	Elliott, Jas. D.	Actg. Sub-Lieut.
Blanchflower, Edward C.	Clerk		
Blomfield, Myles A.	Midn.		
Bremner, Charles	Gunner	Ford, Robt.	Bosn.
Brooke, Basil R.	Midn.	Fairbairn, Bernd. W.	Midn.
Bluett, Bertie W.	,,	Falkiner, Richd. H.	,,
Boxer, Hy. P.	,,	Fletcher, Hugh U.	,,
Baker, Arthur B. A.	Actg. Sub-Lieut.	Gillett, Owen F.	Commr. N.
Bouchier, Af. E.	Staff Payr.	Goodwin, Frank R.	Asst. Engr.
		Gaskell, Arthur	Surgeon
Crean, Francis	Lieut.	Gowan, Cecil N. B.	Midn.
Cullinan, Willm. F.	Asst. Payr.	Grant, Albt. D.	,,

Name.	Rank.	Name.	Rank.
Grant, Hbt. C. J.	Lieut.	Martin, Geo. H.	Commr.
		Messenger, Ar. W. B.	Clerk
Hughes, Sidney	Commr. N.	McCarthy, Edward	{Captain / R.M.A.
Hutchinson, Reginald	Midn.		
Hallwright, Willm. W.	,,	Mullins, Geo. J. H.	{Captain / R.M.L.I.
Hodson, Gerald L.	,,		
Higgins, Chas.	Gunner	Morley, Harold S.	Asst. Engr.
Henson, Geoffrey W.	Midn.	Macmillan, Chas. C.	Surgeon
Hutchinson, Henry	{Lieut. / R.N.R.	Mayhew, Chas. L.	{Lieut. / R.M.L.I.
Hodgson, Fdk.	Gunner	Maher, G. W. E.	Midn.
Hewitt, Heathcote G.	Midn.	Marton, Ronald G.	Asst. Engr.
Howard, Alan F. W.	{Actg. Sub- / Lieut.	Mitford, Hon. Bertram T. C.	Sub-Lieut.
Heycock, Cecil C.	,,		
Hughes-Onslow, Constantine H.	Lieut. N.	Newcome, Stephen	,,
		Ogilvy, Fdk. C. A.	Commr.
Jameson, Thos. O.	Engr.	Osborne, Smyth N.	Sub-Lieut.
Johns, James	Carpr.		
Jeremy, Alf. H.	Surgeon	Prowse, Alf. B.	Midn.
Jones, James	Sub-Lieut.	Page, Geo. F. L.	,,
		Price, Augustus R.	Chaplain
Kirby, Rcd. E. W.	Midn.	Paterson, Herbt. J.	{Lieut. / R.N.R.
		Prickett, Cecil B.	Midn.
Limpus, Arthur H.	Commr.	Pownall, Geo. H.	,,
Lomas, Ernest C.	Surgeon		
Lyne, Thos. J. S.	Gunner		
Lawrie, Frank B. A.	Lieut. R.M.	Robinson, Chas. G.	Captain
Lucas, Walt. C.	{Naval / Cadet	Rees, Jno. S.	Fleet Engr.
		Rush, Henry C.	Engr.
Laughton, Ed.	Naval Inst.	Robertson, Gordon	Asst. Engr.
Ley, Arthur E. H.	Midn.	Roberts, C. Betton	Clerk.
Laycock, Regd. A.	Clerk	Reyne, Cecil N.	Midn.
Leir, Erst. W.	Midn.	Rosvenan, R. R.	{Sub-Lieut. / R.N.R.
Litchfield, F. Shirley	Lieut.		
Legard, Geo. P.	Sub-Lieut.	Raskruge, Francis J.	Asst. Engr.
Lamb, Francis E.	Engr.	Rice, Robt. A.	Lieut.
Law, Wm. J. B.	Lieut.	Rider, Robt. T.	{Artifir. / Engr.
Loftie, J. Henry	,,		
Lane-Poole, Rcd. H. O.	{Actg.Sub- / Lieut.	Richards, Spencer R. H.	Lieut.
		Reinold, Basil E.	Midn.
		Rock, Carl B. F. L.	Asst. Engr.
Molteno, Vincent B.	Lieut.	Rolfe, Clife N.	Midn.
Montmorency, Jno. P. De	,,	Reed, Archd. N.	{Lieut. / R.N.R.
Murray, Af. E. J.	Engr.		
Massey, Josiah S.	Asst. Engr.	Rogers, James A.	{Sub-Lieut / R.N.R.
Mather, Willm. B.	Gunner		
Moore, Hartley R. G.	Midn.		
Murray, Herbert P. W. G.	Asst. Clerk	Stewart, Archd T.	Lieut.

Name.	Rank.	Name.	Rank.
Short, Edward A.	Chief Engr.	Veasey, Robt. F.	Naval Cadet
Swabey, Geo. T. C. P.	Midn.		
Smart, Robt. C. C.	,,		
Somerville, Jas. F.	,,	Woolcombe, Alfred	Surgeon
Scott, Thos. B.	,,	Wood, Arthur W.	Midn.
Syson, Jno. L.	Clerk	Willis, Frank R.	,,
Sumner, Charles G. C.	Midn.	Whatley Chas. L.	Chaplain
Sharp, Charles R.	,,	Whapham, Richd. H.	Naval Inst.
Skinner, Geo. M.	,,	Willoughby, Percival I.	Midn.
Sherrin, Alwyne E.	,,	Wright, Joseph	Gunner
Scott, Percy M.	Captain	Wilde, Jas. S.	Lieut.
Swainson, Jas. M. G.	Surgeon	Whyte, Herbt. E. W.	Midn.
		Woolf, Thos. A.	Clerk
Trousdale, Chas. W.	Lieut.	Williams, Ernest	Gunner
Thomas, Aubrey	Midn.	Wheater, Percy	Engr.
Troup, Jas. A. G.	,,	Woollcombe, Maurice	Lieut.
Tatham, Horace H.	,,	Wynter, Gerald C.	Midn.
		Wilson, Jas. H. G.	Lieut. R.M.
Vaudin, Matthew, L. M.	Surgeon	Wahab, Jas. C.	Midn.

List of Officers and Men Belonging to the "Terrible" Who Landed With the Naval Brigade in South Africa and China

(Exclusive of officers and men borne for passage to China. Officers commanding units of *Terrible's* guns have their ships' names shown in brackets.)

SOUTH AFRICA.

Captain Percy Scott, Commandant of Durban
Assistant-Paymaster Cullinan, Secretary to Commandant

Mr. Laycock, clerk
,, Blanchflower, clerk
Chief Writer Elliott
Second Writer Shepherd
Petty Officer Porch

} Commandant's Staff in Durban

DURBAN DEFENCE FORCE, AND RELIEF OF LADYSMITH CONTINGENT.

Captain E. P. Jones (*Forte*), commanding Naval Brigade
Commander Limpus (second in command of Naval Brigade)
Midshipman Hutchinson (A.D.C. to Captain Jones)

Surgeon Lomas, R.N.
Engineer Arthur, R.N.
Mr. Cole, Gunner, R.N.
Master-at-Arms Crowe
Chief Gunnery Instructor Baldwin

} Staff duties with naval headquarters under Captain Jones

No. 1 4·7-inch Gun.

Lieutenant England, R.N., in command	Seaman	Powell
Midshipman Sherrin	,,	Dennis
	,,	Palmer
Chief Petty Officer Bate (Capt. of Gun)	,,	Lindridge
Petty Officer Honniball	,,	Lovelady
,, Skinner	,,	Hicks
Ldg. Seaman Grounds	,,	Brennan
Seaman Weippart	,,	Williams
,, Moloney	,,	Cotton
,, Kewell	,,	Shepard
,, Starling	,,	Helman
,, Sandry	,,	Legg
,, Elliott	,,	Nethercoat
,, Murray	,,	Kimber
	,,	Benn

No. 2 4·7-inch Gun.

Lieutenant Hunt (*Forte*) in command	Seaman	Tucker
Midshipman Troup	,,	Symes
	,,	McLeod
Chief Petty Officer Stephens (Capt. of Gun)	,,	Pearce
	,,	Simmons
Petty Officer Dear	,,	Howe
,, Wright	,,	Pope
Ldg. Seaman Gardner	,,	Gardner
Seaman Towers	,,	Livermore
,, Grady	,,	Carpenter
,, Burnham	,,	Cotcher
,, Rood	,,	Channen
,, Curtis	,,	Plummer
,, Rowe	,,	Salter

Miscellaneous, attached to 4·7 Battery.

Sick-berth Steward Stewart	} Ambulance Section	Armourer Ellis	} Special Duties
Ldg. Stoker Clark		Carpenter's Mate Brown	
Stoker Miles		Blacksmith Burnett	
,, Clifton		Carpenter's Crew, Adams	
,, Skene		Ldg. Signalman Large	
,, Austin			
,, McGuire			
,, Morgan			

Lieutenant Richard's 12-pounder Unit (Two Guns).

Midshipman Down

(1)		(2)	
Ldg. Seaman Beatty (Capt. of Gun)		Sergeant Roper (Capt. of Gun)	
Seaman Ashton		Lance-Corpl. Porteous	
,, Lintern		Private Mills	
,, Perkis		,, Annetts	
,, Allison		,, Stubbington	
,, Hurl		,, Nowell	
,, Bird		,· Gulliver	
,, Dennis		,, Fazackerly	
,, Marsh		Shipwright McLeod	} Special duties
,, Sales		Armourer Murray	
		Petty Officer Jeffery	

Lieut. Wilde's 12-pounder Unit (Two Guns).

Midshipman Ackland

(1)
Petty Officer	Metcalfe (Capt. of Gun)
Seaman	Murphy
,,	Warren
,,	Stansmore
,,	Fisher
,,	Jones
,,	Alexander
,,	Terry
,,	Lock
,,	Wilson
,,	White

(2)
Petty Officer	H. Mitchell (Capt. of Gun)
Seaman	Barrett
,,	Roman
,,	Stones
,,	Talbot
,,	Cook
,,	Smith
,,	Gurr
,,	Pellett
,,	Harris
,,	Hughes
,,	Maloney

Lieut. Burne's ("Philomel") 12-pounder Unit (Two Guns).

Midshipman White

(1)
Petty Officer	Mitchell (Capt. of Gun)
Seaman	House
,,	Shepherd
,,	Ratcliffe
,,	Webber
,,	Tuck
,,	Moyse
,,	Long
,,	Phillips
Stoker	Dunstall

(2)
Petty Officer	Mullis (Capt. of Gun)
Seaman	Treharne
,,	Elms
,,	Gurney
,,	Fegan
,,	Kirby
,,	Russell
,,	Patten
,,	Jones
Stoker	Taylor

Lieut. Melville's ("Forte") 12-pounder Unit (Two Guns).

Mr. Williams, Gunner, R.N.

(1)
Petty Officer	Brimble (Capt. of Gun)
Ldg. Seamen	White
Seaman	Dews
,,	Nightingale
,,	Gould
,,	Leniham
,,	Robertson
,,	Bonnick
,,	Judd
,,	Cooke

(2)
Petty Officer	Strudwick (Capt of Gun)
Seaman	Evans
,,	Harwood
,,	Reading
,,	Frood
,,	Alexander
,,	Dyer
,,	Woodward
,,	Caws
,,	Wiltshire
Stoker	Sears

Lieut. Ogilvy's 12-pounder Battery (Four Guns).
Officers.

Lieutenant Deas, R.N. (*Philomel*)	
Surgeon Macmillan, R.N.	
Mr. Wright, Gunner	

Midshipman	Willoughby
,,	Boldero
,,	Hallwright
,,	Hodson

(1)
Petty Officer	Venness (Capt. of Gun)
,,	Peckett
Seaman	Ryall
,,	Randall
,,	Knight
,,	Campling
,,	Marjoran
,,	Hayles
Stoker	King
,,	Willey

(3)
Petty Officer	Ward (Capt. of Gun)
,,	Hunt
Seaman	Bobbett
,,	Ousley
,,	Webster
,,	Leach
,,	Courtney
,,	Edney
,,	Haynes
Stoker	Howard

	(2)		(4)
Petty Officer	Taylor (Capt. of Gun at Colenso)	Petty Officer	Symons (Capt. of Gun)
,,	Challoner (Capt. of Gun)	,,	Fitzgerald
Seaman	Dibden	Seaman	Pledge
,,	Melbourne	,,	Vosper
,,	Bradbury	,,	Rovery
,,	Smith	,,	Aylsbury
,,	Thomas	,,	Funnell
,,	Sawyers	,,	Davis
,,	Cox	,,	Ball
,,	Newstead	Stoker	Riddle
Stoker	Aldworth		

Miscellaneous, attached to Ogilvy's Battery.

Sick-Berth Steward Attree	}		Ldg. Signalman Brown	}
Stoker Ross			,, Shipwright Harvey	
,, Gouge	Ambu-		Armourer's Mate Ford	Special
,, Curtis	lance		Cook's Mate Couzins	duties
,, Bailey	Section		Private (R.M.L.I.) Lessey	
,, Sterck			,, ,, Lovall	
,, Yeomans				

Lieut. Drummond, 6-inch Gun.

Midshipman Skinner		Stoker	Hooker
Petty Officer	Connor (Gunnery Instructor)	,,	Johnson
		,,	Sheldon
,,	Allen (Capt. of Gun)	,,	White
,,	Carey (Second of Gun)	,,	Sweeney
Seaman	Rees	,,	Belsey
,,	Orr	,,	Haberfield
,,	Cole	,,	Arnell
,,	Osbourne	,,	Vickers
,,	Smithen	,,	Knight
,,	Reed	,,	Wilkins
,,	Lavers	,,	Goldsmith
,,	Tuttle	,,	Lane
,,	Shouler	,,	Stone
,,	Thomas	,,	Weir
,,	Toms	,,	French
,,	Shergold	,,	Eames
,,	Varnham	,,	Stevenson
,,	Bryant	,,	Bishop
,,	Silver	,,	Cooper
,,	Stevens	,,	Foord
,,	Elston	,,	Burns
,,	Harris	,,	Evans
,,	Ford	,,	Stevens
Ldg. Stoker	Cripps	,,	Maurice
,,	Parham	,,	Woolley
Stoker	Murray	Armourer	Whitlock

Searchlight Train, with Ladysmith Relief Column.

Sub-Lieutenant Newcome, R.N.	Yeoman of Signals Arnold
Engineer Murray, R.N.	Petty Officer Prince
	Stoker Cox
Artificer Jones	,, Aughton

Ammunition Guard at Frere.

Petty Officer	Horner	Seaman	Hamon
Seaman	Hunter	,,	Thomas

403

Captain Percy Scott, C.B., the officers and warrant officers of H.M.S. "Terrible," 1902

Zululand Expeditionary Force.

Lieutenant Dooner, R.N.		Ldg. Stoker	Denham
Midshipman Kirby		,,	Daniells
Petty Officer	Sparks (Capt. of Field Gun)	Stoker	H. Cooper
,,	Neil	,,	Newland
,,	Bicker	,,	Shepherd
Seaman	Brady	,,	Gardner
,,	Royce	,,	Hart
,,	Johnson	,,	Smith
,,	Parrott	,,	Murray
,,	Giles	,,	Skinner
,,	Clements	,,	Ford
,,	Burke	,,	Clemens
,,	Luckham	,,	Hovell
,,	Bright	,,	Palmer
,,	Shorrock	,,	Copplestone
,,	Cousins	,,	Stevenson
,,	Eaton	,,	Holman
,,	Elton	,,	Bull
,,	Underwood	,,	Sullivan
,,	Trevitt	,,	Harding
,,	Childs	,,	Grant
,,	Webster	,,	Martin
,,	Wedmore	,,	Morse
,,	Franklin	,,	W. Cooper
,,	Dean	,,	Smith
,,	Major	Armourer	Nash

Special Service (Durban).

Lieutenant Hughes-Onslow, R.N.		Seaman	Easson
,,	Bogle, R.N.	,,	Barnett
Staff-Surgeon Andrews, R.N.		,,	Pollard
Petty Officer	Kent	,,	Welling
,,	Beard	,,	Endean
Ldg. Seaman	Donovon	,,	Trim
,,	Hefferman	,,	Creese
,,	Abrahams	,,	Novis
,,	Hutchence	Qualified Signalman	Newman
Seaman	Alesbury	,,	Marsh
,,	Harber	Stoker	Vickers
,,	Griggs	,,	Sack
,,	Bush	Cook's Mate	Hayward

Naval Transport Service (Durban).

Mr. Higgins, Gunner, R.N.		Seaman	Boland
Petty Officer	Pinkerton	,,	Bolt
Ldg. Seaman	Nunn	,,	Daniells
Seaman	Swift	,,	Buckett
,,	Holland	,,	Wood
,,	Goodwin	,,	Sears
,,	Fisher	,,	Sherwin
,,	Goulter	,,	Baker
,,	England	,,	Knight
,,	Scarlett	,,	Randall
,,	Butler	,,	Vail
,,	Dodd	,,	Hawkins
,,	Stickland	,,	Slater
		,,	Dugdale

For Special Service on Shore at Durban.

Mr. Johns, Carpenter, R.N.
Artificer Collins
  ,,   Downton
  ,,   Warburton
Ship's Steward Hopkins
Chief Armourer Burke
Chief Cook Crawford
Ship's Corporal Huckle

Ship's Corporal Wyman
    ,,   Long
Petty Officer Trengrove
Stoker   Wilton
  ,,   Wright
  ,,   Plumb
Carpenter's Mate Pellett
Blacksmith's Mate Everett
Captain's Steward Meredith

CHINA.

TIENTSIN DEFENCE FORCE, AND RELIEF OF PEKIN.

Officers.

Lieutenant Drummond, R.N.
    ,,   Wilde, R.N.
    ,,   Hutchinson, R.N.R.
Staff-Surgeon Andrews, R.N.
Assistant-Paymaster Cullinan, R.N.
Mr. Wright, Gunner, R.N.
Midshipman Sherrin
    ,,   Dorling
    ,,   Troup

Midshipman Hutchinson
    ,,   Reinold
    ,,   Leir
    ,,   Cargill
    ,,   Sumner
    ,,   Willoughby
    ,,   Down
    ,,   Ackland

No. 1 12-pounder.

Petty Officer Allen (Capt. of Gun)
Ldg. Seaman Herriott
    ,,   Rowe
    ,,   Shepherd
Seaman   Sherwin
  ,,   Stones
  ,,   Pinkerton
  ,,   Tucker
  ,,   Rees

Seaman   Dugdale
  ,,   Knight
  ,,   Pollard
  ,,   Ford
  ,,   Griggs
  ,,   Jones
  ,,   Wiltshire
  ,,   Franklin
  ,,   French

No. 2 12-pounder.

Petty Officer Symons (Capt. of Gun)
    ,,   Skinner
Ldg. Seaman Rood
Seaman   Toms
  ,,   Brennan
  ,,   Grady
  ,,   Dennis
  ,,   Walker
  ,,   Barrett

Seaman   Roman
  ,,   Hicks
  ,,   Whyte
  ,,   Cox
Stoker   Wells
  ,,   Ross
  ,,   Forbes
  ,,   Woodgate

No. 3 12-pounder.

Petty Officer Metcalfe (Capt. of Gun)
Ldg. Seaman Starling
Seaman   Lovelady
  ,,   Shepherd
  ,,   Lock
  ,,   Clifton
  ,,   Saunders
  ,,   Thomas

Seaman   Maloney
Stoker   Porter
  ,,   Burns
  ,,   Newland
  ,,   Pankhurst
  ,,   Davis
  ,,   Bennett

No. 4 12-pounder.

Petty Officer	Strudwick (Capt. of Gun)	Seaman	Ashton
Ldg. Seaman	Kewell	,,	Ratcliffe
Seaman	Sandry	,,	Webster
,,	Novis	,,	Alsbury
,,	Holland	,,	Flaherty
,,	Fisher	Stoker	Payne
,,	Elton	,,	Carter
,,	Balls		

No. 5 12-pounder (for Service at Shanghai).

Petty Officer	Mitchell (Capt. of Gun)	Seaman	Maloney
Ldg. Seaman	Hefferman	,,	Sawyers

For Special Duties.

Ship's Corporal Huckle, general duties
Petty Officer Trengrove } Gunnery
   ,,   Connor } Instructors
Sick-berth Steward }
   Stewart   } Naval Hospital
Sick-berth Steward } Staff, Tientsin
   Blake   }
Armourer Whitlock

Armourer's Crew Macey
   ,,   ,,   Hide
Carpenter's Mate Scott
Shipwright McLeod
   ,,   Cooke
Yeoman of Signals Bowbyes
Qualified Signalman Maple
Ship's Steward Assistant Light

Service Company.

Petty Officer	Mullis	Seaman	Pledge
,,	Dear	,,	Bobbett
,,	Beard	,,	Kirby
,,	Burtenshaw	,,	Marsh
,,	White	,,	Warren
,,	Gardiner	,,	Barnett
,,	Lenihan	,,	Reed
Seaman	Stickland	,,	Gardner
,,	Randall	,,	Campling
,,	Edney	,,	Blake
,,	Neil	,,	Underwood
,,	Weldon	,,	Bolt
,,	Scarlett	Ldg. Stoker	Johnstone
,,	Vail	,,	Clark
,,	Stansmore	,,	Cassell
,,	Stark	,,	Foley
,,	Cotton	Stoker	Seymour
,,	White	,,	Clarke
,,	Channon	,,	Day
,,	Knight	,,	Kemp
,,	McDonald	,,	Byron
,,	Smithen	,,	Norman
,,	Rayner	,,	Baldwin
,,	Elliott	,,	Owens
,,	Fegan	,,	Vine
,,	Courtney	,,	Gregory
,,	Robertson	,,	Bell
,,	Benn	,,	Morgan
,,	Stevens	,,	Lambert
,,	Hughes	,,	Cushion
,,	Bland	,,	Creedon
,,	Leach	,,	Boyd

Service Company—continued.

Stoker	Cooper	Stoker	Murphy
,,	Copplestone	,,	Weir
,,	Martin	,,	Gibb
,,	Pagett	,,	Sheridan
,,	Blackwell	,,	Fowler
,,	Foote	,,	Woodgate
,,	Harding	,,	Morrison
,,	Hubbard	,,	Chittenden
,,	Hardy	,,	McCormick
,,	Cooper	,,	Voar
,,	Cummings	,,	Williams
,,	Holman	,,	Flyde

"*Terrible's*" *Royal Marine Detachment.*

Landed with Stormberg Naval Brigade (Cape Colony). With Durban Defence Force (Natal). Marched to Relief of Tientsin. With Tientsin Defence Force until fall of Native City. Relief of Pekin Expeditionary Force.

Captain Mullins, R.M.L.I. (commanding Detachment)
Lieutenant Lawrie, R.M.L.I.

Sergeant	Peck	Private	Harris
,,	York	,,	Stubbington
,,	Roper	,,	Cooper
,,	Jones	,,	Relf
,,	Stanbridge	,,	Ashley
Corporal	Lester	,,	Edwards
Lance-Corporal	Silvers	,,	Farley
,,	Barnard	,,	Yeomans
,,	Smith	,,	Hughes
,,	Horsley	,,	Houghton
,,	Tomkins	,,	G. Ellis
,,	Whitter	,,	Harrison
Bugler	Armitage	,,	Pasker
,,	Carter	,,	Rose
Private	Penn	,,	Hook
,,	Southard	,,	Burt
,,	Foote	,,	Collins
,,	Briggs	,,	Osborne
,,	Wright	,,	Tovey
,,	Thompson	,,	C. Ellis
,,	Nowell	,,	Chalmers
,,	Gulliver	,,	Rielly
,,	Walker	,,	Lidstone
,,	Dellow	,,	Dedman
,,	Hopkins	,,	Abraham
,,	Haysom	,,	Dighton
,,	Watt	,,	Porteous
,,	Annett	,,	Blake
,,	Case	,,	Brown
,,	White	,,	Nicholson
,,	Denny	,,	Howard
,,	Werndley	,,	Riley
,,	Prime	,,	Foster
,,	O'mara	,,	Rayner
,,	Rudgley	,,	Clark
,,	Mills	,,	Hayes
,,	Legg	,,	Jones
,,	Boyes	,,	Cuell
,,	Parker	,,	Lawes
		,,	Roper
		,,	Butler

Landed South Africa.

Private	Turberfield	Private	Fazackerly
,,	Laker	,,	Lovell
,,	Cox	,,	Scrivens
,,	Haddrell		

Landed China.

| Private | Lessey | Private | Barritt |
| ,, | Waltens | | |

Ambulance Section with Marines (Cape Colony).

Stoker	Cashman	,,	Pashley
,,	Manwaring	,,	Grant
,,	Cooper	Sick-berth Steward Blake	
,,	Ford		

SOUTH AFRICA.

Mentioned in General Sir Redvers Buller's Despatches of March 30th, 1900, after the Relief of Ladysmith.

Extracts From the *London Gazette,*
February 8th, 1901.

Capt. P. Scott, C.B., H.M.S. *Terrible,* has discharged the difficult duties of Commandant of Durban with the greatest tact and ability, and has been most helpful in every way.

Capt. E. P. Jones, H.M.S. *Forte,* as Senior Officer of the Naval Brigade he has earned my most heartfelt thanks. The assistance they have rendered to me has been invaluable; the spirit of their leader was reflected in the men, and at any time, day or night, they were always ready, and their work was excellent. (C.B. conferred afterwards.)

Com. A. H. Limpus and Lieut. F. C. A. Ogilvy, H.M.S. *Terrible,* and Lieut. H. W. James, H.M.S. *Tartar:*—These three officers were indefatigable. There never was a moment in the day that they were not working hard and well to advance the work in hand. (Each officer afterwards promoted.)

Lieut. N. W. Chiazzari, Natal Naval Volunteers, was in charge of a detachment who were associated with the Naval Brigade, and took their full share of the good work done by the Naval Brigade. (D.S.O. conferred afterwards.)

★★★★★★

Lieut. C. P. Hunt, H.M.S. *Forte.* (Promoted Commander and received D.S.O.)

Lieut. C. R. N. Burne, H.M.S. *Philomel*. (Promoted Commander.)
Staff-Surg. F. J. Lilly, H.M.S. *Forte*. (Promoted Fleet Surgeon.)
Surg. C. C. Macmillan, H.M.S. *Terrible*, (Received D.S.O.)
Surg. E. C. Lomas, H.M.S. *Terrible*, (Promoted Staff-Surgeon and received D.S.O.)
Acting-Gnr. J. Wright, H.M.S. *Terrible*, (Received Conspicuous Service Cross.)
Midshipman R. B. Hutchinson, H.M.S. *Terrible*, (Received Conspicuous Service Cross.)
Midshipman H. S. Boldero, H.M.S. *Terrible*.
Midshipman G. L. Hodson, H.M.S. *Terrible*.
Clerk W. T. Hollins, H.M.S. *Philomel*,
Master-at-Arms G. Crowe, H.M.S. *Terrible*,
Chief Petty Officer T. Baldwin, H.M.S. *Terrible*,
Chief Petty Officer W. Bate, H.M.S. *Terrible*.
Chief Petty Officer B. Stephens, H.M.S. *Terrible*.
1st Class Petty Officer P. Cashman, H.M.S. *Philomel*.
Armourer Ellis, H.M.S. *Terrible*.
2nd Class Petty Officer C. Challoner, H.M.S. *Terrible*. (Promoted Petty Officer, 1st Class.)
2nd Class Petty Officer J. J. Frennett, H.M.S. *Philomel*.
A.B. F. Moore, H.M.S. *Forte*.

CHINA.

Mentioned in Admiral Sir Edward Seymour's Despatches for Service at Tientsin—North China War.

Lieut. John E. Drummond. (Already promoted Commander.)
Mr. Joseph Wright, Gunner.

The White Era

The appointment of Sir William White as Chief Constructor more or less synchronised with a considerable revolution in naval construction and ideas. The institution of naval manoeuvres drew great attention to the sea-going quality of various types of ships. The manoeuvres of 1887 mostly centred around the *Polyphemus*, and her charging a boom at Berehaven. Little was here proved except that boom defences were easily to be annihilated. In 1888, however, the manoeuvres were of a much more extensive nature, and a Committee was appointed to consider and report upon them, especially with regard to the following points:—

The feasibility or otherwise of maintaining an effective blockade in war of an enemy's squadron or fast cruisers in strongly fortified ports, including the advantages and disadvantages of—
(a) Keeping the main body of the blockading Fleets off the ports to be blockaded with an inshore squadron.
(b) Keeping the main body of the blockading Fleets at a base, with a squadron of fast cruisers and scouts off the blockaded ports, having means of rapid communication with the Fleet.
(c) In both cases the approximate relative number of battleships and cruisers that should be
employed by the blockading Fleet, as compared with those of the blockaded Fleet.
The value of torpedo-gunboats and first-class torpedo boats both with the blockading and blockaded Fleets, and the most efficient manner of utilising them.
As to the arrangements made by B squadron for the attack of commerce in the Channel, and by A squadron for its protection.
As to the feasibility and expediency of cruisers making raids

Sir William White

on an enemy's coasts and unprotected towns for the purpose of levying contribution.

As to the claims and counterclaims made by the admirals in command of both squadrons with regard to captures made during the operation.

As to any defects of importance which were developed in any of the vessels employed, and their cause.

As Supplementary Instructions there were:—

(1) As to the behaviour and sea-going qualities of, or the defects in, the new and most recently commissioned vessels, as obtained from the reports of the Admirals in command of the respective squadrons.

(2) The general conclusion to be drawn from the recent operations.

A summary of the findings[1], is as follows:—

That to maintain an effective blockade of a Fleet in a strongly fortified port a proportion of at least five to three would be essential and possibly an even larger proportion, unless a good anchorage could be found near the blockaded port which could be used as a base, in which case a proportion of four to three might suffice, supposing the blockading squadron to be very amply supplied with look-out ships and colliers.

Torpedo boats were condemned as being of little value to blockaders, though useful to the blockaded. For blockade purposes the torpedo-gunboats of the *Rattlesnake* class were highly commended.

Attention was drawn to the large number of deck hands employed down below on account of the insufficient engine-room complements, and the excess of untrained stokers. The case of the *Warspite* was specifically mentioned. In order to break the blockade at sixteen knots she sent thirty-six deck hands down below at a time when every available deck hand would have been required above had the operations been real war.

A special supplementary report was called for as to the sea-going qualities of the ships. Considerable historical interest attaches to this particular report, and the following extracts are especially interesting:—

---

1. The full report is to be found in Part IV of *Brassey's Naval Annual*, 1888-9.

Admiral class.

So far as could be judged, these vessels are good sea-boats, and their speed is not affected when steaming against a moderate wind and sea; but we are of opinion that their low freeboard renders them unsuitable as sea-going armour-clads for general service with the Fleet, as their speed must be rapidly reduced when it is necessary to force them against a head sea or swell.

On the only occasion on which the *Collingwood* experienced any considerable beam swell she is reported to have rolled 20 degrees each way; this does not make it appear as if the *Admiral* class will be very steady gun-platforms in bad weather.

They are said to be 'handy' at 6 knots and over.

In the *Benbow* much difficulty was experienced in stowing the bower anchors. This is the case in all low freeboard vessels, more or less, but the evil appears to have been intensified in this instance by defective fittings, and by the fact of her being supplied with the old-fashioned iron-stocked anchors instead of improved Martins.

Serious complaints are made from these ships that the forecastles leak badly, and that the mess-deck is made uninhabitable whenever the sea breaks over the forecastle at all; it would seem that this defect might be remedied.

This opinion was not shared by Admiral Sir Arthur Hood, who commented as follows:—

> I cannot concur in this opinion, my view being that the objects of primary importance to be fulfilled in a first-class battleship are: (1) That, on a given displacement, the combined powers of offence and defence shall be as great as can be given; (2) that she shall be handy and possess good speed in ordinary weather, combined with sea-worthiness; (3) that she shall have large coal-carrying capacity'. I certainly do not consider that the *Admiral* class, which, on account of their comparatively low freeboard forward, must have their speed reduced when steaming against a heavy head sea or swell to a greater extent than is the case with the long, high freeboard, older armour-clads, as the *Minotaur, Northumberland, Black Prince* are for this reason rendered unsuitable as sea-going armour-clads for general service with a Fleet. The power of being able to force a first-class battleship at full speed against a head sea is not, in my opinion,

a point of the first importance, although in the case of a fast cruiser it certainly is.

Admiral Tryon draws an unfavourable comparison between the speed of the new battleships and that of the long ships of the old type, when steaming against a head sea. I admit at once that vessels like the *Minotaur* class would maintain their speed and make better weather of it when being forced against a head sea than would the *Admirals*; but this advantage, under these exceptional conditions, cannot for a moment be compared with the enormous increase in the power of offence and defence possessed by the *Admirals*.

The *Conqueror* and *Hero* were reported to roll a great deal. Being short they felt a head sea quickly, and on account of their low freeboard it was found impossible to drive them against a heavy sea at anything approaching full speed. Incidentally these ships were known as half-boots."

Here, again, Admiral Sir Arthur Hood dissented. In connection with these points, Admiral Tryon submitted a report in which he emphasised, as he had done with the *Admirals*, that however fast these short ships might be in smooth water, their speeds fell off rapidly in a seaway.

The *Mersey* class were described as being handy, steady gun platforms and able to fight their guns longer than most ships.[2] The captain of the *Severn*, however, reported a view that the 8-inch guns should be removed and lighter pieces substituted. Admiral Baird agreed with this. Sir Arthur Hood, in his comments, stated that he was "decidedly opposed" to any reduction of armament, both in this case and that of the other cruisers.

The *Arethusa* type were reported to roll so heavily when the sea was abeam or abaft that "accurate shooting would be impossible and machine guns in the tops would be useless."

The committee concurred with Admiral Baird that the armament of these should be reduced.

For the *Archer* class it was unanimously suggested that lighter guns should be fitted forward. Sir Arthur Hood agreed with this view, which, however, was never carried into effect.

---

2. It is worthy of note that these ships were abnormally "over-gunned "according to the ideas which were then in official favour, and which, later on, came more into favour still. The same applies to the *Arethusa* class.

Particular interest attaches to the *Rattlesnake* [3] class of torpedo-gunboats—these vessels being really prototypes of the destroyers of the present day. They were reported as "safe, provided they were handled with care." Their handiness was unfavourably reported on. It was strongly urged that the 4-inch gun mounted forward should be removed. This, however, was never done.

With reference to any new vessels of this type, the committee reported as deserving immediate consideration:—

(1) Generally strengthen the hull in this type of vessel.
(2) Raise the freeboard forward.
or (3) "Turtle-back" the forecastle.

In the gunboats that followed the freeboard forward was considerably raised; but when destroyers came to be built several years later, it is interesting to observe that the turtle-back forecastle was adopted, and it was not till after over a hundred had been built that the high forecastle, recommended so long before, appeared in the *River* class.

The report concluded:—

The proportion of untrained (2nd class) stokers which were drafted to several of the ships appears to have been too large; in point of physique they are reported as unequal to their work, and in many instances the experience of these men in stokehold (or any other work on board ship) was nil.

As a means of affording opportunities for training newly-raised stokers we recommend that at least one year should be served by them as supernumerary in a sea-going ship before they are considered fit to be draughted as part complement to any vessel; we further are of opinion that a Committee should be appointed to inquire into the sufficiency or otherwise of the complements allowed in the steam department of each class of ship, the proportion of 2nd class stokers which should be borne, and the amount of training which they should be required to undergo before they can usefully be borne as part complement in a fighting ship.

An agitation as to the state of the navy, which was commenced in

---

3. It is interesting to note that the Laird firm, who built the *Rattlesnake*, which was easily the fastest of her class, made her engines considerably heavier than Admiralty specifications. For this they were fined £1,000, which sum, however, was remitted after the brilliant success of the ship in the manoeuvres above referred to.

the year 1887, mainly by the initiative of the *Pall Mall Gazette*[4] finally resulted in the passing of the Naval Defence Act of 1889. This provided for the construction of a total of seventy vessels, consisting of ten armoured ships, nine first-class cruisers, twenty-nine second-class cruisers, four third-class and eighteen torpedo gunboats, to be built as quickly as possible at the estimated cost of £21,500,000.

The substantial part of the programme of 1886 had consisted of two big turret ships, the *Nile* and *Trafalgar*, and two armoured cruisers, *Immortalité* and *Aurora* of the *Orlando* class. In 1887 nothing larger than second-class cruisers was laid down; and in 1888 the most important vessels on the programme were only the protected cruisers, *Blake* and *Blenheim*. There was, therefore, ample material for panic.

Details of the *Blake* class:—

Length (*p.p.*)— 375 ft.
Beam—65 ft.
Guns—Two 9-2 in., 22-ton B.L.R., ten 6-in. Q.F., eighteen 3-pdr.
H.P.—20,000.
Designed speed—22.0 kts.
Coal—1500 tons.
Builder of Ship—*Blake*, Chatham; *Blenheim*, Thames Ironworks.
Builder of machinery—*Blake*, Maudsley; *Blenheim*, Thames Ironworks.
Launched—*Blake*, 1889; *Blenheim*, 1890.

Special features of these ships were a combination of the armament of the *Orlando* class with greatly increased speed secured by the development of deck armour in place of the belts of the *Orlando* class. In so far as a special type of ship may be said to be the development of some predecessor, the *Blake* and *Blenheim* may be described as enlarged *Merseys*. They were, however, unique on account of their relatively great length and great increase of displacement as compared with preceding vessels. In them the armoured casemate, a leading characteristic of nearly all Sir William White's ships, made its first appearance. It was employed in the *Blake* and *Blenheim* for four main deck guns, the upper deck guns being behind the usual shields.

---

4. Mr. W. T. Stead, who edited the *Pall Mall Gazette* at that time, intimated some twenty yearn later that Lord Fisher was behind him in commencing the agitation. Lord Charles Beresford, then in political life, brought the Bill forward.

The coming of the casemate, curiously enough, attracted little attention, compared to its importance. It may be said to have rendered possible the return to main deck guns in unarmoured ships. In the *Orlando* class, ten 6-inch guns were all bunched together on the upper deck amidships. Since these ships were designed the 6-inch quickfirer had made its first appearance, and the largest possible distribution of armament was therefore desirable. The adoption of the two-deck system of the *Blake* and *Blenheim* secured this much larger distribution, rendering it impossible for a single shell to put more than one of the five broadside 6-inch out of action, whereas in the *Orlando* class at least three guns were at the mercy of a single shell.

Another novelty of the type was the introduction of a special armoured glacis around the engine hatches. This system had, of course, been used before in the Italian monster ships *Italia* and *Lepanto*, but it was first introduced in the British Navy in the *Blakes*.[5]

The ships were very successful steamers, for all that neither made her expected twenty-two knots on trial.

Trial results:—

Blake: Eight hours' natural draught, mean I.H.P.-14,525=19.4 knots.

Blenheim: Eight hours' natural draught, mean I. H. P.—14,925 =20.4 knots.

Blake: Four hours' force draught, mean I.H.P.—19,579=21.5 knots.

Blenheim: Four hours' forced draught, mean I.H.P.—21,411=21.8 knots.

The principal item of the Naval Defence Act was eight first-class and two second-class battleships. All these ships were designed by Sir William White, and may be described as battleship editions of the *Blake* and *Blenheim*, so far as the disposition of their armament was concerned. For the rest they may be described as attempts to combine in one ship the best features of the Read and Barnaby ideals. In place of the low freeboard of the *Admiral* class, seven of the *Royal Sovereign*s were given high freeboard fore and aft, with the big guns about twenty-three feet above water. The eighth ship, the *Hood*, was modified to

---

5. In 1899 the *Blake* was re-boilered. The ships remained upon the effective list till 1906, when they were converted into sea-going depot ships for destroyers, most of their guns being removed. They now carry each 670 tons of coal of their own. and 470 tons stowed in one cwt. bags for use by destroyers.

suit the ideals of Admiral Hood, and was to some extent an improved *Trafalgar*, her big guns being in turrets some seventeen feet above the water, in turrets instead of *en barbette*, with guns exposed as in the rest of the class.

In them, among other special features, 18-inch torpedo tubes were first introduced instead of 14-inch, and a stern torpedo tube appeared.

The original idea of end-on torpedo tubes was torpedo attack from the bow in place of the ram. The *Polyphemus* was the first ship in which an end-on tube appeared (submerged). In cruisers of a later date the bow tube was found to injure speed, and there was always the danger of a ship over-nmning her own torpedo. On this account the bow-tube never secured in the British Navy that vogue which it obtained, and still has, in Germany.

The stern-tube appears to owe its origin to an idea that a defeated or overpowered ship, running from an enemy, might save herself by it: dim ideas of "runaway tactics" had also begun to appear.

Sir William White never claimed for himself that he had anticipated the future in any way in his torpedo armament, even when defending himself against criticisms, to the effect that he "gave too little for the displacement." Yet his torpedo innovations, besides discounting the future, all helped to swell the total weight; as also did many internal strengthenings of the kind which do not show on paper. Possibly he did not realise his own greatness as the designer of a class of ship which was so much better than any contemporary vessel, that even in these days of "Super-Dreadnoughts" the *Royal Sovereig*ns are still looked back upon with respect, and invariably regarded as marking the beginning of an entirely new phase in ship construction.

In April, 1889, their designer read a paper about them at the Institution of Naval Architects, in which the principal points which he claimed were that much superior command of guns was given, and that the auxiliary armament was nearly three times the weight of that of the *Trafalgars*. The following points were also mentioned by him:—

> (a) 'That (it was officially decided that) it was preferable to have two separate strongly protected stations for the four heavy guns, rather than to have a single citadel.'
> (b) 'That on the whole the 4-inch armour amidships, from the belt deck to the main deck, associated as it would be with the

internal coal bunkers, sub-divided into numerous compartments, might be considered satisfactory; but that if armour weight became available, it could be profitably utilised in thickening the 4-inch steel above the middle portion of the belt.'

I would draw particular attention to the first of these conclusions, since it expresses a most important distinction between the two systems of protection.

With separate redoubts, placed far apart, the two stations are isolated, and there is practically no risk of simultaneous disablement by the explosion of shells, or perforation of projectiles from the heaviest guns. Each redoubt offers a small target to the fire of an enemy, and its weakest part—the thick steel protective plating on the top—is of so small extent that the chance of its being struck is extremely remote. Serious damage to the unarmoured turret bases therefore involves the perforation of the thick vertical armour on the redoubts.

With a single citadel, extending the full breadth of a ship, the case is widely different.

Over a comparatively large area of the protective deck-plating in the neighbourhood of each turret, perforation of the deck, or its disruption by shell explosions at any point, involves very serious risk of damage to the turret bases and the loading apparatus. In fact, such damage may be effected and the heavy guns put out of action while the thick vertical armour on the citadel is uninjured. Moreover, as the turrets stand at the ends of a single citadel, there is a possibility of their simultaneous disablement by the explosion of heavy shell within the citadel.

This last risk may be minimised (as in the *Nile* and Trafalgar) by constructing armoured 'traverses' within the citadel; but it cannot be wholly overcome, so long as both turrets stand in one armoured enclosure.

It may be thought that the risk of damage to a 3-inch steel deck situated 11 ft. above water is remote; but I think the facts are as stated, when actions at sea are taken into account.

For example, if a ship of 70 to 75 ft. beam is rolling only to 10 degrees from the vertical, which is by no means a heavy roll, she presents a target having a vertical (projected) height of 13 to 14 ft. to an enemy's fire, and even if she is a steady, slow-moving ship, she will do this four or five times in each minute.

Now, at this angle of inclination, assuming the flight of projectiles to be practically horizontal, even the thickest protective steel decks yet fitted in battleships are liable to serious damage from the fire of guns of moderate calibre, and this danger is increased by the employment of high explosives. Of course, I do not mean to say that this damage is to follow from fire intentionally aimed at the protective deck; but with a great and sustained volume of fire, such as is possible with a powerful auxiliary armament, and especially with quick-firing guns, it is obvious that there is a very real danger of chance shots injuring seriously the wide expanse of the protective deck at the top of a long citadel.

Again, it must be noted that the chances of damage to a deck placed 10 or 11 ft. above water, and with large exposed surfaces in the neighbourhood of the turrets when a ship is inclined or rolling, are greater far than those of a deck 7 or 8 ft. lower, and with 5-inch armour on the sides protecting the deck from the direct impact of shells containing heavy bursters. It is for the naval gunner to estimate these chances of injury; but, unless I am greatly mistaken, their verdict will be that a far greater number of shots are likely to strike at a height of 8 to 10 ft. above water than at a height of 4 to 5 ft.

These considerations, I submit, amply justify the selection of the separate redoubt system, in association with the thin side armour above the belt, and the lowering of the protective deck to the top of the belt in the new designs.

It may be urged that, if the redoubt system be adopted, it should be associated with side armour and screen bulkheads of greater thickness than 5-inch steel, and more strongly backed. This is perfectly practicable, but necessarily costly, involving an additional load of armour, and a corresponding increase in the size of the ship.

The designs were vigorously criticised by Sir Edward Reed, whose chief objections centred on the fact that the lower-deck protection was thin armour only. Sir William White combated this idea, and proved very conclusively that, according to the needs of the moment, his views were correct. It is, however, worthy of record that at a later date with the *Majestic* class (see a few pages further on), he effected modifications which brought his ships more into line with what Sir Edward Reed had advocated. It should, however, be mentioned that this was not done until improvements in armour construction rendered possible things that were certainly impossible in the days of the *Royal Sovereigns*.

In connection with the later career of the *Royal Sovereign* class these items may be added. On completion they were found to be singularly simple in all their internal arrangements, and extraordinarily strong. When they went to the scrap-heap in 1911-12, they were, constructionally, practically as good as when built. They proved to be good sea boats, but at first rolled very badly, which resulted in their getting an unenviable notoriety in this respect. This was, however, completely cured by the fitting of bilge keels, after which the ships were everything that could be desired in the way of being steady gun platforms.

The ever increasing vogue of the quickfirer tended to render them rather quickly obsolescent over things which today would count much less than they did in the past. The defects of the *Sovereigns*, as realised not very long after completion, were:—

(1) That the big guns' crews were practically unprotected, and easily to be annihilated by the newly-introduced high explosive shells of the secondary armament of an enemy.

(2) Only four of the ten 6-inch were armour protected, which also was considered a fatal drawback. In the first case nothing was ever done; but in the second, about the year 1900, casemates were fitted for the upper-deck guns of all ships except the *Hood*,[6] which on survey was found unsuitable for such reconstruction.

The only thing that remains to add is that although in the course of years the ships lost the speeds for which they were designed, up to the very end they proved capable of doing about thirteen knots indefinitely.

In addition to the *Sovereigns* two "second-class battleships" were built, the *Centurion* and *Barfleur*, of which details are:—

Displacement—10,500 tons. Complement, 620.
Length— (Waterline) 360 ft.

---

6. This ship very greatly exceeded her nominal displacement of 14,200 tons. She was actually 15,400 tons. The essentially White ships were, on the other hand, of about their nominal displacement. Of the Hood it may further be added that she was greatly inferior to the others as a sea-boat—a serious set-off against her superior big gun protection.

Beam—70 ft.

Draught—(Maximum) 27 ft.

Armament—Four 10-inch, ten 4.7-inch, eight 6-pounders twelve 3-pounders, two Maxims, two 9-pounder boat guns. Torpedo tubes (18-inch)—two submerged and one above water in the stern.

The *Barfleur* was laid down at Chatham in November, 1890, launched in August, 1892, and completed two years later. The *Centurion*, laid down at Portsmouth in March, 1891, was launched a year later, but completed before her sister.

The ships were armoured generally on the *Royal Sovereign* plan, with 12-inch belts which, however, were only 200 ft. long, instead of 250 ft. The bulkheads were six inches only, and the upper belt (nickel steel) an inch less than in the big ships. The barbettes were reduced to nine inches only, but on the other hand were made circular instead of pear-shaped, and 6-inch shields were provided for the big guns— probably as the result of criticisms of the unprotected big guns of the *Sovereigns*. With a few early exceptions as to the shape of the base, and with certain variation in form, this kind of "turret" has been adhered to ever since in the British Navy and copied into every other.

Both ships were engined by the Greenock Foundry Company, and designed for 13,000 H.P., with forced draught, giving a speed of 18.5 knots, which speed both exceeded on trial. This high speed and their coal endurance—they carried a maximum of 1,125 tons, sufficient for a nominal 9750 mile radius—makes them something more than the "second-class battleships" which they nominally were.

Compared to the *Sovereigns* they were:—

	Barfleurs.	Sovereigns.
Minus Points :		
Displacement (tons)	10,500	14,100
Principal guns	4-10in., 10-4.7	4-13.5, 10-6in.
Armour belt	12 inches.	18 inches.
Plus Points :		
Horse Power	13,000	13,000
Speed	18.5	17
Nominal endurance (kts.).	9,750	7,900

From which the existence of an elementary conception of the "battle-cruiser" of today seems fairly apparent. Today the battle-cruiser, instead of having guns of reduced calibre, carries a reduced number, but the general principle of "moderate sacrifices for increased speed" obtains.

The *Barfleur* and *Centurion* proved excellent steamers and good sea-boats. Their defect was their weak armament, and in 1903 it was decided to remedy this. In that year they were "reconstructed." Their 4.7's were taken out and 6-inch guns substituted, and the six on the upper deck were put into casemates. As a species of make-weight the foremast was taken out of both ships; but this made little difference. The "improvements" were a total failure; the ships were immersed far below what they had been designed for, and they never thereafter realised much more than about sixteen knots. Within seven years they were removed from the Navy List altogether, and such service as they performed after modernising was entirely of a subsidiary order.

For the first-class cruisers of the Naval Defence Act reduced examples of the *Blenheim* were decided on. These vessels were the *Edgar, Endymion, Grafton, Hawke, St. George, Gibraltar, Crescent,* and *Royal Arthur* (formerly designated as the *Centaur*). They were launched between 1891 and 1892, averaging 7,350 tons (unsheathed) and 7,700 tons (sheathed and coppered, in the case of the last four mentioned). Except the two last, all had the *Blenheim* armament of two 9.2 and ten 6-inch. The two latter had a couple of extra 6-inch on a raised forecastle substituted for the forward 9.2.

No attempt was made to obtain the high speed of the *Blenheims*— 19.5 knots being the utmost aimed at. Not only, however, did the *Edgar* class exceed expectations on trial, but they proved most remarkably good steamers in service. No engine-room defects of moment were ever encountered in any of them, and twenty years after launch most were still able to steam at little short of the designed speed. Like the battleships, they were given 18-inch torpedoes in place of the 14-inch of the *Blenheims*.

In the course of their service careers, the *St. George* (or rather her crew) earned distinction in the Benin Expedition. The *Crescent* was served in by King George V, and the *Hawke* achieved notoriety by ramming the *Olympic* in the Solent in 1911.

The lesser cruisers of the Naval Defence Act numbered altogether 28. Of these twenty belonged to the *Apollo* class of 3,400 tons (unsheathed) and 3,600 tons (sheathed). They were *Apollo, Andromache, Latona, Melampus, Naiad, Sappho, Scylla, Terpsichore, Thetis, Tribune* (unsheathed), and *Aeolus, Brilliant,* Indefatigable (named *Melpomene* in 1911), *Intrepid, Iphegnia, Pique, Rainbow, Retribution, Sirius,* and *Spartan* (sheathed).

In all, the armament was two 6-inch and six 4.7, with lesser guns, and, above-water, 14-inch torpedo tubes. The speed was twenty knots in the unsheathed, and a quarter of a knot less in the sheathed ones.

When built all proved able to steam very well, but after some years service certain of them fell off very badly in speed. Others, however, remained as fast as when they were built—the *Terpsichore*, in 1908, averaging 20.1 knots, and the *Aeolus*, in 1909, nearly nineteen knots.

During their service, the *Melampus* was commanded by King George as Prince George, while the *Scylla*, under Captain Percy Scott, gave birth to the "dotter," and the "gunnery boom" which followed. In 1904 and onwards seven of them, scrapped from regular service— the *Latona*, *Thetis*, *Apollo*, *Andromache*, *Iphegnia Intrepid*, and *Thetis*— were totally or partially disarmed and converted into mine layers.

The remaining eight cruisers of the Act—*Astroea, Bonaventure, Cambrian, Charybdis, Flora, Forte, Fox,* and *Hermione*—were increased in size up to 4,360 tons, and given a couple of extra 4.7, and 18-inch in place of 14-inch tubes. Instead of their 4.7's being mounted in the well amidships, they were placed on the upper deck level, a much better position in a sea-way, but they never proved themselves quite such good ships for their size as did the earlier type. They served to illustrate the general rule that slight improvements on a design are rarely satisfactory, and that while every staple design has its defects, it is extremely difficult to remove one drawback without creating another. Moreover, such improvements invariably cause increased cost, and an essential with the small cruiser is that she shall be cheap enough to be numerically strong. Four *Astroeas* cost as much as five *Apollos*. They were rather more seaworthy, but no faster—if as fast. The total broadsides obtained were only *one* 4.7 more and *two* 6-inch *less*.[7] A considerably greater possible bunker capacity was obtained; but the normal supply (400 tons) was the same for both.

In the British Navy, in 1908-11, a precisely similar thing obtained. It was probably inevitable. In the German Navy, between 1897 and 1907, displacement for small cruisers rose from 2,645 to 4,350 tons, with practically the same armament. But here the horse-power rose from about 8,500 or less to 20,000, and designed speeds in proportion, from a twenty-one knots (not made) to a 25.5, which, on trial, turned out to be 27,000 I.H.P. and over twenty-seven knots.

Here, however, there was a definite aim—increased speed, with only trivial improvements in any other direction. With similar Brit-

---

7. 4 *Aatroeas* = 8—6 ins., 16—4.7. 5 *Apollos* = 10—6 in., 15—4.7

Second class cruiser of the Naval Defence Act era, now converted into a minelayer.

ish cruisers the defect has invariably been "general improvements" on what the original design *might have been* if plotted a year or two later than it actually was. There is no question—or very little—but that Germany in its ultra-conservative policy gauged the situation better than any British Admiralty ever did till just before the war.

Minor cruisers *must* be cheap to construct. Any improvement in them *must* have a definite intrinsic value. Lacking that, it is worth very little. The *Astroeas*, as. cited, indicated how a supposed advantage may even be a real deficit from another point of view.

The value of increased speed cannot be put into £ s. d., but armament easily can be. Like reconstruction, minor "improvements" on a design rarely pay. With the original conception the naval architect is given certain data for which he arranges accordingly. Ordered to improve upon it in any direction he can only add displacement and upset the balance of everything.

The Naval Defence Act also included a certain number of third-class cruisers—*Pallas, Pearl, Philomel,* and *Phoebe*—for the ordinary service, and five similar ships for the Australian station, originally named *Pandora, Pelorus, Persian, Phoenix,* and *Psyche*. These were later altered to Australian names, *Katoomba, Mildura, Wallaroo, Tauranga,* and *Ringarooma*. They were of 2,575 tons, with 2½ decks, armaments of eight 4.7-inch and four above-water 14-inch tubes. The designed speed was 19 knots.

Thirteen torpedo gunboats, improved *Rattlesnakes*, were laid down under the act, corresponding to nine others of the normal programme, of which two were for Australia. The Naval Defence boats were *Alarm, Antelope, Circe, Gleaner, Gossamer, Hebe, Renard, Speedy*—all laid down in 1889, as also were the *Whiting* (afterwards *Boomerang*) and *Wizard* (renamed *Karahatta*) for Australia. Those laid down normally in the previous year were the *Salamander, Seagull, Sheldrake, Skipjack, Spanker, Speedwell,* for the British Navy. Two others, *Assaye* and *Plassy*, were built for the Indian Marine at and about this time. All carried a couple of 4.7-inch guns, were of about 750-850 tons displacement, and were first known as "catchers." They were all intended to steam at 19 knots or over with locomotive boilers; but in service none ever did. At a later date, re-boilered with water-tubes, many reached or exceeded the designed speed, and the majority of them are still in service for auxiliary purposes—many being specially fitted as mine sweepers, and the rest used as tenders for various services.

They are of considerable interest on account of the fact that the destroyers of 1909-12 were practically the same displacement and general shape, with a not very dissimilar armament—two 4-inch instead of two 4.7. The modern destroyers, however, were approximately ten knots faster—an interesting commentary on engineering improvements in the course of twenty years!

More interesting still, however, is the fact that Sir William White should have evolved twenty years ago almost exactly what—except in the matter of modern speed possibilities—is today, (as at time of first publication), the recognised ideal for destroyers.

In the British Navy the torpedo gun-boats never get beyond the "catcher" stage—they never had the opportunity; but it is worthy of note that the first two ships to be torpedoed under anything like modern war conditions—the Chilian *Blanco Encalada* and the Brazilian *Aquidaban*—were both sunk by vessels of almost exactly the same type as the "catchers," and not by torpedo boats.

So far as the British Navy was concerned, the "catchers" tested in the "secret manoeuvres" of 1891 did uncommonly well. They hung about off the torpedo bases, and though only about one to four, accounted for at least 90 *per cent*, of the hostile torpedo boats. To this very success, perhaps, was due the fact that in their own day they were not thought of as an offensive arm against big ships—destruction of the torpedo boat was then the principal aim in view. This they fulfilled. The South American Republics discovered their "other uses," and so really led the way to the evolution of the destroyer of a later era.

Perhaps the only nation which really read the lesson involved was Germany. So long ago as 1895 she had launched the 2,000-ton "small cruiser" *Hela*; in 1898 the *Gazelle* of 2,645 tons was set afloat. For years Germany added to the *Gazelle* class, at a time when all the rest of the world had decreed that "third-class cruisers" were useless. Not for many a year did the British Admiralty discover that Germany had seen the matter of the *Lynch* and the *Sampaio* [8] better than any other power.

Neither of these ships in attacking got hit. They got home without. But they might have been hit. Germany evolved something that even if hit badly would still float long enough to get off her torpedoes.

Till the Chilian "catchers" in 1891 proved their offensive abilities, no one had ever considered that side of the question. To this day, (1912), Germany has never really received her meed of credit for per-

---

8. The *Lynch* and *Condell* (launched 1890) sank the Chilian *Blanco Encalada* in 1891; the *G. Sampaio* (1893) the Brazilian *Aquidaban* in 1894.

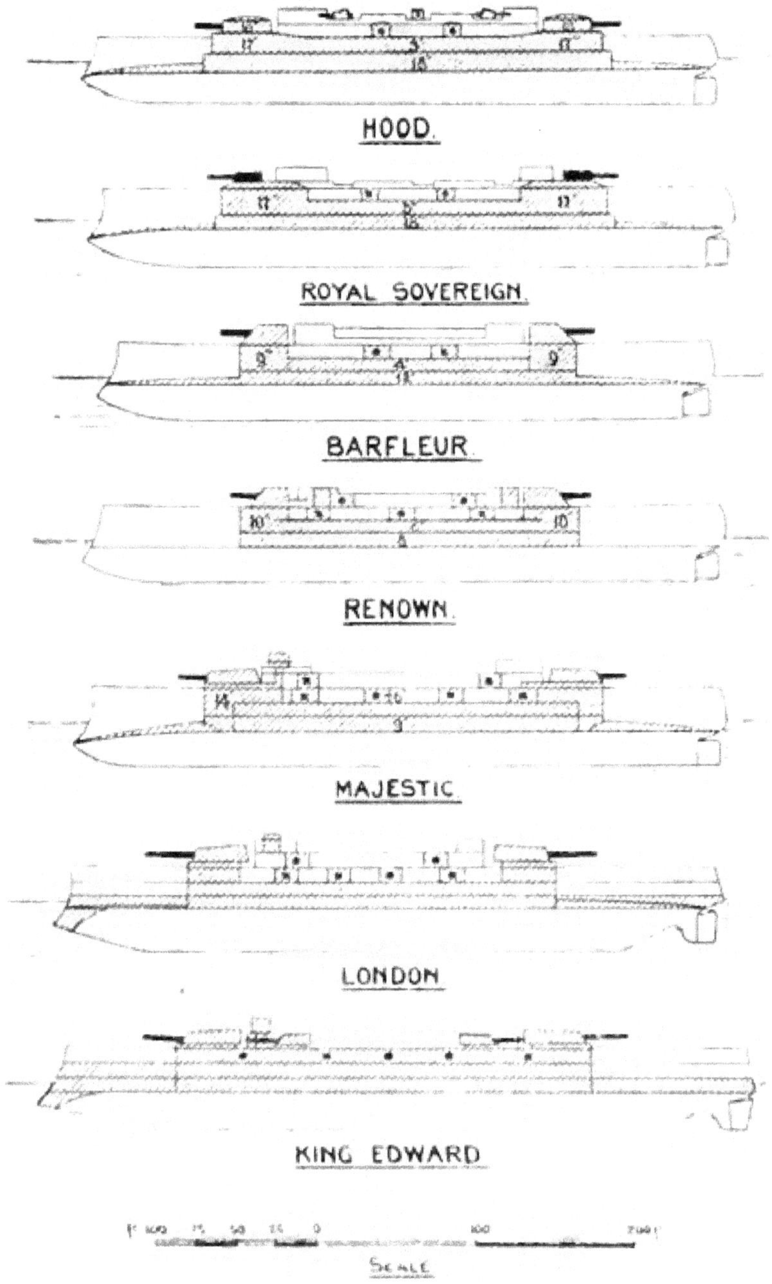

Battleships of the White Era

HOOD.

ROYAL SOVEREIGN.

BARFLEUR.

RENOWN.

MAJESTIC

LONDON

KING EDWARD

Scale

ceiving that a small third-class cruiser has potentialities with torpedoes against a battleship at night.

So late as the present day much comment about German small cruisers being inadequately gunned, a clear indication that just as in the past there was a difficulty in conceiving of the torpedo-gunboat for other than her nominal use, so the possibilities of the small cruiser in the role of destroyer were still apt to be generally overlooked.

In February, 1893, there was laid down the *Renown*, the only armoured ship of the 1892-93 Estimates; an improved *Centurion*, with thinner belt armour. Harvey armour—three inches of which had the resisting value of four inches of compound or six inches of iron—was adopted in this ship for the first time. Influences other than taking advantage of the reduced weight required for a given protective value were, however, at work, for in the *Renown* sacrifices were made at the waterline in order to secure better protection to the lower deck side.

Details of the *Renown*:—

Displacement—12,350 tons.
Length (between perpendiculars)—380 ft.
Beam—72 1/3 f t.
Draught—(maximum) 27 ft.
Armament—Four 10-inch, ten 6-inch 40 cal., twelve
    12-pounders, four submerged 18-inch tubes, and one
    above water-line in stern.
Armour—8-6 in. belt, 200 ft. long amidships, 6 in. side above.
Bulkheads 10-6 in., barbettes 10 in., casemates, main deck
    ones 6 in., upper deck ones, 4 in.
Horse-power—12,000—18 knots.
Coal—(normal) 800 tons; (maximum) 1,760 tons=nominal
    7,200 miles at ton knots.

Built at Pembroke; engined by Maudslay; she was launched in May, 1895, and completed for sea in April, 1897, having taken no less than 4¼ years to build. Cost, £746,247.

She proved one of the best steamers ever built for the Navy. On a four-hour trial she made 18.75 knots, with 12,901 I.H.P. Her economical speed proved to be fifteen knots. She always steamed well, and after thirteen years' service did 17.4 knots with ease.

The special feature of this ship was that in her instead of the ordinary flat deck on top of the belt, a sloping deck behind the belt was first introduced. This system—rigidly adhered to in the British

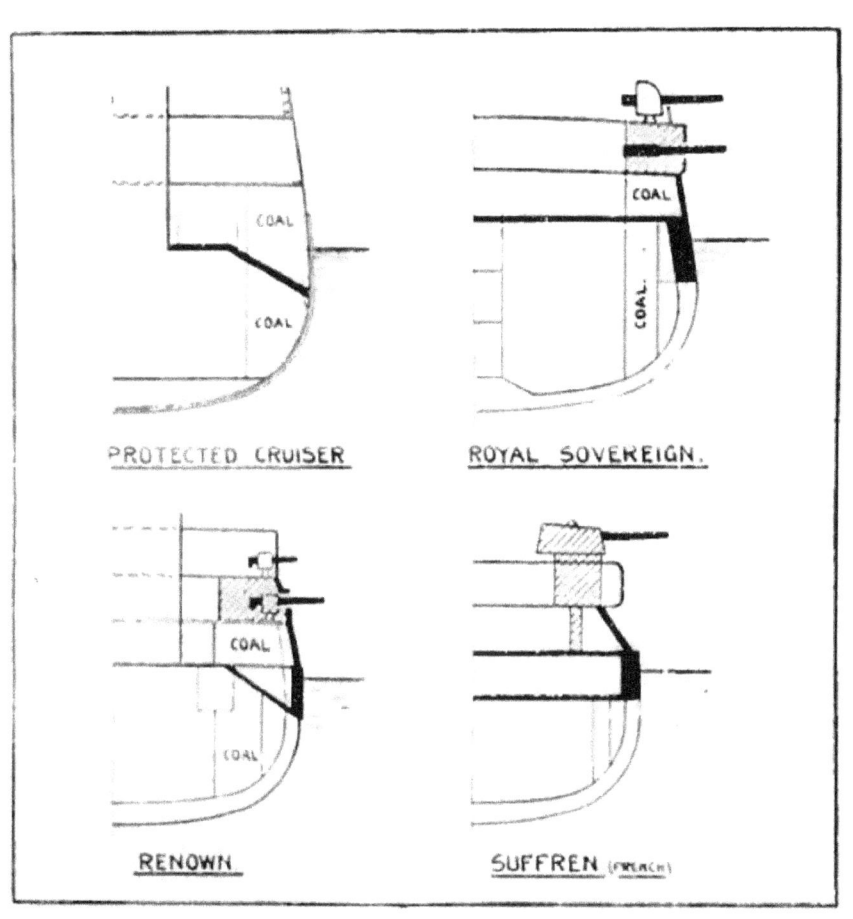

Systems of water-line protection

Navy ever since, and copied eventually into every other Navy—was based upon the idea of reinforcing the deck-protected cruiser with side armour. The principle involved was that at whatever angle the belt might be hit and penetrated, the incoming projectile would then meet a further obstruction at a 45° angle, calculated to present a maximum of deflecting resistance. Professor Hovgaard and others have since indicated that, weight for weight, three inches of inclined deck armour, having to be spread more, represent as much or more tons as six inches of vertical armour (the nominal equivalent), and protective decks behind armour are today, (1912), much thinner than of yore and little better than "splinter decks." The principle, however, remains, as originated by Sir William White, and is, perhaps, the most characteristic feature of his era: seeing how universally the idea was copied.

The French were the last to adopt it. Instead, they used the flat deck below the belt in addition to the one on top of it. This was made use of so late as the *République* and *Liberté* class. While ideally better for resisting projectiles which might penetrate the belt, it was impossible of really practical application amidships on account of the difficulty of keeping the engines entirely below it.

The *Renown* was the first ship to carry all her secondary guns in casemates. She was fitted as a flagship, and first served on the North American Station. When Admiral Fisher went from there to the Mediterranean he took the *Renown* with him as flagship, presumably with the idea that speed was better than power in a flagship. The *Renown's* fighting power was small even then, but she was well fitted for the social side of flagship work—so nicely, indeed, that the flash-plates of the big guns had been taken up so as not to interfere with ladies' shoes in dances!

After leaving the Mediterranean the *Renown* was still further converted into a "battleship yacht," the six-inch guns being removed. She was painted white, and used to convey the then Prince of Wales to India. Thereafter she practically disappeared from the effective list and eventually became a training ship for stokers.

The *Renown* was followed by the ships of the Spencer programme, nine battleships of the *Majestic* class, which were spread over the 1893-94 Estimates, and those of the next year. The *Majestics* were in substance amplified *Renowns*, their special and particular feature being that in place of the two amidships belt of varying thickness a single belt of 16 ft. wide of a uniform 9 in. thickness was substituted.

In the *Majestics*, the 13.5, which had been for so long the standard gun for first-class battleships, disappeared in favour of a new type of 12-inch, a Mark VIII. of 35 calibres. The two types compare as follows:—

Bore. Inch.	Length. Cals.	Weight. Tons.	Projectile. lbs.	Maximum Penetration against K.C (capped projectiles). at 5000 yds. in.	at 3000 yds. in.
13.5	30	67	1250	9	12
12	35	46	850	11½	14¼

The new gun was, therefore, superior in everything except weight of projectile, and that was not considered much in those days. Today, of course, it has quite a special meaning.

In the *Majestics*, except in the first two, all-round loading positions for the big guns were introduced in place of the cumbersome old system whereby, after firing, the guns had to return to an end-on position, tilt up,, and at a fixed angle take their charges at what was little but an adaption for breechloaders of the loading system evolved twenty years before for the old *Inflexible*.

Details of these ships:—

Displacement—14,900 tons.
Length—(between perpendiculars) 390 ft., (over-all) 413 ft.
Beam—75 ft.
Draught—(mean), 27½ ft., (maximum) about 30 ft.
Armament—Four 12-inch 35 cal., twelve 6-inch 40 cal.,
    sixteen 12-pounders, twelve 3-pounders. Torpedo tubes
    (18-inch), four submerged and one above water in stern.
Armour (Harvey)—Belt, (220 ft. by 16 ft.) 9 in. Bulkheads,
    14 in. Barbettes, 14 in. with 10 in. turrets. Casemates,
    6 in.
Horse-power—12,000=17.5 knots.
Coal—(normal) 1,200 tons; (maximum) 2,200 tons =
    nominal radius of 7,600 miles at 10 knots and 4,000 at
    15 knots.

The ships were built, etc., as follows:—

Name.	Laid down.	Builder.	Engined by
Magnificent	Dec. '93	Chatham	Penn
Majestic	Feb. '94	Portsmouth	Vickers

Hannibal	April,	'94	Pembroke	Harland & Wolff
Victorious	May,	'94	Chatham	Hawthorn, Leslie
Mars	June,	'94	Laird	Laird
Prince George	Sept.	'94	Portsmouth	Humphrys
Jupiter	Oct.	'94	Clydebank	Clydebank
Cæsar	March,	'95	Portsmouth	Maudslay
Illustrious	March,	'95	Chatham	Penn

Mostly they were completed inside two years, the only ones which took appreciably longer being the *Hannibal* and the *Illustrious*. In these and the *Caesar* an innovation introduced in the others—the placing of the chart house round the base of the foremast with the conning tower well clear ahead—was done away with, and the old system of the bridge over the conning tower reverted to. In the *Caesar* and *Illustrious*, laid down later than the others, an improvement was effected by the introduction of circular instead of pear-shaped barbettes. The *Majestic, Magnificent,* and *Caesar* were built in dry dock instead of on slips—the first instance of this since the days of early coast-defence monitors.

The total cost was approximately a million per ship.

On trials most of them exceeded the designed speed, but all were light on trials. They proved very handy ships, with circles of 450 yards at fifteen knots. Coal consumption was always high.

Compared to the *Sovereigns*, the following figures are of interest:—

Name.	Displacement (tons).	Weight of Armour (tons).	Weight of Armament & Ammunition (tons).	H.P.	Normal Coal (tons).
Majestics	14,900	4260	1500	12,000	1200
Sovereigns	14,100	4600	1410	13,000	900

The total dead weight carried in armament, armour, and coal thus works out at practically the same figure, despite the rise of 800 tons in displacement. On these grounds certain attacks were made upon the ships, mainly by those who argued against the unarmoured ends. The criticisms were, however, mainly of the captious order—the ships were certainly the finest specimens of naval architecture of their day.

At a later date electric hoists were fitted to the 6-inch guns, and 400 tons of oil fuel were added to the fuel capacity (the maximum coal capacity being reduced by 200 tons). The first ship to be so fitted was the *Mars*. Another innovation was shifting the torpedo nets, first in the *Mars*, then in all the others, from the upper deck to the main deck level; the idea being to keep the nets clear of the 6-inch guns.

The *Majestic* and *Magnificent* served for a long time as flagships in the Channel Fleet. Admiral Sir F. Stephenson and Sir A. K. Wilson flew their flags in the *Majestic*, of which ship Prince Louis of Battenberg was at one time captain.

It was during the early service of the *Majestics* in the Channel Fleet that "invisible" colours for warships first came into consideration, all ships up to that date being painted with black hulls, white upper works, and yellow masts and funnels. For these experiments the *Magnificent* was painted black all over, the *Majestic* and *Hannibal* were given grey and light green upper works respectively. The latter was really the more "invisible" of the two, but both ships were left with black hulls. Ultimately a grey, a little darker than that which the Germans had long used, was adopted as the regulation, though for some time it varied greatly between ship and ship, following the old system under which a good deal of latitude in painting was allowed.[9]

To this era, 1894-95, belong two groups of protected cruisers, the *Powerfuls* and the *Talbots*. The latter, nine in all, were merely enlarged (5,600 tons) editions of the later cruisers of the Naval Defence Act, and call for no comment. The former group were the *Powerful* and *Terrible*, "replies" to the Russian *Rurik* and *Rossiya*. They displaced nearly as much as the battleships—14,200 tons—and ran to the then unheard of length of 500 ft. between perpendiculars. They carried no belt armour whatever, but were given stout protective decks, no less than 6in. on the slopes amidships. The two big guns (40 calibre, 9.2) were given 6 in. Harvey barbettes, the twelve other guns [10] (6-inch) being in 6-inch casemates. Sixteen 12-pounders were disposed about the upper works. Designed horse-power 25,000=22 knots. Total bunker capacity of 3,000 tons, equal to a nominal 7,000 miles at fourteen knots. Both ships were laid down in 1894, the *Powerful* by Vickers and the *Terrible* at Clydebank. They were launched in the following year.

In service the *Powerfuls* proved capable of keeping up a speed of twenty knots almost indefinitely. For the rest, they were unhandy ships with large turning circles. At the time of the South African War, both

---

9. In 1894 the *Thunderer* had her upper works painted in black and white chequers, like the old three-deckers of the Nelson era. Ships with the top of their upper works yellow were also not uncommon.
10. About 1902-3 four additional casemates for 6-inch guns were added on top of the four amidship casemates.

of them were at the Cape, and did service with landed naval brigades. Of these, one from the *Powerful*, with some 4.7's on special Percy Scott gun-carriages, materially assisted in the defence of Ladysmith.

During the year 1911 the decision was come to that it was not worth while preserving either ship, on account of the large crews required and their comparatively small fighting value under modern conditions.

Two considerable novelties were embodied in these ships. The first of these was the adoption of electrical gear for the big guns. The other and more far-reaching was the adoption of Belleville boilers.

THE BATTLE OF THE BOILERS.

Owing to favourable reports of their use in the French Navy, Belleville boilers were in 1895 experimentally fitted to the *Sharpshooter*, torpedo gunboat; but the decision to adopt them in large ships was taken from French rather than any British experience. Trouble and failure were freely predicted. With the result frequently attending lugubrious predictions, very little trouble has ever been experienced with any type and then only in the very early stage when the water-tube boiler was an almost unknown curiosity to the engine-room staff.

The chief advantages claimed for Belleville boilers were the higher working pressures, economy in maintenance and fuel consumption, saving of weight, rapid steam raising, and great facility for repairs.

The Belleville was the first water-tube boiler to come into prominence; other types, however, soon appeared. In the period 1895-98, torpedo gunboats were experimentally fitted as follows:—*Sharpshooter, Belleville*; *Sheldrake*, Babcock; *Seagull*, Niclausse; *Spanker*, Du Temple; *Salamander*, Mumford; *Speedy*, Thornycroft—these three last being of the small tube type. Other existing types were the Yarrow, White-Foster, Normand, Reed, Blechynden, all these being of the small tube type also, and regarded as suitable for small craft only.[11]

In the matter of big ships, so far as the British Navy was concerned, "water-tube boiler" for some years meant Bellevilles only, whence it came that in the insensate "Battle of the Boilers," which presently broke out, Bellevilles were the main object of attack in Parliament and elsewhere. Actually, of course, the whole principle was in the melting pot. All the elements opposed to change in any form rallied to the attack, led on and influenced in some cases by those whose interests

---

11. The large tube Yarrow, now so general, did not appear till at a later date.

White Era battleships of the Majestic class

were bound up with the old style cylindrical boilers. It was all over again the old story of the fight for the retention of the paddle against the screw propeller, with an equal disregard for facts.

Unfortunately the party of progress played somewhat into the hands of the reactionaries. In fitting the Belleville type only, they had not much alternative, other types being then in a less forward state. The error made was that in the wholesale adoption of a new type of steam generator, requiring twice the skill and intelligence necessary for the old type, it was practically impossible to train quickly enough a sufficiency of engineers and stokers. Hence troubles soon arose. An even greater error was that the boilers were mostly built in England to the French specifications, without, in many case, sufficient experienced supervision; and minor "improvements," such as fusible plugs and restricting regulations, were introduced by more or less amateur Admiralty authorities—which also produced trouble.

For example, French practice had taught that adding lime to the feed water was desirable; but in many British ships this rule was ignored. Again, one Belleville essential was to throw on coal in very small quantities at a time, in contradistinction to the old cylindrical practice in which shovelling on enormous quantities of coal was the recipe for increased speed. This feature was often disregarded.

The Belleville, ever a complicated and delicate mechanism, if its full efficiency is to be secured, was a worse boiler for the experiments than many of the simpler types of today would have been. But no water-tube boiler of any type would have stood any chance of success against the opposition. There were some terrible times in the boiler rooms in those days. One or two ships whose chief engineers had been specially trained in France secured marvellous results, usually by ignoring Admiralty improvements and regulations.[12] But for one success there were many early failures.

The agitation triumphed to the extent of a Committee of Inquiry being appointed. An interim report of this committee made a scapegoat of the Belleville, to the extent of recommending that no

---

12. Comparatively recently, (1912), a ship—best left unnamed—made wonderful speed. With a new Engineer commander she suddenly lost 25 *per cent.* of her horsepower. The newcomer was rather inexperienced in the type, and closely followed Admiralty regulations. Presently the ship recovered her power—he had given up following the book! It is only fair to say that the restrictive regulations of the Admiralty were mostly forced upon them by people ashore, who probably had not even a nodding acquaintance with the engine-room of a warship, or warship requirements.

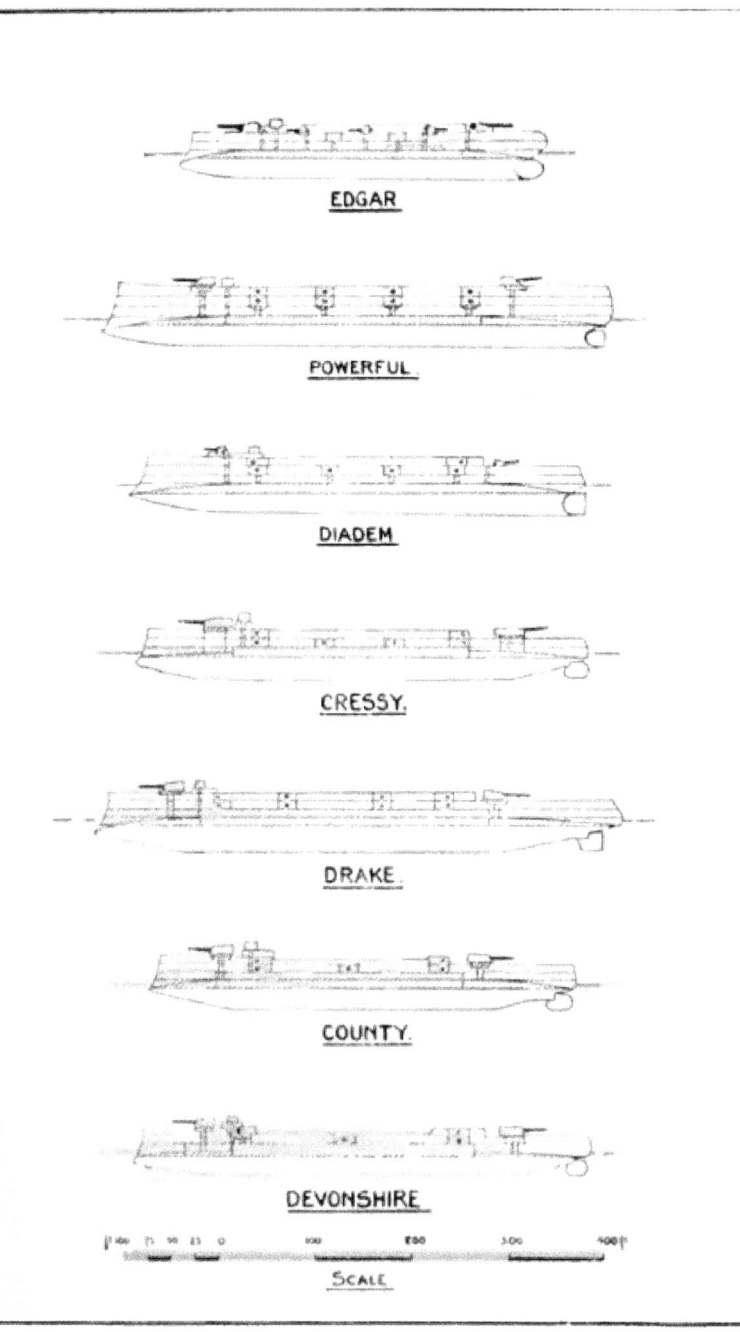

PRINCIPLE CRUISERS IN THE WHITE ERA

more should be fitted. But the victory of the retrogrades ended there. A species of compromise with public opinion inflamed against the water-tube system was temporarily adopted, and absurd mixed installations of cylindrical and water-tube boilers were fitted to some ships. Four large tube types were selected as substitutes for Bellevilles, the Niclausse, Dürr (a German variant of the Niclausse), the Babcock and Wilcox, and the Yarrow large tube.

It may approximately be said that every water-tube boiler is a species of compromise between facility for rapid repair on board ship and complication, and the need of great care in using and working. It is usual to put the Belleville at one end of this scale and the Yarrow (large tube) at the other, this last boiler now requiring little, if any, more care than the old type of cylindrical.

In the course of comparatively short experiments, both the Niclausse and the Dürr were found to possess most of the alleged deficiencies of the Belleville without its advantages; and it was decided to fit all future types of large ships with the Babcock and Yarrow types only. The absurd mixture of cylindrical and water-tube boilers was wisely done away with. Curiously enough, the Belleville boiler, once the agitation had ceased, also ceased to be troublesome. This was no doubt due to the increased experience which had been gained in the interim.

Both the Babcock and Yarrow boilers have been immensely improved since the days when they were first brought out. Something of the same sort is, of course, true of all the standard types, and there is today, (1912), hardly any question as to which of them may be the best or worst. Each type has some special advantage of its own, and in no case, probably, is that advantage sufficiently pronounced to render any one type absolutely the best. When adopted by the Admiralty the Belleville was certainly the best water-tube boiler available. Had it been persisted in and not "improved" by amateurs it would probably have done quite as well as any type adopted today. The real issue was mainly not one of type, but of principle. That principle was the water-tube boiler as opposed to the old type cylindrical.

The Estimates for 1896-97 provided for five battleships which were somewhat sarcastically alluded to as "improved" *Majestics*. These ships were the *Canopus* class, and they mark a species of early striving after the ideal of the battle-cruisers of today. That is to say, certain sacrifices were made in them with a view to securing increased speed.

Particulars of these ships:—

Displacement—12,950 tons.
Length— (over all) 418 ft.
Beam—74 ft.
Draught—(maximum) 26½ ft.
Armament—Four 12 in., 35 cal., twelve 6 in. 40 cal., ten 12-pounders, four submerged tubes (18 in.)
Armour—Harvey-Nickel. Belt amidships 6 in. with 2 in. extension to the bow and 1½ in. skin aft on the waterline. Bulkheads and barbettes 12 in. Turrets 8 in.
Horse-power—31,500=18.25 knots.
Coal—(normal) 1,000 tons; (maximum) 2,300 tons = nominal radius of 8,000 miles at 10 knots.

The adoption of Harvey-Nickel armour, which was of superior resisting power to Harvey armour in the ratio of about 5 to 4, partly, but not entirely accounted for the thinning of the armour of this class. Theoretically, the 9 in. armour belt of the *Majestic* was equal to 18 in. of iron, while the belt of the *Canopus* class was equal to about 1oin, of iron. In place of the 4 in. deck of the *Majestics*, the *Canopus* class had only a 2½ in. deck. The thin bow (2 in.) plating was introduced as a sop to a public agitation against soft-ended ships. Such a belt is, of course, perfectly useless against any heavy projectile, or, for that matter, against 6 in., except at very long range indeed. Sir William White never made any secret of his cynical disbelief in these bow belts. They were and always have been what doctors call a "placebo."

In the following year the sixth ship of this class was built—the *Vengeance*. She differed from the others in the form of her turrets, which were flat sided for the first time. In her also a mounting was first introduced, whereby, in addition to being loaded in any position, big guns could also be loaded at any elevation.

Some other details of the *Canopus* class are:—

Name.	Built by	Engines by	Laid down.	Completed
Canopus	Portsmouth	Greenock	Jan. '97	1900
Goliath	Chatham	Penn	Jan. '97	1900
Albion	Thames I.W.	Maudslay	Dec. '96	1902
Ocean	Devonport	Hawthorn Leslie	Feb. '97	1900
Glory	Laird	Laird	Dec. '96	1901
Vengeance	Vickers	Vickers	Aug. '97	1901

The cruisers of the following year were eight cruisers of the much discussed *Diadem* class, small editions of the *Powerful* (11,000 tons), and carrying a pair of 6-inch guns in place of the 9.2's of the *Powerfuls*. For the first four (the *Diadem*, *Andromeda*, *Europa*, and *Niobe*) a speed of 20.5 knots only was provided, but in the late four (the *Argonaut*, *Ariadne*, *Amphitrite*, and *Spartiate*) the horse-power was increased to 18,000, in order to provide twenty-one knots. At the present time (1912) these ships have for all practical purposes already passed from the effective list, all the weak points of the *Powerfuls* being exaggerated in them.

In the Estimates for the years 1895 to 1898, provision was made also for eleven small third-class cruisers of the "P" class of 2135 tons and twenty knot speed. The armament consisted of eight 4-inch guns. On trials most of them did well, but in a very short time their speeds fell off, and at the present time, such of them as remain on the active list are slower than the far older cruisers of the *Apollo* class.

In the Estimates for 1897-98, in addition to the *Vengeance*, already mentioned, three improved copies of the *Majestic* were provided. These ships were:—

Name.	Laid down.	Built at.	Engines by.
Formidable	March, '98	Portsmouth	Earle
Irresistible	April, '98	Chatham	Maudslay
Implacable	July, '98	Devonport	Laird

The only difference between them and the *Majestics* lies in advantage being taken of improvements in gunnery and armour to increase the offensive and defensive items. The absurd 2-inch bow belt of the *Canopus* was repeated in them, but raised within 2½ ft. of the main deck. A 40-calibre 12-inch was mounted, also a 45-calibre 6-inch.

These were the first ships of the British Navy in which Krupp cemented armour was used. This armour, generally known as "K.C.," has approximately a resisting power three times that of iron armour. That is to say, the 9 in. belts of the *Formidables* were approximately 33 *per cent*, more effective than the similar belts of the *Majestics*. These ships proved faster and more handy, easily exceeding their designed eighteen knots. The superior handiness was brought about by a superior form of hull—the deadwood aft being cut away for the first time in them.

In this year's Estimates armoured cruisers definitely re-appeared, six ships of the *Cressy* type being laid down.

Particulars of these:—

Displacement—12,000 tons.
Length—454 ft.
Beam— 69½ ft.
Draught—(maximum) 28 ft.
Armament—Two 9.2, 40 cal., twelve 6-inch, 45 cal., twelve 12-pounders, two 18 in. submerged tubes.
Armour—6 in. Krupp belt amidships, 250 ft. long by 11½ ft. wide, 2 in. continuation to the bow. Barbettes 6 in. casemates 5 in.
Horse power—21,000=21 knots.
Coal—(normal) 800 tons; (maximum) 1,600 tons.

Name.	Laid down.	Built at.	Engined by.
Sutlej	Aug. '98	Clydebank	Clydebank
Cressy	Oct. '98	Fairfield	Fairfield
Aboukir	Nov. '98	Fairfield	Fairfield
Hogue	July, '98	Vickers	Vickers
Bacchante	Dec. '99	Clydebank	Clydebank
Euryalus	July, '99	Vickers	Vickers

In substance these ships were armoured editions of the *Powerful*. They steamed very well in their time, but have now fallen off considerably and are no longer of any importance. Total weight of armour 2,100 tons. An innovation introduced in these ships was the fitting of non-flammable wood, which at a later date was objected to on the grounds that it deteriorated the gold lace of the uniforms stored in drawers made of it. The *Cressy* was completed in 1901; the others, excepting the *Euryalus*, in 1902. This latter ship was greatly delayed from various causes, and not completed until 1903.

The 1898-99 Estimates consisted of three battleships and four armoured cruisers. The battleships were practically sisters to the *Formidable*, but differed from her in that the main belt, instead of being a patch amidships, has a total length of 300 ft. from the bow. At the bow it is 2 in., quickly increasing to 4 in., 5 in., 6 in., and finally to 9 in., and this provided a measure of protection that the 2 in. belts of preceding ships could never afford. The flat-sided turrets, first introduced in the *Vengeance*, were also fitted in these ships, the *Formidables* having the old pattern turrets.

The advantages of flat-sided turrets lie in the fact that K.C. can be used for them instead of the relatively softer non-cemented. K.C. is not applicable to curved surfaces, for which reason barbettes, casemates, and batteries with curved portholes in them and rounded turrets cannot be constructed of it. Flat-sided turrets consist of a number of flat plates placed to meet each other at predetermined angles, thus forming one homogeneous whole.

These battleships were:—

Name.	Laid down.	Built at	Engines by.
London	Dec. '98	Portsmouth	Earle
Bulwark	March, '99	Devonport	Hawthorn
Venerable	Nov. '99	Chatham	Maudslay

All were completed in 1902. The cruisers of the same year, the *Drake* class, were "improved" *Cressies*, with increased displacement, power and speed. The increased displacement allowed of four extra 6-inch guns being mounted, these being placed in casemates on top of the amidships casemates. Particulars of the *Drake* class:—

Displacement—14,000 tons.
Length—(over all) 529½ ft.
Beam—71 ft.
Draught—(maximum) 28 ft.
Armament—Two 9.2, 45 cal. (instead of 40 cal., as in the *Cressies*), sixteen 6-inch, 45 cal., and fourteen 12-pounders, two submerged tubes (18 in.).
Armour—2,700 tons, as in *Cressy*, except that the casemates are 6 in. thick.
Horse-power—30,000 = 23 knots. Boilers, 43 Belleville.
Coal—(normal) 1,250 tons; (maximum) 2,500.

These ships were altogether superior to the *Cressy* class. On trial they all easily made their contract speeds and subsequently greatly exceeded them. It was discovered that increased speed was to be obtained by additional weight aft, and this was so much brought to a fine art that weights were adjusted accordingly, and in one of them, seeking to make a speed record, the entire crew were once mustered aft in order to vary the trim! Building details are as follows:—

Name.	Laid down.	Completed	Built at.	Engines by.
Good Hope	Sept. '99	1902	Fairfield	Fairfield
Drake	April, '99	1902	Pembroke	Humphrys & T
Leviathan	Nov. '99	1903	Clydebank	Clydebank
King Alfred	Aug. '99	1903	Vickers	Vickers

For some years these were the fastest ships in the world. In 1905, in a race by the Second Cruiser Squadron across the Atlantic, with ships of nominally equal speed, the *Drake* came in first. In December, 1906, at four-fifths power for thirty hours, she averaged 22.5 knots. In 1907, the *King Alfred* averaged 25.1 knots for one hour, and made an eight hours' mean of 24.8. They proved very economical steamers, being able to do nineteen knots at an expenditure of eleven tons of coal an hour, and though they are now getting old, as warships go, they have never yet been beaten on the results achieved by horse-power per ton of displacement.

The Estimates of 1898-99 included a supplementary programme of four armoured ships which, like the *Canopus* class, again foreshadowed the battle cruisers of today. These were the famous *Duncan* class, and may be described as slightly smaller editions of the *London*, with armour thickness sacrificed for superior speed. The belt amidships was reduced from 9 in. to 7 in., but against this the belt at the extreme bow was made an inch thicker, and 25 ft. away from the ram became 5 in. thick. The displacement sank by 1,000 tons, the horse-power was increased by 3,000, and the speed by one knot.

The total weight of armour is about 3,500 against 4,300 tons in the *Londons*. The *Duncans* may be regarded as a species of recrudescence of Barnaby ideas, plus a later notion that a well-extended partial protection was better than a more concentrated protection of less area. Generally speaking, they were improved duplicates of the *Canopus* class, in the same way that the *Formidable* and the ships that followed her were duplicates of the *Majestic*. Two ideas were obviously at work. In other forms these two ideas have (with variations) existed to the present day. Then it was purely a question between ratios devoted to speed and protection. Today (1912) matters have been so far modified that increased displacements are given to secure speed advantages, but protection remains proportionately as it was. Reduced armament has always been accepted.

Construction details of the *Duncans*, of which two more figured in the estimates for 1899-1900:—

Name.	Laid down.	Built at.	Engines by.
Duncan	July, '99	Thames, I.W.	Thames, I.W.
Russell	March, '99	Palmer	Palmer
Cornwallis	July, '99	Thames, I.W.	Thames, I.W.
Exmouth	Aug. '99	Laird	Laird
Albemarle	Jan. '00	Chatham	Thames, I.W.
Montagu	Nov. '99	Devonport	Laird

The *Montagu* was wrecked on Lundy Island in 1906.

Contemporaneous with the *Drakes*, and extending over four ships in the Estimates of 1898-99 to two in the following and four in the year later, ten armoured cruisers were provided for, which in essence were little but an attempt to provide a normal second-class protected cruiser of the *Talbot* class, with armour protection. These ships—the *County* class—are of 9,800 tons displacement, and may also be regarded as diminutives of the *Drake* and *Cressy* classes, with a touch of the *Diadems* thrown in. In place of the fore and aft 9.2's of the *Drake* and *Cressy*, they were supplied with a couple of pairs of 6-inch guns mounted in turrets fore and aft. The belt amidships was reduced to 4 in. (a thickness in K.C. which has no virtues over armour of earlier type) with the usual extension of 2 in. to the bow. The twin turrets, in which, like those of the *Powerful*, electrical control was once more introduced, have never given satisfaction, being very cramped for working purposes, and probably no more efficient than single gun turrets would have been, certainly less than the single gun 7.5 in. turrets, originally proposed as an alternative, would have been.

Had the ships been regarded frankly as modern variants of the second-class protected cruisers, they probably would have been esteemed more than they were. Unfortunately they have always been regarded as "armoured ships" and discounted on account of their obvious inferiority to the *Drakes*. In the matter of steaming all of them have invariably done well (except in the case of the *Essex*, over which a mistake in design was made). The anticipated twenty-three knots was made quite easily, once certain early propeller difficulties were overcome. The Boiler Commission, already referred to, affected these ships, in so far that, instead of the hitherto inevitable Bellevilles, the *Berwick* and *Suffolk* were given Niclausse boilers and the *Cornwall* Babcocks. The total weight of armour is 1,800 tons.

Details of the construction of this class are:—

Name.	Laid down.	Built at.	Engines by.
Essex	Jan. '00	Pembroke	Clydebank
Kent	Feb. '00	Portsmouth	Hawthorn
Bedford	Feb. '00	Fairfield	Fairfield
Monmouth	Aug. '99	L. & Glasgow	L. & Glasgow
Lancaster	Mar. '01	Elswick	Hawthorn L.
Berwick	April, '01	Beardmore	Humphrys
Donegal	Feb. '01	Fairfield	Fairfield
Cornwall	Mar. '01	Pembroke	Hawthorn
Cumberland	Feb. '01	L. & Glasgow	L. & Glasgow
Suffolk	Mar. '02	Portsmouth	Humphrys & T.

All were completed during 1903 and 1904.

For the year 1900-01 only two battleships were provided: the *Queen*, built at Devonport and engined by Harland and Wolff, and the *Prince of Wales*, built at Chatham and engined by the Greenock Foundry Co. These were laid down in 1901 and completed in 1904. They were copies of the *Londons* in every detail, saving that, instead of being enclosed, their upper deck batteries were left open as in the *Duncans*. The *Queen* was given Babcock boilers instead of Bellevilles.

The 1901-02 Estimates provided three battleships and six armoured cruisers of the *County* class. These were the last ships designed by Sir William White. The battleships, of which eight were built altogether—three for 1901-02, two for the next year—were of a different type from any which had preceded them, and to some extent may be said to mark the birth of the *Dreadnought* era. That is to say, in them the old idea of the two calibres, 12 in. and 6 in., died out, and heavier auxiliary guns began to appear.

Particulars of these ships, the *King Edward VII* class, are as follows:—

Displacement—16,350 tons.
Length—(over all) 453¾ ft.
Beam—78ft.
Draughts—(maximum) 26¾ ft.
Armament—Four 12-inch, 40 cal., four 9.2, 45 cal.,
    ten 6-inch, 45 cal., twelve 12-pounders, fourteen
    3-pounders, five 18-inch submerged tubes (of which
    one is in the stern).
Armour—As in the *London* (but a 6 in. battery instead of
    casemates).
Horse-power—18,000=18.9 knots.
Coal—(normal) 950 tons; (maximum) 2,150 tons, also
    400 tons of oil, except in the *New Zealand*.

Name.	Laid down.	Built at.	Engines by.
Commonwealth	June, '01	Fairfield	Fairfield
King Edward	Mar. '02	Devonport	Harland & W.
Dominion	May, '02	Vickers	Vickers
Hindustan	Oct. '02	Clydebank	Clydebank
New Zealand (now Zelandia)	Feb. '03	Portsmouth	Humphrys & T.
Africa	Jan. '04	Chatham	Clydebank
Britannia	Feb. '04	Portsmouth	Humphrys & T.
Hibernia	Jan. '04	Devonport	Harland & W.

Except the last three, all were completed in 1905. The others were completed very shortly afterwards.

The boilers fitted to these ships varied considerably. The *King Edward, Hindustan,* and *Britannia* were given a mixed installation of Babcocks and cylindricals; the *New Zealand* Niclausse boilers; the other ships Babcock only. In the *Britannia,* super-heaters were also fitted to six of her boilers. The point differentiating these ships from their predecessors was the mounting of four 9.2 guns in single turrets at the angles of the superstructure. Equally novel was the placing of 6-inch guns in a battery behind the armour on the main deck.[13] Fighting tops, a feature of all previous ships, disappeared, and in place of them fire-control platforms were substituted.

When produced, these ships were considered as something like the "last word"; but in service later on it was very soon found that the two calibres of big guns rendered fire-control extremely difficult, and they have been a somewhat costly lesson in that respect. They cost about £1,500,000 each, and were found to be all that could be desired tactically, their turning circles with engines being only about 340 yds. at fifteen knots. All of them did not make their speeds on trials, and some have never quite come up to expectations in that respect, but they have all proved remarkably reliable steamers.

Six armoured cruisers provided for in the 1901-02 Estimates were the *Devonshires.* These were originally intended to have been enlarged *Counties,* carrying a single 7.5 fore and aft, in place of the twin 6-inch turrets of the prototype ships. The design was, however, modified to the extent of substituting a single 7.5 for each of the forward pairs of 6-inch casemates.

Details of these ships are:—

Displacement—10,850 tons.
Length (between perpendiculars)—450 ft.
Beam—68½ ft.
Draught—(maximum) 25½ ft.
Armament—Four 7.5, six 6-inch, 45 cal.; two
    12-pounders, twenty-two 3-pounders, two 18 in.
    torpedo tubes submerged.
Armour Belt—(length 325 ft. from the bow, width 10½ ft.),
    6 in. amidships, thinning to 2 in. right forward.

---

13. This idea was borrowed from the Continent. Germany had long adopted batteries, and nearly every other nation had followed suit.

Barbettes 6 in. Turrets 5 in. Casemates 6 in.
Horse-power—21,000=22.5 knots.
Coal—(normal) 800; (maximum) 1,800 tons.

Other details are:—

Name.	Laid down.	Built at.	Engined by.
Devonshire	Mar. '02	Chatham	Thames I.W.
Antrim	Aug. '02	Clydebank	Clydebank
Argyll	Sept. '02	Greenock Foundry	Greenock F.C.
Carnarvon	Oct. '02	Beardmore	Beardmore
Hampshire	Sept. '02	Elswick	Elswick
Roxburgh	June, '02	L. & Glasgow	L. & Glasgow

Like the *King Edwards*, various boilers were given to them. All of them have one-fifth cylindrical boilers. The *Devonshire* and *Carnarvon*, were otherwise given Niclausse; *Antrim* and *Hampshire*, Yarrow; *Argyll*, Babcock; and *Roxburgh*, Dürr. The designed speed was exceeded by all on trials, but none have proved successful steamers ever since. They were completed between 1904 and 1905.

These were the last ships to be designed by Sir William White. He resigned his position from ill-health; but, like his predecessors, left under a cloud—at any rate, with his services not really appreciated. He had created a magnificent fleet; but its very magnificence made many of his designs look poor on paper against any foreign construction of less displacement, but—*on paper*—of equal or superior qualities. It is the fate of the naval architect in peace-time to be judged on paper with small regard to issues such as nautical qualities, constructional strength, and a score of other details which are not to be expressed by any statistical formulae, but yet make all the difference between efficiency and the absence of it.

Sir William White's period of office was marked by an almost complete naval revolution. It began with the quick-firer and the disappearance of the low freeboard battleships. It ended with the coming of submarines, fire-control, and wireless. In between, it included the coming of the destroyer, the re-birth of the armoured cruiser; the arrival of the water-tube boiler, new forms of hull, unprecedented advances in both guns and armour—in fact, almost every conceivable change. Through these troubled waters with a steady hand and cool brain Sir William White guided the destiny of the Fleet and the millions of pounds expended in shipbuilding. Already his era is "the pre-*Dreadnought*" one, and to present-day ideas the term "pre-*Dreadnought*"

Early type of 27 knot destroyers

is already very nearly akin to "pre-historic." His creations preserved the peace, for which very reason they failed to secure glory. Already some have gone to the scrap-heap, and others are well on their way thither to join the Reed and Barnaby ships in that oblivion to which modern *Dreadnoughts* will just as surely go in their season.

More might be said: but *cui bono?* Such public epitaph as Sir William White received when he retired was of the "about time, too!" order. The creator of the finest fleet that the world has ever seen left office with less honour and no more public interest than did half-a-dozen mediocre admirals who had chanced to fly their flags in some of his creations. It is not given for the stage manager to stand in the lime-light reserved for the principal actors. But the historian of a hundred years hence, placing great Englishmen in perspective, will assuredly place Sir William White far ahead of many who loom greater in the public eye today, (1912).

Guns in the Era

The guns which especially belong to the White Era are as follows:—

Designation.	Weight. Tons.	Projectile. lbs.	Velocity. f.s.	Maximum Penetration with capped shot against K.C. at	
				5000 yds.	3000 yds.
13.5, 30 cal.	67	1250	2016	9	12
12in., 35 cal.	46	850	2367	$11\frac{1}{4}$	$14\frac{1}{4}$
12in., 40 cal.	50	850	2750	16	20
10in., 32 cal.	29	500	2040	$5\frac{1}{4}$	$7\frac{1}{4}$
9.2, 30 cal.	24	380	2065	4	6
9.2, 40 cal.	25	380	2347	$6\frac{3}{4}$	$9\frac{1}{4}$
9.2, 45 cal.	27	380	2640	$8\frac{3}{4}$	$11\frac{1}{4}$
7.5, 45 cal.	14	200	2600	$5\frac{3}{4}$	$7\frac{1}{2}$
6in., 40 cal.	$7\frac{1}{2}$	100	2200	—	—
6in., 45 cal.	7	100	2535	—	$4\frac{1}{4}$

Purchased Ships.

In the year 1902 two ships, the *Constitucion* and *Libertad*, were laid down at Elswick and Vickers-Maxims' respectively for the Chilian Government. They were designed by Sir Edward Reed, and compare interestingly with the *King Edwards* in being much longer and narrower. It will be remembered that in the past Reed ideals had always centred round a "short handy ship." They had also always embodied the maximum of protection, while these ships carried medium armour only. His ships had, further, always been characterised by extremely strong construction, while these verged on the flimsy, the scantlings being far lighter than in British naval practice.

Out of all which it has been held that they represented the Reed ideal of armoured cruisers interlaced with what- ever limitations the Chilian authorities may have specified. Particulars of these ships, which in 1903 were purchased for the British Navy and renamed *Swiftsure* (ex *Constitucion*) and *Triumph* (ex *Libertad*):—

Displacement—11,800. Complement, 700.
Length—(over all) 470 ft.
Beam—71 ft.
Draught—(Maximum) 24 ft. 8 in.
Armament—Four 10-inch, 45 cal.; fourteen 7.5-inch, 50 cal.; fourteen 14-pounders, four 6-pounders, four Maxims; two 18-inch submerged tubes.
Armour—Practically complete belt 8 ft. wide, 7-inch thick amidships, reduced to 3-inch at ends. 10-inch bulkheads at ends of thick portion of belt. Redoubt above (250 ft. long), 7-inch on sides 6-inch bulkheads to it. Deck 1½-inch on slopes amidships, 3-inch on slopes at ends. Barbettes 10-inch, with 8 to 6-inch turrets. Battery and upper deck casemates, 7-inch.
Horse-power—14,000=20 knots. Yarrow boilers.
Coal—(normal) 800 tons; (maximum) 2,000 tons.

These ships compare interestingly with the *King Edwards* and *Devonshires*, between which they struck a mean, as follows:—

	King Edward.	Swiftsure.	Devonshire.
Displacement	16,350	11,800	10,850
Principal Guns....	4—12in.	4—10in.	4—7.5.
	4—9.2	14—7.5	6—6in.
	16—6in.		
	5—18in. tubes	2—18in. tubes.	2—18in. tubes
Armour belt	9—2in.	7—3in.	6—2in.
Speed	18.9 knots	20 knots	22.25 knots
Coal (Normal)	950	800	800
Coal (Maximum) .	2,150—400 (oil)	2,000	1,800

Other items of interest are that the armament of the *Swiftsures* (10-inch and 7.5's) had somewhere about that time been laid down by Admiral Fisher as the ideal armament of the future, on the principle that the best possible was "the smallest effective big gun, and the largest possible secondary gun." In service these ships never proved brilliantly successful. They rarely managed to make their speeds successfully, and there was a great deal of vibration with them. They were shored up internally in places with a view to strengthening them. On the other hand, it should be mentioned that some of these alleged defects have been put down to conservatism in nautical ideas, and that the shoring up was not really required. Their great drawback was that so far as the British Navy was concerned they were neither one thing nor the other, being too light in heavy guns to be satisfactory with the battleships, and too slow to act with the cruisers. Had there been six or so of them they would, possibly enough, have formed an ideal squadron. Being two ships only, they of necessity became round pegs in square holes.

NAVAL ESTIMATES IN THE ERA.

Financial Year.	Amount.	Personnel.	Ships.		
			Battleships.	Armoured Cruisers.	Protected Cruisers.
1887-88	12,476,800	62,500	—	—	3
1888-89*	13,082,800	62,500	—	—	2
1889-90	13,685,400	62,400	—	—	—
1890-91	13,786,600	65,400	8	—	4
1891-92	14,557,856	68,800	2	—	2
1892-93	14,240,200	67,700	1	—	—
1893-94	14,340,000	70,500	6	—	2
1894-95	17,365,900	83,000	3	—	9
1895-96	18,701,000	88,850	—	—	8
1896-97	21,823,000	93,750	6	—	3
1897-98	21,838,000	100,050	7	6	—
1898-99	23,780,000	106,390	3	4	—
1899-00	26,594,000	110,640	2	2	1
1900-01	28,791,900	114,880	2	6	1
1901-02	30,875,500	118,625	3	6	—
1902-03	31,255,500	122,500	2	2	—

* *Also under Naval Defence Act an additional sum of £10,000,000, spread over seven years.*

In the following year 1903-04 three ships (the last of the *King Edwards*) were provided for. The total number of battleships designed for the British Navy by Sir William White was therefore 48. There were in addition 26 armoured cruisers—making a total of 74 armoured ships, and about as many protected cruisers, including some for Colonial service.

ALSO FROM LEONAUR
AVAILABLE IN SOFTCOVER OR HARDCOVER WITH DUST JACKET

ESCAPE FROM THE FRENCH *by Edward Boys*—A Young Royal Navy Midshipman's Adventures During the Napoleonic War.

THE VOYAGE OF H.M.S. PANDORA *by Edward Edwards R. N. & George Hamilton, edited by Basil Thomson*—In Pursuit of the Mutineers of the Bounty in the South Seas—1790-1791.

MEDUSA *by J. B. Henry Savigny and Alexander Correard and Charlotte-Adélaïde Dard* —Narrative of a Voyage to Senegal in 1816 & The Sufferings of the Picard Family After the Shipwreck of the Medusa.

THE SEA WAR OF 1812 VOLUME 1 *by A. T. Mahan*—A History of the Maritime Conflict.

THE SEA WAR OF 1812 VOLUME 2 *by A. T. Mahan*—A History of the Maritime Conflict.

WETHERELL OF H. M. S. HUSSAR *by John Wetherell*—The Recollections of an Ordinary Seaman of the Royal Navy During the Napoleonic Wars.

THE NAVAL BRIGADE IN NATAL *by C. R. N. Burne*—With the Guns of H. M. S. Terrible & H. M. S. Tartar during the Boer War 1899-1900.

THE VOYAGE OF H. M. S. BOUNTY *by William Bligh*—The True Story of an 18th Century Voyage of Exploration and Mutiny.

SHIPWRECK! *by William Gilly*—The Royal Navy's Disasters at Sea 1793-1849.

KING'S CUTTERS AND SMUGGLERS: 1700-1855 *by E. Keble Chatterton*—A unique period of maritime history-from the beginning of the eighteenth to the middle of the nineteenth century when British seamen risked all to smuggle valuable goods from wool to tea and spirits from and to the Continent.

CONFEDERATE BLOCKADE RUNNER *by John Wilkinson*—The Personal Recollections of an Officer of the Confederate Navy.

NAVAL BATTLES OF THE NAPOLEONIC WARS *by W. H. Fitchett*—Cape St. Vincent, the Nile, Cadiz, Copenhagen, Trafalgar & Others.

PRISONERS OF THE RED DESERT *by R. S. Gwatkin-Williams*—The Adventures of the Crew of the Tara During the First World War.

U-BOAT WAR 1914-1918 *by James B. Connolly/Karl von Schenk*—Two Contrasting Accounts from Both Sides of the Conflict at Sea D uring the Great War.

AVAILABLE ONLINE AT **www.leonaur.com**
AND FROM ALL GOOD BOOK STORES

www.ingramcontent.com/pod-product-compliance
Lightning Source LLC
Chambersburg PA
CBHW031306150426
43191CB00005B/96